Gift

of the

Friends of the

Aiken County

Public Library

1 8 6 6 - 1 9 9 1

125th

ANNIVERSARY

The Lightship
The German Lesson
The Heritage

THE TRAINING GROUND

*Translated from the German
by Geoffrey Skelton*

■ ■ ■

SIEGFRIED LENZ

HENRY HOLT AND COMPANY · NEW YORK

First published in the United States in 1991 by
Henry Holt and Company, Inc., 115 West 18th Street,
New York, New York 10011.
Originally published in Germany in 1985 under the title
Exerzierplatz.

Library of Congress Cataloging-in-Publication Data
Lenz, Siegfried.
[Exerzierplatz. English]
The training ground / Siegfried Lenz; translated from the German
by Geoffrey Skelton. — First American ed.
p.   cm.
Translation of: Exerzierplatz.
I. Title.
PT2623.E583E9713 1991   91-34203
833'.914—dc20   CIP
ISBN 0-8050-0943-4

Henry Holt books are available at special discounts
for bulk purchases for sales promotions, premiums,
fund-raising, or educational use. Special editions
or book excerpts can also be created to specification.

For details contact:
Special Sales Director, Henry Holt and Company, Inc.,
115 West 18th Street, New York, New York 10011.

First American Edition—1991

Recognizing the importance of preserving the written word,
Henry Holt and Company, Inc., by policy, prints all its
first editions on acid-free paper. ∞

Printed in the United States of America

1 3 5 7 9 10 8 6 4 2

THE
TRAINING
GROUND

They have taken away his rights. I don't know exactly what that means, but Magda says they have given him a guardian – a guardian for someone who owns a million trees and other plants and understands better than anyone else how to make them grow here, in the mild easterly winds of the Baltic! As long as I can remember he has taken care that I have enough to eat, and I'm sure he knows – maybe even suggested it – that Magda brings me bits from the kitchen late in the evening – the remains of a loaf, slices of sausage and cheese – to ease my hunger pangs during the night. He knows everything about me, not just my perpetual hunger, and it seems his feelings for me are such that he once called me his friend, his only friend. That was when he put me in charge of all the knives and clippers, the lovely grafting and layering knives, the quick-budder and the bill-hooks. When I come to think of it, Bruno, he said, you are my only friend. Then he sat down in the little old toolshed he had turned into a home for me, complete with safety locks – he sat down and looked at me for a long time in a brooding sort of way.

If Magda hadn't told me they've taken his rights away, I wouldn't have known how to account for certain changes in him, but now I know where that long-suffering smile comes from, that weariness and that shyness I never noticed in him before. One evening at dusk he caught me pulling young needles from the spruce-trees and sucking the sweetness from their resinous ends, a ruse for relieving hunger and warding off gout. In earlier times he would have flared up and his skin have turned red under his shaggy, stubbly hair, but now he just smiled in a long-suffering sort of way and looked shyly down at his dog, as if unwilling to take me to task. Oh, Bruno, he said, and that was all. I made for the new toolshed as quickly as I could, so as to get the disc coulter cleaned before darkness fell, and maybe the disc harrow and the ploughs as well.

When darkness comes I'm happiest in my own home. I lie on my bed or sit in the brown armchair the chief gave me many years ago as a reward for some service I was supposed to have done him. I don't often put on the light, knowing I can depend on the two safety locks. The sapling beds, the endless rows of conifers and shrubs, they then stand deserted, all the plants seeming to bow down as they await the arrival of the Hookman, whom I see so often in my dreams. He is a small, barefooted man who walks silently through our plantations and, following a plan known only to himself, bends the heads of the young stems with his hook. Usually I wait till I hear, far off in the distance behind our nursery garden, the whistle of the railway engine as it drags its line of trucks through the hilly countryside towards Schleswig, and I then make up my mind to set out one day to see what a town looks like.

In better times Magda would bring me rolls and slices of ham that had been put aside as too dry. Though I could always see Magda's shadow as she emerged from the big house, I would let her knock seven times on my door and open it only after she'd shown herself at the window. She enjoyed watching me eat and was amazed by the speed with which I got it all down. How often would she then drag my open palm under the lamp to read the lines on it! But at some point she always sighed and shook her head in vexation, because a planetary mount was seemingly missing and a cross-line leading in the wrong direction. That, she declared, was reason enough to be wary of me. All the same, she often stayed with me till morning; she would put her hand on my chest and breathe against my neck. I don't know why she kept asking me about my parents, for I'd told her more than once how they'd been swept away on a yellow raft after the big landing barge went down, while I was left swimming among soldiers and horses until the old paddle steamer *Stradaune* came chugging up.

Not even Magda could tell me whether I would have to leave now the chief has lost his rights. Though she works in the big house – the stronghold, as we call it – she has heard nothing that need make me feel uneasy. He who has always been so good to me and who once called me his only friend, he still sits at the head of the table, drinking the double Wacholder his son pours out for him before every meal. He still follows the custom of carving the joint and leads the conversation, with only his wife, Dorothea Zeller, challenging him if necessary. I only hope Magda doesn't forget to bring me the latest news from the stronghold. Since this Serbian fellow who always lays a hand on my shoulder when he speaks to me, since this red-eyed Mirko has been working with us she only rarely pays me a visit. Maybe I should pluck up my courage and ask the chief himself: he could tell me better than anyone whether I shall now have to leave Hollenhusen, leave my favourite plantation, the grafted blue spruces, all of which I staked myself. Our relations being what they are, it is not impossible he might even tell me why they're taking his rights away, and what that will mean for him, to whom everyone here owes something. All I want is to stay by his side.

I am happiest of all when working to his instructions. When he has told me to thin out our shelter belt, my shears twitter and snap and sing among the thuya branches, and the hedge soon repays us with the thickness and swiftness of its growth. I work almost as happily for Ewaldsen, our foreman, who goes around in patched gumboots even in summer, repeats his instructions several times, and is always amazed by the number of plants I manage to pot on. With the chief's son Joachim I have my difficulties. After giving me his orders, he keeps turning up unexpectedly, checking, looking at his watch, measuring progress. Usually then he'll stride off in his leather-

3

trimmed knee-breeches, shaking his head. If it was left to him, I could hardly expect to stay on, though I have seen him grow up and have often enough taken the blame for things he has done wrong. My heart always beats quicker when the chief's wife sends for me, maybe to saw and split logs for the fire, or at another time because she wants me to sort the potatoes in her cellar. She always stays at my side – not to keep watch over me, but to help with the job. Her open face, which I secretly watch as I work, clearly shows her independent character. I would give a lot to stop Ina's children having the right to boss me around, but she is the chief's daughter and even after the accident she has continued to live here with us. And, though I know they're her sons who from their hiding-places keep pelting me with clods of earth, sticks and even stones, I still help them put up a tent, if that's what they want, fix up their swing, or go down to the sunless little river Holle to catch tadpoles for their aquarium.

But I can't make up my mind to speak to the chief. Maybe, that evening when he caught me chewing pine-needles, he said so little only because he'd still not forgiven me for refusing his gift. Though I've come to expect almost anything from him, I was never more surprised in my life: he just came into my hut one Sunday, sat down and looked at me for a long time through his ice-blue eyes. Then he began recalling memories: how together we had paced out this land that for many years, up to the end of the war, had been a military training ground; how we had tested the mineral properties of the soil by poking and kneading it between our fingers; how we had worried whether the seeds they'd brought with them from far off in the east would sprout here. Then suddenly he pulled out his gold pocket-watch and pushed it towards me, its spring cover open. As I hesitated to touch it, he said: So you'll have something to remind you of our beginnings. I still didn't dare take the watch in my hand, for there was something engraved on the cover. In spite of all his nodding and urging I didn't touch the watch, because having it would at once have drawn attention to me

4

or laid suspicion on me, and if there is one thing I try to avoid it is drawing attention to myself. I kept a finger pointing to the inscription, and at last he read it. He seemed only a bit surprised. He pressed the spring cover shut and went off without a further word.

There's one person I can think of who would tell me straight out what I must now expect, and if only he were here I'd seek him out at once, because he has always been good to me and because he himself suggested I should go to him when anything is worrying me. But Max, our curly-head, is not here: the chief's eldest son is in the town, giving lectures to hundreds of students, and writing to him would only put an extra burden on him. Magda says there are sometimes pictures of him in the newspapers lying around the stronghold. Nobody lived more simply than he did when he was here, but that was how he wanted it: just a chair, a bed and a table. The bricks and planks he used to make his bookcases I got for him in Hollenhusen. He only rarely pays us a visit – not even for the main holidays can we be sure to see him – but, whenever he does let us know he's coming, I go to our dreary railway station in plenty of time so as to be there to meet him, to carry his bags and walk beside him and speak with him: that alone would be reward enough. If I now and again address him by his doctor's title, he scoffs and reminds me of the past we share – once he even spoke of our rich past – and, though I try to avoid addressing him directly, I call him Max in my thoughts, just as he wants.

Since it has never crossed anyone's mind that the chief could be deprived of his rights, I've made no list of the hiding-places in which I keep the things that are no business of anyone else's, and which may one day help me to take care of myself and to savour once again the things that mean most to me. The money – or at least the little bit they pay me – I've buried behind the juniper. It is safe there, for that bit of ground gets trampled on only every other winter when they're gathering the fruits with a mane-comb – yes, they do actually comb it out. What the

5

soil itself has yielded up to me, all the bits and pieces left behind by generations of soldiers – these are split up between at least three hiding-places. The cartridges and the cartridge-cases and the shell fragments are buried at the edge of the pit from which we used to fetch sand for the seed sowings; the brass buttons, the coins, the rosettes and the bayonet should be close to the monkey-puzzle trees, also the hand grenade and the officer's belt clasp. It is only the two thunderer-whistles on plaited cords I keep here under my pillow. Beneath the soil where the plot of tall-trunked lime-trees ends are all the presents Max once gave me, also the things Joachim and Ina slipped into my hand when I was living with them in the house. Almost all of them are the products of a guilty conscience, their efforts to make up to me for their having blamed me for something they had done. Oh yes, I still remember what the mouth-organ was for and the penknife with a corkscrew attached, and the little case of coloured pencils from Ina – I still remember both the gifts and the reasons for them. If I do have to go, I shall clear out all my hiding-places; nothing will be left behind, for I want to be able to take each of the things in my hand, to let them speak and bring back memories. But I must be careful, very careful: what Magda told me in confidence must not be spread around among the people – and particularly not those from Hollenhusen who are now happy enough to work here. Quite a few from that wretched nest depend entirely on the chief today, all those grumbleguts who in the early years treated him with suspicion and unconcealed scorn. But the foreign workers, for whom the chief had a fine wooden house specially built, they mustn't know either. I shall keep my mouth tightly shut, for it's easy enough to imagine the rumours and the gossip when the Hollenhusen people come to hear of it, and also the shock and fear that will spread among Elef and his people, for it was the chief alone who smoothed the way from their home country to us here. Elef is the only one who doffs his cap when he speaks to me, and when from a distance I see him standing there in his baggy

6

trousers, surrounded by a few others in peaked caps or oversize headscarves, it always makes me hope he'll one day invite me to their house.

What I'd like most of all would be to call Magda back and get her to repeat what she told me, for I just can't bring myself to believe the news she brought, let alone accept it. There's always the chance of a misunderstanding: a garbled sentence, the way you hear things wrong when you're excited, a certain kind of glance, an unintended silence – all these can lead to mistakes: I've made such mistakes myself, many times. I just can't believe the chief has been given a guardian to think for him and sign in his name. Even if they do manage to find one in Schleswig, no guardian could ever measure up to the chief, who has more in his little finger than all the guardians in the world in their whole hands. Nobody knows more than he does. He only needs take a leaf or a twig in his hand to see at once what's wrong with it. Nobody knows the secrets of trees and plants as he does.

Let this guardian go round our young plantations just once with the chief, let him walk as I do through the different plots and listen to the chief, who, always ready to talk, will prove to him that everything that grows has its own appointed enemy, some other creature made specially for it that waits, moves in and then causes its death. I didn't really believe him at first, but he soon proved to me that every species of plant, every one, has its own special, intimate enemy, and, since we were standing among the pine-trees, he said: Take just the pines, Bruno, and then he spoke of the pine-shoot moth, the pine-bud moth and the double shoot moth, ravenous caterpillars that live in the resin chambers and attack the young shoots and buds. He reeled off a list of all the pests that confine their attention to pine-trees, from the pine branch louse to the pine sawfly. He knows all the pine's enemies, and he knows just as well what threatens the broad-leaved trees, each and every one of them. Wherever we went together in our walk over the land, and whatever I pointed to (sometimes just to test him), the closest enemies of every species came to his mind without effort, and, while my head was already ringing with the names he named, he kept on mentioning new ones, talking of the ash-bark beetle and the lilac-leaf miner. He named at least a hundred names, they fell on me like raindrops, pear-sucker, poplar longhorn, green oak tortrix moth, and, since in the end I was using all my efforts just to remember the names, I no longer took note of the signs of damage these moths and weevils leave behind, what they smother or cause to shrivel or reduce to a skeleton. But, as I say, I should be interested to know how long a guardian would want to remain a guardian after a walk with the chief and a conversation about close and mortal enemies – that would be interesting indeed.

I must bolt my door tonight. Though I can rely on the two safety locks, it may be better to fasten the iron bolt as well, for the tracks, which (as always) come from the birch plot, lead directly to my window, bare foot prints whose origin no one can guess, whose purpose no one can explain. They begin suddenly and they end suddenly, just as if whoever has left them behind let himself down on a rope and, when he thought it time, climbed up it again, high into the skies. However often I have followed these tracks, all I knew in the end was that whoever it is making them has no big toe on his right foot; the heel print is always clearer and more revealing.

I haven't told the chief that the tracks lead more often than not from my window to the stronghold: I noticed that after a light fall of rain, also in summer when dew has settled on the dusty terrace. Every time they lead over the grass mound and past the rose borders to the three lime-trees, from where you can see into the rooms in which Ina and her children live. Even if I could show the chief the tracks, he'd only say what he always says: You think too much, Bruno, and your thoughts bring you nothing but uneasiness. And, knowing him as I do, he would then run a friendly hand over my hair, as if in that way he could soothe my thoughts and cure my uneasiness.

That wasn't the whistle of the engine that disturbed the

rooks in their sleep: something else must have alarmed them in their old windswept pines by the railway cutting. They rose with warning cries from their loveless nests, and now they're circling above the young plantations, over the dispatch hall and the new toolshed. They'll circle as far as the stronghold, where the whole family will surely now be sitting around a table, discussing how to manage things in the future, things both big and small. I can't make out more than shadowy movements, but I can imagine them passing papers around and putting their heads together over some documents, studying it and looking for its meaning until they're satisfied, until their eyes meet and they exchange relieved nods, maybe over the head of the one person it most affects, sitting there silent among them, silent and ready to oblige.

He won't let me be sent away, even if his son Joachim demands it, he will point out that from the very first day I helped him take possession of this land, to work on it and change its appearance, and that together we chose the hill on which the house would one day stand, his stronghold. He will surely recall that moment: how we stood on the old, scarred soldiers' land and looked around for a place for the house. Everything was covered in a haze, the practice bunkers, the dummies, the practice tank, the stillness throbbed and hammered, and then, without having exchanged a word, we walked through scattered pines to the top of a hill, where we sat down and ate our sandwiches. Here, Bruno, the chief said, this is where we'll one day build our stronghold, here we stay. Playfully he lay down on his stomach and put the steel rod we'd been pushing into the ground to take soil samples to his shoulder like a gun. He aimed it here and he aimed it there, and in the end said there couldn't be a better field of fire anywhere.

Yet again I can hear that voice behind me, yet again I have begun to talk, yet again I catch myself listening to my own voice. No, there is no one behind me, I am alone and can trust the safety locks and the bolt. I know this uneasiness is only due to my perpetual hunger: a slice of raw turnip would calm me down all right, but better still would be rye bread soaked in curdled milk. I don't often feel as full as I would always like to be; even when Magda came after dark with all those tasty leftovers, my hunger was only eased for a time, never completely stilled. Magda has told me that these days the chief is eating less and less, sometimes a single slice of meat is enough for him, sometimes just a couple of apples, and in the morning a cup of milky coffee. It's easy to see he isn't woken up by hunger as I am. Every morning I'm woken by a griping in my innards, I can feel it even in my dreams, and as soon as I wake I run my hand along the windowsill to find whatever bit of food I've managed to put there in readiness. When you're around, Magda once said to me, everything eatable must be put under lock and key.

If old Lauritzen, our stooping, pig-headed neighbour, who in the early years showed nothing but contempt for us, if Lauritzen were still alive, I'd know where to go: whenever and wherever I met him, he would offer to take me on, whether it was at the railway station in Hollenhusen where I was waiting for Max, by the year-old morello cherries near the big pond, or more than once in Danes' Wood, for the possession of which he and the chief waged a long battle. When are you coming over to me? he would always ask, and, when I shrugged my shoulders, he'd growl: You'll live to regret it, blockhead. He managed to persuade two men to leave the chief for him, but not me, though he promised me work which would have nothing to do with horses. All right, all right, he said, when I told him I could never work with horses, we'll find something else for you, there's work enough. Maybe he would have been good to me, I don't know; all I know is that there was something not quite right between us, for the flowers I took to his funeral faded and withered on the short way from the cemetery gate to the grave.

It was not often I saw the chief as happy and content as on the day old Lauritzen granted him all the rights to Danes'

Wood, this gloomy patch of trees disfigured by the wind to which strangers hardly ever go. Because in the rare north winds you could hear the weak moans of the wounded Danish soldiers who had hidden in these woods a hundred years ago, I often made my way there, and I would sit down on a tree stump or lie in the grass to await the groans and wails. When the chief's dog sniffed me out in a ditch, I was prepared for anything, but the chief just took me by the arm in a friendly way and led me over to a fallen pine. We sat down on it and drank a little from his flask, and then I felt a bit scared, for suddenly he asked me whether I was happy. Never before had he put such a question to me, he to whom I owe everything, the first rescue after the big landing barge went down and the second rescue after the wreck of the paddle steamer *Stradaune*. I must have looked at him in a confused sort of way, for he made a smiling gesture of dismissal and directed my eyes to the wild growth of Danes' Wood, saying: You see, Bruno, Nature never forgets it was once a wilderness; but we must stop it recalling that too often.

And then once again he told me about the plantations, stretching further than the eye could see, which his father once owned in the east, and about the poor soil at the edge of the Rominter heath, where they grew the toughest conifers: poor soil is sometimes good soil. I could listen to him for days on end when he talks of those times, of the winters there, the planting schemes, the wolf he killed. I sometimes have the feeling I was there with him, though I know very well I come from still farther away, from the river Memel, which would always silently suck down anything I threw in from the bank. We sat a long time on the fallen pine, the chief and I, and, when he felt we'd talked enough, he thumped me on the back, and we walked side by side through Danes' Wood, which had on some occasion been made over to him as a mark of reconciliation. He was very happy. Now and again he showed his high spirits by ramming the toe of his boot into the soil. Before we left the wood he gave me another little drink and, as

I returned the slim flask to him, he said: Believe me, Bruno, if you want security you must expand.

Nobody now, I feel sure, will be coming over today to bring me any news, so I can undress and get things ready for the night. The green jacket the chief gave me has got heavier with the years, the arms seem to have shrunk even shorter, and the edges are already frayed: all the same I enjoy wearing it just as much as the raw leather boots Max brought me at Easter. Once, when I had turned the collar of the jacket up – I was standing in the shade of the young cedars – Elef's men mistook me for the chief and sent one over to ask for something; I couldn't understand why they took such delight in their mistake. What I have sewn into the lining is nobody's business but mine, the empty shotgun cartridge case will never be seen by anyone else. My trousers: I don't know why I wear out more trousers than jackets, even the dark ones the chief's wife gave me are already frayed again, have bags over the knees and have rubbed so thin I shall soon have to patch them. I manage best with socks, since in the summer I don't wear any.

That's Joachim: the beam from his flash-lamp wanders across beds and young plantations, comes to rest on the paths, swings over to the buildings which, ever since he has had the say here, have to be kept locked. He is making his final tour of inspection, which he does almost every evening. The chief puts his trust, not in Max, who has always stayed in the background, but in Joachim, who seems to have been born mistrustful and who always shakes his head as he leaves me, as if there was no use talking to me. Even on a day such as this he can't give up his tour of inspection; I think, if it were left to him, he would even claim the right to order us when to go to sleep – a quiet order, since he is not a man for loud words. At times, when I am potting or pruning, he watches me so long in silence that I get nervous and my hands begin to shake. They used once to call him the little gosling, because he was so delicate and had such a sensitive skin. He for sure would be glad to see me go.

There's no point in trying to sleep until the night train has gone through; I can't drop off before I hear the engine whistle. I drop off easiest when I think of the wind sweeping softly through the fir-trees, or when I think of the silent training ground, over which two buzzards are circling in the warm air on motionless wings. Often I never get round to thinking I'm going off to sleep, because I already am asleep, maybe even dreaming that I am lying at the bottom of the river Memel, watching slow thick clouds pass high above my head, bulging like sacks of potatoes. The engine whistle must be coming any moment now.

When Ewaldsen, our foreman, sees me slip a few seeds into my mouth, he threatens me, or he screws up his face and turns away. His threats are only joking ones, for he is as good-natured and forbearing as anyone you could hope to find, and he screws up his face because he probably thinks the seeds taste bitter or mouldy, even (some of them) fermented. He says I have a stomach like a thrush, since nothing ever upsets me, foam doesn't burst from the corners of my lips, the pupils of my eyes don't freeze, I don't go into convulsions. I'd have been dead long ago, Bruno, he has often said, if I'd swallowed all the pods and capsules you've swallowed. I admit some seeds make me giddy, others bring out a rash on my skin, and, whenever I eat the pulpy privet, yew and berberis seeds (which we always let go slightly rotten), I feel as if a hundred crickets were ticking and chirping inside my head. But so far nothing has done me any harm. I like eating the seeds from fir-cones, so long as they haven't yet shed their wings: then I sometimes get the feeling that my voice is becoming stronger and more rounded, and more and more words come into my head. It's different with spirea and magnolia, whose seeds mustn't dry out before sowing: after eating them I see myself gliding quietly along in a boat, past familiar banks. Bruno, Bruno, our foreman Ewaldsen says, take it easy, or there'll be nothing left for the seedbeds.

Here from the seedbeds I can keep the stronghold in view, but no one has appeared yet, not on the paths and not on the terrace, though the mist has already cleared and the sun is gleaming in the upper windows. On any ordinary day the chief would have joined us long ago, would have ruffled my hair and demonstrated something to us in the seedbed. He would for sure have asked after Ewaldsen's sick wife and then, with a word of praise for us both, have gone on his way, drawn by his need to be everywhere at the same time. But now he just will not come. Maybe the guardian they have got for him is keeping him back, I don't know.

Our foreman Ewaldsen just gave me a surprised look when I asked what a guardian was needed for. He had to think awhile, and then all he said was: What questions you ask, Bruno! But then suddenly, as if he had remembered some particular case in Hollenhusen, he thought of an answer and said people could appoint a guardian in cases of feeble-mindedness or drunkenness or illness of some kind. But a lot would need to happen first, he said. I am now even more at a loss, since I know for certain the chief can't be accused of any of these things: he is still his own best guardian and can run rings round everyone here. If I were to confront our foreman Ewaldsen with what Magda told me, he would probably just dismiss it with a wave of his hand and go on working, for Ewaldsen has been with the chief for twenty-seven years – just four fewer than me – and for that reason he'll believe only what his experience tells him.

No, no one has been with the chief as long as I have, no one else has made it to thirty-one years. At the beginning I used to cut a notch in my fine juniper stick, one for every year. I meant the stick for my parents, so as to have something to give them on the day they turned up in Hollenhusen to fetch me, but they never came, never, the yellow raft had carried them off for good and all. At that time, though still counting the years with notches, I cried a lot, simply because I thought my tears would make it easier for my parents to find me in Hollenhusen. What today I find difficult, I could do then whenever I wanted: I could cry my heart out anywhere and at any time, not just dry sobs, but real tears that wetted my face and hands: I only needed to think of the eyes of the horses and of the yellow raft with my parents crouched on it, and I would grow hot behind the eyes and the tears would fall – never mind whether I was in bed or outside on the land. When the chief caught me weeping he never said a word or showed any wish to comfort me, he would just look at me and nod, not to cheer me up, but simply to show he understood. It was not he who told me the horses had forced me under the water and struck me with their hooves; they are good, but heedless swimmers, they swim with eyes rolling and teeth bared, puffing and snorting steadily through their nostrils while thrashing the water with their hooves. Max told me this later, and it is also through him that I know how the chief dived down after me, brought me to the surface and kept hold of me until he was able to lift me on to some floating planks. And then he stayed with me until the *Stradaune* fished us out of the water: they said I was all green and blue. Though Max had not been there, he knew all about it, knew anyway more than I did, he was the only one who comforted me, and, to stop my crying, all I needed to do was to think of him, of his fondness, which I felt from the very first day, when he came back from the war in his blue uniform.

I don't turn around, but stoop even lower over the seedbed, though for some time now I've been hearing that rubbing noise behind me, the hissing sound that comes from Joachim's leather-trimmed breeches. He can think, if he wants, that he has taken me by surprise, and to show my surprise I'll spit three times to overcome my shock. He's making his first round as the new chief, I suppose; it wouldn't surprise me if he were to tell me and our foreman Ewaldsen that significant changes are on the way, for we are after all the senior people here, assistants from the very beginning. He looks the same as usual, his greeting is short and friendly as always, and nothing shows in his narrow face, no secret suffering, no embarrassment, no grief, nothing. How calmly he looks me in the eye! Much longer and I shall grow nervous. My mother's expecting you,

Bruno. I nod, and then hear myself asking: Is anything wrong with the chief? He starts, gives me a surprised look, and that shake of his head is meant just to show how out of place my question is, that shake of his head already contains the answer: Oh, Bruno. There's nothing to be seen either in the way he goes off. He isn't stooping more than usual, his step isn't unduly heavy, but I know it is all just self-control. So sure is his control over himself that he can hold his hand back in the middle of a blow – as I saw once when I gave him occasion to hit me: his hand was already raised, I had already ducked my head, when at the last moment he stopped the blow in full flight, tightened his lips and walked off.

Whenever I see the big house, which here is always called the stronghold, from far away, I clearly recognise the former command hill of the training ground. The rose-beds, the winding paths, the lime-trees, they suddenly vanish, and in their place I see coarse grass and tough weeds, a churned-up, track-covered soil defiantly laying siege to the house. It is the roomiest house in Hollenhusen, its floors are of polished stone, the walls are covered with browning photographs, the corridors contain many stools and chairs, and in the entrance hall stands a large bowl of fruit, which the chief's wife herself keeps filled.

Now I'll continue walking in the shelter of the wind-break hedge, so they won't see me immediately, and, once I step on to the main path behind the dispatch hall, I shall be almost there, and Ina's children won't have time to think anything up. They once hit me over the eye with a lump of clay, it bled a little without my noticing, but the chief never found out from me the cause of my slight wound. If he'd had his way, I should still be living in the stronghold, in the dry and cosy basement apartment he planned especially for me – he even had a separate staircase built in the shadow of a clump of rhododendrons. But I couldn't stand it for long and stayed there only a month. Do what I could, every evening when I went down to my apartment I met my parents, usually they were crouching behind the barred window, calling softly to me, they tapped first on the windowpane, then called out and made signs, slowly, as if exhausted. I couldn't understand their signs. They were wearing shabby clothing and looked as if they'd come a long way. Sometimes I found the imprint of a body on my bed, which made me think one of them must have taken a rest there, and now and again the door of the wardrobe was wide open. Speak or call as loudly as I could, they never understood me; they just couldn't understand, and they went off disappointed in their worn-out clothing. For a whole month I had no sleep. The chief soon agreed to give me back my old home beside the greenhouse when I asked him; he didn't even try to persuade me to stay.

Maybe the chief's wife will tell me what has happened and what I must be prepared for. If now and again she lost patience, she has always been good to me, has seen to it that I got my fair share and said more than once that I belong to them. I just can't help looking at her open face, it is so fine and regular, and I should dearly like to touch it, but she will never know that, not for all her intelligence. Hiding your desires is difficult, maybe the most difficult thing in the world. In my mind I call her Dorothea. Often, when secretly I gaze at her, I remember how she once kissed me, one winter long ago, when we were all still living in the barracks, in a single room divided in two with the help of a tent awning and a blanket. I fell off a moving goods train during a snowstorm. I had waited for it on the long curve behind the training ground, jumped aboard and hastily thrown down a few huge lumps of coal, which Max and the chief picked up; then I slipped and fell. They put me to bed close to the cast iron stove, an old doctor came from a barrack hut nearby, I thought I was going to die. Dorothea sat with me longer than any of the others, she dried my sweating face and smiled at me, brought me milk, camomile tea, once a bar of chocolate, which I had to eat straight away. The winter fog hung over the barrack huts, draining the colour from the camouflage paint; every morning the window was covered in ice-flowers, which I tried putting names to before they melted in the slowly rising temperature. The old doctor never spoke to me, he just held a whispered conversation with Dorothea at the door and then tripped away down the echoing passage, which had been worn right down in many places by the soldiers' boots, particularly near the entrance. And when one evening I asked him if I would soon die he just pinched my cheek, and after he was gone Dorothea sat down on the edge of my bed and kissed me on both eyes. You'll be getting up soon, Bruno, she said, quite soon.

How I should like to take a couple of apples from the bowl! But the chief's father is looking down on me from his shiny dark frame on the wall, he seems to be guarding the apples, to be watching the door out and in. How happy I'd have been to see him here in Hollenhusen: from what I know of him he must have been a kind man of few words, going his own way in his chosen field.

She is scolding Ina: that is Dorothea's voice, scolding her daughter. I mustn't stand listening. I must draw their attention, tell them I'm here, even though I might otherwise hear something that could be of importance to me. They're talking about a newspaper advertisement, that I'm sure of, an announcement that Dorothea thinks has something vulgar about it, it sounds vulgar. I don't know what it is that's vulgar, whether it's true or untrue, I have never really thought what vulgar means.

So there you are, Bruno, she says, and she's already coming towards me. Her face betrays nothing, tiredness maybe, a slight nervousness, but nothing suggesting some big decision. Ina gives me just a single nod, then turns away to the window, showing me her thin back. Are you unwell, Bruno? Dorothea asks. You look so run down. All I can do is shake my head, I can never say much in her presence.

So Max is coming. He'll be arriving on the noon train, and as always he will sleep in his former room, on the campbed, just for a few days. I know what's to be done, and she probably sees in my face my pleasure over the expected visit, for she says: We're looking forward to it too.

If Max sits upright on his campbed, he can see right over our plantations to the place where the soldiers' barracks used to stand, eight wooden huts with tarred felt roofs and camouflage paint, and, if he gets up and goes to the other window, he can make out Danes' Wood and the big pond. Now they are gone; the old pines in which the rooks nest are still there, but the barracks are gone, and nothing remains to remind us that once we ourselves lived there with a thousand or so other people who had come from some place or other and were now occupying a room there, living and waiting.

The chief simply brought me with him. He, who finds out everything, learned that Dorothea was living there with Joachim and Ina, and he led me into their room as if I was already one of them, letting me see the reunion and the weeping and the comforting and everything. Then he said: I have brought someone who'll be staying with us for the time being. That was all he said on the first day. Ina knew where a straw mattress could be got, we carried it away together after dark, and, after it had all gone off without a hitch, we sat down side by side and rejoiced together. The chief chose to sleep nearest the wall, I slept between him and Joachim, and Dorothea and Ina slept behind the awning and the blanket.

They have surely sent for Max because he must be allowed a say in the discussions. They may even have need of his help, for I can imagine how much they now depend on him. Though I can always go to him when I have something on my mind, I don't want to bother him with my questions right away, and, if I do so later, I must take care not to betray Magda. If you betray me, Bruno, Magda said, I'll be sorry for every piece of bread I ever brought you.

Maybe Max will ask me, as he so often does, to go for a walk with him – always the same path along the river Holle to the judgement tree and the twin dolmens: I can't remember how many times I've sat on those stones and listened to him. I could ask him there, in front of the crumbling hollow lime, the judgement tree to which I was once fastened with ropes, tied upright as if on the cross, and I managed to stick it out for a whole night without calling for help, without giving any names away. I could ask him there, because it's the place where he also used to ask *me* countless questions, about my earliest memories, for instance, about my needs and my disappointments and so-called goals at which I'm aiming.

Joachim has never put such questions to me. All he wanted to be told in the beginning was about the risks his father had taken to rescue me, first, when the big landing barge went down, and then when the kind-hearted *Stradaune*, the steamer that had taken us on board, ran on a submerged wreck in the early morning light, and the whole forecastle was split in two – split as if by a knife. He very rarely interrupted me, and listened in a reflective sort of way, as if constantly comparing and considering things, and in the end I took care always to use the same words. It didn't escape my notice how closely he inspected the scars on my cheek – this reddish-blue calyx-like gathering of scar tissue beneath my leaking eye – that's what he himself once called it: leaky eye – and he just nodded when I told him it was the chief, his father, who put the first bandages on it: that was on the *Stradaune*, the old paddle-steamer that in the end didn't go to the bottom, but just filled with water and settled on top of some unknown wreck. If I left anything out of my account, Joachim knew at once what it was, and I would then dutifully say: Oh, yes, that's right, and put in a description of how, after the *Stradaune*'s overloaded rubber dinghy had capsized in the breakers, the chief had carried me over the last stretch through water reaching up to his hips. I could have told the whole thing backwards and, if he'd wanted, could have begun with the words the chief said to me as he laid me on the sand and bent over me: Let's wait and see, lad, what the third thing will be. He said that on the last day of the war.

I couldn't fall asleep on this campbed. I only need to lie on it for a short while and my head begins to buzz, as if a swarm of excited wasps were trying to get out, and my arms begin to itch. How Max could spend whole days in this modest room, lying down, reading and thinking – I suppose he has inherited his sound sleep from the chief, a deep untroubled sleep he can call on wherever he may be, even under the dwarf mountain pines on the training ground. When I recall our times in the barracks, what I always see is the chief lying on the straw mattress with his legs drawn up, his face to the wall, never irritable or angry when hammering or quarrelling was going on somewhere. He would lie there as if he'd just died a peaceful death, dressed in a uniform from which he'd cut off the badges of rank. When we roused him to eat, he would empty his plate, lie down again against the wall and stare straight ahead. At times, when his eyes fell on me, he would smile weakly and then he might say: Well, lad, it seems we'll never see the back of each other. He never got cross with Ina when she tickled him in his sleep, he just growled good-humouredly. Even when someone trod on him or dropped something on him, he would just growl in that good-humoured way. The only person to show consideration while he was sleeping was Dorothea: she'd go about her work carefully, treading softly, hissing warnings to us. She knew that at some time there'd be a final awakening – once he'd had the rest he certainly needed. No lasting plans were made; the things we thought important were put off till the day of his final awakening, and when Joachim once asked me: How long are you going to stay?, Dorothea answered for him: Wait till Daddy gets up, then everything will be sorted out.

There's time yet before the midday train, but it's not worth starting anything. I shall walk through the conifer plantations to the sandpit, climb on to the rail track and listen to the rails, then walk between them to the station. I can never be too early at the station; even here in Hollenhusen, where the trains seldom stop and there's nothing going on except when we're dispatching a big load of trees and plants, I like to arrive early.

I look around, read the notices and wonder where the few travellers dressed in their Sunday best can be going.

One day I too shall go into town, maybe on the midday train, and maybe, like Max, I'll travel in the end carriage and let the window down as we near a station and hold my head out in the draught we're making; that may well be. When I stoop down to lift his luggage, he'll surely say once again: Not such a hurry, Bruno, I must first take a look whether you've changed, and he'll put his hands on my shoulders and make certain I'm still as I always was. But I shall see that he's still carrying a secret grief around with him, his smile won't entirely wipe out the bitterness, that calm bitterness that comes, I suppose, from so much understanding. Who knows how things would now be if he had gone along with the chief's hopes? Everyone knew the chief was reckoning on him from the first and had great plans for him, that was already clear from the day Max returned home in his blue uniform. The sleep, the weariness, the depression, all were gone. The chief, who up till then had spoken as if in a dream, finally woke up, he embraced and patted Max in his joy and remembered that he had hidden away a small tin of coffee for this moment, and he fished it out of the creaking depths of his straw mattress. At last, Max, at last! the chief said at one point, and Max replied: Yes, father, at last, and they looked at each other happily, shaking their heads in disbelief. And later, in the middle of his account, he got to his feet to fetch his kitbag, from which he brought out several cloth-lined cases, each containing six sterling silver fruit knives, lovely knives with wide curving blades. Each of us was given one of the cases, which he had brought back from the war, from the officers' mess in which he served as a steward.

I hope the pyramid of apples won't collapse if I grab a few of them in passing. It's true Dorothea has given me permission to help myself from any of the fruit bowls standing around in the stronghold, but she doesn't know how often I do it. Dorothea is talking softly to Ina, who is sitting in a leather armchair and weeping. I won't say anything, but just go past, and, if they hear me, they'll know it was just me walking through.

During our time in the barracks Ina once showed me how to endure pain; she pushed a darning needle – a big one of the kind used for sewing sacks – into her hand, into the fleshy part beneath the thumb, she pressed it in quite slowly as I watched her thin, absorbed face, and I was able to assure her that not a single tear came. Usually at that time she was good to me. How often did she secretly pass over to me things she could not or did not want to eat! We sat beside each other at the table, and immediately she dropped a slice of bread from which she'd taken a bite on to her lap, as if by accident, I knew it was meant for me. But she could also make me sad, particularly one Sunday in winter, when I was pulling her over the glistening snow on her homemade sledge and, on our return from Danes' Wood, we met her two friends. These friends asked her about me, and Ina said I was her new horse, her horse Bruno, who could go through all the paces. To prove it, she invited her friends to sit on the sledge and, though I was tired and my shoulder was hurting, I dragged them through the snow, trotting when Ina ordered it, making little galloping hops, tugging and panting. It was hard work up the hill, while downhill the sledge knocked heavily against the back of my knees. All for their delight. Ina declared that later, when we were alone, I had tried to strangle her; she said it was under the old fir-trees, when according to her wish we were 'soaping' ourselves with snow, but I know nothing of it: she must have made it up. All the same, she told about it at home. I was lying on my straw mattress and I heard their whispered conversation. In spite of my exhaustion I couldn't sleep, and I heard Dorothea comforting her and the chief making gentle reproaches, telling her she must show consideration and forbearance towards me.

It may be he's now standing at his window watching me as I walk down the main path. I won't look round, though I should like to wave to him. Yes, he is certainly watching me, for my legs are growing stiff and my skin feels rough as if covered in goose-flesh. I can imagine he has locked himself in, so as to think undisturbed, about himself and all the rest of us, and particularly about what's being done to him. Perhaps he'll also be remembering how we walked over the land here together, over this bruised soldiers' country, he in front with a hammer and a steel rod in place of a proper soil-borer, I behind with the bag of rattling tin cans.

After his final awakening he felt drawn every day to the deserted training ground. He paced it out, marching between bushes and dwarf pines, I saw him sitting alone on the hill, discovered him examining old tank tracks, watched him from a distance gathering shattered fragments of metal together, but in a purposeful sort of way. He said nothing to us about his daily excursions. I am sure he'd have welcomed it if Max had gone along with him, he asked him every day before setting out whether he'd not like to come, often even invited him directly, but Max always had urgent work to attend to, Max expressed his regrets and remained seated in front of his homemade writing-board, which he placed on the windowsill, with a batten to support it on. I don't know why he never invited Joachim to go with him, for you could see he wanted a companion. He had so much pent up inside him, but maybe he felt nothing would come of taking Joachim, since he was so delicate, and leggy as a foal. So at first he went alone, not knowing that sometimes I would follow him and keep him in sight, until one day he surprised me beneath a hazel bush. When he pulled me out by my legs from under the hazel bush, I was afraid he would hit me, but the chief has never hit me, not in all these many years; and on that occasion he just laughed in triumph and said: You see, Bruno, you must make sure your rear is covered too. And next morning it was me he invited to go with him before all the rest.

I was happy, I liked carrying the bag of tin cans, and I would have carried the hammer and the steel rod too, if he'd let me. With him, there was always something to see; he pointed out rare birds to me and a slow-worm, and once even two badgers at play; he needed only to stop suddenly in a certain way, and I'd know at once there was something worth looking at. In the end the fact that he knew everything by name and saw a meaning everywhere, in the colour of the grasses, the colour of the soil, ceased to surprise me. He hammered the steel rod a meter into the ground, loosened it, pulled it gently out with all the various layers of earth it contained. With a little stick I would push them carefully into his hand, he would rub the little samples, knead them, then tip them into the tin cans, and about every one he had something to say.

He asked me once to do as he did, I had to shut my eyes, and he put all kinds of soil samples into my hand, sticky ones, grainy ones, heavy, rough and greasy ones, but I was unable to name the group to which they belonged, only the sandy soil I managed to guess. What pleased him most were the layers of grey-black earth, he said if he'd been a tree and allowed to choose a place to grow in, he wouldn't have wanted to stand in yellow or brown soil, but on grey-black, for there the ground is best aired, and in dry weather the water rises more easily, while in long periods of rain the superfluous water drains away more swiftly.

We probed the whole of the training ground, drove the steel rod into the earth where defence dugouts had formerly been, took soil samples in the trench where the soldiers had maybe gathered before a surprise attack, and any further information he needed the chief got the plant colonies to tell him, the golden thistle, the cock's-foot grass and, where the ground slopes down to the little river Holle, the marsh bedstraw. And one day – we were sitting in the shade of the half-sunken practice tank, eating our sandwiches – he said to me: Bruno, we'll make something out of this soldiers' land. He spent a little more time in thought, then we walked very quickly back home without a further word.

Now I shall just pretend I haven't seen Mirko on his new muck spreader. He has already whistled, but I shan't have heard it. All he wants to do is show me how nippy his machine is between the plots and how easily he can control it, and by doing that he hopes to remind me that I'm not allowed to use any kind of machine, neither his muck spreader nor the grubber. I shall never take another drink from his bottle, for it always knocks me over, but I shall always sit down beside him when he starts talking about his village, the mountains and the dancing and the hunters banging away in the autumn woods. Maybe that's the only reason Magda visits him so often, because she enjoys listening to him when he talks about his village. There beside the monkey-puzzle trees I have buried the coins and the buttons and cockades. I must make a list of all my hiding-places, and a sketch, which I shall sew into the lining of my jacket, as I've already done with that other thing, with the cartridge-case. If I die and haven't been able to clear the hiding-places out myself, then others must be able to find them.

For a while it's fun walking between the rails, for all steps have to be of the same length, the sleepers allow no rest, they drive you on, and I don't like to stop on a sleeper. But after a time I get tired, feel like changing my step or dawdling or trotting, and then I hop out from between the rails on to the gravel path. The rails are not signalling anything yet, there's just a distant singing and crackling; the rhythmic beat with which a train gives notice of its approach can't yet be heard. But it won't be long now: there's a loaded trolley already waiting on the platform and in front of the big sign 'Hollenhusen' an old man in black is standing, reading the station name and unable to take his eyes off it; maybe he's wondering how he got there. I shall go to the far end of the station, for Max will as always be sitting in the rear coach. Probably he won't bring me a present this time, I can imagine he had no time to spare in the hurry of his departure. Still, what he doesn't bring me I can't lose, and somehow it has often been his presents I've lost: the cap, the fine handkerchieves. If anyone asks me what has happened to a present, I must usually reckon on having lost it; sometimes I get to thinking things don't want to stay with me, not even Dorothea's presents.

Hollenhusen is growing and growing. Earlier there was just the one street leading in and out, but now there are side roads and ring roads and even a ramblers' route; I hardly dare go in. Earlier, too, I knew almost everybody in Hollenhusen, and they all replied to my greeting; now there are too many people I don't know, strangers who nudge one another when I pass and stare silently after me, as if not knowing what to make of my greeting. The new council office they've built has so many rooms that even the chief lost his way when he was once summoned there on my account; we had first to be told the room number, and even then we had to sit on chairs and wait.

Once, when we were still in the barracks, the chief said: Come along, Bruno, we're going to see the council clerk. Then we went and fetched Detlefsen, the council clerk, from his chaff-chopper and followed him into a low room in his house – that was the council office. He still had chaff clinging to his sleeves and collar as he sat opposite us with his long peevish face and fixed his eyes, not on us, but on a framed photograph of the Hollenhusen dolmens. The chief had brought nothing with him, no papers or anything like that, he just said he wanted to take over the former training ground to grow trees and plants of many different kinds, and he knew there would probably be conditions to be discussed with the council. There is good soil there for outdoor plantations, the chief said, broad-leaved trees, conifers and fruit trees could be grown, it is good cultivating land and it would bring in something for Hollen-husen. That's what he said, and added that he was ready to come before the council and lay papers in front of them, if that's what they wanted. The clerk said nothing, just listened, and he didn't move at all, just crouched there long and stiff like a heron, but in the end he dropped his gaze and said very slowly that he had taken note of it all. He also said, in exactly the same slow way, that he would lay the chief's proposal before the council at the proper time. He could give no guarantees, he went on, for on the list were already two other interested parties to be considered before the chief: they too had plans for the use of the old training ground – plans of a different kind.

He swallowed, looked at us in a manner that gave nothing away and bared his teeth, big decayed teeth with a yellowish film over them, and I felt my throat swelling and contracting, and something inside me began to throb, faster and faster, my hands broke into a sweat, there was a humming in my temples as the blood suddenly rose, and, while the chief just sat there in disappointment, I heard the clerk's voice, muffled and monotonous, as if coming out of a tomb. I heard his voice, though he was not moving his lips, and the voice said: Not you, our land is for our own people, we'll soon find a couple willing to take it over. I looked at his bent fingers jerking uneasily and knew I hadn't misheard him: it was his voice, speaking inside him to himself.

At first I found it impossible to believe the chief had heard nothing of all this, but so it was: on the way home he was utterly silent, disappointed at knowing there were two other interested parties to be reckoned with, and he had almost got to the stage of giving up altogether. Having to stop several times for a piss, I kept lagging behind, but as soon as I caught up with him again I repeated what I knew, just kept repeating the words the voice had spoken, and at last he stopped, looked at me in a brooding sort of way and bit gently on his underlip. Then he said: I believe you, Bruno, it's odd, but I have the feeling you're right; we won't give up. He was very earnest. He put his arm round my shoulder, and we walked out of our way down to the river Holle, where we sat on the grassy bank and the chief talked of the plantations on the edge of the Rominter heath and of his father, who had made a big mistake by specialising – specialising in big trees. We won't do that, Bruno, the chief said, not we, and he gave me a nod, as if he'd already won.

There are five people on the platform now, and I can't

understand why they look so vexed and disappointed. The man in uniform has said the train is running twenty minutes late, which gives time to sit down on one of the benches and think of all kinds of things: what's to be seen through the compartment window, what people in the place you're going to will say to your presents, what there'll be to eat. I like waiting; waiting is one of my favourite occupations. Here I can sit undisturbed, looking in the direction from which Max is coming, and I don't even have to close my eyes to see him already here, to choose how he'll look when he comes towards me, either silent and depressed, or with that sad smile he has for all occasions. The air is shimmering over the rails, there's still no sound of an approaching train, but I can already see Max, I'm holding his hand and questioning him with my eyes.

This is where he stopped, here by the new toolshed, and I thought he was just taking a short rest, but suddenly he took the hold-all out of my hand and said: Right, Bruno, now I'd better go on alone, and off he went along the main path to the stronghold with the heavy suitcase – which he'd insisted on carrying himself – and the hold-all, without once turning round to look at me. This time he didn't ask: Everything still standing in Hollenhusen?, nor did he leave the suitcase to me as he usually does, knowing that, when it comes to it, I can carry more than anyone else here. He has put on weight; his chin now rests on swelling flesh, his belt cuts into the bulky body below his navel, and when he walks I can't help thinking of a duck. He hasn't much to say: he just briefly made sure I was still the same as ever, then he nodded towards the rail track and set off ahead of me along the forbidden path. He did stop more often than usual among our plantations, and I don't know whether he was just getting his breath back or thinking of something, trying to remember something. I didn't venture to eat the stick of marzipan he'd given me at the station; as long as he remained wrapped up in his thoughts, I just didn't dare. Not a word did he say about the chief. Neither of us even mentioned him, and the longer we kept silent, the more insistently did my thoughts turn to him who had called me his only friend.

It seems they just can't find a way through to each other, Max and the chief, not in the beginning and not since. They've drifted apart like two rafts blown by contrary winds, and it has many times saddened me to see how the chief could never manage to bring Max over to his side, in spite of all the requests and suggestions and all the discussions they carried on even in my presence.

But one day the chief gave it up, and that was not on any ordinary day, but on the happiest day of his life, as he himself said: that Friday when he signed the leasehold agreement for the whole training ground, including the damp ground leading down to the river Holle. We had scrambled eggs with bacon and fried potatoes – that was his own choice – and I still remember how in my eagerness I climbed up into the old fir-tree to watch out for him and to be the first to wave as soon as he appeared on the little bridge, a white rag fluttering on the end of my juniper stick. I liked sitting in the old fir-tree; when they jeered at me or chased me, I would climb up to the highest branch that would bear my weight, and none of the boys from the neighbouring barracks would dare follow. The branches hid me from sight, and I was quite content to stay in my green hiding-place for as long as it took for my fear to die down. The chief knew at once that it was me up in the fir-tree waving the rag, and from the bridge he waved back – no, he didn't wave, he raised his clenched fist and punched the air a few times; then I knew everything had gone just as he'd wanted. I ran to meet him, he ruffled my hair, his hand closed like a vice around my neck and, when I looked up at him, I saw in his broad, stern face nothing but grim satisfaction. It was not at all easy to keep pace, I just kept trotting along beside him, and at times I thought he'd forgotten me, but then, near the half-buried practice tank in which I'd found the skeletons of three birds, he suddenly stopped, looked long at me and said: You were right, Bruno, no doubt of it! A good thing I listened to you. He said that, and then we walked on home and had our meal, and afterwards he laid the leasehold agreement on the table: it was made out for ninety-nine years and it gave the chief the first refusal if it was decided to sell the former soldiers' land. Dorothea read it first. You could see how pleased she was, but it was a cautious kind of pleasure, I remember that, and, while Joachim and Ina were staring at the agreement, she rummaged around in a cardboard box and brought out some small leather pouches, three or four pouches in which lay the winged seeds of conifers, also of broad-leaved trees. From home, she said, I just had to bring them. The chief looked at her in amazement, then he tipped a few seeds into his hand, lifted them up to the light and declared: They're still viable, though they'll have to wait a few more years yet.

I had already noticed how he kept glancing towards Max, who after the meal had quietly sat down at his writing board, where he was now copying things out of books and comparing them. All of a sudden the chief took the leasehold agreement and laid it down in front of Max, simply laid it on top of the writing board and the open books and asked in a very friendly way: Wouldn't you like to take a look at it, son? Here's what I've got. We're there now. Max nodded and started to read, and the chief fished around for a stool and sat down likewise at the writing board, took a flask from his breast pocket and placed it on the windowsill. Because Max took so long to read, we thought he had discovered some mistake in the lease agreement – he has only to run his eyes over something to see at once what is wrong, what is inconsistent. But he found nothing to object to in it, he thought it sound – yes, that's what he said: a sound agreement. Since Max didn't wish to drink with him, the chief drank alone, and he gazed out at the land he had taken over and rejoiced. Believe it or not, he said, this is one of the happiest days of my life. And he said too: We'll show them, now all this mess is over, we'll show them what can be done with this land that has so far known nothing but words of command and hob-nailed boots. And then he told us what would come of it in time, when all had been carried out according to his plans, to his wishes.

It was all mapped out in his head, and, as he divided the land up and decided what should go where, I could already see

33

the young plantations, the shrubberies, the seedbeds stretching out as far as the horizon, I saw the sheds and the greenhouse in the places he had chosen for them; paths emerged, whole schools of plants growing according to his will, and the whole surrounded by a dark protecting ring, the shelter belt. I was filled with excitement as he moulded the training ground to fit his plans. He was drawing on all the knowledge and experience he had brought from far away, from the edge of the Rominter heath, and, with his confidence in himself and his way of always getting things right I had no doubt he'd succeed in what he was setting out to do.

At one point he said: I have my hopes, Max, as you see. I could have had the land for forty-eight years, but that wasn't long enough, I raised it to ninety-nine and made sure of the first option to buy. He took two small sips from his flask, then added: Land, Max, the only thing that gives us security is land. At that Max turned his face towards him and looked at him in wonder, just as if he'd misheard him. He looked at him so long that the chief asked: Aren't I right? Max just shook his head. Remember grandpa, he said, and that was all. It didn't escape my notice that all the chief's words were addressed to Max alone, even when he was looking over his head towards the shadowy land. I could feel him trying to infect Max with his own excitement, but it was the last time he spoke in that way, spoke of the big task ahead and of the future, saying that if they stuck together they couldn't be beaten and that one day it could all be handed on and taken over. It was the very last time, and at the end he asked: What do you think, Max?, and Max said quietly: Each of us must play on the instrument made for him. That's what he said.

Every time I think of it I feel sad, and I see the chief getting to his feet and staring through the window. A few times he dropped his hand on the edge of the writing board, he seemed to be having difficulty in breathing, his eyes narrowed, and I could see what it meant to him to be left on his own and what efforts he was making to come to terms with his disappoint-

34

ment. It seemed he would not succeed: he who could hardly ever bring himself to accept things seemed, this time too, unable to accept Max's answer. He walked slowly away from the window. He opened the lid of the stove and slammed it shut. He picked up a piece of firewood, weighed it in his hand and threw it back. He aimed a little kick at a cardboard box sticking out from under the iron bedstead, sending it scuttling back. I couldn't move for fright. With nodding head he eyed the divided barrack-room, our sleeping place, the rucksacks, the cardboard boxes, the crate and the kitbag that contained everything that remained to them, that the war had left them with, and suddenly he said: As you like, son. Then he went off. We waited, but he didn't pass beneath the window. Ina and Joachim, who at a sign from Dorothea went after him, didn't pass under the window either, all we heard was their voices as spray from the communal water-pipe wetted them.

I don't know whether Dorothea was trying to comfort Max or just to calm him down, but she went up behind him, leaned over him and began to whisper, and I made no attempt to understand what she was saying, for it was not meant for me. I'd dearly have liked to go outside myself, but at that time I was afraid of a boy whose evil intentions could be read in his eyes. His name was Heiner Walendy, and once already he had started a fire. So I stayed where I was. I lay on my straw mattress without moving, shut my eyes and thought of the big pond and the creaking and croaking of the frogs, and the sound was soon echoing so loudly in my head that I had to stop my ears. But then I heard Max rubbing Dorothea's hands, something he frequently did, even in summer, for Dorothea often had ice-cold hands, fingers completely without feeling. Sometimes Max rubbed so hard that Dorothea laughingly protested. I too would have liked to rub her hands warm, but she never asked me, and I didn't dare offer of my own accord.

Once they were in harmony again, she left Max's side and knelt down to pull the cardboard box out from under the bed: I suppose to see what damage the chief's kick had done. She lifted the lid and took out a number of papers and envelopes, and she also fetched out two painted wooden birds, hanging on a rod. She came at last on an album which she couldn't help looking through straight away, turning the pages forwards and backwards, sometimes unbelieving, sometimes smiling. What she found there so absorbed her that she sat on the edge of the bed and placed the album in her lap, and suddenly with a splutter of laughter she said: Come, Bruno, take a look at this. We then sat side by side, and with great enjoyment she showed me the many photos pasted in the album. They were old, brownish photos, some faded, fogged at the edges, and some also sprinkled with little dots. At first I couldn't believe that the baby with the big head, staring out of a high-wheeled hooded pram and brandishing a rattle was the chief, but it was him: I recognised him by his eyes. It was also him lying on a fur rug and trying hard to hold his head up, with folds of fat round his neck and fingers like sausages, and he was also the little horn-player just about to put the horn to his lips as he sat on the knee of a man with a guilty expression on his face. Dorothea showed me the chief dressed for his first day at school and the chief riding a horse. In one photo a neat gravestone could be seen: it stood above the chief's sister, who had gone out on to the ice with him too soon; both had fallen through, but he alone was saved. Easiest to recognise was the chief standing in an open shirt against a background of plantations, one foot resting on a wheelbarrow, or with a spade over his shoulder. I can still remember them all, and I also recall two pictures showing the chief with Dorothea. On one of these they were holding hands on a bridge with a railing that was surely birchwood; on the other the chief was wearing a uniform and walking with Dorothea through a cordon of men, all of whom looked like hunters. As Dorothea closed the album, all she said was: What's past is past, but she also said: Tomorrow we'll fetch your photos, Bruno.

After that I remained sitting by myself, thinking as I often did of the Memel, of the dark river which each spring would carry past all kinds of things: chairs and dead cats and bottles and bits of timber without end, sometimes a swollen cow carcase circling stiff-legged in the whirlpools, then, caught once more by the current, drifting gently on. Broad, tarred boats with brown sails glided past in my mind's eye. An old woman walked across the bark-covered courtyard of our sawmill, she was lugging two baskets, one filled with fresh pike, the other with smoked flounder, she came right up to the gate, then my father appeared and looked in the baskets and sent the woman away, because he wanted perch, never anything but perch. Teams of horses hauled great tree trunks out of the river and dragged them up to the gate. My mother called from inside the white-painted manager's house: my extra lessons teacher had arrived and was sitting at the table, eating plain cake and drinking a cup of coffee. The steam whistle blew, and down by the river a man dropped the long boat-hook.

Then all of a sudden we were sitting in the fading evening light. Ina and Joachim had already returned a few times and then gone out again. A haze of rain hung over the training ground, and now Dorothea sent me and Max out once more to look for the chief. She must have been worried, for up till now he had never neglected to tell her what he was about to do and where he was going. I decided straight away to find the chief by myself, and I raced off without paying heed to Max, ran through the barracks out to the sandy road and then on to the flimsy plantation of dwarf pines, where I stopped for the first time to listen. I had never been out on the training ground in the dark before. It was quite still, nothing moved, yet I felt someone must be watching me, from the bushes, from the top of the hill, from the dummy houses. I couldn't help thinking of the sergeant who at that time was said to have vanished on this ground – now we know the whole story, even the names of the soldiers who caused the sergeant to vanish – and I crept cautiously down to the drain, doubled back and approached the half-buried practice tank from behind. The three bird skeletons were still lying in their nest beside the driver's seat:

probably the young chicks had starved to death because someone had closed the turret hatch – I don't know, I just assume it. The chief was not there, and so I continued my search, pushing the undergrowth aside, peering down along the rail track, following the churned-up path that led to the dummy houses. Once I startled a hare, at another time I threw myself on the ground as a rushing draught of air passed close above my head, a sharp fluttering as of very large wings.

And suddenly, in one of the dummy houses, I saw a match flare up. It was not followed by the glow of tobacco, but wandered along a wall, along a wooden beam that had not yet been carried off for firewood like everything else burnable. Three, four matches flared up, all of them throwing their modest light on the beam, which was no doubt being tested for use of some kind. I crept nearer, thinking a crowbar would soon be applied to the wall, that the wall would collapse and free the beam, but not a sound came.

He grabbed me from behind, his stranglehold so tight that I could scarcely breathe, and slowly he lifted me up from the ground and shook me. My heart beat against my ribs, I wanted to cry out, but couldn't. Then, as I was already expecting the worst, he let me go, pulled me round by my shirt and asked: Who are you, hm? Who are you? At first I was so frightened I could say nothing at all, and it was quite a while before I could answer: From the barracks, over there, and I pointed to the dim lights. Hearing this, he no longer demanded to know what I was doing there, he said: There's nothing more for you to steal, what there was you've already carted off long ago, and then he added: Don't let me ever see you here again. You people have nothing to seek here, you don't belong. It was Lauritzen who said that. I recognised him at once the next time we met by his voice: that stooping, pig-headed Lauritzen who never found out who it was he threatened that time on the training ground.

They were all back home, Max as well, waiting and waiting for the chief, who had still not returned, though it had long been dark and nothing looked as it really was. We kept watch at the window, listened to all sounds out in the corridor, and gradually we began to think some accident might have befallen him: Say that he . . . say if somebody . . . maybe he could have . . . : these were the sort of questions we were asking ourselves. Once a woman called out so loudly in her sleep that it could be heard across the whole barracks, but no doors opened, no feet scurried to and fro, we were familiar with it already. It must have been very late when Dorothea went outside with a flash-lamp. All we could see was the jerking, swinging beam of light stabbing the darkness this way and that, even straying up to the crowns of the pine-trees, but the chief could not be found by a flash-lamp either. We then switched off the electric light and waited. Nobody spoke, except for Max, who at one point asked if he could help himself to a gherkin out of a stone jar, and we listened as he felt his way towards the jar, took off the greaseproof paper cover and fished around, and suddenly I too felt a dripping gherkin in my hand.

The two men who brought the chief home were strangers to us. Both of them were wearing dyed uniforms and soldiers' boots. They held the chief beneath his arms and they dragged him in, dragged him across to his straw mattress and dropped him carefully on it so he would not hurt himself, then gave Dorothea a military salute and clumped off down the long corridor. The chief kept hiccuping, spit dribbled from his mouth, and now and again he wiped a hand over his face, as if brushing off flies, and made shuffling movements with his feet. He was breathing heavily, making gurgling noises, and a few times a faint smile crossed his face. We all sat down on Joachim's bed and watched Dorothea take off his clothes, first the boots, then the socks and the jacket and the shirt. Last of all she took off his trousers, which were covered in mud, and for the first time I became aware of all the scars on the chief's body, a long curving one above his hips, two star-shaped ones on his shoulders; he had a scar on his thigh and another angry red one on his chest. I counted nine scars altogether. His body was broad, compact and lean, the skin tautly stretched; in the way he was lying, his arms looked surprisingly long. He made no resistance, and he also remained supple and yielding as Dorothea sat him up and pulled a nightshirt over his head. He swayed and let out a belch before he fell back on his straw mattress, grunting something that sounded like: Tomorrow we'll get started, tomorrow. He was fast asleep almost before the blanket was put over him, and Max, who had just sat watching, shaking his head, said to Dorothea: What a fine old mess! She fixed her narrowed eyes on him and said: Don't you put on such airs! You haven't the least idea, you don't know what he's taking on – and for the sake of us all.

That was then – at the time he signed the leasehold agreement for ninety-nine years and spoke to Max for the last time about the land he'd won the right one day to buy.

If only I can stay with him, by his side! He surely doesn't mean to stop working, even if they've taken away his rights. Maybe they'll set something aside for him, the damp ground beside the Holle maybe, which he'll be allowed to work as he thinks best, that sour unused land that he alone can turn into a garden to wonder at. I could begin with him like in the old days in the barracks, I could help with the drainage, and with the clearing, the tilling and the dunging, we would have something for ourselves alone, and his knowledge wouldn't need go waste.

But who knows what Max will say to that, Max, whom they were in such a hurry to call in? He was different this time. He wished to walk the last stretch alone with his heavy suitcase, and he didn't ask: Everything still standing in Hollenhusen? Nor did he mention the judgement lime or suggest I should go there with him, to the place where we have already discussed so many other important matters, where he once said it is only the things we consider important that are important. But maybe he'll come back, so I'd better stay here by the toolshed, where he left me.

There's the iron bar signalling the midday break, with Ewaldsen striking it, or moody Löbsack. The vibrating tones of that bit of iron hanging on a rope reach everybody, whether they're working in the sand-pit or in the greenhouse: when the wind's from the east you can even hear midday being struck in Danes' Wood. Its notes are so high, so penetrating, that it hurts when you're standing close by, and sometimes too my skin gets very hot and I feel a kind of pressure on my temples, as if they're about to split open. And really it's just a strip of worn-out rail, hanging free beside the shed. What I'd like to do now would be to run quickly past the rhododendrons to the stronghold and through the side entrance to my table, but then old Lisbeth is sure to start moaning again: Typical, Greedyguts is the first to arrive, so I'll finish off the drilling tool before I go. It's only thanks to the chief that I'm allowed to eat in the room beside the kitchen; he gave the orders, and he has also eaten a few times in this room himself, when he was wet from the rain or had too much soil on his clothes and was in a hurry. It's the room where everything is washed before it comes to the table, and it has pale blue tiles up to eye level. The food would taste even better if Lisbeth didn't always keep her eyes fixed on me. The minute I sit down at the table and Magda puts the plate down in front of me, the wide hatch flies open and Lisbeth turns round on her chair so as to have me in sight, and her looks are never anything but gloomy and bad-tempered. Although she's so heavy and so short of breath that she can scarcely walk, she is only rarely ill. The flesh on her face hangs down in wobbling folds, and when she speaks her voice emerges like an organ from her bulk, frightening the life out of you. I once noticed she was sitting on two chairs at the same time. No one dares say a word to her, not even Magda, whom she sometimes snaps at and scolds, for everyone knows that Lisbeth was with the chief's family in earlier days, when they were still living on the edge of the Rominter heath. Except for the years she was in prison she has always worked for the Zeller family and, when one day she turned up in Hollenhusen, the chief promptly took her on, almost as if he'd been waiting for her.

This time she didn't grumble, she just nodded in reply to my greeting, and now she is sitting on her chair beside the cooking range, stirring and tasting things with hardly a glance at me. She didn't ask to see the plate Magda had filled for me either, she just told Magda to remove the string round the stuffed cabbage, or I'd be eating that too. The hatch is not even opened wide, I can make signs to Magda without Lisbeth seeing, and Magda has taken the risk of bringing me a second helping – something she usually daren't do. She even managed to whisper something to me without Lisbeth demanding to know what we're whispering about. But now she herself is whispering to Magda and putting something into a dish, which she places on a tray. I'll bet that's for the chief, something light and simple, a mash that certainly won't cause bad dreams. She is always trying to frighten me with forebodings of bad dreams: it's as if she thinks she knows exactly what I'll dream after eating pork chops with pears, and what after streaky bacon and what after mince loaf. But when she tells me, as she sometimes does, that I'll dream of being buried alive, all I then see is the Hookman and the way he walks barefoot through our plantations, bending the heads of the young plants.

Why not? I say, for it was her voice asking me whether I'd like a dollop of stewed apple. There's a bit too much, she says, and I should come and fetch the little glass bowl. When you see her sitting there, with her arched nose and her thinning hair, you feel she's someone you could rely on and would like to help, and it's impossible to believe she's such a moaner. Now, even before grabbing the glass bowl, I've asked her whether the chief is ill maybe, having ordered up stewed apple. Ill, she snorts, you're ill, and now get out of here. She doesn't ask whether I find the stewed apple tasty, just crouches there unmoving, staring, her eyes fixed on the kitchen towels, her hands folded in her lap. Her miserable bun of hair sits like a mouse on the back of her neck. This time she'll certainly not be watching to see that I rinse my plate in the sink and wipe the table.

When Magda comes to me after dark – and she will come, for she said she would – I shall ask her once again why Lisbeth was in prison. I can't bring myself to believe she killed her baby by lying on it in her sleep, but that is what Magda has told me, and she is always right. Why is Lisbeth looking at me like that? I only asked if there was anything that needed grinding, knives or scissors. She has very small eyes like currants, and she gives me a nod, though I haven't yet said goodbye, I can see she wants to be alone. It was very tasty, I say, then: I'm going back to my grinding.

They won't find me here in the rhododendrons, I can sit and wait. I'll be safe from them here, from Ina's children, for even from this distance I can see they're looking for me and have something up their sleeves. How delicate their school satchels make them look! Both of them are narrow-chested, their matchstick legs seem always on the point of snapping and their necks are so thin I could circle them with one hand. Tim and Tobias: for sure they're after me. They once offered me a rusty mousetrap and tried to talk me into taking the sweet that was fixed to the little bait board, but I pushed the board down with a stick and took the sweet after the trap had snapped shut.

I'd like to know what happened to the school satchel the chief gave me: I suppose I've lost it, like all my other presents, the cap, the fine handkerchieves and the little telescope. Ina

43

said at the time that I was too big for a school satchel and should have a leather case with a lot of compartments, but the chief had already bought the satchel secondhand, and he insisted on taking me personally to the school in Hollenhusen, where he had entered me for the final year.

At that time there were two classes, one for the small childen, the other for the bigger ones. I was put with the big ones, who at once formed a ring round me, put their heads together and were obviously plotting what to do. None of them came higher than my shoulder, as I saw when we were made to line up in the bumpy school yard, and I found it hard to keep their faces apart: they were all smooth, with fair eyelashes and a knowing look in their eyes. Even before we reached the classroom with its narrow desks they had tried to find out how sensitive I was at the back of my knees and neck, and by blowing up a paperbag and bursting it behind my head they also found how easily I could be startled. I felt sad that nobody wanted to sit beside me; neither Jens Redlefsen nor Lars Luderjahn were willing to change places in order to be near me, not on the first day and not later either. Our teacher, Fräulein Ratzum, made me sit in the front row, close to the door. Fräulein Ratzum always called me just 'our Bruno'. When she wanted my opinion, she would ask: What does our Bruno say to that? or: Would our Bruno like to add anything? And sometimes she just asked: And our Bruno?

She once told us about the invention of the wheel. The wheel, she said, was one of the finest and most important of all inventions, in its effect on transport, for instance, and forward motion in general: in fact, it was the wheel that first helped us to conquer distance. Then she suddenly asked: What does our Bruno think of that? I said plants had already invented many different ways of transporting their seeds and conquering distances: dandelions, for instance, which send out parachutes, burrs that cling to a fox's hide, the propeller seeds of the lime-tree and the ears of wild oats that can crawl and hop and travel quite a long way. Fräulein Ratzum was at first surprised, then she agreed that I was right, and said in front of the whole class: Our Bruno has given thought to a great mystery. That was what she said, and she looked at me thoughtfully through both eyes, one of which was pale blue and the other green.

Fräulein Ratzum was covered all over with freckles – her forehead and her neck as well as her plump arms sprinkled with dots and patches; she wore buttoned walking shoes and usually grey woollen dresses; when rehearsing us in a song, two little lights would flash in the depths of her differently coloured eyes. She lived by herself in the annex of a farm – Steenberg's, I remember – and, if you peeped over the hedge, you could see her washing or eating all by herself and correcting our schoolbooks. When it was snowing, I would come to the hedge very early and wait there in the dark till she came out, and then I would offer to carry her case, and she would wipe the snow from my hair and say: Our Bruno is a true cavalier. I waited for her quite often when the ground was icy, when it was thawing, when the road was flooded. Once, hand in hand, we jumped over slush and puddles, and, when the mornings got lighter and warmer, we made a detour past Danes' Wood, and I showed her how ants carried off the seeds of the violets. I should dearly have liked to have had her to myself as a teacher.

It was never discovered who smeared her chair with so much glue that her woollen dress stuck to it, but the tube turned up in my satchel. Fräulein Ratzum herself fished it out during the search, and she held it in her hand and looked at me unbelievingly for a long time, and her differently coloured eyes grew moist. No tears came, but her chin trembled for an instant and her lips twitched, and that was all. She pulled the back of her skirt towards the front and examined the stain, which was already turning darker, and she also tried rubbing it a bit, but that only gave her sticky fingers and brought giggles and gurgles from the gang behind me. I jumped to my feet and tried to say something, but my throat swelled and became constricted, my hands broke out in a sweat and I felt a throbbing in my temples, and, although my teacher was now standing right in front of me, I saw her as if through a veil, and I heard her say in a muffled voice: Why, Bruno, why have you done this? I could never make up my mind about you, but now I see you're just like the others. And she also said, without moving her lips: I'm sad, very sad, and you can expect nothing more from me. She went back to her desk and started to write, and the class became very still. I just stayed standing there, listening to the knocking inside my head. I was made to remain on my feet until the lesson ended, and when she left the classroom she didn't give me her usual nod.

Next morning, before the birds were awake, I was crouching behind the hedge. The curtains in her room were still drawn, Steenberg's dog was lying on the hard clay soil in front of his kennel, blinking at me – we already knew each other so well that he no longer barked. Then the birds began to sing, just odd ones trying out their voices, chaffinches and flycatchers, also thrushes and larks and yellowhammers, but gradually they got their voices in harmony, and I found myself thinking Fräulein Ratzum must have rehearsed all their entries with them, in fact, arranged the whole chorus. I could hardly contain my impatience and, unable to crouch behind the hedge any longer, began walking up and down. Then at last I heard Fräulein Ratzum open a window, and in a flash I was standing in front of her, wishing her good morning.

First she gave a surprised smile, but then her face clouded over and she said quietly: I think it would be better, Bruno, if we each go alone. I wanted quickly to tell her what she ought to know. I'd already worked it out in my mind, each word carefully chosen, but all at once I was unable to speak, for I found my eyes resting on the grey woollen dress, which was hanging on a coat-hanger before the wardrobe. There were some rust-brown stains on it, and it looked as if it had been singed, singed by an overheated iron. Our teacher gave me a pat on my cheek – it was neither a warning nor a punishment, but seemed more like an appeal – and then she said: Our

Bruno will now go to school by himself for a while, like a good boy. That's all she said.

I ran off, ran across the fields and along the Holle to Danes' Wood. I couldn't stop, all I wanted was to keep running, on and on, but then at the big pond some alder roots tripped me up, and I fell down and stayed lying on the grass. The water was peat-brown with a shimmer of gold beneath the surface, and, from places where the reeds had strayed into it, there came flashes as if from little moving mirrors; clouds of slime floated over the shallow, weedy bottom. I crept very close to the water, and the roaring I'd felt in my head as I ran slowly died down; it stopped altogether when I broke a shrivelled flag root open and ate a bit of its bitter flesh. Water spiders. Dragonflies. Beetles that just let themselves sink to the bottom. Movement everywhere, scampering, paddling, stalking. A couple of coots, ceaselessly nodding. Tench leaping suddenly. On the opposite bank a polecat, listening with twitching nose. I tried to trail it, but it lured me only as far as Danes' Wood, then suddenly vanished.

I don't know why the others grinned so widely when I entered the classroom: maybe because I was dirty and caked and covered in burrs. I no longer remember: all I know is that it was the first time I was ever late for a lesson. I was at once made to pick up a pointer and go to the map of Europe, coloured blue, green and pink, and Fräulein Ratzum immediately demanded to know where the Goths came from, where they spread to and the names of the tribes into which they decayed, yes, decayed: Our Bruno will now tell us. Then the pointer began uneasily to wobble, it reared up, tapped down here and there on mountains and lakes, described vague circles and refused to settle down. My hand grew heavier and heavier and finally lost all feeling for the pointer. Another feeling took its place: a kind of tightening, squeezing. The pulses in my fingers began beating, and before my eyes I clearly saw a spiral, turning and turning. Scandinavia, said a voice that could only have been our teacher's, and, gathering my wits together, I tapped Scandinavia. Fräulein Ratzum praised me and confirmed it: Yes, the Goths came from Scandinavia and spread first to the coast of Samland and to the Vistula flats. Good, now go on. But I knew nothing more. I let the pointer droop and I thought and I listened, and once again I heard that voice, coming as if from far away, until it was clear enough for me to hear it say: You're very close now, Bruno – one of their domains was between the Carpathians and the Dnieper. I at once traced a wide circle between the Carpathians and the Dnieper, and Fräulein Ratzum said in a pleased tone: You see, and then, turning to the class: Now remember the things our Bruno has pointed out.

I gazed into her freckled face and waited. My left eye was smarting and there was a sour taste in my mouth, but I kept a hold on myself and waited, and I heard the words Ostrogoths and Visigoths – no, I was no longer hearing the words, they were just coming into my mind, because our teacher was willing them there loudly enough: So the Ostrogoths established an empire on the southern steppes of Russia, and they made great raiding excursions and defeated several emperors and sacked Thrace. Our Bruno has done his homework well, Fräulein Ratzum said, then suddenly she gave me a concerned look and asked: Is anything the matter, are you ill, have you got a temperature? You're bathed in sweat. She guided me to my desk in the front row, and I was not called on again that day: even during the singing lesson I was allowed to stay in my seat. And not only that: at the end of the final lesson she gave me a nod as she used to do. Maybe that was why Heiner Walendy was lying in wait for me, his bad intentions showing clearly in his eyes, but I saw him in good time and climbed up my Scots pine, to the highest branch that would bear my weight.

They've gone, Bruno, that skinny couple of pests, the coast's clear and you can go back to your grinding. Now I shall draw the blades across the oilstone till they're so clean, so smooth, so clear that the wood won't even feel the cuts they make.

48

Since the chief put me in charge of knives, shears, saws and all the grafting tools, no one has ever grumbled about blunt blades or dirty saw-teeth, everything in my care has its proper sharpness, its bite, because I grind angles where angles belong and leave cutting edges flat where they were flat in the beginning. Blunt tools can easily lead to bruising, the chief told me, and that's why I test every edge for its sharpness, take a soft piece of wood and practise making upward strokes with it. It wasn't easy at first to remember all the names: you must know the difference between a budding knife and a grafting knife, we've got bill-hooks and quick-budders as well as anvil pruners and parrot-beak pruners, and I don't know how many saws, but it was not long before I knew them all, and now I have only to take one in my hand to know at once, even in the dark, which cutting instrument it is. I enjoy grinding even more than potting, the grinding noise is so lovely as the oilstone works the steel, it rasps and hisses, and that sets up a tingling in my stomach, just like being tickled. Here is the sandpaper and here the leather strop, the rag, the little oil can from which each joint and each spring will receive a little drop, measured according to its needs. I once missed a cuttings knife with a polished point, I noticed it at once when I opened the drawer, and I searched and searched the whole toolshed from top to bottom and the plantations too without finding it. It then turned out that the chief himself had taken the knife, just to make sure I was keeping a watchful eye on all the things he'd put in my care.

The knife Joachim once gave me had no high-grade steel blade, no brass inlay, and its handle was also not of walnut: it was just a flat silver knife with a corkscrew. I hadn't told the chief that Joachim was present when I was tied to the judgement lime-tree and stayed there all night without calling for help. I was fearful of remembering any names, since the chief was in such a rage, swearing to deal individually with all who had had a hand in tying me up. He would wring their necks: that's what he said. Joachim crouched on his mattress, making himself small and not saying a word, and I could see he was frightened too. Afterwards, when we were alone, he showed me the knife, he showed it me and asked whether I liked it; then I knew he meant to give it to me and why. You can keep it, he said, and that was all.

Lost now, this knife I have lost too: I suppose somewhere near the railway station in Hollenhusen, in the tulip bed beneath the poplar, to which they dragged me after school, winking and making mysterious remarks. Redlefsen was one of them, Luderjahn too and Heiner Walendy, looking innocent. They could hardly wait for the last lesson to end and kept making signs to me as Fräulein Ratzum stood writing on the blackboard. The signs meant: Done! Hurry up, we'll be waiting for you in the school yard.

It's only when you have to walk to the station from the school in the rain that you notice how far it is; we walked and walked, and they didn't breathe a word about what they wanted to show me, they just answered my questions with soothing nods: You'll soon see, just keep going. It didn't escape my notice how they kept secretly nudging each other. They were cooking something up: that was obvious enough. We were wet through by the time we reached the station, and they led me straight over a thin patch of grass to the poplar-tree, which everybody has to pass on leaving the station.

A poster. Yes, that was all I saw at first: a poster fixed to the tree at eye level with drawing-pins, and I was puzzled and glanced over my shoulder at the others, who were now standing close behind me. They avoided my eyes, directing them instead towards the poster: Take a closer look at it. I read the inscription: Children seeking their parents. I cast a quick glance over the faces of the six children shown below it. They could have been my own brothers and sisters, all with snub noses and fixed stares, all with large heads – but that was probably just the way the photos had been taken. The Red Cross was seeking helpful information, that I still remember. And then, talking right into my ear, Heiner Walendy said: The one in the middle with the wonky eye – doesn't he look familiar? And suddenly I recognised myself. Beneath the photo was written: Bruno Messmer – my name, my birthday. They could only make a guess where I came from: maybe Schlohmitten on the Memel. Children seeking their parents, that was written in large letters on the poster. That's me, I said to the others, that's me, and all of a sudden I felt hot all over, and I pulled out my knife to loosen the drawing-pins, which were driven firmly into the wood. You mustn't do that, said Heiner Walendy, you mustn't take the poster down, and he seized my wrist and forced it away, and the others laughed. They laughed, and one of them said: Our Bruno doesn't even know where he comes from. Another said: Our Bruno, they found him in a crow's nest. And, with Heiner Walendy still holding my wrist tight, they decided to hang the poster up in the school: they'd pin it to the blackboard, put a ring round my photo and colour it. I gave them a push backwards and tore the poster down. It was damaged only at the edges and, before they regained their balance and fell on me, I had stuffed it inside my shirt, my wet shirt. They threw me to the ground, and Heiner Walendy pressed my face into the tulip bed, demanding the poster back. He was riding on me, threatening and shouting, thumping my satchel with his fists. There was earth in my mouth and a roaring in my head. I don't know how I suddenly found the strength to brace my body and throw myself to one side, I kicked and lashed out and was suddenly free, and Heiner Walendy, who had been riding on my back, slowly tipped over and lay on the ground without moving. The others had already run off, and I ran too, sped across the rails and along the gravel path, spitting out earth as I went, the poster still inside my muddy shirt. I ran to the dwarf pines on the training ground with the idea of hiding there, but then I thought I'd find better cover in the half-buried practice tank which the chief meant to blow up, but hadn't yet got round to it. In the cool half-light I sat in the gunner's seat; the turret hatch was closed, and light came only through the peep-hole, but that was enough to enable me to find my picture again on the poster, which I put across my knee. It was one of the photos Dorothea had had taken of me, and which she had never shown me. I looked long at my picture, reading the words beneath it over and over again, and so great was my grief that I had only one wish, and that was to disappear, to disappear for a whole year into a crack in the ground or never mind where. I imagined the ground opening, simply splitting apart, and the practice tank sinking deeper and deeper, until it touched the bottom and the earth tumbling down after it would cover it entirely, so that no one would ever trace us. To be forgotten for a while, that was what I was longing for. But then I heard voices, shouts, muffled as if coming from far away, out of the darkness that lay over the training ground. Flares flickered, beams from flash-lamps wandered over the ground. Through the peep-hole I could see the line of searchers moving down towards the damp ground, to the Holle. At one point a dog barked quite close to me, but a voice from the distance called it back and it obeyed. Though I couldn't understand the calls, I knew at once that they were to do with me, that the men were looking for me. I made the levers of the turret hatch fast. Now nobody would be able to open it from the outside. I folded the poster and pushed it inside my shirt and waited, determined not to answer any of the calls and to keep as still as the grave if they should come back and examine the place where I was hiding. And after a while they did come back: they came straight towards me, but didn't call out my name. Closer and closer they came with their flares, then unleashed their dog, which promptly sprang on to the platform and began to whine. At that, one of the men mounted the platform and tried to open the hatch. He tugged and swore, hammered with something hard against the steel, but the hatch held firm. I heard them discussing what to do. I lay quite still and listened to them with this throbbing in my temples, with this weight in my stomach, and suddenly the chief said: It's my opinion we should blow it up. He spoke so loudly that everyone could hear him, and it seemed no one had anything against it, for no more questions were asked. My hands were shaking like mad as I tried to move the hatch levers, they resisted my efforts, got stuck, and suddenly I felt a crackling and a ticking inside my head, and I screamed and screamed again. And then the turret hatch opened.

When I think of that night, I can see the chief lifting me down from the practice tank and rubbing my shoulders and my back and hanging his jacket over them. Then he is seizing me by the back of the neck and saying: Never do that again, Bruno, never. We walked along between the flares, which one after the other dropped behind or went out, accompanied each time by a short greeting, a brief word of thanks. The last to take his leave, close to the barracks, was old Gollup, who in wet weather often cursed the bits of shrapnel that were wandering around inside his chest.

Dorothea was already expecting us, I had to undress, to hand over the poster, which she carefully ironed and hung up to dry, and then I had to drink something hot and bitter that made me feel giddy, and wrap myself in a grey blanket. Since my hands were still shaking, Dorothea took them and held them firmly enclosed in her own, and she sat down beside me and told me a few times I had nothing to fear. I belonged to them, she also said, and I could stay with them always if my parents didn't come to fetch me. We don't want to be rid of you, she said, but maybe your parents are looking for you, and we sent your picture to the Red Cross so they can find their way here. Later the chief came and said nothing more than that school would stop for the time being. Not a word did he say about my having stabbed Heiner Walendy in the back, that big blade right into his back: it wasn't till next morning I heard that, when the chief, instead of going out to the training ground as usual, went to the school. When he told me what I'd done, I didn't want at first to believe him, but the chief has always been truthful, so there could be no doubt my blade had gone into Heiner Walendy's shoulder, easy as can be and without my even noticing. Who knows who found my knife?

But now they will surely send me away. The chief is the only one to have taken care of me and protected me when necessary, but now they have taken away his rights, and that surely means his word no longer counts for anything here in Hollenhusen. From now on, I suppose, he'll be getting nothing but his bare keep, with now and again a sip of Wacholder; they'll see to it that he keeps to his room as much as possible, doesn't give orders, doesn't take customers round the plantations, nothing. If only he would come out on the terrace, or at least show himself at the window, if only I could once speak to him alone! Maybe Magda can think of a way, Magda, who has promised to come after dark with some leftovers – I hope with leftovers. The chief is the only one who can prevent my having to leave, he to whom all of us here owe everything, whose word was always listened to. Surely they haven't forgotten that it was he who took over this land and worked it at the beginning with borrowed tools and hired horses? They surely can't ignore the fact that everything here is linked with his name.

And I was with him from the very start: at first, only in the afternoons, and then, after he took me away from school, from morning till evening. I was there when he divided up the land according to his plan, drained it bit by bit, then ploughed and harrowed it. He arranged for me not to have to go to school any more, and on waking I would quickly swallow two plates of porridge and then run out to the training ground, where he would already be striding along behind the plough or clearing or digging trenches. Sometimes I had to search him out in the mist, sometimes he would wave to me from the hill bare of bushes. Hardly a day passed without his finding something for me; before I started work, I would take a peep at the rusty steel helmet into which he threw it all: buttons, shell splinters, rosettes, every day cartridge cases. Since I couldn't bring myself to walk behind the horses, I would collect up stones in a basket, collect the last scrapings from the dynamited dummy houses and scraps of iron and sheet metal, and when the heap came up to my chest, I would wheel it off in the handcart, the barrow. There, in the place where our land bordered on Lauritzen's fields, I built a wall, piling up the stuff I had collected and levelling it out so you could comfortably sit on it and take a rest. Just the flintstones I put to one side: I used the gleaming black flints to mark out a little garden of my own, with a dwarf birch-tree at the centre. It was a dry summer, with a light breeze blowing steadily from the east and just flimsy wisps of cloud in the sky. Whenever we drew close, the chief and I, or passed one another with plough and handcart, we would nod to each other, smile and nod, and sometimes make little gestures to express our happiness and sense of togetherness, and then I would scarcely feel the strap cutting into my chest. At that time I never felt tired, not the whole day through. Ina, when she sometimes helped me gather stones and clear wood after school, tired very quickly, and Joachim needed only to stoop a couple of times and he'd have to take a rest, but I felt tired only when I got into bed in the evenings.

Whichever of us was the first to spot Dorothea with the basket would give a whistle – that hadn't been planned, it just happened that way – and, hearing the whistle, we would drop our work and walk across to my wall, where Dorothea would share out the food: bread and dripping and apples and unsweetened rosehip tea, and on a few occasions broad beans and potato cakes. Then she would sit on the wall with us and watch us eat, making sure the chief and I first put on our shirts, and before going off with the empty basket she always had a word of praise for what we'd done. When the chief listed all the things that still remained to be done, from sanding through to dunging, she said: How on earth will you manage it all? And the chief said: Bit by bit, and with Bruno's help, and he gave me a wink. That was a rare time of happiness: I needed nothing, I missed nothing, and with every day that passed we could see we had achieved something, gained something. When we finished work, we wouldn't always go straight home: often enough we'd sit down on the wall, and the chief, whom nobody here can hold a candle to, would talk of the lost plantations on the edge of the Rominter heath, the plantations of the rising sun, as he called them, or he would pick up the stones I had gathered and tell me which was feldspar, which granite or gneis. He told me how stones were formed, how they travelled on the backs of glaciers, and I felt as if I was there when the ice came down from the north and smoothed the mountains and dug out long valleys and pushed the stony rubble along in front of it – whatever he described, I always felt at once I was there. And often enough I'd then wish I were a tree on the plain, standing alone and free, or a little river like the Holle, or an erratic block, that's to say, a boulder the melting glaciers had lost hold of. That's what I wanted to be, so as always to be able just to watch and listen.

We once came on an erratic block among the junipers. It was raising its mossy back just slightly above the soil, a grey, lichen-covered back that had a few dents in it, as if made by very heavy blows, and there were also scratch marks running across its surface, thin and sharp, as if someone had dragged a pointed iron stake across it. The chief saw at once that the boulder reached far down into the earth. He measured it with a piece of wire which he used as a probe, he stabbed and poked and felt around until he had established the size of the stone, but he wasn't content just to leave it at that, he decided to dig it up and cart it away. And so we dug and dug, and the boulder grew bigger and bigger both downwards and lengthways. It looked a bit like a whale – the lumpy, cudgel-like head, the gradual slimming towards the end – and, because it was wrapped around in several places with fine roots, it looked to me as if it had been caught in a net. Our arms and necks and chests were thickly smeared with earth as we worked right up against the stone, this obstinate boulder that didn't even stir when we leaned on it with all our weight. If I'd had any say in the matter, the stone could have stayed in its bed, but the chief had his reasons for moving it, so we dug it free and set up a slide, sloping down into the earth, over which the horses could be used to drag the boulder out.

We had just fixed the chain around it – a chain lengthened by a shackle, which ran in two loops round the stone and was knotted in several places – when Lauritzen appeared above our heads. There he stood in his green jacket, stooping as always, his stick rammed into the soil, and as always he just stared in contempt and took his time before speaking. The wall – he wanted the wall I had built with the stones and all the rubbish I had collected to be taken down. The fact that it ran along the border between his land and ours didn't satisfy him: there'd never been a wall separating the fields in Hollenhusen from each other, not as long as he could remember, and he was not prepared to put up with our elongated rubbish heap. That is what he said, and then he demanded the instant removal of the wall, staring down at the chief, who, as he adjusted the chain around the boulder, was pressing himself against it, breathing heavily and grunting. The chief just went on working in his own way without answering Lauritzen, and without letting him know how much of what had been said he'd taken in.

A gesture with his hand, yes, that he did make towards our pig-headed neighbour, but that could have meant: All right, all right, just as well as: Get out of here, and Lauritzen went off without a word. I moved away too and watched from a distance as the chief harnessed the horses and urged them to haul, again and yet again. Since they couldn't make it with strenuous heaves, he started them at a gallop. Clods of earth flew from under their hooves, they rose on their hindlegs, they shook themselves, thrashed around and tossed their heads, but the boulder didn't move until the chief placed two tree trunks on the sloping slide. Then, hauling steadily, they dragged the boulder out of its hole and on without stopping to the edge of our land. The chief gave me a wave: he was so exhausted he wouldn't or couldn't say a word; the upper part of his body was all wet, and under the skin of one of his nine scars the

57

pulse was beating hard. I rubbed his back with his shirt, and then he sat down on the boulder and I went across to the hole and began filling it, filled it halfway up with the dark grey earth. The chief watched me blankly, and when I returned to his side he slapped the boulder with his palm and said he had just dug out his gravestone. Under that anyone can rest in peace, he also said.

We gave no more thought to Lauritzen, and it was only when one morning we found nothing but the remains of my wall that we were reminded of him. The wall had been knocked down during the night, not all of it, but all the same a great deal of the section we sat on to eat, and all the stones and bits of wood I had gathered hadn't disappeared, but lay strewn over our land, which looked as if it was pitted with smallpox. A fresh cart track led across the land. I pointed it out to the chief, and he patiently followed it, walking this way and that and in a circle and finally down to the Holle, or rather to the makeshift bridge Lauritzen had had built there for himself. There he stopped and gave himself up to thought. And then together we collected up all the scattered bits and without a word raised the wall high again – this time not directly on the borderline, but clearly on our side of it. All that could be heard was the clicking and crashing of stone, and when Dorothea arrived with the basket, the wall was already casting a low shadow.

That wall stood for only a few days, then one morning we found it knocked down again. All the things we had used to build it lay scattered in a wide circle, hurled all over the place in rage, and it looked to me as if a further load of stones had been dumped on our land, together with rusty bits of machinery and a few tree stumps and barbed wire and a tin bath with holes in it. I couldn't utter a word, I felt so shocked, so helpless. All I could do was look at the chief, whose face was dark with fury. He was gazing silently over the land, taking it all in, as if trying to measure the damage that had been done to us, and after a while he nodded and said in a voice that contained neither rage nor indignation: Well, let's get started – and that was all.

He did not listen to me: he simply ignored my suggestion that we dig a few mantraps along the way down to the Holle and cover them up well, and he also had nothing to say to my plan of keeping a watch through the night. As if his thoughts were elsewhere, he slowly dragged all the scattered objects together, leaving me no choice but to do the same.

So we dragged and carted and raised our wall high yet again, and this time it took us a whole day to get it done. We rested in the light of the setting sun. There was a glow behind Hollenhusen, a reddish-yellow sky giving off a curious reflection. The chief said: Slow us down, Bruno, that's all the people here can do, just slow us down, but they'll never finish us off. That's what he said, and it made me think of his nine scars and the two shipwrecks, also that he had survived being buried alive in Russia, an attack on a train in Belgium, and that he alone had escaped an ambush his company ran into in Croatia.

We walked home in silence, and during the night I dreamed of the largest erratic block in the world; a whole village was spread across it: there were farms, a church, a school, a village hall. The boulder had only a gentle slope and, where the sun caught it, there was a sparkle of quartz and mica. And I dreamed that the chief and I secretly measured the boulder and fixed round it, in a way that wouldn't be seen, the longest and strongest chain it's possible to imagine, a chain that came together in Danes' Wood. Here in the darkness the chief brought together all the horses he had found in the paddocks in Schleswig, and, when he had collected a hundred horses, he harnessed them during a thunderstorm, and with only a single word of command got them to pull together, and their combined strength loosened the boulder and started it sliding, with everything still on its back. At one time I asked the chief how far he meant to drag the boulder, and he said: Beyond the horizon to the sea. But we didn't get that far, because from the hole the boulder had left behind soldiers in very strange

59

uniforms rose up. They were most of them soldiers with beards, and they swarmed out without a word of command and began to shoot at the horses. With their lively ratatat they decimated the largest team the world has ever seen: in the end only two horses remained. As they were about to bind the chief and me to the two horses, I woke up, and peered across at once to the chief's mattress. It was empty.

And it's hard to say how confused I felt when next morning we walked to the top of what we called the command hill. As so often, a light morning mist lay over the training ground, and above the mist, which was already dispersing, rose the backs of trotting horses and the silhouettes of grazing cattle, between them two men who were waving and shouting in an attempt to drive them down to the Holle, to the meadows and paddocks that belonged to Lauritzen. The animals were not eager to be caught: they played with their pursuers and made fools of them. It was fun to watch how from a standing position they would swing their heavy shoulders round or gain ground with a sudden trot. The chief seemed to be enjoying it too, for he smiled and was in no hurry to begin work. He gave me a nudge and pointed across to the oats and barley fields. There were animals standing in those too – no, they weren't standing, but wading through the corn, carving lanes in it as they bundled up the ears with their long tongues and stripped them off. He also drew my attention to the gates, which were all open, and to the makeshift bridge, which had lost its beams and its boards: some of them had drifted a short way down the Holle, had piled up at the bend and were blocking the water. I saw, as he pointed all this out, what a long detour they'd now have to make with the animals to get them back inside the fenced pasture land.

I would dearly have liked to lie on the hill and watch their attempts to drive the obstinate beasts off our land, but, once the sun was up, the chief was unwilling to stay there doing nothing. He led the way down the hill to the dwarf pines, which had still to be cleared, and he was not prepared to help the two men whose Halloos and Brrrs and Whoas could be heard coming from all directions. At times the ground vibrated with the hoofbeats of running beasts, and sometimes a lone animal would break off and come close to us, only to shy and turn back at the sight of a pickaxe or a spade. We took no notice of all these rounding-up efforts. Side by side, we felled and we cleared, and it was my job to pull at the thinner, creeping side-roots, which usually tore off with a pop. The tap-roots we dug out. I always felt sorry for the fine white hair-roots; when I held them up to the wind and blew off the crumbs of soil, they would start to quiver, to lash around, and it looked as if they were trying to run away. Quite often I plucked them off and ate them; I could hardly feel them between my teeth, and I couldn't make out any particular taste, though, as the chief said, they kept the tree alive, taking up moisture and salts and all the other things it needed and passing them on.

Without the help of the horse-rider they would never have got the beasts away. He was a young man with a face that didn't give his thoughts away, and he rode past us without a greeting. First of all he rounded the animals up and forced them close together, but only in order to put the horses on a rein. They then set off at a walking pace down to the Holle and along the Holle to the next makeshift bridge, and the cattle trotted after them, kept on the move by shouts and threats. We could still hear their shouts at noon, and we saw men running across the fields to catch odd stubborn beasts, and I was pleased each time their attempts failed. When at last they got it done, they went across to the bridge, fished the beams and boards out of the river and put it all back in order. After that they just stood there for a long time watching us. Probably they were trying to think of some way of getting their own back, but couldn't decide what.

The chief, who missed nothing of what was going on, just once gave a fleeting smile and said: I've got the feeling, Bruno, that from now on our wall will stay as it is. He said nothing more, and I wasn't surprised to find he was right.

61

Max hasn't forgotten me: there's no doubt that now, there on the terrace after having greeted them all and given his advice, he's keeping an eye out for me. Maybe he'll invite me to go with him to the judgement lime or to the dolmen, and tell me the latest news from the stronghold. Maybe too he'll tell me why he was not his usual self when we met, he who most times has been so good to me and always patient. The fact that he has gone down to the main path and is now heading in the direction of the glasshouse can surely only mean he's expecting to find me in my home, so I'd better make my way there, for I don't want him to knock in vain on my door, to knock, wait and then turn away. It could be that he just needs me to listen, as so often before. The knives and shears I can clear away later; by the time Joachim makes his evening round everything will be back in its proper place.

He has seen me and understood my sign. Not so fast, old chap, he says, not so fast, and he stops in front of my door and points with a smile to the two locks, points so fixedly that there's nothing else to do but unlock them before his eyes. Something is worrying him, he's got something on his mind, I can see that from his movements, the way he walks inside: not expectant, curious, but hesitant, as if he's hiding something – no, it's rather the manner of someone with a guilty conscience: he's intending something he can't excuse even to himself – I know Max. So this is where you live, Bruno, a cosy little place you've got. He says this with only half-hearted interest and walks around, tapping the back of the armchair, sizing up the view, before sitting down on the only stool. How hurriedly he eyes it all, hurriedly and coldly: however unconcerned he makes himself out to be, I can see he is searching around for something he's hoping to find here in my home. I can feel that what he really wants to do is to pull open the drawers of my chest and look inside the dark-blue trunk Dorothea gave me for my twenty-first birthday. How practical he finds the rack on which, behind a curtain, my clothes are hanging and my shoes and gumboots standing! And the little clock in its marble case pleases him so much that he takes it off the windowsill. No, it's not worth repairing. He wants to know whether I haven't got a pocket watch – a watch with a spring cover, for instance. No, no.

He shakes his head, less at me than at himself. He probably regrets his question, regrets, I have the feeling, having come to see me at all. At last he has found his book, the only book I keep in my home, and by a wonder it hasn't yet been lost. It was his first book, and in it he wrote: To Bruno, the most patient of listeners, in memory of our years together. He reads the inscription with a sad smile, looks at me and nods, just as if wanting to show he is still satisfied with the words he wrote then. Much has happened, he says, with the book, with me, with my 'theory of property' – well, you know all about that. He turns the pages of the book he gave me; I have read it five times already, and each time I've had the feeling of falling down a hole, a hole with smooth sides. Yes, five times already, but I shall certainly read it a sixth time, I say, and he puts the book back in its place and gets to his feet and sighs and doesn't know how to begin.

Bruno? Yes? You're one of us, after all, Bruno, he says, you've been living with us so long – just think of the past years and all the things you owe to the chief. He reflects, screws up his fingers, and I can see how hard he finds it to go on speaking. Is the chief ill? I ask. He doesn't reply, but gives me a pleading look, then whispers: Only you, Bruno, you are the only one I can take into my confidence: you should be told that they're worried in the stronghold. About the chief? I ask. Several things are missing, he says, personal things, valuable things, they have simply disappeared. Stolen? I ask. No, he says, not stolen, Bruno, at least they don't think so; they believe everything is here somewhere, here in Hollenhusen. I should keep my eyes open, he tells me, I should go around and find out whether anybody has anything that doesn't belong to him, and I should at once report any property that looks out of place or suspicious to him, Max, who has taken me into his confidence. Yes, I say. Don't forget, he says, you're one of us, we must hold together, we mustn't allow everything to be scattered and lost. But most important of all: keep it to yourself. He gives me his hand, and I am sad, because he is sad. How long he holds my hand in his, how intently he gazes into my eyes! It's as if he'd like to confide even more to me, but first has to make sure it would all be safe with me. Do you remember, Bruno, he asks, how long you have been calling my father the chief? From the beginning, I say. Because everyone called him the chief, I called him that too, from the beginning and always. The chief has done a lot for us, he says, and it looks as if we must now do something for him.

He goes off with lowered head, and I can't watch him go, for there's a buzzing in my head like a swarm of June bugs, I have first to sit down and wait till it's gone, till I can put everything in place and sort it out. If I still had that bit of glass from the bottom of a green bottle, I could start my search for the missing things at once; with that piece of glass, ground smooth by the sand after a long time in the sea, I could surely get some of them back: all I'd have needed to do was to follow the sparkling arrows that always showed up inside it. But a bullet from Joachim's shotgun put an end to that helpful piece of glass, it just shattered into a shower of splinters. In the few days I had it I could find almost everything I'd lost. Simon, that ex-soldier tramp, who had brought it from far away and who gave it to me when I first came on him digging on our land one evening – Simon hadn't been wrong in his promise. If it turns out I shan't be able to stay here any longer, I shall maybe have to take to the road like him. I don't know how much power a guardian has, but if he's allowed to lock the chief up, I shall always be ready to open the door for him, so softly that no one would hear, and I'd go with him anywhere, if that's what he wants. The chief must surely know that, he who knows me better than anyone else here and who has always listened to me when I had something important to tell him; however far away from each other we might have been, he understood me. When once I was running out of strength in the big pond, I simply turned to him: I didn't let out a shout, just told myself he must be coming, and, though before he'd been nowhere in sight, he did come running from Danes' Wood and at once had a rope in his hand to throw to me.

It wasn't Ina's fault that I ran out of strength: she had been throwing sticks into the water for her own amusement, and for *my* amusement I was carrying them back to Ina, who had surprised me while I was naked, trying to cool off. She was sitting in her bathing costume on my clothes, and each time I laid the piece of wood on the bank she praised me.

With the piece of green bottle-glass you could only find things that had been lost above the soil; things lying beneath it, things that had been covered up or buried or had sunk to the bottom wouldn't show up in that glass polished by the waves, Simon had told me, and that was probably the reason why the roving ex-soldier gave it to me and why, the next time he turned up on our land, he was trailing behind him a heavy magnet attached to a string, a piece of iron painted red and blue that hopped and leaped around as he doggedly traced his circles. He didn't mind having me close to him. However often he dug and however often he consulted his grubby sketch, he didn't find what he was looking for: his short-handled spade never struck the regimental strongbox that was said to be buried on our land. But I don't know whether that was what drew him to us: maybe he was looking for something else. He didn't dig just anywhere: it was always close to the place where the erratic block had been. Five times he dug, then he gave up, and after sitting for a while in dejection, he beckoned me over and had nothing more to tell me than that this land was well dunged, very well dunged, and he himself had done his bit towards that in former times. He didn't want to go with me to greet the chief, he had to get moving at once. I should just tell the chief Simon had been here, that was all. His scaly, lizard-like skin grew red as he got to his feet and gulped down air, and then he simply walked off after making a note of my name on the edge of a grubby sketch.

The chief knew nobody called Simon, he just shook his head when I told him about the man in the long soldier's greatcoat, and I remember he didn't pause to give it any further thought as he stood in our shed checking whether the seeds were ready to germinate. This was a flat wooden lock-up shed we had built down in the hollow out of stuff lying around in the dummy houses, and the path leading to it had been trodden by ourselves. Here there was no wind, and the sun was baking. Nothing escaped the chief's eye: when he removed the husks from the seeds, when he watered the seeds or laid them in a solution that turned them red, when he cut open the conifer and beech seeds lengthways and freed the embryo, then he at once knew what had happened to them in the dormancy period, and he could tell at once whether they were right for an experimental sowing. He watered in the dark, he brought things into the light, he made longitudinal sections and cross sections to confirm what he must already have known, and nearly everything he sowed in exact numbers in pots or trays came up and was good for planting outdoors.

Much of the seed Dorothea had brought with her in leather bags from the lost plantations in the east came up too and grew tall and broad beneath the glass covers the chief laid over the pots and trays. While sitting on his three-legged stool contemplating what had come up, he didn't like being talked to. I had to keep quite still, I mustn't walk about or do any work, nor was I allowed to get too close to him, I don't know why, but I do know that his lips would sometimes move, that he would speak softly to the seed-leaves, the cotyledons. Sometimes, as I sat on the rough working-top watching him, I felt as if I were no longer in my body, and I forgot to breathe. Then everything would begin to hum and to feel light, and I would come to with a start when the chief got up and said: Come along, Bruno. Not once did I see Joachim or Max in our shed, Dorothea rarely and Ina even more rarely. I believe the chief liked it best with just me there, and that mainly because after a while he stopped noticing me. One evening, after he had nearly locked me in, he said: Sorry, Bruno, but it's easy enough to forget you, I didn't realise you were there.

At that time, just as I had to have a garden of my own, which I ringed around with flint-stones, I had to have my own seedbed as well. The chief nodded his approval and made no objection to my carrying humus to the skeleton of an old boat we had dug up on the damp ground and tipping it on the bottom boards, which were well-preserved. The boat was maybe a hundred years old, its ribs so hard that no knife would leave a mark on them, but after only a few days the wood began to fade in the sun, losing its blackness and turning a greyish-brown. Since it had no thwarts, I was able to spread the bed over the whole length of the boat, and there I sowed elderberry, mountain ash and gorse, the one pre-sown, the other washed, and most of it came up in its own time, sheltered from the wind by bits of sacking tied to the boat's ribs. In order to keep my little plantation safe from rabbits, I put out some wire snares, but the chief was against that: without saying a word, he collected the snares up and carried them off to the wooden shed in the hollow.

What I best liked doing was sitting in the fading light on the earth above the boat's keel. I would imagine a brown sail and a wheelhouse of plaited twigs and let the Holle grow wider and wider until there was room for us on it, and then it was not long before my floating garden was heading for distant coastlands, to the mouth of the river Memel. And as soon as I thought of the Memel, the swollen river, I would also begin to feel the pain. It would rise up from my stomach and press on my heart, and at first I didn't know how to fight it off. I would just crouch there as if completely stunned, racked. But then I came on the idea of answering the pain quite simply by lying down and knocking my head against the ground, again and again, until I could hear a kind of roaring inside me. Then, when the roaring at last died away, the pain was gone.

The chief once found me doing this. He came up close beside me, but didn't pull me to my feet; he just stood and waited, and when I raised myself up he sat down beside me and ruffled my hair. Not a word did he say; only on our way home together, as once again we looked out over the cultivated land from the top of the hill, he muttered something to himself. I didn't catch it all, just that each of us carries around something he'd like to thrash out of himself. That's what he said, up there on the hill where the stronghold now stands, where they are probably holding him prisoner, he who has always led the way and made the decisions, he to whom everyone here owes something. If only he would now show himself at the window or on the terrace! I would at once run to him and, without saying a word, drag him here to my home, where I could ask him all my questions, for it is surely he who can tell me whether I shall have to leave Hollenhusen. He knows there's nobody here who has stood by him and worked together with him as I have done, Dorothea maybe excepted, and he will surely still remember how well I have carried out the hundreds of tasks he has given me over these many years.

I have only to think of that winter when he sent me with the sledge to Danes' Wood to fetch firewood: not for ourselves, since we had enough piled up beneath our two barrack-room windows, but for old Magnussen, who lived by himself on a tumbledown farm with just his guinea fowls. They'd only spoken to each other a few times, the chief and the old man, across the leaning, gaping fence – just in passing, so to speak – and, when the first snow arrived, the chief sent me with a sledge-load of firewood to the neglected farm everyone calls the Kollerhof, why I don't know either. None of us had ever been in the house, neither Joachim nor Max nor Ina, not even Heiner Walendy had ever dared follow the old man. I dragged the sledge up to the house and didn't hang about to unload and stack it. In order to make a quick get-away, I just turned the sledge over so that the wood fell into the snow, but Magnussen, who likely enough sat by his window all day, had already seen me and was tapping urgently on the glass, and before I'd adjusted the leather strap round my shoulder he was already at the door, holding out a tin of biscuits to me. I approached him warily and, because I didn't put out my hand, he put his biscuits into my pocket, stuffing it full. Never have I eaten better biscuits, they tasted of aniseed and attar of roses. After that I brought him several loads of firewood, each time showing less haste in unloading it, and sometimes I even gave a whistle as I came near, so as to attract his attention, but he had always seen me already and would be standing there with his biscuit-tin, urging me to help myself. I didn't enter his house.

But one Sunday, when the snow was falling in thick flakes, he was not at the window and not at the door. In fact, he didn't appear at all, though I made a lot of noise while unloading and was in no hurry to leave. Since I had been looking forward all day to his biscuits, I walked round the house to look for him, but all I found was his snow-covered box-cart and some snow-covered ploughs and water-pipes. Something warned Bruno, something advised him to make off with his sledge. But after I'd noticed how the wind was playing around with the unlatched door, I slipped into the passage-way, which had a floor of hard clay, groped my way forward and startled a few guinea fowls sleeping in a corner; the birds flew outside between my legs.

When Magnussen called out to me, my first thought was to

run away, but he knew it was me standing outside his living-room, and since his calls continued and were becoming more pressing, I went in. I could smell at once the stale sour air, and I saw him lying on his bed, fully dressed with a horse-blanket wrapped around his feet. Above the bed a big mirror hung, its frame stuck all around with countless postcards, and a stuffed polecat glared at me from a low chest of drawers. What my eyes at once fell on were the spring-traps and snares lying in an open closet, together with eel-prongs and harpoons and pick-rods, things with which you can pick sleeping pheasants off branches, first dazzling them, then picking them off.

He beckoned me over. He was now very friendly, and there was an unexpected warmth in his look as he told me to reload the firewood and take it away. I've got enough for the time that still remains, he said, I don't need any more. Then he gave me the closed biscuit-tin and stared at his blanket and was reluctant to say anything more, and I went out and loaded up the firewood as he'd said: the pile he already had was maybe enough for a week. And so I took my load home, piled it up under the window where we could always keep an eye on it and, when the chief came along, I told him that old Magnussen had refused the wood and that he was lying motionless on his bed. Hearing that, the chief went off alone in the snowstorm to the Kollerhof, he didn't want me with him, not then and not on the following days. Just Dorothea: he did take her along once, but I don't know what they did there. Anyway, before Magnussen could use up his little woodpile he was dead.

And soon afterwards we left the barracks and moved into the Kollerhof. The thaw had set in, and we loaded up the sledge and the two-wheeled cart while our neighbours stood looking on, some of them unbelieving, others grudging, and none of them offered to help, though, as we went off with our last load, a few wished us good luck and walked with us as far as the railway cutting, where they stood for a long time watching us go.

Max was the only one of us unaffected by the move; he

collected and bundled up his belongings at the very last minute, and the way he trotted along behind the cart gave you the feeling that any new home would be all the same to him. Ina and Joachim squabbled the whole way about which of them would occupy the big room in the loft whose windows looked out over Danes' Wood; they had paid a secret visit to the Kollerhof before, or at any rate had crept around the house to inspect it all. I was sorry most of all for Dorothea; before our departure she sat quite motionless on the piled straw mattresses. Her lips were pale, she was shivering, and I could see she wanted to cry, but couldn't; maybe she was finding it very hard to leave this room. But then, as the chief and I swept out the barrack-room, as our brooms collided and we set them sparring with each other like two little enemy dogs, Dorothea did lift her head and smile, and the chief threw down his broom, pulled her to her feet and held her very tight. Ah, Dotti, he said, and that was all, and then together they dragged the mattresses outside.

Magnussen's nephew was waiting for us in the living-room, a proud giant of a man in old-fashioned clothes who regretted not having been able to hand over the house in a clean condition, free of all the junk and strange stuff that had accumulated in a lifetime, and he pointed to two heaps on to which he had thrown all the things he took to be useless, ready for carting away. I made up my mind at once to rescue the stuffed polecat and some picture frames and moulds for shaping biscuits; but first we followed Magnussen's nephew through the house, peered into all the rooms and closets, laid our hands on the tiled stove, tried out the privy, which was made of rough planks, filed through stable and sheds, and at the end of it the chief was given the only key the Kollerhof possessed. Then Magnussen's nephew wished us a pleasant stay and went off along the edge of the flooded fields to Hollenhusen's railway station.

Wind: that was the very first time I saw the wind in its moving shape. I saw it through the only window in my room, a dim attic window that looked out on the sky: it passed greyish-white above my head, it twisted and contorted itself, causing sheets and sacks to flutter in its wake, while at the same time it whistled and strummed on creaking wires. Hardly was I alone in the little attic room the chief had put me in when I saw it, and I wanted to run at once to Ina, who had been given the big room in the loft. I wanted to show her what I had seen, but then the wind broke away and headed for a flock of rooks, which it no doubt hurled down on to Danes' Wood. When I cast my eyes over my room, I knew I would often lie awake in the nights: the walls kept up a constant creaking, from the moss-covered roof there came a growling sound from time to time, and since around the fireplace there were gaps betwen the floor-boards, I could hear what was going on down below, in the living-room. Max and Joachim agreed to share a room only when the chief promised to knock down a wall and to turn the roomy larder into a work-room. To find out whether Ina could overhear me I tapped a few times on the whitewashed wooden wall. She soon tapped back, and then I knew.

The first evening we had fried potatoes and beetroot for supper. We sighed in the warmth the tiled stove gave off, we ate and sighed and took off our jackets and pullovers. The chief undid his shirt buttons, so we could see the fiery red scar on his chest, and all of a sudden Joachim asked him whether he was drawing a pension like Redlefsen's father, who had had an arm shot off. At that the chief just grinned and said his scars were worth more to him than what he'd been offered for them: scars like this weren't to be sold off cheap. That's what he said. Later on, biting smoke came out of the kitchen stove, billowing clouds wrapped us around and we all had tears in our eyes, but we stayed where we were and listened to the chief talking about the war, about a man he called Boris, whom he met far away in Russia by the Black Sea.

They had captured a lot of land, the chief and his company, and on the Black Sea they captured some big plantations with broad-leaved trees and conifers and fields of sweet-smelling shrubs, but then they were unable to move on, because a lot of the men had become feverish and were suffering from boils and pains of all kinds. They set up camp at the edge of the plantations. It was a dry summer and the ground was hard and cracked, and all they had to eat was canned meat and bread. The plantations were deserted, or looked deserted when the chief wandered through them, when he got lost in them. He was suffering less than the others and needed to take a walk each evening in order to make himself sleepy. On one of these walks in the dusk he met Boris, who was thin and bearded and humble; he was living in a leaf-hut, and, when the chief took him by surprise, he offered him some berries, and also some cold tea – not in a frightened or over-hasty way, but relaxed and with natural hospitality. They couldn't understand everything each of them said, but the chief did gather that Boris had been there many years: some institute had sent him out and then seemingly forgotten him, so he was able to devote himself entirely to work of his own choice. He lived in the winter in the village hall, in the summer in the leaf-hut. Not just once but several times the chief told us that Boris spent his whole life finding out all he could about the way plants feel.

Since the rest period on the edge of the plantations lasted some time, he paid Boris quite a lot more visits. They would drink tea, walk together across the land, comparing, judging and exchanging ideas as far as they could. Though little of what there was to see was new to the chief, one thing did make him wonder, and that was Boris's habit of taking selected plants by surprise, of touching them or of talking to them in different ways. Some he just tapped lightly, others he would flick with a finger against a leaf or a stem, or he would suddenly cast a shadow over them, speak directly to them, making them feel his satisfaction or disappointment with them, and in response to his touch, his scolding and his words of praise, little leaf buds filled out, a young silver lime raised its leaves, a mimosa shed several stems in fright, and there were even blossoms that showed they felt something, either by opening or by closing their petals. On one occasion Boris maintained that plants can feel fear, and he showed the chief that they can even fall in a faint if, quick as lightning, you pull up a few neighbouring plants. Boris could also send some plants into convulsions, and he made the ivy drunk by dipping its air roots in diluted alcohol, which produced a sort of reeling and rustling.

Often, when they were walking together through the deserted plantations, Boris would pluck off leaves and blossoms, he would hold them in his hand and seem to be waiting for something. Occasionally he would lay them on his tongue and stand there quite still and expectant: the chief thought he must have been examining what effect they would have. How well Boris understood such effects was clearly shown after he saw the soldiers shivering from fever and plagued with boils. Without saying a word, he picked some leaves and blossoms and put them in glass containers half-filled with spring water. He left the containers standing in the sun for three days, then gave them to the chief, who made the soldiers drink at the intervals Boris had laid down, and after only a short time one soldier after another began to recover his health. The chief asked himself what he could give Boris in return. He racked his brains, but neither he nor the soldiers had anything among their possessions that seemed suitable. In the end he could think of nothing better than to make a cash collection, and the soldiers gave willingly. The leaf-hut was empty when the chief arrived with the money and, after waiting a while, he laid the envelope on the table and went away, resolving to come again the next day. Boris was nowhere to be seen, however often the chief returned to the leaf-hut on the following days, though he looked and called everywhere. In the plantations nothing moved, no one answered.

Shortly before he and his company moved off, he paid a last visit to the leaf-hut. It was very early in the morning, and this time he did see Boris again: his thin figure was leaning up against one of the wooden posts that supported the leaf-hut, and it did not move. The chief waved and walked towards him, his steps getting faster and faster and when he was close enough, he saw that Boris's feet were not on the ground: stretched full out, the toes pointing downwards, they dangled a hand's width above it, and the shoulders were drooping, the head to one side as if he was listening. Boris was hanging from a noose. He was already dead, and strewn around him, in the grass, between the bushes, pressed by the wind against a pile of cut branches, lay the banknotes the chief and the soldiers had collected.

This was the tale the chief told us all as we sat together for the first time beneath the roof of the Kollerhof, and after hearing it we laid no more wood on the fire, but made plans for the following day, deciding what to do first and what next, each one satisfied with the work the chief had given him to do, even Max. I was allowed to scrape the pan and finish the remaining potatoes, and from the pile of junk I was allowed to fish out the things I had marked out for myself at first glance, and, beside these, the mirror plastered over with postcards and a round pocket lamp, which (like so many other things) I seem to have lost.

In my room there was more than enough space for them all. I just laid them on the floor and then sat down on my bed and in the dark began to listen to the room. The noises were already familiar – the creaking, the rustling and murmuring – only the scuttling was new. It came from two hard black beetles, which I squashed in the light of my pocket lamp. In the next room Ina was hurriedly undressing, she plumped down on her mattress and then there was no further sound from her. In the living-room below the chief was still talking with Dorothea: I could clearly hear their voices beside the fireplace, coming through the gaps between the floorboards. Dorothea wanted to settle, at last to settle down somewhere for keeps, to stay put and to make do with what they had. The chief didn't disagree with her entirely, he just felt it was too early to be content with what they had, and for that reason he was ready to put up with the period of drought that now lay ahead. That's what he called it: period of drought. And he said; With that behind us, we'll be in a position where nothing can shake us and pull us down. Dorothea was freezing, and the chief offered to fetch her a rug, but she didn't wish to stay up any longer, and she was curious what she would dream about on her first night in the Kollerhof.

I must go back to the shed and clear away the sharpened knives and shears and put the oilstone where it belongs, for Joachim will soon be making his round and, if all isn't neat and tidy, he's quite capable of losing his temper and scattering everything I've left lying around, even of hiding it; he has already done that once. He would certainly be the first to send me away from Hollenhusen. If it had been left to him, I would never have been put in charge of the knives and shears and all the grafting equipment. The only one I have to thank for that is the chief, who once called me his only friend.

If Magda doesn't come, I'll read Max's book again, for the sixth time. But she will come, she has promised, and soon I shall have to keep my ears open for the arranged signal, count the number of knocks, for sometimes Magda forgets she must knock seven times before I will open. If I hear only two or three knocks, I put out the light and raise a corner of the black paper blind so I can see who it is standing there; the rays from the big lamp on the main path reach as far as my door. I don't know why there are so often knocks at my door, it's not just those little pests, Ina's children, who knock and run away, there are others too who creep up in the darkness and, when I'm least expecting it, hammer on the door in order to scare me. Usually there's no one to be seen, and the sound of fleeing footsteps is only rarely to be heard. If I do ever catch sight of a figure, it is wearing a long cloak or a hood and it makes off into the plantation before I can get a clear view of it.

Magda just says: Somebody seems to have it in for you, and that's all she says. I believe she quite likes me to be frightened occasionally, and now and again she even pretends to be scared herself, just in order to make me uneasy. One night, just as she was about to leave, she took a quick look out of the window. There was a cold moon hanging over the plantations, and suddenly she let out a scream and pointed towards the young conifers, saying she could see a big shaggy animal with gleaming eyes standing there, an animal such as had never been seen before: it had huge curved horns and a fleece of silvery-white. Where? I asked, where? and she: There, can't you see it? There in the espaliers, and she kept on pointing as she pressed herself against me and held me tight. I didn't see anything, and next morning there were no tracks among the conifers, however hard I searched.

In the Kollerhof there was not a single safety lock anywhere, no bar I could push across my bedroom door. All I had to fasten it with was a catch, a bent catch that would give if the door was firmly shaken or pushed. The chief just laughed when I asked him for a lock, wanting to know whether I no longer trusted them, and Dorothea, who in the summer even slept with the door open, asked me what treasure I was trying to hide. Everything had been improved and made to look nice, so that scarcely a trace of Magnussen's neglected property remained to be seen, but by locks and keys they set no store. We patched the roof and cleared away the sparrows' nests; we broke down a wall, gave the kitchen stove a new brick overlay, put down wooden floorboards in the passage, plugged the cracks round the window frames with moss, replaced the broken palings in the fence with sound ones, we swept and planed and whitewashed, but no one gave a thought to locks, and when they found I had secured my door with a catch, they just shook their heads.

The gaps around my fireplace were not filled in. It didn't disturb me, hearing them talk in the living-room below. Often the sound of their voices sent me off to sleep: it was like the murmuring of the Holle in springtime; and often I learned something of their hidden worries. On one occasion Dorothea had worked out that we could be living in debt for the next twenty years, but the chief's answer to that was: You forget we may have good luck. That was what he said, and then he went out in the rain to thin out the old hedge, in which hawthorn, elderberry and hazel bushes were cramping each other's growth. I learned a lot through listening: I always knew what was afoot and could prepare myself for what was coming.

I was sad when I heard they wanted to send me somewhere for training, to send me away from the Kollerhof and our land, to Paulsen, the roofer, who still knew how to thatch, and, if not to him, then to Boom, the last of the whip-makers, who supplied a good half of the Baltic coast; they also considered Tordsen with his grocer's shop. The boy can't just drift along beside us, Dorothea said. We can't just leave him to his own devices, she said. And she also said: We are, after all, responsible for his development – an odd word, but that's the one she used: development. The chief had in the end to agree with her, though he didn't find it easy. He admitted he would miss me in his work, he praised my willingness, my perseverance, he even said he found pleasure in having me near him, but all the same he was not prepared to stand in the way of my development. They were quick to agree it wouldn't be easy to find anything for me, they foresaw all kinds of difficulties and obstacles. Don't forget, the chief said, our Bruno is different from all the others, and that remark was always sufficient reason for dismissing some plan or other. Dorothea was willing to take it on herself to find out first of all from me what my wishes were, and then together they would try to persuade me that an apprenticeship or a training in some other place would help me later to get on, to make progress.

The frozen meadow was creaking and crackling beneath our feet that morning when at first light the chief took me to Jakob Ewaldsen, the brother of our foreman, when he led me in a clean shirt, my hair cut short and watertight raw-leather boots on my feet, to my new workplace, the sub-post office in Hollenhusen. Jakob Ewaldsen looked after the post office in the mornings, and the afternoons he spent repairing farm machines. He was the only one prepared to take me on: Paulsen, the travelling roofer, wouldn't, and nor would Tordsen: he just took one look at me in his shop and then stood in front of his wares as if to protect them. I had cried only a little during the night, and I was already washed and dressed by the time the chief came to fetch me, and after a silent breakfast –

Dorothea smuggled a few raisins into my porridge – we set out, across meadows, across a lumpy field and then along the road between the poplars to Hollenhusen.

Two magpies flew in front of us, settled, waited for us, flew off and then settled down again. Both of us, the chief and I, knew we were sad, so we didn't say much.

The man who had taken me on gave us a joyless greeting as we entered the dim post office workroom; he grabbed the small packet of tobacco the chief pushed towards him with no sign of gratitude, invited us to sit down on a much battered bench, and went on sorting a pile of mail into three bags suspended open in racks. When that was done, he tied the bags with string and put them beside the door, ready for the bus that was expected any moment. Jakob Ewaldsen was not like his brother: he was broad and squat, his skin shone like melted fat, and the expression on his face was always sullen. As he turned all that sullenness on me in the stare he gave me, I found myself hoping he'd go back on his word and send me away, but all he did was tell me to go to the door and keep an eye out for the bus. I could see he wanted to have another word with the chief alone. But before the lights of the bus came swerving into view between the poplars I was called back into the room, the chief put an arm round my shoulders and after a few moments of silence I learned I had become an assistant postman on probation – but only on probation, said Jakob Ewaldsen, that must be quite clear.

In the beginning Bruno found it difficult to breathe in that low bare room – whether I was sweeping or polishing the leather postbag, whether counting, sorting letters for delivery, checking the postal charges or rubber-stamping, after a certain time I always began gasping for breath. Then I would simply drop my work and go outside, breathe in deeply again and again, filling myself full of refreshing air.

Jakob Ewaldsen didn't pay much attention to me, he just told me what he wanted done, threw me the book of instructions for postal employees, maybe telling me to read up the necessary instructions in cases of doubt, then he would settle down to his notebooks and tables, or he would go into the adjoining living-room to cross-examine his wife and to show her figures that proved she was squandering his money. He often hit her too, always the same two sharp blows, and his wife would cry out each time in exactly the same tone of voice; sometimes she would cry out even before the blows fell, just in case, but while he was hitting her there never came a word from him. Once, after I'd counted fourteen blows, there was suddenly a complete silence; I got up then and cautiously opened the door, and I saw Jakob Ewaldsen and his wife sitting opposite each other at the table, drinking coffee out of blue enamel mugs. He was able in an instant to regain his calm and lose his angry colour, as he had shown me often enough, when he broke off some punishment to attend to one of his rare morning customers.

What I enjoyed most was setting out with the canvas bag to empty the Hollenhusen pillar-boxes, one near Tordsen the grocer's, one at the station and lastly the one at our home; I would shake the letters up several times, mix them and stir them, raising a miniature snowstorm inside the bag, and back in the post office I would tip them all into a basket and at once set about finding their destination. Where they were all wanting to go! Redlefsen's letters were always for Schleswig, Tordsen wanted his overweight letters, often understamped, sent to Flensburg, Fräulein Ratzum's neatly written envelopes did not go, like Lauritzen's, to Kappeln, but to Doctor Ringleb in Husum. If now and again red and blue stripes indicated an airmail letter, I knew at once that it was off to America, to Wyoming, the place from which Kraske, the stationmaster, was always receiving parcels that had got damaged in the post. If a letter was addressed to Hamburg, to Heide or Harrislee, I would at once picture in my mind what those places might look like, and with a few letters I would ask myself whether its receiver would laugh or would he cry. Only a few postcards came our way, they contained either just greetings or the date of a forthcoming visit. Once, by the handwriting, I recognised a letter from Ina, addressed to herself from the Kollerhof. The chief rarely wrote; if he did, it was to Rellingen or Bremen. Max sent off the largest number of letters, and in return received more mail than all the others.

The rounds, the long rounds Ewaldsen took me on when he delivered the letters in Hollenhusen and in the barracks and out to the most distant of farms. He let me push his bicycle, with its locked postbag and its swaying load of parcels. He always followed on behind, dressed at times of rain and storm in an old dispatch-rider's coat, on frosty days in a loden jacket and on the first warm days of spring in a faded postman's uniform. However far we went, he never walked beside me. I often asked myself what we must look like from far off as we trotted along field paths beneath ragged clouds or crossed the Holle under a dark sky at the place where it flows along beside Boom the whip-maker's lonely farm. When we skirted the edge of the old training ground, a part of which was now common land, in order to get to the barracks, we would now and again see the chief in the distance. He was always the first to wave, to wave in a reserved sort of way, and it made me think he wished I was there at his side.

In how many different ways would the people in Hollenhusen react when we brought them their post! Some were unbelieving, confused, reluctant to take their letters; others ran indoors as if they couldn't wait to read them; Paulsen just told us to leave them on the windowsill on top of a pile of unopened letters; and in the barracks there were two people who came each day to meet us, quite ill with expectation: Frau Schmundt and the limping captain. There was never anything for either of them, though they were just the ones most in need of a letter: it was the only thing they longed for.

One morning Jakob Ewaldsen woke up with a high temperature and from his bed told me to deliver the mail by myself. I loaded up the bicycle in the usual way, the parcels on the handlebars, the postbag on the carrier, then went in to him once more to receive his final instructions and warnings. Money orders he would not trust me with, but I could use his bicycle and with it I set off alone along the familiar paths. How excited I was, how anxious to do well and how watchful! Some welcomed me as the new postman, I was given a glass of fruit juice, a thick slice of freshly baked bread, I was told I'd soon be wearing a postman's cap. It was a bright day and the first starlings had already arrived. Only in the barracks did things become tricky, and that was because Heiner Walendy and a few others in his gang saw me at once and followed me, yelling and laughing at me. They aimed kicks at the bicycle and tried to snatch the postbag, and they would have succeeded in the end if Kukeitis, our old neighbour, hadn't chased them off. It didn't worry me that on the way home I still had some mail left over: I just decided to follow Jakob Ewaldsen's example – he would always just throw what he hadn't delivered into the basket for the following day, muttering: You'll find out soon enough.

His fever lingered on, and I was allowed to continue my rounds alone, without instructions, without warnings. I began to find some enjoyment in it. Several of the people I brought mail to smiled encouragingly and were kind to me, and I was sad only when I saw Frau Schmundt and the limping captain walking towards me: there was never anything for them, however fervently I joined them in their wish. To save them the trouble of coming, I made them a sign from a distance, scything a slow 'No' across the air. I had done that too on the morning the accident happened to me on the bridge, the brick bridge across the Holle at the spot where vegetable fields go down to the water's edge.

My sign meaning 'No, sorry, nothing' had once again persuaded them to give up. Disappointed, they went back to the barracks, and I placed a foot on the pedal and free-wheeled down the gentle slope. That gave me a good start for crossing the bridge which, since I'd been on my own, I always took at a brisk pace. Everything was bumping and rattling as I rode over the uneven brick surface, the parcels on the handlebars jerking and banging against each other, and I didn't hear, I didn't see what was coming towards me, from the Erlenhof, the biggest farm in Hollenhusen, over which Lauritzen's sister ruled.

The shaft of a cart: the horse was dragging a loose shaft behind it in a wild gallop, and the shaft was being hurled from side to side, its metal fittings striking sparks from the stones as it churned them up. I saw the horse's hooves, the awful whites of its eyes, its tossing mane, froth was flying, the air was filled with a wild snorting. The runaway was heading straight for me, it didn't turn aside, didn't check its pace when it saw me on the arching bridge, it was surely after me, intent on running me over, mowing me down with the whirling shaft. I must jump for it, there was no other way – must push the bicycle up against the bridge railings, jump over the granite support and duck down behind it. With eyes shut tight I waited for the storm to pass. There was a rumbling noise and a bang as the hurtling shaft gave the bicycle a glancing blow and then struck the granite post head on.

Everywhere on the dark little river letters floating, white letters, brown letters, packets in postal wrappers, and the postbag itself, slowly sinking – I took it all in with a single glance: the river bank sprinkled with paper, the carrier that had been wrenched off the bicycle, whose back wheel had caught it too and been knocked into a figure eight. Even the bridge's iron railing was dented, I was the only object the shaft had missed altogether – I alone! The horse had not stopped its mad gallop and had already vanished behind the poplars. My first act was to spring down the bank and rescue the postbag. Then I ran downstream to the letters the current had carried farthest. I needed a stick, a stick with a forked tip, to scoop it all up, but I couldn't find one, and, since some of the envelopes had already filled with water and were floating beneath the surface, I jumped into the water and, groping, gathered up all the gentle current brought my way. The water reached up to my thighs, I felt neither the drag nor the cold as I waded towards the bridge, grabbing and dipping my arms down to the elbows. There wasn't time to carry each single letter to the dry bank: I just slapped the wet envelopes down one on top of the other like wet handkerchieves, and, like wet handkerchieves, I slowly wrung them out on the river bank – no, I didn't wring them, but just squeezed them and was alarmed to see how much of the writing began to smear and fade. Using my pullover, I wiped the inside of the postbag and packed the wet letters into it. I climbed up the bank to the bicycle, or was just about to when a kingfisher flew down to the Holle near the bridge pier. It dived under close to a clump of weed, and the river didn't let on whether it swam off upstream or downstream.

The back wheel of the bicycle was wobbling and scraping against the mudguard. I couldn't go on with my round, couldn't deliver the wet mail, so I turned back, the bag over my shoulder, already planning in my mind to spread the letters out to dry in the yard behind the post office and afterwards to iron them out with Frau Ewaldsen's heavy flatiron. A man went running past me: he must surely have come from the Erlenhof and was trying to catch the horse. The two girls who passed me on new bicycles were just as surely from the Erlenhof, strapping girls who made fun of me, suddenly turned round and rode back, just in order to view me from the front and, as they were cycling round me, I heard one of the girls say: What a sight, and him a postman! I turned aside and waited till they'd gone, and then I walked to the post office along a bumpy footpath and at once put the letters, now baked into a cake, out to dry, my socks as well.

Unobserved, for Jakob Ewaldsen was still in bed with his fever and his wife was over at Tordsen's helping to cook for a wedding. I slipped through the grass barefoot, turned the letters over, fanned them and waved them about, and in the bright sunshine everything dried quite quickly – I was surprised how quickly it all dried. The sun was so strong that the paper shrank, it crumpled, curled, some of the letters looked as if they were full of bubbles and, when I turned them over, I noticed that the gum was no longer sticking and a lot of the envelope flaps had opened.

The postbag wasn't so quick to dry, though I laid it down slantways and wedged it open, so the sun could get right inside down to the bottom. When a banknote peeped out from one of the open envelopes, I got a bit alarmed and tried to stick it down with spit, but my spit wouldn't hold, the curling flap soon opened up again, the Holle and the sun having destroyed its stickiness. And that's the reason why, after drying it, I collected all the mail together and took it to our workroom, so as to stick the letters together again with the help of our gum-pot. I wanted them all to be properly gummed before I ironed them.

I tipped my load on to the old shop-counter that was our work table, arranged them, tested them and gummed them as necessary. The gum smelled so sweet that I should dearly have liked to taste it: a stringy, honey-coloured gum that spread more easily the longer I worked with it. At one point a customer came to the door and knocked and shouted. Though there was a cardboard notice on the door saying we were temporarily closed, he wouldn't go away and, when I at last opened up for him, all he did was hand me a stamped letter he could easily have dropped into the mail-box by the door. Now and again I stopped work to listen, for the post office was a house of echoes: if you heard a sigh, a weaker sigh would soon answer it, a distinct knock would be followed by an indistinct one, and a raised voice would bring some response from a well-worn voice in the distance. Just as I was listening out for an echo, the handle of the door to the living-room turned downwards, bare feet appeared, the hem of a nightshirt, and Jakob Ewaldsen was standing before me. At first he was puzzled, for he expected me to be out on my round, but that very soon changed to mistrust and growing suspicion. He moved closer without saying a word, then, as he reached my side, he snatched that letter the Holle had opened from my hand, put his fingers inside the envelope and drew out a banknote, which he held in front of my nose and then slapped down on the table. And before I could say anything at all, he said: So that's it! And they call you half-witted and dopey. So that's it! He said no more.

Then he hit me, a sharp blow, exactly placed. I did not see his fist coming, but, even if I had seen it, I wouldn't have dodged aside, for something was holding me fast, making me stiff and unable to move, so that I didn't even duck my head when he landed his first blow. I don't remember how often he hit me before I fell, all I know is he hit me on the chin, on the head, and there was a warm feeling in my mouth, my mouth filled with something thick and creamy which I had to swallow down before I could breathe. All of a sudden I was lying on the floor, lying beside the sorting-bag rack, and I saw him, Jakob Ewaldsen, floating in the air above me in his greyish-white nightshirt, his fever shirt. Then I was on my feet again: he suddenly pulled me to my feet and, pinning me against the wall with one hand, went over me with the other, feeling, tapping, turning pockets inside out. He even searched under my shirt without finding what he was looking for. I couldn't say what I wanted to say to him because of all the stuff flowing in my mouth. I'd bitten the tip of my tongue during one of his blows, and the pain of it would have sent me running helter-skelter, if only I could have stayed on my feet. I didn't at once think of calling for the chief. I suppose I was too dazed to send out a wish for him to come, and when at last I did, it was ages before he came. He didn't lead me away immediately: first he had a few things to say to Jakob Ewaldsen, and so excited and so angry was he that I felt they must soon set about each other. At one point the chief said: A child, to attack a child like that, and to end with: You'll be made to pay for this, just you wait.

It was nice being ill – not at first, but later. The chief came to my room twice a day, sat down and always had something to tell me. Dorothea came five times even, came with soup and bread pudding and porridge and watched me eat it all up. The others came too and sometimes brought me things. Max shared an orange with me. Through my attic window I watched the big birds, the buzzards, as they circled the skies without once beating their wings and then suddenly flew off at all angles as if just for fun. In the night the moon stood there, throwing its light, its greenish-yellow light straight into my room. Often I listened to them talking down below, at mealtimes or in the evenings: all I had to do was move close to the wall, and then I heard everything. They didn't often talk about me, it was mostly Ina who did the talking, telling them about Rolf and Dieter, her two schoolmates with whom she travelled by train to Schleswig each day. They must both have been good runners, for they could both sprint along beside the train for quite a distance as it moved off. From Joachim there came scarcely a sound, and Max, who was on the point of leaving us, spoke only just about enough for me to know he was still there. Once, at the very end of a conversation, I clearly heard Dorothea say: Very well, keep the boy here with you, and the chief reply: Nothing I'd like better. Then it was all I could do to stop myself running downstairs.

Magda had gone to sleep, so now I mustn't talk, mustn't move. I must lie quite still, so her arm doesn't slide off my chest, so her feet stay covered. The slightest movement is enough to wake her and, once awake, she is bad-tempered and says she'll go. In her sleep Magda always looks different from when she's awake. Her face loses its severity, her lips part and grow thicker, a little wrinkle appears above the bridge of her nose, as if she's having difficulty in thinking something out, but after a while this expression changes too: her face becomes relaxed and looks just contented and slightly crumpled. Even if she doesn't like hearing me say so, she smells like rice-pudding when she's asleep.

If only I knew what she was looking for! She'd hardly come in when she started pulling out all the drawers, arranging and smoothing things out, sorting and bringing together whatever belonged together, and after that she unpacked the trunk, laid everything out on the floor and shook her head, not as she normally does in an amused sort of way, but in disappointment and perplexity, and she did the same after diving behind my curtain and examining the shelves. She'd surely been hoping, like Max, to find something in my home, something special, but neither has said what it is, neither of them. I'm wary of asking Magda too many questions, for she can't stand much questioning and quickly becomes vexed and snappish. Often all she says is: If you go on asking questions, I shall leave. It's better to wait for her to begin of her own accord.

The really important thing: she has seen the chief, she was in the room while he was sitting at table with the others, drinking his Wacholder and being served stewed apple by Dorothea as the others ate sandwiches and drank tea. Magda clearly heard them talking, in his presence, about household expenses. Joachim had a sheet of paper in front of him and was reading out sums, which he sometimes repeated without comment, and the chief sat there, quiet and self-absorbed, as if it were no concern of his. I can imagine he was just smiling to himself as they went through the household expenses without consulting him, the one person to whom everybody here – and not just those in the stronghold either – owes something. When Magda brought in a second pot of tea they were still at it, naming and examining figures. None of them showed any further interest in eating and none of them had very much to say, just a word or two of doubt or agreement, which Joachim noted down on his sheet of paper, sitting beside an absent-minded chief who never once joined in and didn't raise his head even when his own name was mentioned. That they were all worried Magda could see from the moment she came in: she had never known Ina look so depressed, and Joachim shrugged his shoulders a few times, as if he could see no way out. Dorothea and Max were the only ones unwilling to accept the situation: they asked and asked again and checked and tried new starts.

It was Joachim who suddenly suggested dismissing Lisbeth. Magda hadn't heard wrong: she was so startled that she turned at the door and looked back, and then Joachim repeated his suggestion of parting with Lisbeth and paying her compensation for all her past services. The others round the table just looked at him in dismay, silent and dismayed, maybe because they'd none of them dared go to such lengths in their thoughts and suggestions. After all, Lisbeth had been working for the chief's family since Rominter times, and, when she turned up in Hollenhusen, she'd been welcomed as if for years they'd been expecting her. In the silence Joachim mentioned the sum

Lisbeth was receiving in wages, he read it out from his sheet of paper and added on a further sum for food and keep.

Just as Magda turned to leave the room, the chief stood up. He looked at each of them in turn, took his time as he always did, letting nothing escape him, and I can imagine how they just sat there uneasily, waiting to hear what he had to say, he who can hear even when he's half asleep and who overlooks nothing of importance. How I should like to have been there as he first took them to task with a look! Then he said: Lisbeth stays, remember that. And that was all. He stood there a while, as if expecting questions, opposition, but none of them dared reply, not even Dorothea, and he then rapped the table, as he sometimes does, before following Magda out of the room.

And out in the passage he suddenly took Magda by the arm and led her along to his room, motioned her to sit down in the easy chair on which I have sometimes sat myself, all this time saying nothing and giving no explanation, which left Magda time to collect her wits. He bent over the bare top of the writing-desk, covered his face with both his hands and stared in front of him as if unable to make up his mind, and Magda began to feel he had already forgotten why he had brought her there. But the chief forgets nothing, as she must surely know – nothing, let them take away as many of his rights as they like. The envelope: he searched in his desk and brought out a large envelope, on which he wrote Lisbeth's name. Then he told Magda to go to the window for a moment and not to turn round. Magda did as he asked; but in a reflection in the window pane she saw him lift the cushion of the easy chair and take from beneath it a leather bag, which he carried to the writing-desk and opened. After that, Magda told me, she was given permission to turn round, and she saw the chief take various things out of the bag: documents and money and some small cases. But these were not what he was looking for: what he was after was a photo of the chief's father and beside him a young Lisbeth, even at that time wrapped in gloom. They were sitting close together on a rough bench, Magda said: the chief's father was smoking a pipe and Lisbeth had a basket in her lap. The chief put this photo in the envelope, added some money to it and asked Magda to take it straight to Lisbeth and give it to her.

I have never been in Lisbeth's room, which I'm told is big and shady. The tall rhododendrons in front of the window keep it always in semi-darkness, there are two clocks facing each other on the walls, and under the bed cardboard suitcases and boxes tied with string. Over the head of the bed a calendar is pinned, and each day is crossed through as it passes. There are no pictures, Magda says, only an embroidered sampler showing two girls swimming among water-lilies. The room is not furnished for visitors, and whoever seeks her out will find her sitting in the one and only armchair, from which, it seems, she never rises except to go to bed. Magda has often been there, and every time found Lisbeth sitting in that decrepit old chair, and that's where she was when Magda came along with the chief's letter, meaning just to hand over the envelope and go away. To her surprise, she was asked to sit on the edge of the bed and wait. What the envelope contained seemed to give very little pleasure: the money Lisbeth didn't even count, and the old photo merely brought a brief smile to her face; she laid both down on the windowsill, reflected a while and then said: A photo and some money – those are farewell presents, aren't they?

Magda has always had the feeling that Lisbeth knows a lot more than anyone else, and, long as she had to wait for it, she found in the end that she was right. Lisbeth began talking about herself, just hints to start with, but then with more and more openness. If Magda hadn't been so excited, she'd have remembered more of what Lisbeth told her – I know how it is with her: nothing sticks in her mind when she's excited. But this much she does claim to have understood: There are hard times ahead for us in Hollenhusen, we shan't be here very much longer, Lisbeth said. It's all still in the air, she said, adding that all we can do now is hope.

What Lisbeth knows can only have come through the others – Ina maybe, or Joachim: she was surely just repeating crumbs that had been scattered before her in explanation. I don't know, but what I do know is that, if anything needs to be saved, the chief is the only one who can do it – there's no one else can hold a candle to him. All he needs is a short moment of reflection and then he feels instinctively what must be done, he sees it all, he sniffs out and identifies everything, no one can match him for persistence, no one can plan as he can, and his plans have always been successful. If things here are still in the air, all they need do is ask him: up till now he has always known the safest paths to take, and he has always been ready to share his knowledge.

Anyone planting cuttings with him will at once be told why cuttings from broad-leaved trees must be taken in the early hours of the morning – not with a knife, that's not at all necessary, but with secateurs – and he'll soon convince you that it's best to make the cut immediately under a node. The nodes, Bruno, he has told me, are where the materials for growth are stored, that's where the root formation is developed. Other people keep what they know to themselves, do something without telling anybody why they are doing it and what they expect from it; he, on the other hand, always says why he's doing something this way and not that. How often has he told me!

I only need think of the times we worked close together in the sheds or on the land, and at once I hear his voice calling me over and showing me how fleshy root cuttings must be severed and stem cuttings planted out. He only needs to tell me why we plant taxus in April and potentilla in June, but conifers, which take a long time to root, not until September. At the start he would let me hold a cutting in my hand and would show me how a scab – he called it a callus – had formed where it had been cut, providing a sort of cover that contained fat, through which the adventitious roots would grow; or he would explain why he bent layers sharply over and deliberately bruised the

93

bark of a tree. It was just that he wanted me to know all the things I was dealing with and understand the jobs he gave me to do – he, whom nobody has yet got the better of, not even those grudging people in Hollenhusen who used to come out to us on Sundays and walk in file past our frames and our beds, inquisitive and disparaging. They wouldn't run the risk of addressing the chief direct, but they took care he heard their jeering remarks when his back was towards them or they themselves had turned aside. So the training ground's blooming at last, one of them said, and another: Just the stuff for broom-makers; and I also heard someone say: You'll see, the saplings will soon be drilling here. Those shaking heads! Those superior grins! The chief saw it all, but it seemed hardly to bother him.

Lauritzen came over once, together with his son, walking across our land as if it all belonged to him. With his stick he drew sketches of the plantation layout, he inspected our beds, scratched around among the layers and the runners, now and again scooped up a handful of earth and blew on it, and, while his son walked along beside him in silence, insisted on spreading his gall, waving his arms in discontent. Well, Zeller, was his greeting for the chief, combined with a scornful look after him, and then, since the chief showed no desire to speak to him, he turned to his son, wanting to know if the soil wouldn't be just right for maize. What do you say, Niels, he asked, isn't that very good soil for maize? His son gave him an embarrassed look and made no reply. Then they stood watching as the chief mixed dark peat and sand together. This was a mixture of his own, designed for cuttings that were slow rooters. The broad spade dug easily into the mixture, stirred it, shook it, releasing little clouds of dust, and bit by bit it lost its streaky appearance, the dark peat completely absorbed the light sand, and the chief ended by pushing his spade into the loose mound. Mischievously Lauritzen pushed his stick into the mound too, boring and screwing it deep down, then he folded his hands across his stomach in an attitude of waiting, sighed and said with a wink at his son: Let's see how long that takes to sprout. Shall I give

94

it a hand? the chief asked in a quiet voice. His face gave nothing away, so I knew something was coming, and, as with a smile Lauritzen gave his permission, the chief pulled the stick out and broke it twice over his knee, broke it carefully and swished the two stumps about. Here, he said, at the nodes: that's where the break must be; that iron ferrule won't let any roots through. As he spoke, he pressed the stumps into the soil and heaped it up around them as if they were cuttings. Then, taking no further notice of Lauritzen, he filled my wheelbarrow and straightened the running boards for me. Lauritzen looked as if he'd like to say quite a lot more: he was getting agitated and blowing himself up, but his son gave him a gentle push with both hands, saying: Come along now, and, without the old man noticing, gave us a friendly nod and a sign that he'd come back alone when he got the chance.

As always we worked until dusk, and, after cleaning all our tools and putting them away, we walked to the railway cutting and sat for a while on the slope overlooking the rails, where the chief let me in on his big plans. Over there, Bruno, will be the packing-shed and sorting-room, he said, and there at the back, that's where we'll build our dispatch hall. The day will come when we'll be sending our plants to all points of the compass from a loading ramp of our own that the railway will build for us. What we produce will speak for itself. We shall never stop wishing, he said, and then he spoke once more of his father, who had been content just to grow large trees and had thus got into difficulties. Before we headed for the Kollerhof he said: Whoever wants to be secure must stand on three legs. I couldn't say anything at all, I was so happy, so full of excitement. I didn't for a moment doubt that things would turn out just as he said, and in my gratitude for his having let me into his plans, I made up my mind always to do more than he would expect of me. At the hedge by the Kollerhof he suddenly said: Don't hop around so much, Bruno, save your strength. I hadn't even noticed I was hopping.

It rained during the night, a silent rain that woke none of us up. The water collected soundlessly, and now it is dripping from the gutters, from the branches; the drops drill neat little holes in the earth, roll along twigs and leaves, stretch out and fall down on other leaves, which quiver, shake themselves and then spring back, until the next drop hits them and either rolls off or bursts. The bushes all shine with a sparkle that doesn't stay steady or fixed, but shifts around with the sliding and falling of the raindrops, and in the plantations the conifers look as if hung with little crystals.

Spiders' webs glint between the plants, and there are raindrops hanging from them heavy enough to make them sag. What would please me best would be for everything to remain just as it is, no sunshine and no wind, but it is going to turn out a bright, windy day. Who knows why our foreman Ewaldsen wants me in the packing hall? Last week there were only a few orders to get ready for dispatch, mainly fruit-bearing plants, pip and stone fruit; I expect I shall just be put to sweeping, clearing, sweeping.

Paddy: that's Paddy roaming the plantations, creeping on his belly and sniffing. The chief has never managed to break him of his habit of roaming by himself, but he won't find anything: the few rabbits that were here at the beginning are long since dead, and the two badgers have moved out. There's no point in calling him, he won't obey me; though he's old now, Paddy will never abandon a chase; maybe if the chief called him, he'd come – maybe.

What's new, Bruno? Ewaldsen asks me, asks with his head turned aside as he pulls a red tab off a rubber boot and sticks it on again. I don't know what to say, all I know is that never before has he asked me what's new, never in twenty-seven years. So, in the way he's approaching me now, he's expecting something special. He winks at me, looks enquiringly at me – a look that lasts long, much too long, but there's nothing I can say. Magda made me give her my word. All the news she brings me from the stronghold must remain between ourselves. How scrawny he looks, how lined! Nothing, Bruno, nothing new? He lights his pipe, drawing so hard on it that the dottle glows red-hot. He slaps a wooden tub: Come on, let's sit down – we're alone. It is so still that I can hear the watch ticking in his waistcoat pocket. Look, Bruno, you asked what anybody would need a guardian for, and I can tell you this: it's for when a person can't look after himself, when there's no knowing what he'll do next. Then people can apply to the courts for legal assistance, and the court appoints a guardian, who takes everything over, the management, the writing of signatures, all the security arrangements. That's what it means. But surely there's no one here in need of a guardian, is there?

He's waiting again. He probably feels I know something. Maybe he has heard something himself, some rumour – or why, without anything leading up to it, should he start talking of courts and guardians? He's trying to sound me out, but I can't let Max down, nor Magda, I promised them both to say nothing. While he's speaking, Ewaldsen keeps looking down at his rubber boots and lightly scratching the back of his hands, which are quite scaly; he strokes the skin, in whose folds the soil looks ingrained. People are whispering, Bruno, he says. All right, they're always finding something to whisper about, someone claiming to have heard something in Schleswig, direct from the law courts, someone else overhearing something in the stronghold. But we two know more than most, I'm thinking, there's no one can fool us. That was all he had to say, and now I must tackle the packing hall, give it a thorough going over, for it looks in need of it, Bruno, this lofty hall with its steel ribs that make you feel you're inside some great fish. He can open the door as wide as he likes, this door that runs on rollers: it needs hardly more than a touch.

Ina, that's Ina; there's no point her calling, Paddy won't respond and go to her: when sniffing around the plantations he recognises no master. She is gathering flowers, picking fruit, her little bags already contain thuya twigs, so someone is having a birthday in the stronghold – probably Tim or Tobias, one or the other of the two pests: the chief and Dorothea have their birthdays in the winter. She'll arrange the flowers, fruit and twigs in pretty patterns where the birthday child sits. That's how it has always been – in the barracks and in the Kollerhof: even on my birthday my cup and my plate were always surrounded by something colourful and every year there was elderberry blossom. If only I knew what has become of all the presents I found lying beside my place at table: the brown case containing a comb and a mirror, the leather strap and the thick box with a lot of pictures which was a history of sailing ships. The feather ball I gave Ina on her sixteenth birthday still lies on her windowsill: that painted clay ball I stuck full of feathers from all kinds of birds – doves, thrushes, jays, rooks as well as wood pigeons and herons. She hasn't lost my gift.

She was still in bed when I brought it to her. I crept into her room very quietly so as to lay the feather ball beside her pillow unnoticed, but Ina was already awake, maybe because of the wind howling under the eaves, or maybe because of her excitement, and she didn't at first recognise what I was trying to give her, asking almost fearfully: What is it, Bruno, what have you got there? Since she was nervous of taking the feather ball in her hand, I laid it down on the blanket, and only after eying it for a long time did she put out a finger to touch it, then she stroked it gently and finally took it up in both hands.

She asked me softly if I had found all the feathers myself, and when I nodded, she sat up quickly and hugged me to her; after that she put a hand on my chest and looked at me wonderingly. She wanted to know what I was wearing on the leather lace round my neck: what was that dangling on my chest? I showed her the oval identity disc I'd found while gathering stones on our land, the old training ground. A soldier lost it, I said, it's got his number on it. At that she laughed unbelievingly and stroked my gift again. It's a lovely gift, Bruno, she said, I shall keep it for ever. All through the day she insisted on having the feather ball beside her place at table.

It was the day on which Elma came: Elma Tordsen from the grocer's shop, Ina's friend. Rolf also came to the birthday party, the sprinter who so often ran along beside the moving train, they all travelled to school together, belonged in the same class, they knew each other well, knew everything about each other, and the smallest hint was enough to set them off laughing. At table they took hardly any notice of me; even when Ina showed them the feather ball, they just gave me a brief and indifferent glance and then continued imitating their teachers and talking about other pupils. Something that had happened on a school outing had also to be gone over again in a sort of private code, and, while they were talking, the chief and I, spurred on by Dorothea's glances, carried out a competition which I won: by the end of it I had eaten two more pieces of crumble cake than he had.

After birthday coffee we went out into the yard, and I was allowed to watch them shooting red and green feathered darts at a target with Rolf's air pistol. They were all unhappy with their shots, except for the chief: he hit the target six times and then left us by ourselves. The second-best shot was Elma. She held the pistol in both hands, placed her legs apart and spent so long taking aim that the others got impatient, then, after at last firing, she hopped up and down a few times. Joachim: all he could ever hit was the stable door, and a shot from Ina even ended up on the roof.

When Rolf, feeling the need for living targets, began to fire little pellets at the flowers in the shrub garden, at the asters and the roses, Elma tried to take the air pistol away from him. She tugged him, hung on him and drummed on his back, but he kept shaking her off, and then all of a sudden we found ourselves standing still looking upwards, for Ack-Ack, the old mallard drake, was sailing around the roof in the gusty wind. Over the months I had tamed him with bits of carrot, and he was probably looking for me as he curved down lower and sailed close over our heads towards the marshy meadow behind the Kollerhof, to the slushy ditches in which I regularly scattered food for him. There he landed, so much overweight that he almost turned right over. Ack-Ack had at one time been caught in a spring trap, certainly laid down by old Magnussen, but his beak was not broken, just split, and after I had freed him he began at once to preen himself. Never at any time did I try to catch hold of him or to stroke him; when I brought his food I would always speak to him, and he would walk to and fro, fly a short distance and then return. One day he forgot his shyness and crossed the line he felt he needed for his own safety. In the end he became so trusting that he would strut around me as soon as I crouched down and kept quite still.

He was waiting for me now by the willows with outstretched neck. I sped into the stable, grabbed a handful of carrot slices and, as I ran towards him, he waddled across, greeting me as usual with his demanding cry of ack-ack. Ina and the others followed me. I knelt down and gave them a sign not to come closer, and they obeyed – except for Rolf: he called out a few times, something sharp and commanding, but the wind carried his words away and I didn't understand them. Ack-Ack was right in front of me, his neck stretched far out as he nibbled at the carrots. The shot Rolf fired I did not hear at all, I just felt a light blow on my chest, against the identity disc, and, even before I could move my hand or turn around, I saw the drake give a little hop and then drag his head violently along the ground as he fluttered wildly around me without flying off. The ricochet had struck him in the eye, right in the eye, and as he continued fluttering and hopping around, the others came running up and Joachim threw himself on the bird and caught him.

In spite of all my pleas he wouldn't give me the injured drake. He pressed it tight to his body, since it would not stop struggling and paddling, and then Rolf and Joachim put their heads together and went down to the willows, where they shot Ack-Ack several times through the head till he was dead. Then I went back to the house, to my room, and I fastened the catch on my door and lay down on my bed.

I wouldn't have opened the door to anyone but Dorothea, that's for sure. She stood outside and called, knocked and called, and when I let her in she at once took my hand, and we sat down together. The peace. The soothing feeling. She was there beside me, and I waited for her to speak. She didn't say much, just pointed out that Ack-Ack had been hurt and must be put out of his pain. And she also said: Pity, Bruno, it sometimes calls for hardness, hardness and courage. And that was all. Then she took me by the arm and reminded me that it was Ina's birthday, they wanted to send something up into the sky, but not without me, they were all waiting for me, and particularly Ina, who had already tried a few times to fetch me down. They were sitting in the big living-room and, when I came in, they all jumped to their feet and showed me the two long-tailed paper kites the chief had built in secret for this day, kites with wide grinning mouths, clown's cheeks and squint-eyes painted on them in bright colours. They were the biggest kites I'd ever seen, and the balls of string were so fat you needed two hands to hold them. Who with whom, who against whom? It was obvious Ina wanted Rolf, the one who was always chosen to sit beside her, the only one she ever had eyes for, but then they tossed for it, and Rolf had to go with Elma, on the other side Ina and me.

Just a run of a few paces across the meadow behind the

Kollerhof, and the wind was pressing the parchment paper against the light wooden crosses. The kites rose up, swinging from side to side to begin with, but the higher they flew, the steadier they became, kept in trim by the waving paper tails.

We paid out the string, the kites rose up and up, and the higher the wind carried them, the harder it was to hold them. Our hands were already smarting, but Ina kept urging me to let the string out faster: our kite must go the highest – we had to win! Her eagerness was catching: everything she wanted I wanted too, and together we tore the string off the ball, handful after handful, we supported each other, held each other tight to prevent ourselves stumbling, and before running into the house a fetch a new ball, I tied the end of the string around her waist and knotted it. While I was doing that Ina put both her arms round my neck and said: Quick, Bruno, quick, we've got to win! Whenever we looked into each other's eyes we felt joyful, and when I was holding her tight I didn't want to let her go, and she didn't seem to mind. She wanted to win, she wanted our kite to fly the highest, to receive the most letters – bits of cardboard with holes in the middle that the wind drove up the string as far as it would go. Once the kite made a downward plunge, turning over and almost getting caught in the overhead power line, but on her hasty word of command we ran back as far as we could and brought wind beneath the tumbling kite, so that it steadied and rose swinging over the Kollerhof.

At times her face was hardly to be seen, because the wind ruffled and blew her fair, her shining hair, over it. At times the little chain around her neck slipped outside her collar, and I could see the piece of amber with the five insects trapped inside. That she could brace herself so firmly on such thin thighs I'd never have thought possible. If I'd had my way we need never have fetched that kite down, but Dorothea called us in for supper, and we rolled the string back into a ball and Ina went back with me to the house.

At supper she sat beside Rolf. There were scrambled eggs

with prawns to begin with, and, no doubt because she knew how much he liked prawns, she gave him an extra spoonful and then another, he could never get enough of them, that sprinter with his freckles and his blond match-stick haircut, and he could eat just as quickly as I could, though he never left off talking: about the school and about the Hollenhusen savings bank where his father was manager. When we came to the waffles, waffles with syrup, Ina asked whether the victor shouldn't be given something for his victory, and, without waiting for an answer, she took the last golden-brown waffle from the pan and put it on my plate, dabbing the syrup on herself. And that was not all: as I held the fork in my right hand, she suddenly laid her hand over my left one, she pressed it flat against the tabletop, slapped it, pressed down on it, and all I felt was this small warm weight, and I didn't dare look down – even less share the waffle. Later I noticed that there was a red stripe running across her hand too, where the string had cut into the skin.

Though Dorothea invited me to stay on after the meal, I said goodnight and went up to my room. I didn't undress, but just lay on the bed listening to the voices below, to her voice. They were playing games I couldn't have joined in anyway: the chief kept on winning and was then told to drop out. I was waiting, I'd left the door of my room slightly open, just a crack. Ina must come up some time, and I was hoping she'd notice my open door and wouldn't shut it before calling out goodnight to me. I could still feel her arms around my neck, see the joy in her eyes; among all the clutter in my head I could still feel her flowing hair in my face and the weight of her hand on my hand; I only had to think of it and again I was holding her very tight and winding the kite string around her waist, tying a knot as excitedly she urged me on.

When she came up at last, she didn't listen outside my door and she didn't close it. She fell on her bed with a sort of puffing noise, lay still for a while, then undressed quickly, more or less flinging her shoes across the room. Before going off to sleep I spent a long time wondering what I could do on the following day to give her pleasure, but I could think of nothing – or rather I thought of so much that I couldn't decide.

In the end I had just to clean the bicycle on which she rode each morning to the station in Hollenhusen, to polish it and pump up the tyres while she sat listlessly over breakfast, chewing slowly and drinking milk. Dorothea sat with her at the kitchen table and saw to it that Ina ate both slices of bread; several times she said, as she did practically every morning: Don't fill your mouth so full, child. I could see them both through the window, see Ina grumbling and Dorothea coaxing. I had long finished with the bicycle, and tightening a few screws was just a pretence, but then, when Ina took up her case and brushed a quick kiss over Dorothea's cheek, I didn't wheel the bicycle to the door as I'd planned, I didn't go up to her to wish her good morning and study her face, all words had vanished from my mind. I left the bicycle against the wooden bench and ran to the hedge to crouch down behind it. She didn't notice the shine on the bicycle, being too tired, I suppose, but I was happy when she rode past me. I didn't need her thanks, it was enough to feel glad I could tell myself no other schoolgirl would be leaving such a well-kept bike at the station as Ina.

How impatiently I used at that time to await her return! Each day I would arrange things so that I could wave to her from afar. When we were sitting together at table I usually didn't dare look straight at her, I don't know why either, and in my mind was just a single wish: that we might meet in a solitary place, maybe at dusk among the plantations, or that we might be partners again in some competition. It was not until we lit the candles so as to save electricity, and the shadows began to move, that I dared look in her direction, and then I couldn't take my eyes off her, off her thin, watchful face, her large eyes and the brightly coloured butterfly slide in her hair; I had to watch her, because I was always hoping for a sign meant for me alone, for a touch that would renew and confirm what had suddenly happened while we were flying that kite. That was my hope.

I once went secretly into her room. I was alone in the Kollerhof and, since her door was open, I went in to see how she lived. She had tied bows round a lot of the things there, blue and yellow bows round a photo of Dorothea, round a vase, round the foot of a globe the chief had given her for Christmas. I would dearly have liked to start tidying her clothes away, putting the shoes, the shawl, the pullover in their proper places, taking the cotton vest off the back of the chair, placing the pyjamas under the pillow, but I didn't dare touch anything, for from the top of the wardrobe I was being watched by a stuffed owl that (like my polecat) came from Magnussen's inheritance. That amber eye. That split glance.

On a wide, smooth board that served as a table several sheets from Ina's drawing block were lying. She had been drawing autumn flowers with coloured chalks, and in each flower there was a hidden face waiting to be discovered. They were merry faces, full of mischief. I sat for a short while on her chair, then went over to her wardrobe and, since it was out of range of the owl's eye, I opened it and breathed in the scent of lavender.

The flowers: it's certain I'd never have begun secretly putting a flower in her school bag if Bruno had never seen all those drawings in her room, all those twinkling, mischievous flower faces. I didn't take them from our Kollerhof flowerbeds, the chrysanthemums, the asters and I don't know what else – I took them from the graveyard in Hollenhusen, plucking them from fresh wreaths or fishing them out of green metal vases before the wind and rain could spoil them. It was always just a single flower, which for the most part I fetched early in the morning. I would vault lightly over the crumbling wall, seek out a decorated grave, careful to ring the changes, pick whatever took my fancy and hide it quickly inside my jacket. If anyone should come into sight in the road or on the forecourt, I would read the inscriptions on the gravestones or sit on a bench like a mourner. Before Ina rode off to the station on her bicycle I would smuggle the flower into her school bag, which would either be lying in the hall or already fixed to the carrier, and each time I'd try to picture her surprise and delight when she opened her bag in the classroom.

At home she said nothing about the flowers. She gave no sign and asked no questions, but all the same I believe she suspected me, for she shook her head over me more often than usual, not reproachfully, just with a sad smile. What pleased me most was when she gave me a task to do. Whether I was cleaning her shoes or repairing the catch on her amber pendant, I would make the job last as long as I could; and I often had to pause in the middle of it, for I had the frightening feeling that I was touching her in person, her foot, her neck. If I was asked to take a letter to the savings bank in Hollenhusen for Rolf, I would hold it in my hand only on the first stretch; as soon as I reached the line of poplars I would push her letter inside the neck of my shirt. How happy I was when I was allowed to lend her some money! Before her eyes I opened up the stuffed polecat in which at that time I kept all the coins I had received from the chief or Dorothea. The sum I shook out of that polecat came to more than eight marks. Ina counted the money up by the light of my pocket lamp, and as a reward I was allowed to go with her next day to the shop. She bought Rolf a game of darts with six arrows.

Ina meant to pay the money back in a month's time, but when that time came she asked to put it off a further month, and I gladly agreed, only wishing she would remain in my debt even longer. It worried her that her pocket-money wasn't enough to pay off the debt, it worried her a lot and, when once she tried to give me two marks in part payment, I wouldn't take the money, but consoled her instead. However, that didn't make her any happier. She was upset at being unable to keep her promise, and sometimes I had the feeling she was keeping out of my way so as not to be reminded of her debt. Then, because that in turn worried me, I thought out a plan to relieve her altogether of the whole sum at once.

Sign-reading: I thought up many different signs that would lead to and fro across our land to my hiding-place, to the old boat-skeleton. With stones, with broken branches, with bits of rag and coloured paper fastened to young plants I marked the route out, and, after hesitation at first on her part and patient persuasion on mine, Ina at last gave in and agreed to my plan: with the help of my signs she would try to track me down in my hiding-place. She took no pleasure in the idea; even after she'd agreed, you could see she had her doubts: maybe she thought I was making it too easy for her to rid herself of her debts all in one go. The search was to begin at the erratic block the chief and I had dug out. A chalked arrow on the weathered hump showed the direction in which Ina had to start out – not of course knowing that my hiding-place lay in fact close to the block itself.

From where I was hiding I observed how well she managed at the start. Her eyes went searching to and fro, from the ground to the plants, the stakes; some of the signs she put in her pocket, and now and then she seemed to be laughing at herself, especially when she threw away something she had at first taken for a sign: a stick or bits of a broken flowerpot. Soon she was among the plantations of young trees. Near the thuyas she became a bit puzzled, but she found the bottle that pointed to the old command hill. She climbed that and then disappeared at once down the hollow. I had no doubt she'd find the white arrow on our shed and would walk around the hut and the seedbeds to the arrow that marked the beginning of the return journey. I was already feeling pleased and working out what to do when she found me in my hiding-place. Pretend to be dead: I would pretend to be dead and jump up only after she gave me a prod. That was my plan.

Ina didn't come. Ina didn't find me. I lay and waited and kept watch for her, I abandoned my hiding-place, showed myself openly, climbed on to the block, finally ran to the top of the command hill, where I could see all around. Ina was nowhere in sight. I sat there a while longer, then set off to look for her. I looked everywhere: on our land, along the Holle, the scorched railway cutting, but Ina didn't show up, and even in the Kollerhof no one could say where she was. As darkness fell, my fear rose, I felt it in my stomach, in my temples, it crawled like a colony of ants over my skin. After supper I went straight up to my room.

It couldn't have been so very late when Ina came home. No reproaches were made. On the contrary, she was praised for eating up her elderberry soup and all the semolina dumplings as well. She didn't ask after me. All the same, she didn't stay with the others, who spent every evening reading their books; she just spoke quietly with the chief for a while and then she came upstairs, moving with an even step that gave nothing away. She stopped for a moment beside our doors, as if she had still to make up her mind.

Then she knocked on my door. With the second knock she entered and asked in a whisper: Are you asleep, Bruno? I sat up and cleared my clothes from the stool, just swept them off it, and in the light of my pocket lamp Ina sat down, smiling in an embarrassed sort of way and keeping her eyes fixed on a piece of paper she was twisting between her fingers. I could see what it was: the little letter I had pinned to the stake to mark the beginning of the return journey, and on it I had written in pencil: To help Ina find me. You needn't be sad, I said, you read most of the signs, and that's enough. Now you don't owe me anything. I also said: You're a good sign reader, I was watching you in secret. Her sudden seriousness, her seriousness and the slow movement of her head from side to side. She bent over me, looked at me, and in her look there was a single urgent plea. Suddenly she put the letter down on my blanket and said: It's not possible, Bruno; I've noticed what you've been thinking in the past few days, but it's not possible. I could see how difficult she was finding it to speak these words.

I felt something had come to an end, a little storm passed

through my head, words were swept away. It was no better when Ina put a hand on my shoulder; I found myself thinking of the river Memel as it carried the last of the ice downstream, floes big enough to carry a man's weight, and I was standing on a floe, being borne away and watching its blue edges melting, faster and faster, fragments breaking off one after another and drifting away, while on the bank my father stood, holding the boat hook that had been too short to reach me.

But you belong to us all the same, Ina said, we are still your family. That was what she said, but it was not all she said. Without moving her dry lips she was speaking with another voice, an inner voice, and I heard clearly what this voice was saying: Poor Bruno. If only I knew exactly what she meant by that, and what the chief and Dorothea meant when at certain moments they would say nothing more than just: Leave Bruno in peace, saying it sadly and warningly and sometimes even anxiously, and always making these pauses after it, as if worried by their own uncertainty. But I do have some idea of what it might be: it's my perpetual hunger and my perpetual thirst that make them feel so helpless.

Once Dorothea came on me as I was drinking from the big pond beside Danes' Wood. I was lying on the bank, the clouds were reflected in the water, and I had the feeling of drinking from the pond and from the sky at the same time. And then Dorothea suddenly cried out: My goodness, Bruno, you'll burst! I told her I'd drink the whole pond dry if that's what she wanted, but she just pulled me to my feet and led me home. And once the chief caught me in Lauritzen's turnip field. He stared unbelievingly at all the stalks I'd left lying on the ground, not thinking it possible I could swallow so many turnips. He felt my tummy in a concerned sort of way, shook his head and said: Bruno, Bruno. And he also said: You seem to work by a different set of rules.

I don't know why all this happened to me, all I know is that Ina gave me her piece of amber: not the chain, just the amber itself, and I held it tight in my hand after she was gone, I squeezed it and pressed it until my hand hurt. If only I knew what has become of it! The amber has vanished like everything else – maybe trodden into the earth, maybe in Danes' Wood, overgrown by moss and fern.

So that *was* someone calling me. I sometimes hear my name being called though nobody is there to call it, or somebody calls and I don't know who. But this time it's Max standing in the doorway, in his hand a paper-bag from which he is pouring nuts and raisins into his mouth, and before long he'll be giving me a handful of his favourite mixture. His shoes are covered in mud, the turn-ups of his trousers are darker than the rest, which means he has been walking somewhere. He'll surely have been among the fruit trees. In the middle of his greeting he holds the paper-bag out to me: Here, Bruno, try some. He praises the morning and draws me out of the packing hall, steers my steps towards the multi-furrow cultivator. I can see he's after something as he offers me more of his favourite mixture and invites me to sit down on the frame of the cultivator.

This is what I sometimes miss in town, he says, nodding his head in the direction of the level ground on which they're lining out the two-year-old spruces. It's only when you're away from it that you're conscious of what you're missing. He wants to know whether I ever walk to the judgement lime, and I say no. Do I still remember our walks together along the banks of the Holle, he wants to know, and I say: Those were nice. And that long, hot summer: do I ever think of that summer when the Holle almost dried up completely and we caught fish with our bare hands? and I say: We ate fish every day then. You know, Bruno, at the beginning Hollenhusen didn't mean very much to me, but the older I get, the more it begins to feel like home. That's what he says as he gazes across our plantations, over which a slight haze is lying here and there. In the end, he says, when all your hopes have come to nothing, you do need to feel there's at least somewhere you belong.

He is breathing with difficulty, now and again letting out a whistling sound, and he can't hold the paper-bag still between his fingers. Something is bothering him, he keeps wiping his eyes and his brow, and his shoes keep tapping lightly together. I don't mean to, but suddenly I ask: When is the chief coming out again? And, since Max turns to me, I say: Some of them are already missing him. He looks at me so searchingly, as if suspecting me of something – Max, from whom I have hardly ever concealed anything. He can't take his eyes off me. His sudden coldness, his curiosity and this slowly growing mistrust: I find it almost unbearable. He moves away a little, so as to get me better in focus, and now he's lowering his head, as if some doubt is paining him. Tell me, Bruno, have you not received a letter, a letter from Schleswig? No, I say, the last letter I received was from that old soldier, Simon, who sent me his sketches and plans nine years ago. When was the last time I spoke with the chief? That I remember exactly: Last Tuesday, it was in the evening, I was pulling the soft needles from the spruces and chewing them, and he caught me at it. And what did he say to you? He just cautioned me, that was all.

Why does he smile in that forced way? Why does he reach for the measuring rod and start scratching a channel between two puddles, a channel with a slope that lets the water flow together? Why does he now want us to walk together through the young plantations, just a short way, down to the Holle perhaps: Don't you feel like it, Bruno? Oh yes, I say, and I look round for Ewaldsen and wave to the foreman, who has already seen whom I'm sitting with.

Why is it not like the other times I was allowed to walk with Max? Why can't I feel the joy I always felt before when he was walking beside me, telling me how to discover happiness, telling me why the less he has, the more a man is himself? Watch the path, I say, it's slippery. Ah, Bruno, he says, nowhere, I believe, does the rain wash the land so clean as it does here. Just look how it's shining! As in past times I'd rather leave the talking to him and just listen, but he says hardly a word, all his attention fixed on adjusting his steps to his weight and his clumsiness.

He stops beside a water-butt, scoops out a few insects, splashes water over his face and blinks at me beneath drenched eyelashes. I can see he wants to ask me something, but is not finding it easy. And now, Bruno, you'll show me something, won't you? What? I ask, and he: Our best land, our most fertile land, the piece you would pick for yourself if given a free choice; come, show me that. The chief, I say, only the chief can decide that; it is his land from the railway cutting down to the Holle, he knows better than anyone else where the poplars like to grow and where the morello cherries and the China fir, he only needs take up a handful of earth to know at once what plant it's good for. That's true, Max says, no one understands his land as well as he does, but what I want to know is which piece *you* think the most valuable, which piece you would choose for yourself if it were given you as a present or signed over to you.

Maybe the hollow, I say, the land from the erratic block down to the hollow and then the grey-white soil up to the stone wall, the whole northern part of the old training ground. I point in the direction of the erratic block, swing round over the young plantations and trace a circle with my hand, marking it all out with signs up to the stone wall, where the damp ground begins. Max communes with himself, recalling something here, comparing something there in his thoughts; if he were not so tired, I couldn't have read all that in his face. Now he nods in a satisfied way, as if he has found out what he wanted to know.

I must quickly tell him my dream. This was it: all of a sudden there was a rustling and a fluttering in the air, snapping sounds in the darkness, a creaking, a clumping, a boring. Tree-trunks were knocking against each other, clouds of leaves rushing past the window. I heard a violent brushing noise, as if bushes were shaking themselves, and, when I looked out, I couldn't believe my eyes: all our trees and bushes and plants were on the move, rushing this way and that in tumultuous haste. They had worked themselves loose of their own accord and now, freed from the places in which they'd been standing, they were creeping on their roots in all directions – not aimlessly or just carried along by the crush, but in an organised way, as if under orders. They weren't trying to escape: the only reason for this hasty night-time migration was their desire to change their living quarters, to try out new habitats and to see the chief, me and all the others left for once standing there speechless. Larches were swiftly digging themselves in where cypresses had just been, the oak was changing place with the slow-growing common beech, the syringa had come to an agreement with the crack willow and was taking over its hole. Those in the greatest hurry were the fruit-trees: quinces, plums and walnuts. In my dreams I remained awake until morning and, when the chief at last arrived, I told him what had happened. He listened in an amused way and certainly didn't seem to think the move in the night would cause us any great trouble. When I'd finished, he just said to me with twinkling eyes: Leave them alone, Bruno, they know themselves what soil is best for them.

A grin is Max's only response to my dream: he wants to move on, maybe to pace out the land I indicated. But why? Why is he walking with me through plantations where he's never before been seen? Why does he look at everything as if he's assessing its worth: the nursery bed, the soft-wood? He once said to me: Nothing is as widespread as the fear of losing what one owns.

The wall is still damp, rainwater sparkling in the hollows of the stones. We seek out a dry spot and on a sign from him sit down with our backs to the Holle and the pasture land. Now that we're alone he could tell me what has happened to the chief, what is going to happen to him, and he could also tell me whether I shall have to leave Hollenhusen. He won't take offence at the question, not Max; he whose only reason for being here is surely to come to the rescue of something is always understanding.

Well, Bruno, he says, imagine this was all your land, from the railway cutting behind us up to where we are now, all of it yours and registered in your name – what would you do? It belongs to the chief, I say, he leased it to begin with and then he bought it, and what has been done with it has all been according to his plans. His word is the only one that counts here or will ever count. All right, he says, but let's just assume it suddenly belongs to you, you are the rightful owner, free to decide in everything concerning plants and plantations – what would you do?

What does he want? Why is he asking such strange questions? This is a different Max, with hidden motives of his own. Maybe he's even trying to set a trap for me, at a time when everything is going downhill, as Magda has said, as Lisbeth has said. What would you do, Bruno? he asks yet again. The chief, I say, I'd make it over to the chief at once with all its rights, because he can do things that no one else can, and because he's the only one with the right to decide.

The tin containing cherry stones: there where he's sitting, in a hollow between the rocks, my tin is hidden, but I can't fetch it out, not now, I wouldn't want to crack the stones open in his sight. I can clearly feel he has some more questions to ask, and the only reason he isn't asking them now is because Joachim is waving to us from the path beside the hedge and hurrying towards us as if he'd been looking for us. I can already hear the hissing of the leather trimmings on his breeches. He always has to carry a swagger-stick, a smooth black wooden stick that he now and then holds against my chest while talking to me or warning me for the second time. They exchange a quick glance – I can see there's something they want to talk over – then Joachim gives me his hand – Joachim, with whom I haven't shaken hands since my last birthday, and now he's asking: Everything in order, Bruno? Yes, we're just sitting here, I say and make to do what he expects me to do, that is, to return to the packing-hall, but his little stick is against it: Listen, Bruno, there's something that must be settled. We must sit down together. Everybody in the stronghold is of the opinion that you must come up one evening. We'll let you know.

So here we are at last! Now, after all this time, they'll be sending me away. Maybe they'll give me a photograph and a sum of money as they've done to Lisbeth, hand it over with a speech and then slam the door shut on Bruno. But before this happens I shall have another word with the chief, to whom I owe everything and who once called me his only friend. I shall beg him to keep me by his side, I shall bring him everything I have in my hiding-places, he needs me, he will show understanding. Have you got that, Bruno? In the stronghold, some evening soon. Yes, I say, and ask: Will I have to leave? They exchange another glance, Joachim looks at me in surprise, just as if I'd asked something I shouldn't. There's been no talk of that, Bruno, he replies, and he doesn't shake his head over me. He gives Max a summoning nod, and Max follows him readily. They have a lot to say to each other.

I can feel my head spinning, I must crack open those cherry stones. A handful of bitterness: the nuts will calm me down, clear my brain. I must work out a plan, and it must be ready by the time they call me. No, not to join the tinkers, nor go to a town, best of all the sea or a place where woods are being planted, maritime pines maybe on some headland. The yellow raft. The shouted orders, the shooting, the screaming. The clatter of horses' hooves. They've taken away the chief's rights. Soldiers are storming the command hill, storming the ship's deck, they hurl themselves down into the hollow, jump into the water with weapons and packs on their backs; the gathering together after the storm, the little jets of water as they dive in.

Maybe he too will just want to leave, and then I'll go with him, simply follow him. If only I still had that ocarina I found under the dwarf pines, on the old bivouac ground! It was full of dirt and stuck fast, but, once I had washed it in soapy water, it gave out notes again. At one time the chief said to me: Once you've heard those notes you feel like following them for ever. Keep on practising, Bruno. And he also said: When you can play it well enough, we shall all follow you, even the beeches and the elms, our entire plantations.

But this is also the place Ina's husband picked on when he found there was no other way out. He, Guntram Glaser, who in his time here took everything over and pushed people aside and lorded it over all but the chief himself, he simply went down to the rail-track, lay down on the rails and waited for the night train to Schleswig.

Soon, Bruno, soon they'll be calling you. The wall must be kept clean. Anyone finding the cracked cherry stones here will probably think it's a mouse's store.

Here, where the packing hall now is, our dispatch shed once stood. I wasn't even there when it was pulled down – but, anyway, we put it up early one autumn for the first of our open days. At that time I didn't know what an open day was. It was the chief's idea: he thought it might be of some help at a time when Dorothea always found something to complain about as soon as we had gone up to our rooms and they were sitting alone in the dim light. Not reproachful, but just concerned, she gave him details of their mounting debts; she told him of her disappointments with some of the people of Hollenhusen, who suggested she'd do better to go back to the place she'd come from – and that just because she'd spoken in the grocer's shop of the number of bilberries and mushrooms to be found in Rominten. She also complained of rebuffs she had received in the council office and the fact that the big Erlenhof farm would no longer sell us eggs or milk. They treat us like strangers, Dorothea said. The chief, who often spent the evening writing in his plantation logbook or going through the home-made card index in which he entered our first meagre sales, never had very much to say in reply, maybe because he was so tired and exhausted. Usually he would just say: We must find a way through to them, Dotti, or: We're not giving up, and, in order to comfort her, he would also say: Don't listen to them, Dotti, one day it'll be them wishing you good morning. Once, very quietly, he asked her whether he should throw it all up and go away with her and all the family, and that gave me such a shock that I slipped back into bed and held my hands over my ears for fear of hearing Dorothea's reply. I suppose she felt in her own mind that the land would let us down and that sooner or later we'd have to admit it had all been in vain, all the plans and efforts and exertions a waste of time, but she never told the chief to stop and clear out while there was still time, she never did that.

One evening when we were all of us still downstairs, our empty plates before us, the chief suddenly declared: We'll arrange an open day. If they won't come along of their own free will, then we'll invite them officially, invite each single one of them to become acquainted with us and our work on the plantations. Since none of us had anything to say to his suggestion, he got to his feet and walked slowly round the table, giving his thoughts up to the kind of things an open day might put on offer, starting with invitations and advertisements and ending with demonstrations and an advisory service for all and sundry. There would be guided tours; Ewaldsen and two part-time workers would show how soft fruit bushes and evergreen shrubs and roses and hard fruit trees should be planted; tips would be given on ways of making bowls, tubs and boxes look pretty; the art of grafting should be demonstrated; and to round it all off the chief came on the idea of a lottery with rare plants as prizes.

What do you say? he asked, and really there'd been no need to ask, for Ina was already busy with plans to design coloured invitations, with trees bowing low and bushes beckoning; she also undertook to put an advertisement in the Schleswig newspaper, and to see to the issue of invitations generally. Joachim was given the job of looking after the cash and arranging the lottery, and he knew at once where to borrow a cash-box and what the lottery tickets should look like, each one carefully cut out and rolled up and held together by a little rubber band. Then, when the chief came to a halt behind me, I could feel he already had a task for me; his hands were lying on my shoulders and, speaking over my head, he said:

Nobody's as skilful at grafting as Bruno; he will show examples of all the different kinds of grafts, he will not just show all the grafting methods, but he will actually carry out a whip and tongue grafting. Bruno will be a real sensation. That's what he said. Since he himself would undertake the two guided tours and also keep an eye on things in general, that left just Dorothea – for, if Max hadn't just departed, the chief would surely have found something for him as well. Dorothea was not prepared to stay in the house: she wanted to contribute something of her own to our open day. When the chief suggested she should welcome each guest with a flower, she said no and smiled and thought a while, and then she made her decision: I shall appear all by myself, in a way that will surprise you all. I shall dress myself up and stage it all myself. Just you wait and see.

When I recall our open day the first thing I always see is Ina sitting over her invitations, and then I hear hammer blows coming from where I am now, here where the chief and two workmen were putting up a makeshift dispatch shed. After that I see Joachim cutting out and inscribing the lottery tickets, and I feel once again the fluttering I felt in my own tummy as I practised with the bill-hook, the quick-budder and the grafting knife.

Dorothea: during the days of preparation she sat a great deal on her own, reading and making notes. Sometimes she would smile to herself, sometimes explode with laughter and, when one of us wanted to know what she was laughing at, she'd put a finger to her lips and lower her eyes. Everyone was in a state of excitement, even the stray cat that had come to join us, hardly had I let it out when it would be miaowing again at the window, wanting to be let in, and then it would jump into everybody's lap in turn. This was Stumpe, our ginger cat.

Because we were all looking forward to it, our open day arrived swiftly: an autumn day, when the wind was gently stripping the leaves off path edgings and hedgerows, and a few late swallows were sewing the last stitches in their patterns. It was bright, the sun was shining, though not strongly enough to dry the dew, and, as we emerged from the Kollerhof into the fresh Sunday morning air, we exchanged happy winks and, full of confidence, hauled our bits and pieces across to the plantations. What Dorothea had in the sack on her back still remained her secret; she wouldn't allow me even to touch it, but carried it down to the hollow herself and disappeared with it into the hut, forbidding us to go in or even to peep through the cracks. Ewaldsen and his two assistants set up their tubs and boxes and got everything ready for their demonstrations, Ina and Joachim dragged a folding table to the place chosen on this occasion as the beginning of the main path. Whoever came to visit us had to pass through a gate hung with garlands of flowers and blue and white pennants, and it was there the chief took his stand, to welcome distinguished guests and maybe walk a short stretch with them. In no time we were in our places, just as if we'd rehearsed it all. Now all that was lacking was visitors, a Sunday morning procession, as I had seen it in my mind's eye, of sceptical, mistrustful and curious Hollenhuseners, some with children in their best clothes who had been warned not to pull things up or trample things down, and, besides those, people from all the surrounding villages, Seespe, Lundby and Klein-Sarup, and finally a train-load of people from Schleswig.

But, however eagerly we kept our eyes fixed on Hollenhusen and its dreary railway station, we saw no one get out, no one set off in our direction. But wait: there was one isolated couple bearing down on our gate: it was Detlefsen, our peevish crane of a council clerk with his dwarfish wife paddling grimly along beside him and having to take at least twice as many steps as he. They were the first to arrive. They listened curiously to the chief's words of greeting, but refused his offer to accompany them; they wanted to take a look around by themselves, so: Come on, let's go, Trude, and off they went, leaving the chief smiling and shrugging his shoulders. The Detlefsens having gone off in the direction of the erratic block, we were once again alone together, waiting, watching, imagining ourselves in Hollenhusen, where our brightly coloured advertisements were hanging on every tree. Joachim could think of nothing to do except sit there shaking the cardboard box containing the lottery tickets, and the chief walked up and down with lowered head, muttering to himself and massaging his wrists. I couldn't tear myself away from him. When he took a turn round a plantation I followed close behind, always in the hope of something happening. Several times I was on the point of speaking to him, but in the end I didn't dare – I don't know why either. Because I had eyes for no one but him and was so busy helping him will people to arrive, I didn't even notice Ina slipping away: she slipped across to the railway cutting and ran to Hollenhusen, and it was not until I saw her light blue figure skipping across the station yard that I realised she had left.

The sudden shouting, the sudden laughter: it was Ewaldsen and his two assistants, calling and laughing and directing our eyes towards the hollow, from which an old crone was emerging and shuffling towards us in galoshes full of holes, bent over like a figure L, her upper body leaning on a knobbly stick. Her jacket was an old sack, her skirt an even older one, and from a cord tied around her middle there bobbed and dangled all kinds of things – dried herbs, kohlrabi, carrots and pale onions strung on thin wire. She was wearing woollen gloves, but each of the fingers had been unravelled. Her head-scarf, on which a calendar was printed, was so large you could make out hardly anything of the earth-brown face beneath, and it must have been her wobbling chin that kept her muttering away to herself all the time.

I ran to the chief and pulled him up from the box on which he was sitting, and then I tried to pluck some of the dangling vegetables from behind the old crone's back, but she hissed at me, a sharp warning hiss louder than any gander, and the chief said: Take care, Bruno, you must watch your step with herb-witches. Not only hiss, she could when she felt like it make circling movements with her hands that kept you rooted to the spot, or she would strike the ground with her stick, making a hollow noise, and when she gave a mournful howl it sent shivers all down your spine. How lightly, though, she skipped on to the crate, and how surely she spun round on her feet, jabbing her stick in all directions of the compass, twice towards the east, and how still we all kept when she called out in a rusty voice: Comes east wind, comes caterpillar, / Comes from far-off Tartarland. / Crush up lupins, bind with horsehair: / Only then will they be banned. Ewaldsen's assistants nudged each other and clapped their hands, but the old crone gave them such a look that their clapping died.

In everything she did and performed in front of us she never once took her eyes off the chief. She sought him out, eyed him reflectively, but also in a concerned way; at one time she plucked herbs from the bunch at her waist and threw them to him, at another she laid the point of her knobbly stick against his chest and murmured: Borage gives all men courage, / Basil restores speech to the tongue, / Marjoram will cure a blockage, / Hellebore bring back songs once sung. That's what she said, and as she did so she raised her head, and I saw how she blinked at him and then at once threatened him, just as if she now expected him to follow the advice her words contained.

Suddenly I heard Ina's voice, she was shouting something encouraging, urging haste, and trailing behind her I recognised a few of her school friends: the boy Rolf was there and Elma and Dieter. They joined us at once, eight visitors at least, they folded their arms in a mild show of interest and considered the recipes the herb-witch was giving to a couple of sisters who had turned up unexpectedly, humorous recipes against snails and greenfly, also against moles, whose tunnels, she advised, should be stopped up with carbide. Then one of Ina's school friends asked amid laughter whether there was also a remedy against a bad memory, for historical dates, for example. The witch began muttering, she was surely racking her brains, going through the pages of her stored experience, and after a while she raised her stick triumphantly towards the questioner and said without hesitation: Lavender worn around the head / Will stop the brain from playing dead. She was thanked with delighted applause, which she cut before adding: Fairies' horse and rosemary / Do wonders for the memory. / Mint at night beneath the pillow / Will sharpen up the dullest fellow.

I should dearly have liked to stay with her, just in order to listen and to note the answers she gave the questioners and which they happily accepted. I should so much have liked to learn them all by heart, but as I stood listening the chief nudged me and pointed to the main path, down which my former teacher, Fräulein Ratzum, was coming with a man in a green uniform who was leading a lumpish boy by the hand. Off you go, Bruno, the chief said, you must now take your seat; and I gathered up my equipment and sped across to the former command hill, where I had fixed up a table-top on which all the things I'd need were now lying, scions and stocks and raffia for binding – the rubber quick-fasteners hadn't yet come into use.

The grafting equipment was laid out in neat rows, and the first to come to a halt in front of my table-top was Fräulein Ratzum, who held out a friendly hand and wanted to know what 'our Bruno' had to offer; before I could answer, the man in the green uniform came up too, that's to say, he was pulled along by the lumpish boy, who had an overlarge head and puffy lips.

I meant to begin with a simple budding job and was just demonstrating how to make a clean T-incision and to carefully lift the rind when Lauritzen called out: Here, Niels, the nitwit wants to teach us something, and they pushed right up to my table, standing so close that I began to shake at the very moment I was about to slice out the bud. Lauritzen's son nodded to me and made a pacifying gesture with his hand, as if begging me not to take too much notice of his father, who was watching my fingers impatiently in a demanding sort of way, but as the old man wouldn't stop calling me nitwit or muddlehead – well, get on with it, muddlehead – my fingers got shakier and shakier. I spoiled the first bud, cut out another and tried to insert it. The shield wouldn't be forced beneath the rind, and I had to cut it; I set the short sharp blade of the quick-budder against it and pressed; the blade slipped and cut cross-wise into my forefinger, right through to the bone. With the pain came the blood. I turned away quickly and wrapped my handkerchief round my finger, and, as Lauritzen was cackling: That didn't quite work, did it? I inserted the bud and put the binding round it, though I couldn't keep bloodstains off the raffia. Eagerly the lumpish boy snatched the twig I'd grafted, put it in his mouth and chewed it. By patient coaxing the man in the green uniform got it away from him, but then the boy began snorting and stamping and clapping his hands, begging me to give him another piece. Lauritzen just grinned and said: You'll all of you be cutting your fingers before long, and he went off with his son, who didn't forget to give me an encouraging nod.

The man in the green uniform also gave me a nod. He was wearing puttees and braided shoulder-straps, and his dark-skinned face was sprinkled with hundreds of bluish dots, as if it had received a blast from a shotgun. He spoke gently to the boy in an effort to calm him down, and then just took my hand and examined the wound, moving my finger to gauge the depth of the cut. Before he could say anything Fräulein Ratzum decided: Bruno must be bandaged, he must be given treatment, come along, Bruno. At that, without saying a word, the man fished a wrapped bandage out of his breast-pocket, tore off the watertight cover and, still in silence, bandaged the wound, tying the ends of the bandage loosely but firmly round my wrist. It was throbbing, it was burning, and a hot stabbing pain shot up to my finger-tip. There, said Fräulein Ratzum, and now our Bruno will break off his demonstration and I shall take him to Herr Zeller. No, no, I said, I'll be all right, and I made an elaborate show of sorting out scions and rootstocks, at the same time becoming aware of Heiner Wal-endy and two of his gang, who I suppose had come up through the plantations. They were all three smoking and were advancing in a cloud of smoke. I could see they were out looking for mischief, anyone could see they had something in mind, and I thought it might be my grafting equipment they were after.

Since the man in the green uniform requested it, I demonstrated wedge grafting. It didn't go as smoothly as usual: every pressure with my fingers was painful, and as I was splitting the stock and cutting out a wedge, the bandage turned red: the blood didn't seep right through, but the redness was clear enough to be seen by all the people round the table. I pulled the raffia tight with my teeth. The stranger praised me and Fräulein Ratzum said: Well done, Bruno, and wanted the graft as a keepsake, but the lumpish boy jumped on me, putting his whole weight on my arm, so I had to give way and deliver it over to him. As before, he bit into it, snorting with delight. The next one I did, a cleft graft which didn't come out quite as even as I wanted, I handed quickly to Fräulein Ratzum, who was so pleased that she opened her old-fashioned handbag and took out a fifty-pfennig piece, which she dropped into my jacket pocket. Seeing that, Heiner Walendy and his two companions exchanged glances and came up so close that they were touching my table.

The searing pain: I still remember wanting to leave off for a while, as I would have done if the chief hadn't appeared with two strange men, silent men whom the man in the green uniform greeted politely. The chief gave me a wink and a private smile, and I knew what that smile meant: under the gaze of those strange men I took two equal-sized bits of scion and rootstock in order to demonstrate a whip and tongue graft. I heard the chief drawing their attention to the difficulty of this method of grafting, I heard that and felt my pain gradually die away: the tongue-shaped incisions must be done correctly, so that the two alien partners fit each other exactly and are given maximum stability. I made my incisions and brought scion and stock together, and was able to insert them so easily into each other that a raffia binding would no longer have been necessary, so complete was their contact.

The two strange men had nothing to say to me, they just waved a hand in my direction, but the chief said: Good work, Bruno, and they then moved on. I fixed the raffia binding in the way it must be done, looked up and found myself staring straight into the eyes of Heiner Walendy. Here, I said, this is for you. It was probably just fear that made me say it, and he was so surprised that he didn't even open his hand. I repeated the words, and I also said: Maybe you'll get some pleasure from it. Then, wonderingly, he took the graft and turned round, and the two others, who were standing there grinning and wanting to have a go at holding it, he pushed roughly back. They followed him off sulkily and came to a halt down in the hollow: there they were allowed to examine the graft, and while they were doing so Heiner Walendy gave me a brief wave.

What's the matter with her? What does Magda want with me now, at this time of day, in the packing hall, where everyone can see us? It's her wish that we should keep out of each other's way, just so as tales won't be told about us, for once they start to talk, their nosiness grows and grows and they pump you and grill you till there's nothing left to hide. What is it, Magda? I ask, and she says: The chemists, I've got to go down to the chemist's in Hollenhusen, and she also said: Nobody's seen me, so keep your hair on. The slight triumph in her eyes, that air of superiority: anybody could see she hasn't wandered in just for the sake of something to do, just to watch my bass broom hissing over the cement floor. Well, what is it, Magda? Get a move on. She still holds back, she pouts and sits down on the edge of the wall, looking as untroubled as someone who holds all the trumps and has nothing to fear. Come on then, tell.

It's nothing, she says, the chief hasn't lost his rights yet; they've only just applied for a hearing. I know now for certain:

it's all been put before the court in Schleswig, and that hasn't made any decision yet. Just ordered a temporary guardianship – I think that's what it's called – for the chief, a temporary guardianship. I was about to ask who had applied for it, but she told me of her own accord: Them in the stronghold, they've started the whole proceedings, they've all of them signed it. She looks at me, then says quietly: Don't ask how I know, I just know, and you can depend on it.

If only it's true! So things haven't yet gone too far, they haven't yet managed to take away the rights of the man to whom they all owe everything; he'll put up a fight, he is cleverer than any of them, which means he'll win in the end, and I shan't have to leave. Not lost his rights, the chief hasn't yet lost his rights!

Why, I ask, do you also know why they're doing all this? Now Magda isn't so sure of herself: she shrugs her shoulders, gets up and peeps outside. It's being said he's suffering from feeblemindedness, she says, then adds quietly: It's also said he's putting the family property at risk, all this here.

I don't know how a family property can be put at risk, that's something I've not yet thought about, but I can't imagine that he'd gamble on something he himself made and built up over many years, I can't believe that, not of a person who has spoken in the name of all nursery gardens, was once mayor of Hollenhusen, has received many decorations and one spring conducted the minister himself through our plantations. He is still the chief, everything here belongs to him, and no one has a larger say in it than he has, no one.

How is he doing that, Magda? In what way is he putting it all at risk? I don't exactly know, she says, but up there they're talking about a deed he drew up in Schleswig, a deed of gift. She has to go, but first the pledge of silence: Yes, Magda, I promise, no one will get anything out of me, never. I'm glad you came, that I know about it now, and, Magda, don't walk between the rails.

How dearly I should like to run to him now, simply run into

the stronghold, past Dorothea and Ina, to the room where he's sitting alone! I wouldn't ask anything, for that wouldn't be right, just my help, all I want to do is offer him that: if there's anything to be taken somewhere or to be ferreted out – that's something I could do.

They've only put in an application, nothing has been decided yet, and they'll surely have to reckon with his resistance, for whoever intends to take away the chief's rights will have to get up early and have quite a bit of proof handy. I at any rate have never seen any signs of his putting the family property at risk or suffering from feeblemindedness: the things people can say about someone! What are they frightened of? Hasn't he always made out the contracts himself, and signed them? Everything has always been done on his signature alone, why have they taken against that all of a sudden? I don't know what's so special about a deed of gift, but, if that's what he's drawn up, it must be for some good reason. If only I'm allowed to stay near him! I'll go anywhere with him, him who's always been so good to me.

He saw at once that the blood had come through that bandage the man in green uniform had put on my hand. He took it off when we were alone, examined the wound and bandaged it again, and then he said: Come along, Bruno, no more work for you today, and that's all he said for the moment. He led me down to the garlanded gateway, where Joachim was dispensing his lottery tickets and Ina handing out the rows of prizes: flowers and shrubs for the most part, but also some soft-fruit bushes. It was mainly strangers who carried off the prizes. From Hollenhusen almost nobody except the tradespeople had come, and they stayed well in the background, showing interest only in ways of improving the appearance of flower bowls and window boxes. The old crone in her rags of sacking still had the largest audience: there comic questions and obscure answers were being bandied to and fro, there was much laughter and mock shows of alarm and aggression, and the crone was always surprising her audience with words of advice they'd never heard before. She had an answer for everything: to make flowers last longer she advised drying and crushing a piece of iris root and putting it in their water; to prevent theft she recommended, after pondering deeply, a bunch of hedge hyssop; to someone very keen to see ghosts she suggested mixing wild thyme and hollyhock buds in his salad; for slugs she knew only one remedy: beer and more beer. That was also written down in the dog-eared little book from which she occasionally read and which in all cases of doubt she held aloft as proof.

When suddenly she sprang from her box, so lightly that everyone was amazed, when she darted towards me, seized my arm and dragged me along with her, I didn't know that the chief had already spoken to her in secret. I had no idea she was just taking me home, to the Kollerhof; so confused was I that I could only stumble along beside her as, to the delight of the onlookers, she hissed and spat.

Thus we fled, she knowing where she was going, I unsure and more dragged along than moving of my own free will, so it could have looked like a kidnapping. That lasted till we reached the shelter belt, when, with that behind us, we held hands and slid down the slope of the railway cutting, where we could no longer be seen. Here we sat down, Dorothea took off her head-scarf and panted until she had got her breath back, and then she said: I think it was worth while, Bruno, we can all be satisfied. And she also said: It would be even easier with them if only they would accept the secrets one tells them, but these Hollenhuseners always want the secrets explained as well. She spluttered with laughter, fluttering her lips like a foal, and then it was she who pulled me to my feet and said: Home now, and fast, we must attend to your wound.

Still dressed in her sacks, she set water on the stove, shredded soap and bathed my finger in warm soapy water, then she brushed on something that burned and stung, and to lessen the pain she stroked my hand, her fingers sliding lightly over mine, so cool, so soothing. She also breathed a few times on the

129

wound, and, after putting on a new bandage, muttered a gay witches' spell over it, made signs in the air and declared the mending had already begun. Then there was black pudding and bread and a bowl of stewed pears and Dorothea sat beside me and was amazed how quickly I dispatched it. She kept bringing me more, and in her happiness she talked to me about the chief, about his ideas and his perseverance, and also how, when he has to, he can face up to anyone, when it's a question of his rights.

Once – this was in Rominten, when they were living among the plantations of the rising sun – some public body, the Chamber of Agriculture, I think, set up a prize competition. It concerned the defoliation of certain plants dug up for dispatch in autumn, the leaf-stripping, which at that time was done by hand: broad-leaved plants, when uprooted, must be stripped of their leaves, otherwise they quickly dry out. Quite by chance the chief saw the conditions of entry on his father's desk: his father was not competing, since he was a member of the commission that would choose the best reply to the question and then award the prize. That had been set at three hundred marks, Dorothea said. Though the chief was only seventeen years old and for that reason was not eligible, he secretly copied out the conditions and, outside the house, in places where he wouldn't be caught, he answered the prize question in his own way. Tree stumps served him as a working base, planks and an old wheelbarrow. It was only the drawings of the leaf-stripping drum he'd thought of that were done in a locked bedroom: this was a standing drum in which his prime concern had been to protect the shoots. Then he sent it all off to the town in a large envelope addressed to the Chamber of Agriculture. Nobody knew a thing about it.

Time passed, the days dragged on, and sometimes he thought his entry must have gone astray. Then, after he had made up his mind to forget all about it, he was called one evening to his father. The first thing he said was just: Congratulations, you've won the competition; but after a while he added: Of course, you won't accept the prize. Then at last the chief had to sit down, feeling as if he was on a rocker grate in a furnace, with his father congratulating him once again on his work, then once again telling him he couldn't accept the prize, simply because everyone would claim the family had had it all worked out from the beginning.

The chief saw the truth of that. He sat down that same evening and wrote the commission a letter in which he asked for the return of his prize work, but his main request was that the prize should be withheld from him, and his father saw to it that this was done. However, the moment the chief got his work back he sent it off again, this time to an old botanist from Johannisburg, who had also taken part in the competition and who now, as the chief had learnt from his father's papers, was to receive the prize that was really his. This botanist's name was Plinski, and he was well-known for his book on tree diseases. He sent no reply, but kept silent, just as if he had never received the chief's letter with the drawing of the leaf-stripping drum. However, a day before the prize-giving in the Chamber of Agriculture, he sent a brief telegram, the first telegram the chief had ever received in his life, and it invited him to come to the town 'for known reasons'.

Not in the company of his father, but all by himself, the chief went to the hall where the ceremony was to take place; he took a seat right at the back under cover of a rubber-plant, and after the music, the greetings and the presentation of certificates Plinski, the old botanist, made a speech. It should have been his speech of thanks, but it wasn't. Important as his own work had been – he had seemingly suggested how the growth element in the leaf could be artificially destroyed – it appeared to him that the answer a young expert had given to the prize question was of still greater significance, and then he repeated the chief's thoughts and ideas, introduced the new leaf-stripping drum in which the shoots were better protected than formerly, and he finished by declaring that with his fifty years' experience he could clearly see to whom the first prize belonged. Then he simply walked across the hall to the rubber-plant, Plinski did, dragged the chief from his hiding-place and introduced him to all those present. And not only that: after handing the money over to him, he turned to the commission and asked them to amend the certificate; he himself, with his fifty years' experience, would be satisfied with the second prize.

They travelled home together, the chief and his father, and not much was said, but when they were back among their own plantations, his father said: This drum, you rascal, this great marvel, we'll keep to ourselves for the time being.

Much more and there'd have been no stewed pears left for the others. With a little cry of alarm Dorothea bore the dish off to the pantry; cheese and blood sausage she also brought into safe keeping, leaving in front of me just the bread she had baked herself for this day, and so much of that did I stuff inside me that I could hardly stand up when Joachim and Ina came home at last, soon after them the chief himself.

Ina wanted to feel my bandage at once, and she sat down beside me and reminded me how pain can be thought away. Meanwhile Joachim was following Dorothea's every footstep: he helped her lay the table, he kept taking hold of her hand and wanted each time to know whether she was pleased with him. At one time, when she quickly stroked his cheek, a gleam of delight lit up his face, and he had to tell us how the people had wrestled with each other for his lottery tickets, and some had wanted an open day to be held regularly, maybe twice a year. How he could gaze at his mother, so ready and willing, so intent on winning a glance from her! Nothing meant so much to him as a word of praise from her.

It wasn't possible to tell whether the chief was satisfied or dissatisfied, not at any rate in the moment he came in and went over to his wall cabinet, which Ina had painted blue and white and decorated with a paeony. He opened the little cabinet, poured himself a drink from his flat bottle and sat down at the table opposite Dorothea. We kept quite still and watched them, and we saw a smile developing, first around the eyes, then in the moving wrinkles in their faces and finally in the opening lips. Carefully, so as not to spill a drop, he raised his glass to Dorothea and said: For my next birthday, Dotti, I've just one wish: that you do your act again – for me alone. Then he drank and, leaning across the table, kissed Dorothea on the brow.

During the meal he had a good word for everybody, even for Ewaldsen and his two assistants, whose bowls of flowers had been so successful that they received many orders for them. But that was just small beer, he said, it just about covered its costs; what really mattered – and gave him the right to another glass – was the consignment he had fixed up at the very end, almost at the point of departure, a consignment of six thousand young monkey-puzzle trees. Then the chief suddenly put an arm round my shoulder and gave me a message. I'm to say hullo to you, Bruno, he said, and to tell you that a whip and tongue grafting can't be done better than that, and the man who asked me to tell you this knows a great deal about it. I asked whether he was maybe wearing a green uniform and had a lumpish boy with him, and the chief nodded, adding quietly that it was this man, the head forester Dähnhardt, who had ordered the young trees from us.

Since the chief had a lot of writing to do as well as things to discuss with Dorothea, we left them by themselves. Joachim and Ina went off to Hollenhusen together, but I didn't feel like it. I went up to my bedroom and saw at once that something was lying on my pillow, something of a handy size, something dog-eared: it was the brown spell book, filled with Dorothea's own handwriting. I was so confused that I just didn't dare open it, I held the little book tight shut in my hand and kept walking up and down, but then I did open it after all and saw what was written there: For Bruno in memory of our open day.

Later I listened to the voices downstairs, and for the first time was unable to make out what they were saying to each other. I just heard the sound of them knocking their hard, thick glasses together. Maybe that was because I still had to keep a tight hold on the brown book and was then hearing other voices, voices that frightened me, and now and again laughter.

If only I knew where Bruno lost that little book! I had already learnt most of it by heart when suddenly it was gone. It was not under my pillow, not in the secret hiding-place under the wide floorboard: it had just vanished into thin air like so many other things. It may be true there are a lot of things that just don't feel at home with me. Magda once said something like that at the time I lost her case with scissors and nail cleaner after hardly more than a day: Really, Bruno, it's no use giving you anything that isn't tied up with string, and even then it must be firmly knotted. And she also said: There must be something wrong with people who lose as many things as you do.

A quick dash to the railway station, to the railway buffet, where cold rissoles are waiting for me, neatly piled under a glass dome. I can be back in a quarter of an hour: two rissoles and a fizzy lemonade. Ewaldsen won't even know I've been away, he always lies down for a while in the shade once he has eaten his sandwiches and folded up the greaseproof paper. Lisbeth didn't give me enough: when it's boiled fish, there's never more than a single piece, but boiled fish only makes my hunger pangs worse, I don't know why either. The pale woman behind the counter doesn't wait for me to order: she knows at once what I want. As I come in she lifts the glass dome off the fried meatballs, gives me a smile and opens a fizzy lemonade. If only there wasn't such a smell of cold smoke and lysol!

There's someone sitting there: this time I'm not alone. Under the rack where the flags of the Hollenhusen savings bank stand gathering dust a man in a creased jacket is sitting drinking beer. Elef? Well, if that isn't Elef: it's certainly his peaked cap hanging on the chair beside him. Now he has seen me too: Ah, Herr Bruno! His bow, his moustache, the question contained in his greeting. Yes, I'm coming, I say, I'm coming. With what a sure hand he balances his beer glass, from which he has drunk scarcely anything. Ah, Herr Bruno. So wife's sister is coming with the train and wife's father too, they will live in the big wooden house, both are quite old, sit a lot on chairs, don't need much room; if the chief wishes, they can both work too, they have always worked on the land, old, yellow land, but too dry. Why must he nod after every bite I take, why is he so pleased? No, I don't take a cigarette, nor do I accept his invitation to a beer: I must be off right away, Elef, much work.

I'd like to know what Duus, the policeman, is looking for here, and why he's standing so long in the entrance door gazing at the empty tables in the buffet. He can surely see there's only the two of us sitting here, myself and Elef. In the way he moves there's nothing that looks like steps: he seems just to glide towards us, weary and glum, showing no clear sign of interest. Can I see your papers? he asks – not me but Elef, who gets up at once and bows and fumbles in his creased jacket, searching one breast pocket, then the other, and now he has found it, his shapeless old artificial leather wallet, and he holds it out to Duus, who doesn't take it, though Elef says politely: If you please.

How quickly Elef grasps that Duus doesn't want to touch the wallet, only to check his work permit and his residence permit. Busily he begins to rummage, pulls out a newspaper cutting, which he lays on the table, pulls out a creased foreign banknote, which he lays on the table. His breath is coming faster now as he fishes out a dry twig of arbor vitae, already crumbling and no more likely to be accepted as a permit than the passport photo of a young girl with black hair. But here, says Elef, if you please, and he hands Duus a rubber-stamped piece of paper.

The paper is in order, Duus reads it and returns it with a nod, but something is still lacking: the work permit, might he see that? Elef fumbles and feels and prises apart the things in his wallet that have got stuck together, but the permit won't show up, in vain Duus stands holding out his open hand. He's with us, I say, Elef has been working with us a long time, and I also say: The chief will bear me out. Duus would like to make do with that, but there's something inside him holding him back, he thinks a while, seeking a way out, and at last says: Bring it to the police station within three days.

He turns away, ignoring Elef's bow, and Elef sits down and helplessly goes through his wallet once again, muttering words I don't understand, and now – There, you see – he finds a stained, pencil-written letter inside which his work permit has been hiding. There, you see. But Duus is already outside on the platform acknowledging the pastor's greeting and exchanging a few words with him. Calm down, Elef, do as he says.

Elef hurriedly stuffs everything back in his wallet; there are people on the platform now, soon train come, he must go outside to welcome wife's sister and wife's father, yes, I know, you must go, is all right. He gives me a quick bow and runs to the door. What's the matter? What has he forgotten? He come back again: So, Herr Bruno, on Sunday small party, much pleasure, expect Herr Bruno towards evening, but truly; and now he is running off again and waving once more from the doorway, Elef in his drain-pipe trousers.

This is something I've often wished for. I hope nothing happens before Sunday. Who knows what they'll think of next in the stronghold? They've started these proceedings against him and they have all given their signatures. And another thing: I hope I won't fall ill. That has happened a few times: when I am particularly looking forward to something I've been taken ill at the last moment, as on the day before the circus came to Hollenhusen, the day before the chief was to set the Midsummer Eve bonfire alight. The pains and the high temperature always wait to the very last moment and then stop me going.

What is Max doing on the platform? Who is he meeting? And there's Joachim too, swinging his car keys like a propeller. If they're using the car for such a short journey, it must be a very special guest arriving on the train from Schleswig. They mustn't see me here, not now. What a lot they have to do, answering all the greetings, and in what different ways they return the greetings: here a hand raised from the elbow, there a stiff bow, a wink here, and that brief nod is surely for Duus, who draws himself up and raises a hand to his cap. They stroll along the platform from one end to the other, the brothers from the stronghold, and it wouldn't surprise me a bit if the lamp-posts also bowed to them in greeting, and the signal box and the Hollenhusen nameboard. Palme: hardly has Palme arrived on the scene with his red cap and his signalling disc – the old stationmaster Kraske was content to send the trains off with just a raised hand and a whistle – when the train gives notice of its arrival. I can feel the shuddering, see the gentle vibrations in Elef's beer glass, which he hasn't emptied, and now comes a darkening, the squeal of brakes. Hollenhusen, this is Hollenhusen: Palme as he shouts it out makes it sound half a greeting, half a warning.

Him I don't know, him I've never seen before, this man in a dark suit Max and Joachim are greeting in a friendly way, and who himself just gives a bitter-sweet smile, revealing huge front teeth: a pompous rabbit who no doubt is used to being met, cautiously holding tight to his travelling bag. The guardian: maybe that's the guardian sent by the court to keep a watch on the chief and to get to know all the things for which he's to take over responsibility for the time being. But he could also be a doctor, carrying remedies in his bag for all pains; though Joachim twice tries to take it from him, the stranger won't let go of it. He walks between them as if under guard. He stops short in front of our nameboard and looks a bit startled, as if he's come to the wrong station, but Max says something to him and he smiles again and allows himself to be guided to the barrier and outside to the station yard.

There they are, the head-scarf and the two balloon-caps: they have found each other, Elef and wife's sister and wife's father, they are joyfully dragging baskets and bags and cardboard boxes tied with string towards the exit, and Elef must of course seek me out with his eyes and give me a sign: that toss of his head is meant to show how pleased he is. If only it were Sunday already!

Now Palme has raised his signalling disc, the engine moves off, a little cloud of steam envelops the stationmaster, who appears to be hovering above the ground – but now it's time to go, high time, straight over the rails to our dispatch ramp. Let him shout, let him hurl his threats after me: nobody has yet followed me this far, and the next time we meet it'll all have been forgotten.

You see, Bruno, there was no need for such haste: Ewaldsen is still asleep in the shade of the young pines, and I won't prod or tickle him awake, that's for sure, not me.

In the early years the chief used sometimes to say to me: All right, Bruno, now we'll take a capful of sleep, and he would stretch himself out wherever we happened to be, on the warm earth, on the grass, would blink a few times in my direction and nod straight off. What he meant by a capful of sleep was something I didn't understand at the time, but that's what he said, just that, and it wasn't my place to ask questions, even if he more than once assured me: If you don't understand something, Bruno, then ask, you can save yourself a lot of trouble by asking, even save your life at times.

Max: he can ply you with questions until you're quite dizzy, he had only to ask me to go with him to the judgement lime or the dolmen and I knew I must resign myself to a hailstorm of questions. When I could no longer follow, I simply agreed with everything, just to put an end to the muddle in my head. The things he could think of in earlier times, when he still wanted me with him on his walks!

Once in springtime, a weak sun shining, he insisted on taking a walk with me, though you could see him shivering with cold after a poor night's sleep. He needed to air his thoughts, he said, and he led me down to the Holle, putting an arm around my shoulders. Since I was the only one with gumboots I walked on the bad side of the path where there were puddles, where the mud squelched and clouded the water. Over the whole stretch to the judgement lime he told me the story of a man who lived alone on his vast property. Many people worked for him and carried out all his wishes, but all the same he was not happy, because he worried too much; and, because every day he had to inspect and defend his property, he became mistrustful of everybody and used force to keep it all together and to increase it still further.

When one day this man was thrown by his horse, he lay ill for a long time and was looked after by a young woman, who every morning was cheerful and untroubled, even when scolded and ordered around; nothing ever got her down. When at last the man was restored to health, he sent for the woman, wanting to give her a special reward, and he asked her what she needed, needed most urgently, and she said: Not much – all I need can be written on the nail of my thumb. So he saved the expense of a reward, but he couldn't stop thinking of the young woman's answer, and often, as he sat over the deeds of his property, he would examine his thumbnail, would turn it this way and that and examine it until, as an experiment, and in small writing, he traced a first word on it and at once saw how much room was left. He was so amazed that, again just as an experiment, he wrote more words on it and then even more, those words that describe what one needs most in life, nothing more and nothing less.

And then one day he put a few things in a shoulder-bag and went off to a distant place, a no man's land, where there were no roads, just forest and a quiet lake, and on the banks of the lake he built himself a hut and cleared a bit of the forest to make a small field; the fish traps he needed he wove for himself with flexible twigs. There he spent his days, and on the very few occasions when he had to walk to a distant shop, he took care only to buy goods whose names could be written all together on one thumbnail. He did not count the winter days on which he went without, the summer made up for those, he adapted himself to the seasons and enjoyed his solitariness. One day he gave food and drink to an empty-handed hunter who had lost his way by the lake and, when the hunter wanted to know the reasons for the man's composure and contentment and peace of mind, he said: Ask yourself what you really need, and when you can list all you need on a thumbnail, then you'll be on the right track.

All the way to the judgement lime Max talked about this man, and when we were sitting on the little mossy bench under the hollow lightning-scarred tree, he started out on his questions, often firing them so fast and so expectantly that I had the feeling he could never get enough and was crazed for answers. He wanted to know whether I'd have behaved like that man, and I said: I don't know; but I also said: With such a vast property a person ought to be content, he only needed to state a wish and at once it would be on the table. Max shook his head and said: But he doesn't come on his true self, Bruno; property breeds suspicion and bitterness and hardheartedness; he discovers his own self only when he rids himself of all the things he doesn't need.

Would I like such a property, he asked me, and I said: No. You see, he said, and why not? Because I'd have a lot to fear, I said. Right, Bruno, he said, and what would you fear? Being noticed, I said, but he was not happy with that and said what I suppose he'd sooner have heard me say: Losing it, Bruno. Every bit of property at once arouses the fear of losing something. And then he asked why so many people set out to gain property and to pile it up, and when I said: Maybe because they have to look to the future, maybe because they find pleasure in it, he shook his head again and said: Endurance, Bruno, whoever piles up property wants to endure, wants to outlast, he can't stand the thought that everything has only a limited amount of time allotted to it. And he also said: He who desires to have, desires it first of all for himself. All this time he would keep offering me his jelly bonbons and, when I now and again fell silent, he would tap me on the shoulder and say soothingly: It's all right, Bruno, it's all right, but then he would go on questioning still with closed eyes: whether that wasn't true independence, when a person needed only as much as could be written on a thumbnail? What can you answer to

141

questions like that? In the end there's nothing else to do but agree, just to put a stop to it.

The things I showed him and told him held hardly any interest for him, and at times I was amazed how little he knew: he didn't know the name of the wood pigeon that suddenly settled on the judgement lime, and he had never heard what can be done with the shiny rotting wood that gathers inside a hollow tree trunk, never. I was so flabbergasted that I should have liked to ask him more, just to find out all the things he didn't know, but I could see from his face that he was deep in thought, his mind elsewhere, so I kept silent.

But all at once it started again, all at once he wanted me to tell him what I owned, I should spell it all out for him, and I named everything I could think of: the jacket and the raincoat, the shirts, the rawhide boots, the working trousers and the rack and the crockery; he just gave a nod, as if making a note of each item, and I still remember: I named everything except the piece of amber Ina gave me. Good, Bruno, he said, and then he wanted to know how much I lacked, and I said: Whenever I need something, I get it from the chief. He didn't seem quite satisfied with my answer, he thought a little and then asked: But free – you do feel unburdened and free? And I said: So long as the chief keeps me by his side, I lack for nothing. He was content only when I told him that I divided my pocket money, received sometimes from the chief, some- times from Dorothea, between two hiding-places – he was not interested in where the hiding-places were, though I would have told Max, who has always been good to me.

And then he told me of a man who had discovered that property is theft, because everything the earth produces belongs, or ought to belong, to all: I could say nothing about that, I couldn't agree with him that it was so, because I thought at once of the chief and of how he took over the scarred land, the soldiers' land, in order to tranform it and to lay out plantations from which not only we but also many people in Hollenhusen live. Max had still more questions to ask, at times he completely ignored the fact that I was sitting quite still beside him, but then, when he found my silences too long, he began to answer himself in a hesitant voice, and as we walked to the meadows and then along the edge of the meadows towards Danes' Wood he was still asking why it is that those who have feel they must have yet more.

The plovers had already arrived, they were flapping over the meadows, changing direction sharply and continuing their jerky flight until we came too close to their nests, when they would attack us. But their attacks and their attempts to divert us were of no use. They couldn't fool me: I had quickly reckoned out where a nest would be, and I fetched the eggs and offered them to Max to taste. I showed him how to make two little holes in the egg, carefully, so as not to break the shell, and how to suck the egg dry in one go, but he was unwilling to try it, he couldn't even look to see how I swallowed the plovers' eggs, he had to shut his eyes and turn away.

Maybe he thought I might swallow a fertilised egg or even a plover chick, maybe that's what he thought, but I can see at a glance and feel after a brief shake how far gone the egg is inside, and it has happened only once that I've tried to suck an egg in which there was a chick. Anything too far gone I put back in the nest at once. There's no need to be afraid of plovers' attacks: they just make a noise, cry and try to frighten you by flapping their wings and creating sharp rushes of air, but set about you or peck you, no, plovers don't do that.

Since he couldn't bring himself to taste the eggs, I wanted to find some other way of pleasing Max, there in Danes' Wood. I wanted to take him to the covered pit in which I kept my root people: snake-men and bulgy-heads and crooked-footed dancers. We had dug or pulled them out while clearing, the chief and I. Washed in the Holle, dried out and bleached over a long period, they were now as hard as the ribs of the boat we'd dug up. No blade could make a mark on them: my root people kept the form in which they'd chosen to grow, and this was in so many different shapes that I could only wonder how a root could be so rich in ideas. The woman with three legs. The kraken-man. The roadsweeper and the man on stilts. I asked Max to choose one for himself.

That was later, though. I gave it to him later, for before we reached Danes' Wood we heard the regular blows of an axe and an indignant voice, and, though we couldn't yet see anybody, we knew it was Lauritzen's voice bawling and uttering threats and at times cracking with fury. We exchanged a glance, Max and I, and then we walked on slowly till we saw the chief, who was calmly felling a few trees, thinnish trunks that he'd earmarked for a fence. He seemed not to be bothering himself at all with Lauritzen, was behaving in fact as if he'd not even noticed him. He just fixed an expert eye on each trunk in turn, ran a hand once over it, then cut it down and began at once to strip the branches.

Seemingly Lauritzen didn't dare block his path or challenge him direct. He kept at a safe distance, growling and barking at the chief from the sidelines, talking all the time of ancient rights and common law and threatening him with Schleswig: We'll meet again in Schleswig, he shouted once, and by that he meant the law courts. As the chief moved on to the next tree, he stamped through the bracken in his wake. One of his puttees had come undone, and it snaked along behind him like a loose bandage, but that didn't stop him continuing his racket, accusing the chief of tampering with another man's property and robbing another man's land. He was behaving as if Danes' Wood belonged to him. He shouted: You'll be sorry for it some day, and he also shouted: You vagabonds. When he said that, the chief set the axe on the ground and for the first time looked at him, just looked at him, which made Lauritzen swallow and then begin winding his puttee in, hand over hand. Without saying a word the chief went on with his work until he had all the trunks he needed; he gave no replies and made no remarks of his own, even though Lauritzen once more threatened him with Schleswig before at last shuffling off. To us all he said was: Someone here seems to have been in a bit of a rage, nothing more than that, and then he put us to work at once, loading four trunks on to our shoulders, two on the left, two on the right, he himself shouldering the broad-bladed axe, and off we went to the Kollerhof, where he began to mend a rotting fence. That Max hadn't time to give him further help he acknowledged with just a curt nod, after which he drove a nail into the wood with such bitter precision that it made my flesh creep.

Ewaldsen is still asleep under the young pines, though someone is now standing beside him and looking down at him. If that isn't Plumbeck, Pastor Plumbeck: he's certainly broad enough, also silver-haired and bullnecked enough, and the black hat could easily be his. He prods our foreman with his foot, he stoops down and shakes him a little, and now Ewaldsen is sitting up, looking as stupid as only he can. He shakes the sleep from his eyes and gets to his feet and seems to be asking Pastor Plumbeck's pardon. There's not much you can say when you're woken up at your place of work at this time of day. Ewaldsen points across to me, makes to go off, must go off, but first, it seems, he must answer a question, probably about the chief, for Pastor Plumbeck is already standing on the main path that leads to the stronghold and pointing with his thumb over his shoulder towards the big house. I suppose Ewaldsen will say what he always says as soon as somebody wants some exact information from him: I've heard nothing and seen even less. If only I knew why Pastor Plumbeck wants to speak to the chief! Up till now he's come only to collect contributions for a new bell tower or for pew repairs. But maybe it's the others who have sent for him, wanting to hear his opinion of the proceedings they've started. He walks up to the stronghold.

Roast: how often during our confirmation lessons did he warn us we would one day roast if we didn't obey the Ten Commandments, if we sinned in small as in large things! As he made his threats he would stamp his feet and his grey, deepset eyes would seek me out – in the end it was always me, I don't know why either; all I know is that, when he spoke of the torments awaiting us, he was aiming it at me. God gave you the Ten Commandments as a mirror, he said, and if you want to know how sinful you are, just look into it. That's what he said, at the same time reeling off the punishments each of us could reckon with for disobeying a commandment. For a time I was so frightened that I fixed a second catch to my door in the Kollerhof, together with a wooden swivel-pin: sin should find no way through to me! I also kept the skylight closed, just so that sin – all the evil that is constantly dragging us down, as he put it – couldn't take me by surprise.

Once I was ordered to relate the parable of the great supper, the story of the rich man who arranged a grand supper and was very angry because the people he's invited cried off at the last moment. But he suppressed his anger and sent his servant out to collect all the cripples, the blind and the lame in the street, and with them the man feasted until all the pots and pans and plates were licked clean, and after it he said he'd never again invite the people who'd refused his invitation. Pastor Plumbeck sat with his purple face close to mine and listened and was satisfied, but then he told me to explain the parable; he maintained that Jesus was a great storyteller and put into each of his stories a hidden truth. This is what I should now bring into the light, but short and to the point.

All I could think of were the excuses the invited guests made to avoid the great supper: one man had bought some oxen and had to go to prove them; another had bought a piece of land and had to go and see it; and yet another had married and had to stay with his wife; and, since the excuses weren't up to much, all I could believe was that the invited guests weren't much taken with the meal the rich man meant to set before them: maybe it was indigestible or too greasy or too spicy – anyway, they must surely have known what they could expect. Pastor Plumbeck was not satisfied with this explanation; he gave me a searching look, his face twitched and an expression came into his eyes, a suspicious expression: he suspected me of not having said what I really believed. The sin, he said, you know well enough that this is about sin, not about eating. So I thought some more, but I couldn't see what he was getting at. I didn't discover the sin, and when the lesson ended he kept me behind and, opening the Bible at Luke, Chapter Fourteen, he commanded: Read until you understand it, and that was all.

Alone in the old Hollenhusen church, in the dim light, the coolness, the silence, I read the parable, read it again and again without managing to find out where the sin lay hidden. To loosen up, I walked around a bit, along beside the thick salt-encrusted wall; I stood beneath a circular window and peered into the evening light; I tapped the pillars; I counted the hymnbooks stacked up on a rickety table. When I found myself by the heavy door, I put my fingers on the handle, just to try it, and then I discovered that the door was locked, I couldn't get it open, tug and shake it all I might. It gave me a real fright, and I went back to my bench, to read and to listen. Then the light began to fade, the letters to shrink on the page, and I stretched myself out on the smooth bench, ready to jump up at the least little noise, the first scrape of a key.

How long I was asleep I no longer know, all I remember is that all of a sudden a light was dazzling me, it flitted to and fro in front of my eyes and I heard the chief's voice, felt his hand under my neck and felt myself being lifted off the bench. So here he is, the chief said, and somewhere in the background Pastor Plumbeck said: That such a thing should happen to me! And in the church doorway he laid a hand on me as if in blessing and said: How could I have forgotten you? It was dark outside. The chief just growled at parting. We walked along the road between the poplars to the Kollerhof, his strides so long I could hardly keep up with him. Only one word did he utter the whole way, and it was not to me, but rather to himself: Lazyguts.

Here knocking-off time takes
nobody unawares. A full half-hour before Ewaldsen sets about
the hanging iron bar they stop working properly, have a smoke
and a rest and then begin cleaning their tools. They scrape and
poke and wipe, but in such a dawdling, unmethodical fashion
that from a distance it's impossible to tell whether they're
engaged on the final cleaning or are just clearing off dirt to
make working easier. As closing time comes nearer, they take
less and less trouble to hide their preparations, they polish and
rub hastily, drift towards the stopcocks to wash their gumboots. Some already start taking off their working gear and
changing into the clothes they'll be going home in.

Their briefcases lie in handy reach or dangle from their
machines. There's little talking, but much looking at watches,
and as always they're amazed how the final five minutes drag.
But the iron bar has begun to sing out at last, and now they're
hurrying from the plantations to the main path, jostling at the
gate before Ewaldsen has finished striking knocking-off time,
and a traffic jam is forming in front of the tool shed, since
chisel plough and trench plough, seeders and sanders, grubbers
and binders have still to be driven in, all the machines that are
the chief's property.

In earlier years, when just a few of us worked here, there
was no knocking-off signal at all; the chief would simply say:
This five hundred must still be staked or repotted, and we
would keep going till all was done, and we two were always

148

the last to leave. He himself would never give up until he could do no more, until he was bent double and nothing went quite as he wanted. Nobody I've ever met could be as weary as he was without becoming cross or silent; he was always content and ready to talk.

What I really enjoyed was being with the chief when he was tired. Then he always looked as if he'd stolen a march on someone: he was happy in his exhaustion and tolerant of almost everything. All the same, nothing escaped him, however tired he was. If after knocking-off time Ewaldsen brought along a few villagers in search of work, the chief would just tell them to plant three young conifers and to transplant three more: tired though he was, he would sit on an upturned wheelbarrow and watch through half-closed eyes, and sometimes I thought he'd fallen asleep, but in the end he chose as I would have chosen myself: You, no, but you and you. Ewaldsen, when the chief left it to him to engage new people, would always begin by asking them their ages, then watch how much each could do – lift, carry or whatever. If one picked up a load of three rather than two boxes, that could prove the deciding factor.

The way everything at once changes after knocking-off time, when the plantations are left to themselves and there's no longer anyone moving around in them! I've often had the thought that the plants stretch themselves a little, look around and exchange signs, sighs of relief; Bruno has often had that thought. Plants do, after all, feel around beneath the soil with their roots till they can touch, catch hold of each other and maybe even change places.

But I must mend this hole in my pocket, which I suppose was made by my knife: the metal presses against the cloth, rubs and presses till suddenly, when I go to fetch something out of my pocket, there's just a hole and nothing besides. The tin box with the sewing things must be under the pillow, the gold and yellow box I was once given by Tim and Tobias, those two little pests who have always picked on me as the butt of their mischief. It was certainly Ina who made them bring me the box filled with chocolate hearts. The evening I ate them I was expecting to find one of them filled with mustard or pepper, but in fact I didn't have to spit any out, they were all good.

Was that a knock? Who wants me now, at this time of day? Who has come along the side-path: surely it can't be him? But it is him, standing there outside my door in his dark suit, his hat in his hand: the pompous rabbit Max and Joachim met at the station, the guardian or the doctor, and now he's knocking again, a timid knock, not like Magda, who knocks with her fist or the palm of her hand. If you're not in, you don't have to open, but of course after closing time I must be at home; maybe they saw me from the stronghold, or he might also have heard my footsteps. If only I knew what he wants with me! The armchair had better be empty, so away with this old shirt, just fling it behind the curtain, the gumboots and the towel and the plate as well, all behind the curtain. Now he can come in. Yes? Who is it?

Herr Messmer? he asks. How does he know my name, this man I've never met? No one has ever called me that before: Herr Messmer. That's a bad sign, surely, but now I must open up. His bittersweet smile, like on the railway platform, his huge front teeth and that pained expression in his eyes, suggesting he's got a load on his mind. Pardon me for disturbing you during your well-earned hours of rest, he says, but I have been instructed to have a talk with you. May I come in for a moment? Instructed? Instructed by whom? That's what I'll be wanting to know, and as soon as he sits down I'll ask him. Come in.

How quickly he glances around! How swiftly the concern leaves his eyes – to be replaced by curiosity: in a twinkling he has taken it all in and made a note of it in his head. Pointing to the broken clock in its marble case, he says: A fine piece. And now he's saying: What a nice place you have here, and he also says in the same tone of voice: My name is Murwitz, and he sits down in the old armchair the chief gave me long ago. I must sit on the stool and leave the talking to him, to this person who has addressed me in a way nobody in Hollenhusen has ever done before. The light seems to dazzle him, he moves a little to the side and looks at me in a friendly way and is already telling me what I meant to ask: Yes, he is Herr Murwitz from Schleswig and he represents the interests of the Zeller family.

What is he trying to say? Whose interests does he mean exactly? I don't understand him, all I know is that I must now look out, even though he's giving me an encouraging nod and praising the wooden chest Dorothea gave me. Is it a fact, he asks quietly, that I've been with the Zeller family for more than twenty years, and I say: It's thirty-one years, I was here from the beginning. Good heavens, he says, thirty-one years! Time for a lot to happen; one learns a great deal, whether one will or not. He closes his eyes, maybe considering all the things he himself has learnt in the last thirty-one years, and now he's shaking his head, amused, unbelieving, as if it were all too much for a short memory. I have been informed, he says, that there is a very close bond between you and Herr Konrad Zeller; I hear he took you into his family at the end of the war.

The landing barge heeling over and starting to sink; the leaping soldiers with their packs and the swimming horses snorting and moaning and thrashing the water with their hooves, and the yellow raft drifting away with people on it waving and screaming, and then the rolling, fear-filled eyeballs, the wet throat, the blows! He pulled me out, I say, when we sank, the chief dived down after me and pulled me out. So I was told, he says, and I also learned that in a second disaster he again saved you from the worst; that's true, isn't it? Without the chief I wouldn't be here, that's for sure.

He has found the book Max dedicated to me, he takes it up, looking at me for permission, which I give, and now he is leafing through it; he reads the inscription and smiles to himself. If he's representing the interests of the Zeller family, then I suppose he has come in the chief's name too. Anyway, he can't be the guardian, the temporary guardian Magda spoke of. It may even be he's come to bring me news of the chief, certainty at last. I must take care now not to let my thoughts wander, I must concentrate, for there are probably more things he'll want to know from me, though he already knows enough; I suppose he just wants me to confirm what he already knows. I like the sound of his voice, his smoky voice.

So one might justly say, Herr Messmer, that you are the man who was in at the birth, the constant companion who has played his part in a life's work? That is what he says, indicating his respect with a movement of his lips. What can I reply? All I can say is: No one has worked for him more willingly than I, no one. I have heard of your dependability, he says, and he says too: It was a good thing that Herr Zeller had someone he could depend on to that extent, to whom he could confide his plans, with whom if need be he could handle matters that had nothing to do with anybody else; anyone engaged on a major task needs someone to lean on. I presume there is much you have experienced and come through together? Yes, I say, we have experienced a lot together through the years, and there are times I fear I shan't be able to remember it all. But I don't think I've forgotten anything yet, because every day at dusk I remind myself of something, every day something different. That's right, he says, that's what one should do, a daily hour for memories: memories constitute a capital that is truly indispensable. How appreciatively he sizes everything up, how pensively his eyes rest on my possessions! Surely he must have come with the chief's knowledge; his friendly manner suggests it. If he doesn't mention it of his own accord, I shall just ask him, ask him in the end how things are with the chief.

Can one say, Herr Messmer, that after all these years you enjoy a position of trust, I might even suggest a very special position of trust? What is he getting at now? I've never given a thought to whether I have a position of trust or not, I've always just accepted the instructions the chief gave me and carried them out, and all I needed was his approval. He has never locked everything up in front of me or put it out of sight, I say, the plantation logbook, for example, he has always left things lying open – if that's what you mean. No, no, he says, you have misunderstood me. By position of trust I mean a position in which you knew more than others, in which you could give advice, use your influence. Then all I can say is: There's nobody in the whole of Hollenhusen who can give the chief advice; if he needs good advice, he gets it from himself. He then wants to know whether it was still like that in the year just past, and at once adds: You would have been the first to notice, Herr Messmer, for hardly anyone is as close to him as you.

When I come to think of it, Bruno, you are my only friend: that's what the chief once said to me, and the chief has always meant what he said. Well? he asks, and I say: Nobody here can hold a candle to him, he's only got to look once and immediately he knows what needs to be known. But that doesn't rule out a change taking place in Herr Zeller's character, his manner, does it? Very well, I'll tell him. The chief has got sadder, I say, sadder and maybe he's bitter as well, anyway, he's not as settled as he was in the beginning. And I also say: It's possible he feels isolated. He considers that, seems to turn it over in his mind, then he nods, as if satisfied with my answer and says, more quietly than before: Pioneers like Herr Zeller, men who have achieved so much in their lives, are lone wolves, after a certain time they are bound to become solitary, that's all according to rule. He considers again, runs his tongue over his big front teeth and grips the arms of the chair so tightly that his knuckles show white. His sudden gravity, his subdued voice.

Could it be, Herr Messmer, that an illness has changed Herr Zeller? What I mean is, has he complained to you of pain of any kind during recent times? Or has he reacted in a strange way, made decisions, for example, that you couldn't understand?

Max said when he was here: The chief has done a lot for us, we must now do something for him, and he also said: You're one of us, after all, Bruno.

Have you perhaps seen signs of depression in Herr Zeller, or of confusion or of feeblemindedness? Most of all, grief, I say, and maybe generosity and consideration. In recent times he has overlooked more than he used to; when he came on me pulling needles from the young pines and sucking them out, he just shook his head and went off without a word. In recent times the chief has spoken less than usual, that's true, I say, and I can see him pricking up his ears, he'll be cutting in directly, seizing this piece of evidence, and sure enough he's already asking: Does that mean he has no longer let you into the secrets of his plans as he used to do, that he has kept his major projects to himself? If I could only know what he's after, why he's probing so into all these things! But I must say something, so he'll be satisfied and go away. I say: The chief has always kept the most important things to himself; he'd work it out in his own way and make it known when he was ready. What is making him smile only he can know, I just hope he's done with me now, my temples are already beginning to throb, and what I'd really like to do is bang my forehead a few times against the doorpost. But he represents the interests of the Zeller family, and so I must of course see it through. And your own plans, he asks in a good-humoured way, can I be told something of your own plans, Herr Messmer? You haven't been thinking of making changes of any kind? I'm staying here, I say quickly, I want to stay where the chief is.

How all at once his friendly manner vanishes as he stands up, how searchingly he looks at me! Then suddenly he turns away and gazes out through the window at the plantations, holding his hat behind his back and turning it in a practised sort of way between his fingers. How long he can stand wrapped in thought! I mustn't disturb him now – but, yes, I must ask him how things are with the chief, and I direct my question to his back: The chief, it's quite a long time since he was last here –

will I be seeing him soon? He doesn't even turn his head in my direction. Maybe he didn't understand me. There are other things too I might be asking, for instance, if it's true they're applying to take away his rights: that's something I might well ask. But now he's drawing himself up and preparing to disclose something. Are you aware, Herr Messmer, that recently, in his solicitor's office in Schleswig, Herr Zeller signed a deed of gift? So Magda was right, she knew about that, she was right! And are you aware, Herr Messmer, that this deed makes over to you one-third of the land, together with an appropriate part of the installations? The deed of gift comes into effect in the event of Herr Zeller's death.

No, it's not true, no – he's just saying that so as to see how I'll take it, how I'll deal with it, he's playing a joke on me to test me out! But why, why is he taking it out on me, this man I don't know who represents the interests of the Zeller family?

He turns to me, he's waiting vexedly for something, his eyes half-closed, his lips twitching. You will understand, Herr Messmer, that the Zeller family is not disposed to consent to this deed.

What a terrible muddle! They surely can't be serious: one-third of the land and some of its installations, maybe the northern part of the old training ground, everything from the erratic block down to the hollow and the greyish-white soil up to the stone wall. Somebody once asked me which is the best earth; it was Max who wanted me, just for fun, to choose for myself the most fertile piece – what had been at the back of his mind then? I know nothing, I say, everything here belongs to the chief, he's the one who makes the decisions, and beside him his wife and Joachim and Ina: they say what's to be done with the plantations. So you really do not know what induced Herr Zeller to go to such lengths? he asks, and he also asks: He has not discussed anything with you? That I shouldn't have to leave Hollenhusen, that he did say once, by the big pond he promised me I could always stay with him.

Bubbles were rising from the soil, there was a babbling as

from a hidden spring as we sat down close together on the rotting tree-trunk and our weight pressed it down. And suddenly he said: Nothing shall ever come between us, Bruno, I promise you that.

Thank God, he's making for the door. I must collect my thoughts, must consider, when I'm alone, the meaning of his guarded manner and mocking expressions. He hesitates, then says: There's a lot of trouble coming your way, Herr Messmer, I fear you can hardly imagine just how much. But he is also saying something with his other voice, with that voice from afar I can distinctly hear, dark and no longer so smoky: This deed will never be put into effect, you can both be sure of that. We shall do all that's necessary to prevent this gift being made. Zeller must be completely out of his senses.

What else can he want from me? His hand is already on the door knob, but something else has come into his mind: If I may ask another question, Herr Messmer, I have been told that you perform certain functions here, that is true? Yes, I say, and he: But you have nothing to do with machines or mechanised tools, have you? Can this be because Herr Zeller does not approve of it? The chief didn't want it, I say, he put me in charge of all cutting tools and grafting instruments. An important task, he says, utters a friendly parting word and keeps his hat in his hand till he reaches the main path, where he carefully puts it on. Then he suddenly comes to a halt and runs his hands over his body. No, he hasn't left anything behind by mistake, he has found what he was looking for, and he walks off towards the stronghold.

Never in his life could the chief have thought up something like this, he knows I can do nothing without him. Never in his life would he sign such a deed. Who on earth has come on the idea and spread it around that the chief means to give me the whole northern part of our land, including some of its installations? Since he knows me better than anyone else, he knows I'm happiest when I work to his instructions. If he'd wanted to give me the land, he'd surely have spoken a word or at least given a hint, even asked me whether I wouldn't like one day to take over the bit from the erratic block to the hollow. Surely he would have done that, and I'd have told him at once I didn't want it.

A mistake, it must be a mistake. The dried prunes: yesterday there were a few left in the bag, I put the bag here on the windowsill and now it's gone – maybe I ate the prunes myself while half-asleep. The chief has signed a deed of gift, that's what Herr Murwitz said, and the deed comes into effect when the chief dies, and then what was his whole pride and joy is to belong to me. I don't want that, I've got no right to it and I don't want it. The very thought makes me giddy.

It was after a storm, it had been blowing hard throughout the night, a turbulence in the air of a kind rare even here, howling in gust after gust, testing the sturdiness of barns and sheds and trees, things flying through the air, not just branches and roof tiles, there were times when you felt you yourself would be lifted up and carried away. It drew a lot of us outside the following morning, we didn't trust the sudden stillness, we walked around uneasily, totting up the damage, though there wasn't very much in the plantations, not as much as on many a still night when the Hookman had gone through with his horrid tool. I felt drawn to Danes' Wood, to the tree dwelling I had built myself high up in the branches of an old beech-tree, everything firmly woven together and with numerous peep-holes. I just wanted to see what the storm had left of my swaying hiding-place, to which the groans of the wounded soldiers penetrated only faintly. As always I took the short cut, walked over the meadow with all its hundreds of molehills towards the big pond, and there I saw the chief, saw at once that he was holding something tight and dragging it behind him, something spotted, something spotted brown and white. I was already running, calling and waving, running as fast as I could.

He was dragging a dead dog by one of its hindlegs. It was one of Lauritzen's spotted dogs, one of the couple that went hunting in our plantations almost every night in successful partnership. Once, when the moon was shining strongly, I saw them myself, saw how one of them would sniff out a hare or a rabbit, put it up and chase it towards the other in wild zigzags over saplings and seedbeds, scattering all before it: in half an hour they could turn three days of hard work into a desert. The chief's requests and demands that Lauritzen should keep his dogs locked up at night remained unanswered.

I was a bit alarmed when I saw the dead hound, and I stopped, but the chief beckoned me quickly and told me to take hold, and together we dragged it to the big pond. There on the bank, where I often lay down to take a drink, there he asked me whether we should bury the dog or sink it. I was at once for sinking and ran to look for stones, heavy, long stones that are easier to bind than round ones. There was a pile of stones at the edge of Danes' Wood, already covered in moss and overgrown by brambles, I ran there and it was while I was pushing back the bramble trailers that I found the shotgun cartridge, its warm case. I took it to the chief, who smelled the case and was about to throw it into the pond, but then he suddenly stopped to consider, gave me a searching look and said: Here, Bruno, you take it, then you'll have something that's as good as a proof. Why he gave me the cartridge case I've never managed to find out, but give it he did, and I resolved to sew it into the lining of my jacket, so I shouldn't lose it easily.

Then we each tied a stone to the hound, the chief round the neck, I round the hindlegs, and we lifted the body, from which blood was dripping through a lot of little wounds, swung it to and fro, the chief counted one-two-three and simultaneously we let go. It made quite a splash, the waves setting up a motion in the reeds and rushes, they swayed to and fro, and at the spot the weighted body reached the bottom, bubbles rose, the water babbled as if from a hidden spring, boiled. Only after everything was still again and the water gave nothing away did we wash our hands and seat ourselves on a rotten alder tree-trunk.

He didn't say much, the chief, but he did say: Nothing shall ever come between us, Bruno, I promise you that.

The stronghold over there: how silent it is, nothing moving, nothing to be seen at the windows. You might easily think they'd left the big house, but I know they're all gathered there, endlessly discussing, checking documents, signing warrants, maybe quarrelling too, and surely one of them is constantly on the telephone, what with all the buzzings and hummings and cracklings coming from the wires that lead from us to the Hollenhusen railway station and from there along the lines to Schleswig. So it is on grounds of feeblemindedness and endangering the family property that the chief is to have his rights taken away: that is what they want, and Herr Murwitz is representing their interests in everything.

If only I knew where this sudden fear comes from! Something is brewing, the spoon is already rattling in the cup. It's he who brought me this fear, this stranger with his questions and statements. Lock myself in, that's what I'd really like to do, lock myself in here and not come out until the chief himself knocks at my door and takes me with him to the Colorado firs and gives me a job to do. But he won't come any more of his own accord, I can feel that. I must go to him, at once.

Even if they're surprised in the stronghold to see me come in without having been sent for, I must go to him, must talk to him, and not just so as to know what's to become of me, I must also put a stop to what he has decided on and decreed or intends to decree. The check shirt and grey trousers, I can visit him in those: he'll probably be sitting in his room by himself. I'll speak only if he's by himself, ask him not to leave anything to me, neither the land nor the installations, assuming anyway that it's even true. But my fear tells me it is true, that he has signed something in my favour, and I've always been able to rely on my fears. Let those who will take the main path, I shall walk along beside the windbreak hedge, hurry past the rose-beds and, once among the rhododendrons, I won't be so easily

159

seen: the rhododendrons around my old basement doorway have often protected me.

Once there were a great many people on the terrace, all thronging round to congratulate the chief. There were at least a hundred people in their Sunday clothes forming a circle round him and admiring the cross on a ribbon, the distinguished service medal he'd just received, and I stood for a long time in the rhododendrons and was able to see it all from close to without being discovered. And later, after some of them had gone into the stronghold, I was even able to fish some good leftovers from the trays without anyone noticing.

Was Magda surprised about that! But better this time not to take any fruit from the bowls in the passage, though Dorothea has given me permission. Even today the coloured bowls have been filled: I'd like to know who gets the fruit when it begins to go bad. Those voices are coming from the big hall, Max's voice and Murwitz's: Do you wish to stand by your proposal, Doctor Murwitz? I consider it a promising one, Professor Zeller. Ina's voice can be heard too, offering tea and biscuits around. For me it will be best to go straight up the stairs, down the long corridor where all the prints hang, the drawings of kinds of broom: dyer's broom, furze and common broom. His door is beside the German broom. I won't announce myself, I'll just knock and go in, and, if anyone stops me before I get there, I'll just say I must see the chief on an urgent matter.

The last time I was here was when the jackdaws invaded us. The whole sky was all of a sudden dark with birds, a noisy sky that swooped down on our plantations, quarrelsome and merciless. Who knows where all the birds came from? At first they just performed their loops and streamed past each other in unexpected patterns as if giving a display, but then they suddenly settled down on the young saplings, so many of them, and landing with such a thud, that the branches broke beneath them. They fought each other for the branches, they were determined to perch close together, and because of their fighting and their weight even more branches bent over and snapped; what couldn't bear their weight was done for. It looked as though the birds were out to lay our plantations waste and, since my clapping did not drive them off, nor my shouts, nor my arm-waving, I ran to the chief, I ran up these stairs and knocked just once and woke him up. He had fallen asleep at his desk, but when he saw what was happening outside, he knew at once what to do. Leaving his guns on their racks he took me down to the shed in which a number of hard, gleaming blocks of tar lay and we dragged these outside, once he had tested the direction of the wind. We quickly set up a number of tubs and grills, the chief poured petrol over the tar blocks, and then it rose up: a cloud of sulphur, yellow and green – no, it didn't rise, it rolled over the saplings, enveloping everything in a stinking fog, and thousands on thousands of jackdaws took to the air and circled screaming above the cloud before following their leader and flying off.

There is someone coming behind me with quick steps, maybe he saw me coming in, I'll just keep going, first of all up the stairs that lead to the bedrooms and to Tim's and Tobias's big play-room. It's Magda: that is her apron. She runs past with a dustpan and brush to the chief's door, she is knocking now and waiting. Please clear this away, says Joachim's voice, all these splinters, and be careful. The chief is not alone, that's for sure, and I can't speak to him now, can't ask him what concerns nobody else but ourselves, not now. The best thing will be to make myself scarce and to wait for another chance; I only hope I can get out without being seen. How cool is this ship's cable that serves here as a handrail! It is dark from the touch of many sweaty hands. It's good for hauling yourself upwards, but going down it swings and gives dangerously. Doors: at times I find myself thinking all these doors are there just for listening, something creeps up behind them and listens and then knows what nobody else knows. If I had a house, I'd only allow a single door, for going in and out, and maybe a secret door just for myself.

Bruno? Is that you, Bruno? Joachim has recognised me from

behind, and there's no reason why I shouldn't stop and look around, for there is no reproach in his voice, not even surprise. He is smiling sadly and holding his hand out to me once again. I suppose you want to see the chief, he says, and I nod and say: I just wanted to have a word with him, just for a moment. You'll have to come another time, Joachim say, I'm sorry, but the doctor's with him now. Ill? Is the chief ill? Nothing serious, says Joachim, just trouble with his balance, a sort of general weakness and problems of balance. He pats me on the shoulder and says: It'll soon be better. You know nothing ever gets him down, a few days' rest and he'll be his old self again. How naturally, as if it was his usual habit, he hooks his arm in mine and leads me off, not even wanting to know whether I'm visiting the chief of my own accord or whether the chief has sent for me. He draws me slowly along, pushing me lightly against the wall so that Magda can get by with a dustpan full of broken glass and a tray on which there's a chipped carafe and two tumblers, also broken. We don't look at each other, Magda and I, we just ignore each other in the way she has always wanted. My stomach turns over at the sight, my mouth suddenly feels quite dry, but she doesn't seem in the least disturbed. She holds the tray out to Joachim and calmly says: Such an expensive carafe – maybe it can be stuck together again. No, he says, it wouldn't be worth it, and she goes off as if there were nothing more to be said.

Never before has Joachim walked beside me for such a distance. It's only here he stops, in the passage, beneath the picture of his grandfather, who stares down at us with a guilty expression on his face. Tcha, he says and voices once more his regret that my visit was in vain, but consoles himself with the arrangement we made earlier up at the stone wall: You'll be coming up one evening, Bruno, we'll soon be letting you know when. What can I do? I can't refuse the apple he takes from the bowl and puts in my pocket.

If only I could now return home unseen, could quickly turn the key and shoot the bolt and open the door to nobody who knocks less than seven times, nobody at all, but I can't get past them, not this time: the little pests have surely been keeping watch for me there in my rhododendrons and still think I haven't spotted them. For sure they'll have gathered a clump of burrs together, at any moment now one of them will say the word and they'll be dancing around me, stretching up to stick burrs all over me, but I'll behave as if I haven't noticed; I won't take them by the scruff of their tender necks, but walk calmly on towards my home, I won't even hear their cries of abuse. So come on out and surprise me, terrors, show what you've got for me this time.

Not now: I'll read Max's book another time, it will be dark soon, and I don't want a light in my home today, not today. If only I knew what to expect, how it will all turn out, if only I knew that! In the Kollerhof it was much easier, I knew everything almost in advance, because hardly a word of what the chief and Dorothea were discussing and deciding downstairs in the living-room escaped me: I knew before any of the others when we would be putting in a tender for woody plants, knew in advance what I'd be getting for Christmas or for my birthday; and, since the chief's biggest deals were with fruit-bearing plants, I knew which plots we'd very soon be extending and adding to; and it wasn't just his plan to buy a secondhand tractor and a new ploughshare I knew about – I also knew his reasons for it.

That important visitors from the famous tree nurseries in Pinneberg were expected; that stock lists were to be introduced; that I'd soon be getting a rise in my pocket money: all this I knew well before it happened, and I also knew that Dorothea wanted to engage a manager, for the work was becoming too much for the chief alone. We want to see something of you as well, that's what she said, and she also said: Someone who has achieved all you have has earned the right to sit back a little. Almost always he agreed with her, yet still he went on doing what he felt had to be done. He was always the first on the plantations and the last to leave, he was everywhere at once, giving good advice, and after closing time he would still spend hours sitting over his plantation logbook and other papers. If a worker was uncertain what to do, he'd just say: Let's ask the chief, and when he came along and gave it a bit of thought, things soon got moving again.

A well: we once had to bore a well, and they all told the chief it should be sunk on the damp ground, on which even in a dry spell little shiny, oily puddles could always be seen. He listened in silence, then he walked up the hill to the wall we'd built in layers, where he first just stood concentrating, then all of a sudden he began walking, cautiously, as if he was treading on splinters of broken glass and in danger of cutting his feet. His eyes fixed on the ground, he paced in circles, and now and again he took a few steps backwards or moved to one side, while the men just stood there watching, one or two of them shaking their heads. After a while he pointed to a patch of blackish-grey soil and said: Here, lads, put a pipe down here.

They screwed an iron clamp-ring to the pipe and positioned the steel bit, which had a lot of little holes in it. With a steam-hammer they sank the pipe vertically into the ground; then, since the sounding-lead they let down inside the pipe still revealed no water, they screwed on a second and then a third pipe, and at last the sounding-lead registered what none of them except for the chief had considered possible. The pump they then put to work brought up only muddy water to begin with, but after a while it began to clear and got clearer and clearer. The chief was the first to drink it; he washed his face and then took another drink, and, since he was the one who found the water, we were allowed to splash him with it; that was good fun. To the head borer, whose wonderment was boundless, he said: You must fix a proper strainer down here, brass wire would be best, and that's all he said.

We were just testing the flow angle for the water supply, for the pipe system, when I caught sight of the strangers. Except for the man with white hair they had all taken off their jackets and were strolling slowly towards us. They were wearing brightly coloured shirts and well-ironed trousers, and I said to the chief: Who can that lot be? He looked up and said nothing, but went straight back to reckoning out how the ditch for the pipe system should run. How friendly were their greetings, with what interest they looked around! The man with white hair asked us very politely where he might find Herr Zeller, and the chief said: That's me, how can I help you?

Soldiers they were, ex-soldiers who had come to Hollenhusen along with many others for a reunion; they were staying in the 'Deutsches Haus', and all they wanted was permission to look around our land, which they knew from previous times. The white-haired man said: It brings back many memories, as you'll well understand, and we'd like to walk around a bit. The chief refused the cigarette he was offered, but he smiled and said: I fear you'll find quite a lot has changed here, and the white-haired man replied: Amazing, quite amazing – he had once been the officer commanding all the soldiers in Hollenhusen. They all expressed their thanks to the chief for letting them walk over his land: it was a sort of general murmur of thanks such as I'd never heard before. The chief also said: I'll give you an escort, and he whispered to me: Watch they don't do any damage, and then we set off in the heat. There was a crackling and a ticking in the air, tiny noises of things bursting, like pods splitting or capsules scattering their seeds. I did not need to turn round to know the chief was watching us with that mysterious smile of his.

Not ahead – I didn't walk ahead of them, but followed behind, stopping when they stopped; I was expecting them to ask me questions, but they asked nothing, just now and again gave me a friendly nod, most often the one-armed man who had tucked his empty shirt-sleeve beneath the belt of his trousers. It was he who suddenly beckoned the others over to show them something on the ground beside the first-year morello cherries. He drew a circle, turned, pointed in the direction where the dummy houses once stood, and the others crowded round him, looked down at the ground, turned and stared in the direction he indicated. It seemed they understood

166

what the one-armed man was urging and inviting them to look at, but from their faces and the way they stood it was clear to me they were hard put to it to recognise anything.

Because I was getting more and more interested in what they were doing, I quietly moved closer to them, walked at the tail of their group, stood among them when they stopped and one of them began searching his memory for the place where the practice tank was buried – our practice tank, the man with the red and white striped shirt called it. It must have been here, he said, it was here, and he pointed to our redcurrant bushes, bent a few twigs aside and let them spring back. He was in no doubt that the practice tank had once stood there, and he turned to the one-armed man and reminded him how they had both had to put the tank out of action from the rear: jump on, limpet bomb, jump off, take cover. Since the one-armed man nodded in agreement, sighed and nodded, I didn't interfere, deciding not to tell them the practice tank had been in an entirely different place: in the middle of our pear-tree plot.

They didn't go into the plantations, but kept to the working tracks we had left for the narrow-gauge tractor. Just now and again they would scrape the soil on the edge of the borders with a foot or a stick, scrape and scratch, but they found nothing. One of them who kept asking himself what had happened to the dwarf pines – he was more intent on finding them than on anything else – traced lines in the air with his fingers from the hollow. At one point he said he'd slept through a night exercise among the dwarf pines and had woken to find he'd won – that's what he said.

By the erratic block, while we were standing beside it, the man in the red and white striped shirt couldn't resist showing us how he had once taken cover, he and his machine-gun, behind the shapeless stone, and he said this spot had always provided him with an ideal field of fire. That must surely have been what he was hoping to find now, but in the end, after spending a long time gazing at the plots of yew and thuya, he got up and said too many things had changed: the ideal field of fire no longer existed. I didn't tell him what we'd done with the erratic block. They were disappointed, they were at a loss, I could see, and I asked myself whether I shouldn't fetch out something from my hiding-places, mementos of the kind they were maybe after: rosettes and buttons, coins and cartridges, the belt clasp or the bayonet. However, since we, the chief and I, had found them all ourselves, they belonged to us, and I thought I'd better keep them.

On the command hill they sat down for a rest. The plantations shimmered beneath a scorching sun, endless rows running from south to north, and one of the men said: They look as if they're lined up for inspection, all these little trees and plants, a sort of never-ending parade; and another said: They're our relief troops.

No one knew what the two men were looking for among the old pines by the railway; they just took off by themselves and walked in that direction. First they paced out a piece of land, but it must have been wrong for, after choosing a group of three trees as a new starting-point, they again measured something out. After that they examined the soil – didn't dig it or rake it, just looked at it and poked it here and there. When they came back to join us, they were unwilling to say much, they sat down and smoked, and one of them said: All gone, you'll find nothing here now, they've wiped out all traces of us.

Then suddenly he caught sight of the identify disc I was wearing at that time on a string round my neck: it must have slipped out of the collar of my shirt, that little oval metal badge I'd found in the rubble of the dummy houses. He asked to see it. He read the letters and figures on it and was so surprised he could hardly speak. At length, without a word, he passed the identity disc to the white-haired man, who wiped it, turned it over and tested it between his fingers and asked me where I had found it. After I'd told him, he asked me whether I'd make him a present of the disc. I said I would, and he placed it carefully in his breast-pocket. When the one-armed man said: Eggers, that was the time Eggers lost it, the white-haired man nodded slowly, as if he'd already known; you could see from his face it meant something to him.

We walked to the stone wall, to my boat skeleton and to the strip of damp ground on which even in a dry spell there were little shiny, oily puddles. We walked a short way along the edge of the railway cutting and looked down into the sandpit, we strolled through the conifer plantations, and the longer we walked, the less attentive and the less talkative they became. They had long given up hope of finding anything to remind them of their own time here: no mark, no trace, nothing once buried and since brought to light by the rain or by our plough. There was nothing to show that this land had once belonged to them, for even the makeshift foundations on which the dummy houses had stood we had dug out. The chief wasn't all that keen on speaking to them again, but, since on their return they had to pass by him, he broke off his work, acknowledged the white-haired man's repeated thanks and said: I hope you found something you could recognise. The white-haired man just shrugged his shoulders, then looked questioningly into the faces of each of the others, as if leaving the answer to them, but, since none of them chose to say anything, he spoke in the end himself: Amazing what has been done here, really quite amazing, we feel almost like strangers. That's how it is sometimes, the chief said, and he also said: There are times when nature puts us out and shuts the door behind us. Before returning to Hollenhusen, to the 'Deutsches Haus', they invited the chief to be their guest that evening, and the white-haired man assured him that his presence would be a particular pleasure, but the chief expressed his regrets, making urgent work his excuse. I don't know why I felt sorry for them as they went off down the main path without even a glance at the nursery beds or the little rose field, I don't know why.

Then suddenly one of them turned back, a narrow-faced man with a casual air, still young. He wanted to know whether he might ask Herr Zeller a question, and the chief said: Of course, go ahead. He had read something, this former soldier, an essay, a paper about trees that exchange signals, that sound a kind of alarm when danger threatens; he could not clearly remember the name of the author, but he thought it was something rather similar to Zeller. Not just similar, the chief said, it was definitely Zeller; it was something I wrote a long time ago, when we were still in the east. The man gave a smile and said nothing more than that it had been a pleasure, and then he went off, leaving the chief shaking his head, maybe because he'd not reckoned on anyone remembering something that happened so long ago. As we worked together I could see he was still thinking of it.

He did not speak of it, however; Dorothea did that in the evening after supper, when we were alone, waiting for the chief, who was sitting beside the new well with the team of borers, who in their enthusiasm over the good new water were wetting their whistles – that was Dorothea's word for it. I simply asked her how the chief had found out that trees give danger signals. She was surprised to begin with and wanted to know how I knew about that. After I'd told her, she thought for a while, and I could see in her face how her thoughts were taking her back farther and farther, right back to those lost plantations in the east in which, though I'd never been there, I could already find my way around quite easily. The big greenhouse, the boundless conifer plantations, the vine-covered house in which they lived: I could see it all before me, even the lake in the woods in which the chief's little sister had been drowned one winter because she ventured on the ice too soon, and also the river, which was broader and clearer than the Holle, and a whole stretch of which belonged to the chief's family.

There, beside the river, healthy willow-trees were growing and, further away from the water's edge on gently rising ground, some sycamores stood. They were growing on both sides of the river, within sight of each other, and it almost looked as if each group was trying to persuade the other that it was better on their side. Once, when the chief went down to the river for a quick swim – just one dive under and out again – he noticed that both the willows and the sycamores were covered in caterpillars. But it wasn't the lackey moth nor the big winter moth that was attacking the trees, nor was it the cute-looking tiger moth caterpillar: it was some unknown caterpillar, handsomely coloured with a horny head, spines and shining eye-spots. With their mobile feelers they were groping their way to the edges of the leaves, in which they then sawed semi-circular holes. They were handsome caterpillars, quite unknown. When the chief took some of them up in his hand, it seemed to him that a peculiar smell was coming from the leaves, a sharp, fleeting smell of decay that he'd never met before. He at once plucked some of the leaves, on which nothing could be seen with the naked eye, but, when he put them under his microscope and placed a few caterpillars on them, he could see how the leaves imperceptibly grew darker in colour, and he again noticed they were giving off this fleeting smell, a substance that after a time made the caterpillars lethargic – not very, just a bit.

That same day he went across to the other side of the river – over the bridge with the birchwood railing: Dorothea and he had once been photographed standing in front of it – he went across and was quite surprised to find that here on this side neither the willows nor the sycamores had been attacked by the unknown caterpillar. Not a single leaf had been sawn through, but he didn't fail to notice that the unaffected trees were giving off the same smell he had discovered among the affected ones. So what else could the chief believe but that the trees were giving off this smell in order to protect themselves? They were taking precautions because the other trees had warned them, had raised the alarm with the aid of this fleeting substance.

The chief's father had only smiled. He said: Maybe one day they'll talk to each other in semaphore, our trees – they've got arms enough, and he also said: It can be allowed that animals sound the alarm, but trees? There we'd better put a question-mark. This didn't stop the chief continuing to watch the affected and the unaffected willows and sycamores and to make comparisons; he noted everything down, he sent leaves off for examination, and one day he received confirmation that in them there were strange substances that were not usually found in willows and sycamores. When he got this news, the chief was satisfied, and he then wrote an account of his discovery in a notebook, putting down everything from the very beginning, and he sent this notebook to the old botanist in Johannisburg, to Plinski, who was known throughout the world for his book on tree diseases.

As with the earlier letter, a long time passed without a reply. Plinski remained so obstinately silent that the chief thought he must be dead, but one Sunday he arrived personally on the doorstep, accompanied by his niece. Having by chance something to do in the neighbourhood, he came himself, because what the chief had discovered had made him curious, and he wanted to speak to him about it. After he had done enough listening and questioning, he asked the chief to continue his observations for two more years, and he also gave him some words of advice. Before he drove off he told the chief's father: What he has discovered, your boy, might one day prove significant for us all; when he's brought it far enough, I'll see it gets through. That's what he said and, when the time came, he kept to his promise and had the chief's discovery printed.

Dorothea told me this that evening when we were alone, waiting for the chief, and I wanted her to tell me more about the plantations of the rising sun, but she was unwilling, she felt too tired. It was only when I said I could never hear enough about that time that she looked at me with a smile and added: So that you'll know this as well, Bruno, the niece who accompanied that botanist was myself. Then she gave me another large glass of buttermilk and started to clear the table, but as she did so she would now and again pause with a smile on her lips, narrow her eyes and, thrusting her lower lip forward, blow gently over her face, her lovely face.

How things come alive in the dark! A sudden flash in the nursery beds as of eyes being opened, a rustling that was not caused by the wind, the two crooked stakes move closer together. A scamper, a chase across the ground, something rolls over in the moonlight, lies huddled, quite dead. A steady breeze is stirring the poplars, green leaf, silver leaf, whoever steps on something out there can reckon on it being soft and running away, running across to the Colorado firs, whose scent is clashing with a scent of hay coming from afar. Now it's time to push the bolt across. A bird calls over the meadows and from outlying farms comes the barking of dogs, asking, listening, answering: Say who you are, we're guarding the horizon.

He sent me in the dark to Hollenhusen, to the 'Deutsches Haus'. He was swaying a bit when he returned from the well-borers, he kissed Dorothea twice, rather inaccurately, had to laugh over the state he was in and wanted nothing but coffee. The chief had no objection to Ina helping out with the service in the 'Deutsches Haus', but, after looking at his watch, he wanted me to go and fetch her. You needn't be in too much of a hurry, Bruno, he said, just see you both get home safely.

Voices – I always heard voices when I was running down the avenue of poplars: there was a sort of leading speaker, whose voice had a quality and a strength of its own; he kept on repeating a sentence, and the other voices would answer him. They went on like that right up to the 'Deutsches Haus', only in the bright light did they fall silent. I didn't dare simply go inside; if it had been the 'Kiek in', the old village inn, I'd have gone inside at once, but with the new 'Deutsches Haus', which was built of red bricks and was tall and wide with a lot of windows, I hadn't the nerve to go straight in, I had first to creep once round the house, keeping close to the wall.

In the yard the cart, the windowsill, the piled beer barrels; in a second I was up on top, crouching down, working my way towards a large window. There they were, sitting and showing each other photographs, writing on little scraps of paper, some of them walking about with large glasses in their hands, drinking each other's health; where they were standing in groups, one man had his hand on his neighbour's shoulder, as Mirko does when he's talking to me. I saw the white-haired man, sitting at the head of a long table, I saw the one-armed man, who seemed always to be in the middle of a circle of comrades, working to keep things cheerful, and I also suddenly recognised the narrow-faced man who had come up to the chief with his far-fetched question; Ina was just carrying a tray past him.

Oh, Ina, if you'd then known who he was and what you would go through with him, if you'd had any idea of what was going to happen to you both, you and this casual, narrow-faced man who was younger than the others and whom I never once saw take a drink. Every time he caught my attention he was standing beside some group, listening, standing there with folded arms, a cigarette dangling from his lips. He never butted in or put in a word of his own. Even though he looked as if nothing interested him particularly, it seemed hardly anything escaped him. He spotted at once that someone had loosened the bands of your apron, had quick as lightning undone the bow as you passed by with the heavy tray. Before you'd noticed it yourself he was standing beside you, taking the tray from you for a moment so you could retie the bow. It may well be that you saw him then for the first time or that he stood out among all those many soldiers, but there he was, standing in front of you with his smile and his superior manner, and you smiled back in an embarrassed way: I saw it myself from the top of the beer barrels.

As the white-haired man rose and began to speak, they all returned to their places and, since he kept his head down as he spoke, it was impossible to understand a word, though I moved very close to the window. In the middle of his speech the furious barking of a dog: the big black dog had discovered me and was trying to mount the pile of barrels, it jumped and fell back, jumped again and fell back again, which only increased its fury, its yowling fury. I had nothing I could throw to it, nothing to drive it off with. In my fright I lay down flat on the barrels, peering over the edge, for I had to keep it in view. That sudden burning feeling, that scorching dampness as the huge black dog stood on its hindlegs against the wall of the house and almost touched the windowsill with its front paws, all the time barking and snapping: I could hear the hard clash of its jaws. I was just about to knock on the window – the ex-soldiers would surely have opened it and let me in – when suddenly a ray of light came from the kitchen door and a white figure came out and called: Asko, then Asko again, and, since the dog didn't obey, the figure crossed the yard, a girl in a white uniform with a white cap. She gave just a quick look round, then seized the dog by the collar and hit it on the muzzle, and I heard her say: Always making such a row, and just for cats. Then she locked it in.

I lay there and didn't dare move, until suddenly music came from the hall; two accordion players, black trousers, shiny silk shirts, were standing on a low platform, as they played they kept their eyes fixed on each other, merrily urging each other on. And then they were dancing in the hall, and the best dancer was the one-armed man. I have danced only a few times myself, with Dorothea at the time we moved into the strong-hold and had a house-warming party, and once more with her when we had a christening party, but I could never dance till the music ended, because I soon got giddy and fell over; I've only got to spin round to music and I always feel giddy, and then I always fall over. Watch, yes, I can always just watch people dancing, but even then for not too long: after a while I have to turn away. Even when Ina was dancing, Bruno had to turn away.

Oh, Ina, the way you stood there with that black tray on the edge of the dance-floor, wondering how to get through the dancing couples, and the way he was suddenly standing beside you, taking the tray from you and carrying it safely to the table, the way he put it down and simply took your hand and drew you on to the dance-floor without any resistance from you. He didn't pull you close to him and hold you tight as many of the ex-soldiers did with their women, he held you quite loosely and a bit away from his body, you laid a hand on his shoulder, your glances mingled, and then it was all so easy, all the awkwardness was gone, it was no longer possible to see what was moving and carrying you along, for everything was movement between you, especially when you leaned right back and were just floating. Not just I, the others too were watching you both.

I didn't see the end of your dance, it was only when they clapped and demanded another that I could look again, but he smiled and led you back to your tray, on which the foam on the beer glasses was already dying. He bowed to you and let go of your hand, which all the time he'd been holding: Guntram Glaser, who turned up suddenly, who vanished for quite a time and then unexpectedly returned, and who after his time with us could think of no way out but to walk to the railtrack and wait for the night train to Schleswig.

Since I didn't dare enter the 'Deutsches Haus', I could think of only one other way: I whistled, I let out our whistle when the musicians took a rest and the windows were opened to air the room, and I saw Ina prick up her ears and leave the hall with a few empty glasses. I'll bet no one ever leaped off that stack quicker than I did: I dashed round the house to the main entrance, hid behind a tree and waited, and when she appeared at the open door and peered out into the dark, I whistled once again our own long-drawn-out, rather mournful whistle, with which in the Kollerhof we always found each other at once. She asked me to give her another ten minutes, not more than ten minutes, and tried to entice me into the lobby, but I was happier waiting outside. I sat down on a bicycle stand and listened to them singing songs in the hall.

What was the matter with her? On our walk home she

hopped, suddenly spun round, gaily bowed low before me and for an instant took my arm, which she pressed so tightly to her that I could feel her ribs; she walked along in mock seriousness, behaved as if she owed me obedience; then she called out: Let's see who's home first, and ran off down the avenue of poplars, leaving me no other choice but to run after her, first to the little brick bridge and from there across the fields. I could have caught her up, but I didn't want to, I just kept close behind her and drove, drove her before me: her breath came ever faster, her gasps were ever louder. At a spot in the fence where there'd once been a gap there was no longer a gap, because they'd straightened the poles and fixed new barbed wire. She climbed on to it, the taut wire creaked and swayed and lashed out, and in the middle of her jump something tore, and she fell into the ditch on the other side. No water, just mud; she stood up to her thighs in mud, gathered her skirt up in one hand and held the other out to me: Come on, do something, and, after I had pulled her out of that sticky bubbling mess, she bawled angrily: To chase me like that! See what's come of it, and in the same breath she commanded: Come on, rub it off.

She stared rigidly in the direction of the Kollerhof and held her skirt high, and I knelt down in front of her and wiped the clods of mud from her legs, at first with my fingers, then with grass, and finally, when no more solid bits remained, I wiped and rubbed with a cloth she gave me. While I was busy cleaning her up we spoke not a single word. It was impossible to get all the mud off her shoes, and when I said: You'll have to wash your shoes, she said sharply: You'll wash them, if you chase someone like that you must do it yourself. But then we made it up again: after she'd told the chief and Dorothea what there was to tell, she came into my room, felt her way to the head of my bed, asked for my hand and gave me one mark from her earnings as a reward for fetching her and everything. It was the first money she had earned for herself since leaving school.

In the stronghold there's only light downstairs, his room lies in darkness. Maybe like me he is standing at his window gazing out over his plantations, in which only mice and night birds are now up and about, hidden in a thin mist coming from the Holle. Maybe he is thinking of me, as I am thinking of him. Tomorrow: I've got the feeling they'll invite me to the stronghold tomorrow, Max or Joachim, and then I'll hear from them what the facts are concerning this deed of gift and shall know what's to become of me. A third of the land together with all the installations belonging to it: he can't have meant that, even though he once called me his only friend; they must surely have made a mistake.

Today I must be properly shaved. Again I've forgotten to buy some razor-blades, but if I wash and whet the old one, it'll be all right: at any rate I won't cut myself on the bottom edge of my scar. With a new blade I've cut myself a few times so deeply that I've bled through at least a dozen of the paper patches I stuck over the tiny wound. Ewaldsen once said to me: You bleed like a stuck pig, and he has also jokingly asked if he couldn't give me a little help in shaving. A new shaving mirror: that's what I'll maybe wish for my birthday, though the crack doesn't bother me, it runs exactly over my mouth, and I've got so used to it that I hardly notice it. The chief also soaps his face with a badger-hair brush like mine, there's no better brush, that's for sure, though I'd like to know whether the hair comes from a live or a dead badger.

Today I must be properly shaved. When I look at myself through the foam, I at once see what surely no one else sees: my right eye is smaller than my left: not only has it dropped a bit as a result of the operation, it's also smaller. That comes, I suppose, from the different skin, which is always so taut, so bare. Nothing grows on the scar itself: that is just smooth and reddish blue and doesn't have to be shaved, but a few strong hairs do always grow on its raised edge, hairs as hard as bristles, and they must go. Leaky-eye, Joachim once said, and he has also called me Bleary-eye. It's my right eye that always leaks and waters. Some people think they're tears, but it's a long time since I last wept. The spots on my forehead are not coming back, that ointment has eaten them away: Dorothea's good ointment that I'd like to rub in every day, because it's so cooling. Dorothea told me that when someone has a forehead as handsome and as rounded as mine, he should take care to keep it unblemished. My teeth: how they all envy me my teeth! Even the chief wanted to buy them off me once, when he was constantly soaking lumps of sugar in rum and putting the pieces on his aching back teeth.

Today I must also dress better – not the check shirt and the grey trousers: I'll wear the pale shirt with the grey trousers, and over it my windcheater, even if the zip fastener no longer works. I'll leave the windcheater open, in the way Joachim wears his, and in the pocket I'll put the bill-hook, my favourite knife that I was allowed to choose from the tools being withdrawn from service. Although there's not much point in cleaning your shoes here, I could give them a rub and a bit of polish, the carefully preserved boots that don't get white toecaps even when I've been out on the damp ground in the rain. It's probably too late now to go to the hairdresser's, but maybe I can cut the tips off myself – the bits that have grown over my ears. Magda won't believe my hair was once the colour of corn, she thinks it has always been as dull as it is now, no proper colour. I'd like to know how all this light gets into water: even the brown bowl looks brighter when I tip the jug into it.

I hope it's not just Joachim I'll have to answer, I hope Max and Dorothea will also talk with me, it's easier with them, thoughts come of their own accord, but Joachim – he only needs to shake his head in that way he has and look around as if seeking help, for everything to freeze inside me, my heart hammers right up to my throat, and I can feel something being closed and screwed down inside me. And if I should maybe see him washing his hands yet again – it's impossible to count the number of times he does that each day, even out in the plantations, in every rainbutt, under every stopcock – then I'd be unable to utter a single word for quite a while.

If anyone here wants to see me leave, it is surely Joachim. From the very start he resented the way the chief wanted me beside him in all he did, how he let me into all his plans and entrusted several secrets to me. And from the very start he made me feel just how much power he had over me, he with his leather-trimmed breeches and his long scarves and those soft riding boots he so often wore. It was no use my telling him the chief had instructed me to cover the seed before evening came, he would just command me to run down to the station restaurant in Hollenhusen and fetch three bottles of lemonade for him and those two strapping great girls from the Erlenhof; he just issued a command. And when he got cold and wanted his jacket, he would send me to the Kollerhof, I had to take his letters to the post office, I had to listen while he practised on his clarinet, I had to pick flowers for him and make them into bouquets, brush his jackets, and once, when he and his friend and the two girls from the Erlenhof wanted to swim in the big pond, he made me follow them, carrying the rug and the basket, and then I had to spread the rug out. The chief, I know, wouldn't have approved of that, but I said nothing. I never complained to him about the things Joachim made me do.

How flabbergasted he was when one evening I said no. He stared at me in disbelief when I made no move, when I didn't take his horse's reins, didn't tie it to the beech-tree as he wanted. They had galloped right up to me, he and the two girls, and I thought at first they were intending to clear the stacked wall, to give me a bit of a fright and then to jump it, as they'd sometimes done before; but just before reaching it they stopped and dismounted, and Joachim held the reins out to me and said: Tie it up, Bruno. I looked into the horse's wide-open eye and refused, instinctively I took a step backwards towards the safety of the wall, so that I could throw myself into the dead corner if need be and hug the ground.

You are to tie it up, Joachim said threateningly and, since I backed off still further, he followed me, slowly, in a determined way, until the wall barred further retreat and I was supporting myself against it with both hands. The girls were watching tensely, holding their horses by the reins and keeping silent. For the last time, Joachim said, tie it up, and, as I just shook my head, he raised his arm to strike me – not even quickly, but in a calm and calculating way. He raised his arm and then, thinking better of it, suddenly let it fall, almost in the very act of striking. Then he said: We'll talk another time, and, after a word to the girls, they mounted and rode down to the meadows.

Not only me: he thought he had the right to order the others about as well. Once he even tried to tell Ewaldsen how often he should water the conifers in our growing frames. I don't know why Dorothea always took his side and praised him long and loud for every little thing: he only had to sweep out the passage in the Kollerhof to have praise showered on him all evening, and if he managed to carry home something from Hollenhusen, Dorothea would at once ask anxiously whether the load hadn't been too much for him, the loaves of bread, the nails, the batteries. The little gosling, our little gosling, who began to feel sorry for himself the minute he found a stain on his shirt or his trousers, everything must be so clean, so proper. If we had happened to be late, the chief or I, Dorothea would probably have had no qualms about going off to sleep. Not so with Joachim: he had to be back from the Erlenhof before she would go to bed, however late he might be.

By the Holle one summer they walked arm in arm along the river bank; from time to time they threw something in and watched the current carry it away, then they linked arms again and walked on, just as if they were married.

Where he got the revolver from I never found out, nor did I know where he kept it; he showed it me by the big pond, a small revolver. He gave it me and told me to shoot one round, but I didn't succeed – though all the chambers were loaded, it didn't go off. He then showed me how to do it, he shot at a water-lily leaf and at a floating piece of wood, and he hit both times; he then gave the revolver back to me, I pressed the trigger too soon, the bullet went into the ground and Joachim shook his head and said: Give it back, for goodness' sake. He cleaned it carefully before putting it in his pocket.

Things were always unpleasant when he came along with his lists: even the others would be on their guard as he pushed back the cardboard cover and started asking questions and making comparisons with what was written in his lists, or when he wanted to know about something down to the smallest detail, and he would then with an expressionless face write it all down in his lists. The chief never did that, and it was surely not he who advised Joachim to write it all down, numbers and hours and remaining stocks. All the same, the chief seemed to have no objection to Joachim going around with his all-knowing lists, the very sight of which could give you a bad conscience; after all, it was he who'd long enough allowed Joachim to sit beside him at the dark-coloured card table he'd had sent from Schleswig, and which was very soon too small to hold all the books, files and papers. In the years when the chief did almost everything himself, orders were pinned to the wall, bills spiked together in batches, and on the floor around the table lay business papers, either fastened together or held down by clean stones; notes hanging on a metal ring from a tightly stretched cord served as reminders. How he found his way through them only he himself knew.

From the day he let Joachim sit beside him everything began gradually to change: the cord and the spike and the metal ring vanished and every inch of the floor could be walked over, for Joachim had arranged for a row of shelves and an open filing cabinet to be put up beside the table. The things that had previously been scattered around or fluttered in the breeze now had their fixed places, not only labelled, but also protected from draughts. I was surprised how little trouble it cost the chief to initiate Joachim: often he would just push papers across to him without a word, or he would draw a circle round a number or just say: What do you think? and it wasn't long before Joachim could give an answer with which the chief would be satisfied. He trusted Joachim and left more and more to him, sometimes expressing his amazement at what Joachim had managed to do all on his own, and I once came on them drinking a bottle of wine together: that was after they had discussed and come to an agreement over a contract which was still lying on the table in front of them.

At supper the chief said to Dorothea: Just to let you know, Dotti, it's my little partner who is sitting there beside you; just you watch out, for that young man knows what he's about. That's what he said, and then I was allowed to try a sip of wine.

When somewhere far off a shot was fired, I felt at once there'd been an accident: a dry crack on a Sunday afternoon, so faint by the time the sound reached us down in the hollow that the chief raised his head and asked: Wasn't that a shot? But he attached no importance to it, he shrugged his shoulders and continued testing the viability of some seeds, while I sat on my stool watching him, as so often in our shed in the hollow.

Joachim — suddenly Joachim came staggering in, he was breathing so heavily he could hardly speak, his face was covered in sweat from running fast, and his hands wouldn't stop shaking: even as he steadied himself against the top of the working table they still shook. The chief dropped everything and drew Joachim close to him, wanting to know what had happened, but Joachim was almost lost for words, all he could say was: Come quickly, or: By the stone wall, quick, nothing more, and as we were running there, the chief and I, he just staggered along behind, and once he even fell down — I saw that when I turned to see if he was coming.

We ran towards the three horses — one was standing quietly by the stone wall, two were tearing leaves from my elderberry bush and eating them — and the closer we came, the more I held back. And then I saw them: one of the girls was lying on the ground, the other was kneeling beside her and speaking to her, she was crying, her face was all smeared, and when she saw the chief she cried even harder, then was suddenly seized by a fit of coughing and continued just to whimper. The chief at once climbed over the wall, bent down over the girl, who was lying there as if dead, and asked her if she could hear him, but the girl's lips didn't move, her eyes were open and they even followed the circling movement of his hand, but it seemed she couldn't speak. I stayed my side of the wall and kept an eye on the horses, which were saddled, and which were moving around in an unconcerned way and stripping my elderberry. Suddenly the chief asked: Did she fall here? and the kneeling girl gave a hesitant nod, she stood up and pointed out the path they'd taken as they rode up to the wall from the meadows, and then she said very softly: Here, and wanted to know if the doctor was already on the way. Did the horses shy, the chief wanted to know. The girl knelt down again without replying, carefully stroked a few long hairs off her friend's face and whispered: Maike, can you hear me, Maike? Only after the chief had repeated his question did she say: The shot, the shot made it bolt, and Maike was thrown here.

That I should be the one to fetch Doctor Ottlinger I knew from the very start: I was just waiting for the chief to say the word. When he sent me off Joachim had not yet reached us, but I saw him and ran towards him, shouting as I ran past that Doctor Ottlinger would soon be here. I scrambled down the slope to the railtrack, then ran along the hard, well-worn path beside the rails to the level crossing, not the one over Hollenhusen's main street, but the one by the forgotten sports field, then on to the dense row of fir-trees with which Doctor Ottlinger had surrounded his big redbrick house, and quickly across the lawn. I rang the bell and kept on ringing until a woman came and said: He's not here, my husband is making his visits. So first of all to Sibbersen's, but he'd already left, then on to Knull's, from which he intended to go on to

Wiermann's. Here I might maybe have found him, but I saw his roomy old car standing in front of Tordsen's grocer's shop. At last I'd caught him: I posted myself beside his car till he came, an old man with scanty hair, friendly, but with buttoned-up lips. While listening, he would always bow his head, as if doubting every word. A brief sign had me sitting in the car beside him.

Nothing, he gave the girl nothing at all. He examined her in silence and did not even look up as Joachim told – couldn't resist telling – how it had happened. Joachim could see absolutely no reason for the fall, since they had ridden up from the meadows at a trot, the two girls in front and he behind, just a trot over country the horses were also familiar with, could have crossed safely in their sleep, they'd often jumped the low wall, nothing easier, and there wasn't a horse far and wide more placid than Maike's horse. For Joachim there was simply no explanation for it. Doctor Ottlinger said nothing throughout, and he was also silent when Joachim asked: She'll pull through, won't she, she'll be all right again? The doctor stroked the girl's cheek and made a sign to the chief, and together they went to the car and got to work on the seats, moving them around, and then both together, the chief and the doctor, lifted the girl and laid her down in the roomy old car so that she was lying almost flat.

How patiently the girl let it all happen! She didn't speak, she didn't groan, there was nothing to show she'd had a fall, just in the corner of her mouth a little blood, and one cheek was roughened and grimy, as if grains of sand had left their mark on it. The other girl asked whether she might go along too – no, she didn't ask, she begged: Please, please, I must go with her, and Doctor Ottlinger nodded, shook the chief by the hand and drove off slowly, jolting over the uneven ground to a working path and then on towards the main road.

Joachim was trembling, never before or since have I seen him tremble so; he kept his eyes fixed on the chief, who still stood there unmoving even after the car had disappeared. The chief didn't say much, he just wanted to know what Joachim had shot with, and Joachim said: Just a single shot into the air, with a revolver; he couldn't hand the revolver over, as the chief at once demanded, because he'd already thrown it away. Find it, the chief said, find it and bring it to me, and that was all; he turned away and went back down to the hollow, and I followed him, but didn't dare catch up with him.

The silence in the Kollerhof. The glances exchanged between Dorothea and the chief. Joachim's footsteps as he paced to and fro in his room. The whispering after the chief returned from the Erlenhof, the shrugging of shoulders. Never before had the ceiling seemed so low, it was as if everything was being squeezed together in the house, the air, the atmosphere, ourselves. Once, as Joachim was bringing his untouched plate back into the kitchen, we bumped into each other, a bit of his milk soup slopped over. It didn't stain his trousers, just splashed on the floor, but he looked at me sourly and said: Damn you, numskull.

Ina was the first to know: we heard from her that Maike was lying in hospital in Schleswig and that she couldn't walk and probably would never walk again. The fall had broken something inside her, I don't know what, in the spine or in the head. Joachim sat there as if stunned as Ina told us, he was staring straight in front of him, while Dorothea and the chief sought each other with their glances. He sat like that for quite a while, then suddenly he got up and went outside, without anyone calling out to him or asking what he was going to do. They let him go, they didn't even mention him the whole day long, were seemingly not concerned, but late after dark Dorothea began working in the kitchen. She must have been warming something up, she pushed open the window that always stuck and closed it again, walked around, clattering and scraping – I heard it all from my bed. It must have been late in the night when Joachim returned, I had gone off to sleep, woke with a start and then went to sleep again, but, since I had resolved to be awake when he returned, I *was* awake. His voice came through to me in my sleep, his subdued voice that had little to report to Dorothea but that he'd been turned away in Schleswig, in the hospital, turned away without any reason being given, no arguing, no urging had helped, he was not allowed into the ward, and now here he was and he simply didn't know what to do. What on earth shall I do? he said several times, and when someone like Joachim says things like that, you can be sure it means a great deal.

It was Dorothea who soon knew what could still be done. She only needed to consult her own thoughts for a while, then each time she'd come on an idea how someone could be helped, whether it was me or Ina or even at times the chief, she would light on something, and one morning she disclosed her plan to us: it was to travel to the south, to a place where there was moorland and woods, she wished for the first time in her life to go away for a good two weeks, together with Joachim, into the land of sheep, the Lüneburg heath. She said: We can both of us do with it; and she also said: When we're away, you'll realise for the first time what you have in us. Joachim took no pleasure in the journey, he just looked on in silence as Dorothea packed his things, and when I carried their luggage to the station and waved goodbye as the train pulled out, it was only Dorothea who waved back, not Joachim.

The smarting will soon wear off: my skin is tighter than Joachim's, rougher and tighter, the artificial eyelid is a bit paler than the other, but there's no great difference between them. Ewaldsen will not be giving me a job to do today; if he sees me clean-shaven and in my good clothes, for sure he'll want to know where I'm going or whom I'm expecting, probably he'll also ask what he has asked several times before: Now, Bruno, who are you out to impress today? But he won't get anything out of me, he won't. It looks as if they're already at work. Maybe I should have my clock repaired, everyone notices it at once, envies me and wants to hold the fine marble casing, but hardly anyone has remarked that my clock has only one hand, the hour hand. The minute hand I broke off myself: it was almost as sharp as a knife, and the thin cut bled heavily and just wouldn't heal up.

Take a look, yes, that's what I must do now: take a look at our land in the north that the chief is said to have made over to me in his deed of gift. Though I only need to close my eyes to see it all at once before me, I feel I want to walk round it in peace, from the hollow to the well, to the erratic block, to the windbreak hedge, and then across to the wall and back beside Lauritzen's meadows to the hollow. Anyone looking for me will soon find me, has always found me. I wish it was midsummer day and that I could stick a bramble twig in my cap, for anyone wearing a bramble twig in his cap on midsummer day is invisible, so the chief has assured me. He once tried it out himself in the place he comes from, in the plantations of the rising sun: unseen, he had listened to what they were saying in the house, had sat on the railings of the bridge and leant against the fence, unseen, and his people passed him by, behaving as if they were alone. That's how I'd now like to walk through the plantations, unnoticed, quietly on my own, without anyone calling me, pointing at me and staring after me.

If what I've been told is correct, then the chief wants me to have the bigger share of the conifer plantations, the firs, the larches, the monkey puzzles and the Colorado firs, my Colorado firs, and whatever else enjoys growing there in the sand. The juniper is also to be mine: I could chew its berries for ever, berries dried in an airy place. The pine-tree there – the chief will hardly have given me his handsome Caucasian fir whose bark becomes whitish after fifty years, but, if what's being said is true, I should be getting the three-year yew seedlings that are so vulnerable to sunburn.

No, it can't be, they're wrong! They are surely just putting me to the test or playing some kind of game with me, but why, why? The chief has never asked me whether I felt up to taking over the land. He is the only one here who can decide, and he knows very well I couldn't do it, couldn't manage things in the way he does, he who recognises everything at first sight and in passing, in the middle of a conversation, pulls up plants that have to be got rid of. He once said to me: In our way of life, Bruno, the most important thing is not what you see, but what you feel. Since he knows me and everything about me better than anyone else, I'm sure he wouldn't entrust me with anything I couldn't manage. But, if it *is* true, then one day the plantations with fruit-trees of various kinds will also belong to me, as well as the apple cordons and over there the sweet cherries, for which the chief favours a weak growth, a slow-growing rootstock, because large trees make cropping difficult.

This is the place – beside the morello cherries – where we once took our soil samples. I can still hear the hammer blows with which he drove the iron pipe into the ground, the simple pipe that took the place of a proper boring-rod, and I can still feel the samples between my fingers, sticky, gritty and heavy. Over there was the practice bunker with its blackened firing slits, we sheltered behind its walls from rain and sharp east winds, but we didn't go inside, for it was full of dried-up turds, we stayed outside and gazed out over the scarred soldiers' land and thought our thoughts. The soil is fresh and nourishing, humous sand and mild clay, and it's given lime when it needs it. There is nothing in the plantations that needs changing or improving, I should leave it exactly as the chief has laid it out, even the tall-trunked limes that will probably be going off soon to make avenues I'd leave where they are.

That's Mirko, yes, yes, I can see you, he's bringing out a weedkiller (Simazine, against the seeds that need light). Though the chief has his friends among the weeds, we have to keep the land free of them, since they are the strongest rivals of cultivated plants, there is a constant battle between them for water and for nourishment, and with the young plants also for light. No, I won't go over to him, I shan't concern myself with him or with his appliance, otherwise he could maybe think I'm trying to check whether the mixture is right, whether he has considered the question of compatibility and the fact that every

190

kind of soil has to be handled in its own way. I can't imagine he knows what I know, that Magda goes to him first with her news, I don't think that. If only he weren't always so cheerful, so full of his own importance! Whatever work he's given to do, he carries it out as if everything, our whole existence, depends on it; even with the smallest job he's always trying to draw attention to himself.

We could understand each other, the plantations and I: there are times already when I talk to them as the chief does. Sometimes I praise them in his words, the yews more than the larches, because they have to stand up to birds and mice, but more than all the rest I praise a Colorado fir after it has been planted out in the bed and staked. They recognise me, the Colorado firs, I can feel it: they don't move or straighten up at my approach, but all the same they know me, offer me their soft green paws, which I can never have enough of holding and cautiously stroking. Maybe, if it was up to me, I'd enlarge the Colorado fir plantations. I could dispense with the limes, the morello cherries too, and plant more Colorado firs in their place, but otherwise nothing need be changed. There are no longer any holes – the chief was right about that: I don't need to be afraid as during the last rainy summer, when time and again deep holes opened up in front of me, dark holes – not just here on our land, but also on the avenue of poplars and even in Hollenhusen itself: with every step I took I had to watch out that a hole didn't suddenly appear and I fall into it. In the end I was just groping my way along, but the chief has seen to it that there are no more holes and that I can now walk around in safety again.

They are greeting me, both taking off their caps. Those are Elef's people who are trimming the green wall, our windbreak hedge; maybe Ewaldsen would have sent me out with them, so I could show them how to do it, but I can see they're dealing severely with the basal shoots and are cutting the laterals back so that it's all nicely tapered. Anything spreading or growing out of line must go, for the leading shoots need space; whatever you do, don't be timid: nothing stimulates growth more than a good cut. You'll be amazed how easily hedge plants can be trained as long as you get them shaped early enough.

The erratic block: I must climb on the erratic block, for from there I can see almost everything. How the lichens crumble! They dissolve into powder and yet they are not dead; if need be, the chief once said, lichens can make do with any kind of stone: they just hold tight and keep going in their own way. How painful the light is! It's shimmering over our sea of trees. So this, this and everything down to the railway cutting and up to the stone wall I built myself as well: this is the land we live from, it is his pride and joy, this land he's said to have set aside for me. Whoever the owner is, he must attract notice, he'll be talked about over and over, his origin and his abilities will be discussed; a lot will be expected of him, advice and instructions, he must prove his superiority, not much can be allowed to fail. Wherever he shows himself the word will be: here he comes, there he goes, people will bend their backs and avoid his eyes, work a bit harder when he's standing by, and, if he now and again asks questions, he'll be told everything is going well. Grief is something he can't give way to. He can't choose when to be alone. If in his tiredness he overlooks something, he will be held responsible for all the consequences. If he makes a claim, it will at once be disputed, for all sorts of reasons.

I am claiming nothing, I can't take over something that's not my due, the very thought of it makes me giddy: the thought that all this will be registered in my name, these profitable plantations that were planned according to his will. Look too long into the light and you'll go blind, someone once said – but who? Maybe it was Simon, that old soldier dressed in an overcoat that dragged him down. They rise up, these ranks of trees; as if set in motion by a gentle swell, they begin to swell, they begin to sway, are borne upwards, sink down into a valley, just as if invisible waves were running through them, gathering up everything in their serene power. Everything is twisting and turning, stretching out and seeking firm ground, and suddenly I hear a wind, high above the woods, a sharp wind like a singing voice. This tight feeling. This churning stomach. This sudden roaring. I must get off this block, back to earth, lie down, stretch out and bang my head against the ground – how good the roaring, the answering roars, the patchy darkness, the rings! A small handful of earth between my teeth, warm earth, gritty and sweet – but don't swallow it: just breathe, quietly, calmly.

They are here, yes, it's them: their skips, their joyful cries. Both are wearing white socks up to their knees. They dance around me on their spindly legs: they've surely been watching me and following me, my two pests dressed in sailor suits. I'll sit up, pretend I was tired and have been dreaming a bit: my smile gives them courage to venture nearer. Come, sit down, I say, sit down here by me and I'll show you something. Here, try it, I say, anyone who wants to be a proper man must once in his life have eaten earth, just a pinch, a little lump, there, take it, I've just been trying it myself, and afterwards you can see seven times as sharply, like a buzzard. They don't trust me. First they want me to swallow some earth, so watch then – did you see? They eye the earth, they smell it, no, they don't believe me and they throw the samples high in the air. Now I can stand on my feet again. I shall turn my back on them: let's see what they've got worked out for me this time – I'll walk very slowly, back to my home.

What did he say, what are they saying? They complete each other's sentences as if they've rehearsed it. This evening: I should come to the stronghold this evening. They've been sent out and told to find me, and that's all it is: uncle Joachim has instructed them to bring me the news. They don't try anything on, though I've turned my back on them and am walking away. Maybe they don't dare, because this evening I have to go to the stronghold, where for a certainty everything will come to a head. I shan't turn round any more, however eagerly you are waiting: I shan't turn round any more, not for you.

Even if there are seven knocks, I shan't open the door to anybody: not to Magda and not to Ewaldsen. I would open to the chief, but he won't come: I suppose he'll be sitting alone and thinking it all over, maybe preparing himself for this evening, rereading papers and documents and placing them in order. If only it were evening already and I knew what is to become of me, whether what I've been told is right, or whether I shall have to leave after all, simply be packed off like Lisbeth with a souvenir snapshot and some money in an envelope. If I must leave, the first thing I'll do is dig up my money – no one knows it's lying close to the juniper. I'll take the grey blanket with me and the clock and the gumboots and the thunderer whistles. I can carry a lot in the suitcase and the two cardboard boxes, it's only the chest and the cabinet and the curtained rack I'll probably have to leave behind or give away. The place will look quite empty when I'm gone.

I ought long ago have looked to see if my money is still there by the juniper: I have always buried it in the dark, waiting, making sure, circling the spot, not even a cat could move more quietly, but there are times when someone comes creeping up unseen, who sees what he wants to see and then, when he's alone, takes from the earth what was buried in it.

Once someone came creeping behind me, at the time I buried my money near the boat skeleton: he followed me secretly and watched and, after I'd gone, he helped himself to what didn't belong to him. Even if I still have nothing to prove it, I know exactly who it was: though at the time the rain had removed all traces, I knew for certain from the very beginning that it could only have been him, he who'd always been nasty to Bruno and who called me his friend only because I helped him after his accident.

He claimed the wind had upset him, a sudden gust, but I saw how he drove too briskly in the three-wheeler delivery van out on to the brick road, at the place where frost had pushed the bricks up. He had turned the steering-wheel too sharply, and the little van toppled over on its side, the tarpaulin cover tore free and flapped and sagged like a sail. Heiner Walendy was supposed to be driving his stepfather's van home from the 'Kiek in', the oldest pub in Hollenhusen, to the new house in which they lived. He had kept on at his stepfather until he at last said yes and gave him the key, though Heiner Walendy didn't have a driving licence. Now there it lay, lay on its side at the edge of a field of rape, and I ran across, but before I reached it he managed to open the door and force his way out. He was so shaken that for a while he couldn't speak. Nothing had happened to him, and not much to the van either, but its load: that had been flung through the air and on to the field. Scattered across the soft black earth were shallow wooden boxes and aluminium bowls and enamel scales, shimmering chips of blue ice, but more important: the fishes themselves. Around the capsized three-wheeler the soil was strewn with grimy, muddy fish that Heiner Walendy's stepfather – known to us all just as Fish Otto, since he delivered fish to Hollenhusen and the outlying farms twice a week – had not managed to sell.

Herring from the Schlei I saw, greyish-white fillets of cod, mackerels, flounders and a few eels; smoked things too: bloaters and sprats, delicately turned fillets of haddock which are called Schiller locks – all lying in a caked mass in the wet field. Only a few flatfish were attempting to work themselves free, their gills opening and shutting, and the few smooth eels were wriggling off to seek refuge in the rape. While Heiner Walendy just stood there, pale and numb, I leaped into the field at once to block the eels' path by just putting a shoe in their way and forcing them to turn back; later, as they began to go limp, I picked them up, wiped them clean with a rag and laid them in a wooden box. Mincemeat, said Heiner Walendy, when he sees this he'll make mincemeat of me, and that showed me how afraid he was of his stepfather. For a while he just watched me collecting up the fish, cleaning them and sorting them into bowls and boxes: with the mackerel and the herrings you couldn't tell any more that they'd been lying in a wet field, and it was the same with the sprats and the bloaters, which were easy to wipe, but the fillets of cod had absorbed the dirt, and crumbs of earth still clung obstinately to the fishes' gills and mouths.

At last he woke up, seized a rag without saying a word and leaped around as if he'd been stung, hastily gathering up scattered fish, which he not only wiped, but also blew clean, and he even licked some of the Schiller locks clean before laying them in a box. The chips of ice were melting before our eyes, we couldn't pick them all up, but what could still be rescued we threw on top of the fillets. The fish had all been gathered up before I had the good luck to find a little brass weight and, when we then checked the weights compartment, we found that all the weights had fallen out. A frantic search began but, however thoroughly we examined everything, two couldn't be found – two out of five. Heiner Walendy was very downcast, he wailed a bit, he cursed and wailed, maybe thinking of what awaited him at home. When I suggested he could buy two new weights, he said he hadn't got any money, and not only that, there was no chance at the moment of getting any, since the odd sum he managed to earn here and there he had to give at once to his stepfather, who took delight in punishing him with fines, not being content with blows alone. Suddenly Heiner Walendy began to sob. It had never entered my thoughts that he, that boy whose badness could be seen in his eyes, could sob: it was a dry kind of sobbing that sounded like hiccups. It was then I promised to give him the money for the two missing weights.

The way he looked at me, as if he couldn't believe his ears, the way he managed to sob and to smile at the same time! He stammered out an admission that he had not always been nice to me, shaking his head as if unable to understand his own behaviour, then all of a sudden he took my hand and said: I'll never forget this, Bruno, from now on you've got a friend. That's what he said, and then he complained of pains in his neck. He walked round the three-wheeler, wondering how to get it back on its wheels. The three-wheeler wasn't all that heavy: with a couple of poles we could have rocked and levered it upright, but there weren't any poles and there wasn't a rope either to help us. We strained and pulled and pushed, but it was no good; it was only when Ewaldsen came along, when we beckoned him over and when he set his lean shoulder against it that it worked, and the three-wheeler stood on its wheels again. We quickly cleaned the tarpaulin and tied it firm, we polished the muddy door – Heiner Walendy thought he could find an excuse for the scratches – and finally we loaded up the fish and restored the floor of the van to its usual order. Bruno, he said as he drove off, and that was all.

At dusk I went along to the 'Kiek in', where he and his friends often spent the evening in a room of their own; there they had their music and they played table football and other games – in summer I had seen them a few times through the open window. I had the money for the lost weights with me, I had taken it from the hiding-place beside the boat skeleton: six marks in separate coins, which I intended to give to Heiner Walendy. He was there and he recognised me at once, he got up from his table and his beer, came towards me and, contrary to the expectations of the others, who surely believed he would play some trick on me, he put a hand on my shoulder and said: Glad you've come, Bruno, come and join us; and then he led me to his table, and they all squashed up and accepted me.

Though I didn't want a drink, Heiner Walendy sent one of his friends into the public bar to fetch me a beer. He was a pale chap with a face like a greyhound, and he slouched out sulkily and took his time. When he returned at last, he came to a halt behind me. I could see from the faces of the others that he had something in mind for me – probably to pour some beer over my head – but even before I sprang up Heiner Walendy said sharply: Stop fooling, Arno, and sit down.

Then we drank the beer they paid for out of a kitty, and Heiner Walendy told them what had happened to him and the delivery van, getting me to confirm the details. The way he described it it was I who'd done most to make good the damage, and he kept on stressing the part I'd played, praising my quick reactions and my presence of mind, and I had to demonstrate which fingers you have to spread in order to keep hold of an eel, he meanwhile giving admiring nods and calling on us all to drink. If it wasn't for Bruno, he said, I wouldn't be here, and he also said: We wouldn't mind if Bruno came here more often. Two of them gave me a wink, which pleased me, and I let them drink up my beer, which was much too bitter for me and made my head feel heavy. Heiner Walendy didn't ask for the money: I gave it him outside in the passage, hurriedly and without a word – nobody saw us. He didn't count it, but put it straight in his pocket and gave me a grateful nod, and then he invited me to come to the 'Kiek in' more often, to join him, to join his friends, who now and again, as he said, set something up, something clever or crazy that gave people something to talk and laugh about. And I did go to join them whenever the chief no longer needed me, and each time they made me welcome, gave me something to drink, taught me their games. None of them tried to make a fool of me or play tricks on me, and, whenever they reminded me of my contributions to the kitty, they always placed the bills in front of me and allowed me to check them for myself.

Once a small circus came to Hollenhusen, and among its artistes was a professional faster, a short man who sat on a sofa in a threadbare black suit and smoked, smoked all the time; on the stroke of every hour he would pour himself a glass of water from a big bottle and drink it, and you could watch him. He had already been fasting forty-four days, and everything about him was shrunken and wasted, only his eyes had grown bigger, sad grey eyes that seemed not to see what was going on close by. We stood for a while admiring him, I and Heiner Walendy and the others, but, since he had nothing to offer but smoking and drinking and since his gaze was always fixed on distant horizons, we decided to make a change in his programme. It was just that we wanted to see more of him, and one of us ran to the 'Kiek in' and fetched a bottle of brandy, half-full. How easy it was to tip that brandy into the bottle of water from which the faster drank on the stroke of each hour! We moved in very close to the sofa and screened Arno so well from view that he could have filled three bottles unnoticed. After that we moved apart again and waited.

Besides us there were a few other villagers who had come to watch the faster drink and, when the hour came, there was a silence, children were lifted up, husbands and wives exchanged glances, all attention was centred on the bony man who moved cautiously, as if he was trying it out, who first carefully crushed out his cigarette, then stretched his legs, then massaged his neck and at last reached out for the bottle and the glass. He'll drink any moment now, said someone behind me. And then he did drink, gave a sudden start, bent double and pressed his hands to his stomach, his gaze numb with horror. At a sign from Heiner Walendy we drifted off one after another, pushing past the little cart out to the street. There was still no hint of laughter: we didn't talk to each other about what we'd succeeded in doing – that we did only when we'd reached our room in the 'Kiek in', when we were alone together.

A celebration: it had to be celebrated, and the first thing we did was to position ourselves around a round table; each of us stretched out his right hand, we laid our hands one on top of the other and stood there with lowered heads – I still don't know why they did that, but I didn't ask, my hand was stuck between theirs, I could hardly feel it, all I was aware of was the warm weight, and I felt happy. At the beginning I hadn't dared lay my hand on theirs, but Heiner Walendy just looked at me and said: What are you waiting for, Bruno? Then I went quickly to the table and knew that I belonged. We stood like that for a moment, and in my excitement I couldn't have said a word, then suddenly Heiner Walendy made a hissing sound, everyone drew his hand back and, at a given signal, everyone made a fist and thumped the table top three times; they didn't take it amiss that I lagged a bit behind. Then we sat down, a bottle with a bit of brandy in it was passed around, each took just a sip, and I had to copy them, though it burned my lips. I was the last to drink from the bottle.

The disappointment when Arno came back from the public bar and declared that the celebration couldn't take place, since the kitty was empty and the innkeeper's wife wouldn't let us chalk up any more till we'd paid last month's debts. Then most of them put on worried expressions and sulked and had no heart for exchanging stories about what had happened to the circus faster. It was useless turning their pockets inside out: nothing fell out, and Heiner Walendy gave me a sorrowful look and said: We'll have to give it up, our celebration.

I shook my head, got up and went to the door, but before I left I said to their astonished faces: Wait for me here, and then I ran off through the dusk, hared across our land to the rock-hard boat skeleton and dug up a tin box, from which I took a handful of coins.

In my haste I forgot to take precautions, I didn't double back on my tracks, I didn't stop and listen; after burying the box again with one hand, I ran back to the 'Kiek in' on the path beside the rails. They were still sitting there without drinks – except for Heiner Walendy, who was outside trying to raise something: that's what they said. It wasn't very long before he came, I gave him the money and he showed it all around and said: Bruno has saved our celebration. Then we ordered; at first they took it badly that I didn't want to drink with them, but later they didn't even notice.

I didn't take enough precautions, that was it, that's why it came about that someone – and it can only have been him – crept along behind me and discovered my hiding-place and dug it up secretly and took what didn't belong to him. Empty: that morning my hiding-place by the boat skeleton was cleared out, though it wasn't on the morning after our celebration that I discovered it, but later, at the beginning of the summer in which our products were given the highest official grading and we got the right to put labels on our plants guaranteeing them true to type, well-rooted and capable of healthy growth. And it was in that same early summer that the chief found it impossible to keep his plan to himself any longer; in a drizzle of rain he took me to the top of the command hill, that gentle rise on which nothing grew and from which you could look down in all directions on our plantations. Here he laid a hand on my shoulder, steered my gaze, lightly turning me this way and that, and waited a long while before speaking.

The stronghold: he had decided to build the stronghold. The time has come, Bruno, he said, and he also said: Now we shall take complete possession of it, the old training ground on which everything used to be practised, both attack and defence. Here our house will stand, raised above the plantations, a house with room enough for us all – the Kollerhof is too old. With a stick he traced a rough diagram in the soil: Here, look, this is the terrace facing south-west, and along its whole length the building, two storeys high, and the main entrance and two side entrances. You'll be getting a room of your own with everything you need, and in the front there'll be rose-beds, look, with rhododendrons along the sides. It will be the house of our dreams, in which we shall all want to stay.

In the Kollerhof that evening after supper the chief spread out on the table a roll of drawings. It had all been designed already according to his ideas and plans, and we gathered around him as he explained it to us, full of amazement at all the things he had thought of and the care he'd taken to provide something for each of us. Even Max was to have his own little kingdom, though he was with us only during the vacations. Continuous lines and dotted lines, cross-sections, arrows and numbers: I couldn't find my way around the drawings, couldn't form a picture – unlike Ina, who understood it at once and saw it all in her mind's eye: she would have preferred to have an entrance for herself alone. Joachim: his main interest was for the position of his rooms, he cared nothing for the view or the direction they would face. Who would be living next to him? He asked about that at least three times, and it was he who wanted to know whether I should also be moving into the new house. He'd surely been reckoning that the chief would find some other place for me, and he just stared straight in front of him as Ina designed a dream-house according to her own ideas: a tall, impregnable house in full sunlight, the east wing covered with vine-leaves, the rose-beds gracefully curved; on the terrace she drew a mastiff as a watchdog, and she had us all gazing happily out of over-large windows – my window was surrounded by vine-leaves. Though she didn't know the chief would one day do it for her, she placed a number of lime-trees, her favourites, in front of her window, and where the hollow is she drew a pond with geese and ducks, but that the chief didn't carry out.

What an occasion that was for planning and asking questions and putting up wishes! Only Dorothea asked few questions: she seemed downcast, she seemed to have worries of her own, though she rejoiced with us and served us tea and coconut biscuits as if to set a seal on it all. Alone in my room before going off to sleep – only the chief and Dorothea were still downstairs – I heard what it was that worried her, I heard her fears, her warnings and her doubts. She was in favour of building the stronghold, was just as pleased as we were, but she wanted it put off for at least a year. It was then that I resolved to go to the boat skeleton next morning to dig up the money I had saved.

The stick I used to scratch and scrape broke twice, and, because it was difficult to dig the clay soil, caked by rain, with my bare fingers, I took the spade with the short handle and dug small holes between the stones I had put there as markers, without once hearing a grating or a clinking sound. Gone, all gone: no gleaming sight greeted my eyes as always before. I sat down and thought for a long time, about my friends and the rain that washes away all traces, and to calm myself I cracked cherry stones open and ate the kernels, and I also swallowed drops of milk from dandelion stems.

Always these calls: how often I think I'm being called! I clearly hear the way they draw my name out, but when I look round to see, there's nobody close by. Bru-no; yes, all right, I'm coming. That was the chief's voice, he was standing at the foot of the command hill, at the spot where the yellow machine was burrowing and dredging, where they were engaged in digging the foundations and had marked out a piece of ground with iron stakes, between which a loosely stretched red ribbon ran. I saw at once that something had happened; not just the chief and the driver of the machine, but Ewaldsen too and a few others were standing on a fresh mound of earth staring down at something, just standing and staring, but you could see in all their faces that something unusual had been discovered. What the yellow machine with its toothed dredging buckets had laid bare was not a complete skeleton: an arm was missing, the dredger had scooped it up and deposited it on the pile of earth, but otherwise there was nothing missing, not a rib, not an ankle-bone. Ewaldsen climbed down and carefully scraped crumbs of earth from the bones, he wiped the skull clean with a handkerchief, he poked around between the ribs and searched with feeling – he could have done with a sieve, but there was none handy. The machine driver rolled himself a cigarette and all he could keep on saying was: That's all I needed. Though I was standing beside him, the chief asked: Where has Bruno got to? And after I made my presence known, he sent me off to the police-station, to Duus: Tell him to come at once.

At first Duus wasn't willing to do what the chief asked. He just looked at me, shaking his head, when I told him we'd found a heap of bones in the place being excavated for the stronghold, and he didn't put on his leather belt until I spoke of a dead human body being brought to light by the bulldozer. Then he came, he couldn't get there fast enough, and from each man on the command hill he wanted to know when and from what point they had discovered the skeleton: there was a great deal for him to note down. When I asked him if it mightn't be the remains of the sergeant who had long ago gone missing here, he just said: What do you know about that? and afterwards he climbed down and scratched around a little and passed a bit of earth through his fingers; he just touched the ribcage, but the skull – that he examined very closely. The chief helped him out of the hole, we clustered round him, but all he could tell us was what we already knew: that this land had previously been a training ground and that the man down there must surely have been buried here during those days, who knows why. Things could get hot here, that he also said. He put a temporary stop to the work, wanting nothing touched before a thorough investigation had been made and the bones removed. On leaving he shook only the chief's hand and said: Here of all places, eh? And the chief shrugged his shoulders and replied: It was a training ground, what can you expect?

In the shed down in the hollow, where we felt like stretching out for a bit, the chief just lay with open eyes – he who could usually go off to sleep anywhere more or less to order. This time he didn't drift off but lay studying the patches of damp on the ceiling, kneading his fingers and now and again letting out a soft moan. It didn't turn out, as so often before by the stacked wall or by the erratic block, that I was left watching over his sleep. His breathing didn't grow more regular and, since he knew I wasn't sleeping either, he suddenly began to speak, telling of another country where mountains sloped gently down to the sea and mousey-grey rocks glistened between sparse cork-trees: the humps looked like scrubbed hides. A railtrack led round the mountains, sometimes disappearing into a tunnel, and in a gorge in which only a few stunted fir-trees grew, a number of upturned waggons lay twisted and shattered, their wheels in the air.

Since the rails were always being torn up or blown up, the chief had the task of guarding them, he and some of the men in his company, but there wasn't much they could do, for the others were everywhere and nowhere at the same time, and once they were surrounded and besieged. Quite a few were shot down. The chief was with his best friend, they shared everything between them, finally a handful of olives. They kept up their resistance for a long time, but one night both of them were hit, and when the chief came round he found himself in a field hospital. His friend was still missing.

When he was on his feet again, he had only a single aim: to find out what had become of his friend, and he searched and enquired, examined lists of missing persons. He spent half of his leave investigating, but it was only two years later, when he was posted back to his old place, that he found anything. In the reddish, rather rough soil beside the rails two little olive trees were growing: they were the last olives the chief had put into his friend's pocket. So now he knew what he wished to know.

This is what the chief told me down in the shed as he lay there unable to sleep, and he expressed a hope that they would find, beside the skeleton at the foot of the command hill, a few things that would help to reveal something of where he came from, his name, the manner of his death. He was thinking of an identity disc or a cigarette lighter with a monogram, but it turned out that the man had been stripped of all he had. They carefully gathered together what was left of him and took it away. Work was not resumed until the car was out of sight, and it was the chief himself who gave the signal and urged the men on.

And he also made sure that he missed nothing of the excavation and the pouring of the foundation walls. He had to be everywhere: he took the plans from the hands of the architect or his foreman, he checked and compared, at one time he'd be dragging up stones, at another crates of beer, he measured, laid bricks, climbed all over the scaffolding, he even mixed mortar. The coins, the newspapers, the documents – these I was allowed to push into the opening in the wall, and they all stood around and clapped as he bricked up the hole. What a time that was, with all its comings and goings, the permanent cloud of dust, the clatter and the cries borne on the wind! Higher and higher the stronghold grew, soon we could see the shell from the Kollerhof, the overhanging brickwork that astonished the Hollenhuseners and made us impatient and proud: Just a little while now, the chief said, and then we'll be here to stay. It will be our training ground then, once and for all. He said that.

Some neighbours came to the topping-out ceremony. A gusty wind was blowing, and it carried off a lot of the foreman's speech. The chief's words of thanks also came over only in fragments, but at least we could hear all the wishes and hopes and vows that were being voiced there, and Dorothea took snaps of the speakers standing by themselves and also exchanging handshakes, and she kept on taking snaps as the festive crown with its gay ribbons was fixed in place and the roofers and carpenters performed the act that is now to be seen only in Hollenhusen: on the last rafter to be trimmed the roofers try to pull the carpenters up to their level, but the carpenters use their weight to prevent them and in turn try to drag the roofers down to theirs. With all the swinging and rocking, our hearts were in our mouths that someone or other would fall or be flung off, but they all knew their game, and so no harm was done.

Although it was so enjoyable, I couldn't stop shaking, and I only calmed down when baskets were carried around, baskets filled with cold rissoles and sausages and cutlets covered in breadcrumbs, and people could take as much as they wanted. Beer and spirits they had to fetch for themselves from a folding table I had set up out of the wind: there couldn't often have been so many bottles standing side by side. There'd surely have been some leftovers if the people from Hollenhusen hadn't been there. It was only envy and nosiness that had brought them, but they helped themselves every time a basket was carried past, and what they didn't want to eat there and then they wrapped up for later; and while they were stuffing themselves and guzzling things not meant for them, they aired their views on the stronghold in their own mean-spirited way, calling it a barracks or the refugees' palace, and one bulgy-eyed old flatfish who'd already devoured at least eight rissoles coined the name 'Villa Bighead'. How I'd have enjoyed turning the lot of them into telegraph poles or milestones!

However, there was one who was not sparing of approval and praise, and that was a man in grey clothes nobody had been expecting. He went up to the chief with an embarrassed smile and gave him a flour sifter and a salt cellar, the handsomest containers I've ever seen, and then modestly turned to go, but the chief, whose face showed as much pleasure as surprise, would not allow it: he quickly called Ina over, gave her the two containers, and then together they led Niels Lauritzen, who had surely come without his father's know-ledge, through the unfinished building, showing him the not yet decorated rooms in which they had to climb over many a trestle bridge. I kept an eye on them during their tour, and when they came out into the open air I snatched up a basket and offered Niels Lauritzen cold cutlets in breadcrumbs. He didn't want to eat anything, but he gave me his hand and said in a friendly way: Thanks, Bruno, and he also said: A splendid house, a fine place to live. He had warm, intelligent eyes like a spaniel's and, though he was still so young, there were already lines across his brow. Whenever he was offered something from a basket he always said no, but Ina got him to drink something. He waited until she had poured a bit out for herself, and then they raised their glasses to each other and sat down on a pile of unused bricks. Here Ina for the second time made him show her how to refill the handsome flour and salt containers.

Lie down – I'll lie down for a while: who knows what they've got in store for me this evening, how long they'll keep working on me – Max too, to whom I owe so much. His book, the faded inscription: To Bruno, the most patient of listeners, in memory of our years together; if I read slowly, I can immediately hear him speaking. Theory of Ownership. The man who wants nothing. The man who knows nothing. I've read it five times already, and it all melts away as if it had never been, the names, the thoughts – though Meister Eckhart I do remember: Max always calls him just Meister and talks a lot about him, about his importance and the fact that everything he wrote so long ago still holds true.

I have always pictured him wearing a leather apron and sitting in front of a table on which lies an open book; a jug filled with water and a mug stand next to the book, on which a ray of light falls directly through a little window. I can't see him any other way. Many people are just the things they possess and they don't wish to be anything else. That is not good: a person must be free, free of all things and all works, inner as well as outer. Free: that is what's good. Possessing or doing something isn't bad in itself, but we shouldn't be bound, fettered, chained to what we possess or what we do.

What can be bringing on this sleepiness? It steals over me with the warmth, evening clouds hang over the fields, over the tear-drenched fields of the Memel as it flows gurgling by, but from the depths there comes a sparkling, as if little stars were bursting; maybe down on the floor of his river the Fish King is stirring, tracing a path between the arrowheads and all the sunken things that have settled on it.

N o, I shan't go over for my lunch, let them wonder as much as they like; I'll not go into the kitchen today to fetch my plate from the hatch – sweet and sour lentils, I expect, garnished with bacon: in earlier times, in the Kollerhof, that was one of the chief's favourite dishes. What my favourite is doesn't need much thought: not jellied eels, not meat loaf in tomato sauce and not smoked knuckle of pork but, now and ever since I can remember, goose giblets boiled up tastily with peas, chopped bits of shiny blue stomach, of neck and wings and skin from the back – the roughness where the quills were doesn't worry me.

Ina always used to pull a face over goose giblets, and she would quickly steer her bits of meat in my direction, finding the pale gooseflesh rather disgusting. Joachim didn't like it either, but he ate it just the same; it was only the bits of stomach he wouldn't touch – those he piled up on the edge of his plate. Ina once said: One of these days you'll all be sprouting wings and flying over the Kollerhof.

It's only rarely Lisbeth cooks my favourite dish, and even then it never tastes as good as the goose giblets Dorothea used to serve up, but Lisbeth is good with pears cooked with broad beans, with stuffed cabbage and with a rice pudding sprinkled with cinnamon: I could eat seven times as much of that as she'll ever give me. When Lisbeth is in a good mood she sometimes turns out something special: pig's trotters with fried potatoes, or bread pudding with vanilla sauce; if all she serves is a stew with bits of beef or gravy or just a potato soup, then I know she's feeling liverish. No, I shan't go there for lunch.

Over there by the yew seedlings: it could be Elef. Who knows whether I'll be able to pay him that visit? Elef can't resist copying some of the Hollenhuseners and walking round the plantations with just wooden clogs on his feet: it's the clumps of earth beneath the soles that make him strut and wobble so. Once he tried to play a joke on me, calling out in an excited way: Quick, Herr Bruno, take a look at this, Herr Bruno. It was his clogs, which appeared to have grown roots overnight, fine hair roots which he showed me and asked me to wonder at. I saw at once that the fine roots were stuck on with clay, but I didn't tell him that, I just said his clogs would now need a lot of watering and, taking up a watering-can, I filled the wooden shoes up to the brim. Elef hadn't been expecting that, but he laughed as I walked off. He has just left the muck-spreader standing there – not like Mirko, who would surely have driven to lunch on it.

Sweat alone is not enough. In earlier times, the chief once said, it was only our sweat that manured the land, but soil needs more than just that to nourish it: to win its favour we must give it stable manure and peat, sphagnum peat: these provide nourishment and humous. There is still more nourishment in chicken dung, but that is too concentrated, and also in hornmeal and horn shavings, but they cost too much. It took the chief four years to work out that broad-leaved trees prefer stable manure, but conifers grow better if they're given peat.

Seven: only Magda knocks seven times, yes, that head-scarf with the anchor, the telescope, the coiled rope is hers. She'll soon knock again, she knows I'm at home, Magda always feels it in her bones. In that battered old breakfast box she has often before brought me a grilled chop or a fillet of fish. I must open up, I must let her in. Come, sit down, I say, sit in the armchair. She doesn't take her head-scarf off, she's clearly in a hurry. How heedlessly she pushes the breakfast box across the table! It's plain she's not come this time just to bring me something to eat: not often has she sat there looking so serious, so concerned. Has anything happened, Magda? With the chief?

I've got something to tell you, Bruno, but don't ask me how I know, I just do, and you can depend on it that it's right. In what a toneless, hesitant way she speaks these words, as if she's bringing me news of a sentence! Come, tell me what's happened. Why is she looking at me like that, as if I'd done God knows what? I've never brought trouble on anybody. Why are you looking at me like that, Magda?

It's because of you, Bruno, and it's also because of you that they've started these legal proceedings, that's what I gathered. They did it and put their signatures to it because the chief has made out a deed of gift in which you are to get the best land here. After his death the best of it will belong to you, and some installations as well. Do you understand what that means? If things happen as the chief wants it, then maybe a third of everything here will belong to you – the bit that's worth more than all the rest together. Just think how it'll be if it all turns out as the chief wants! All of a sudden you'd have a say in things.

So it's beginning all over again, this muddle! I'd be glad to know who started it, the chief hasn't said a word to me about it, never even a hint that a deed of gift was being drawn up and signed, and, just so you'll know, I tell you I wish for nothing and I expect nothing, all I want is to stay with him as long as I can, that and nothing else. Why is she shaking her head? Now listen to me, Bruno: what's done is done. This deed, this deed of gift exists, but the others in the stronghold, they can't bring themselves to accept it, they're not prepared to allow what the chief has arranged, and that's why they're taking steps against him. And you too, Bruno, will have to look out for yourself, mark my words. Since it's too much for them to lose, they'll be taking steps against you as well, I heard enough to know that. Simpleton, a man they've got there as a guest said, and he was surely meaning you: This simpleton has no sense of responsibility, and whoever takes over this land must at least be aware of the obligations he's assuming.

How softly Magda speaks, how far away she is! Everything has become hazy and unclear, and through the buzzing Magda's voice: I don't know, Bruno, I don't know what you should do, but you must speak to the chief, you must.

This evening, Magda, I've got to go to the stronghold, they've sent for me. Don't go yet, stay a bit longer, you must tell me what I should do, how I should answer them – Yes, I know you must go. I feel calmer with her hand lying on my shoulder. Take your time, Bruno, she says, listen carefully and take your time and don't be too quick to say yes or no. There's a lot at stake for all of you, so you mustn't answer too hastily. And she says: You must make a note of everything and tell it all to me, I'll knock, however late it is. Yes.

No sound comes as she closes the door behind her. So gently, so silently. Two skips and she is out on the path, and this time she certainly won't be turning to wave.

That man with the yellow rabbit's teeth, Murwitz – sitting here he said: There's a lot of trouble coming your way, Herr Messmer; and he also said the Zeller family was not disposed to consent to the deed of gift. If only I knew what he meant by that, what it is that will be coming my way! But it won't be anything pleasant, that's for sure. They'll be working something out for me. Maybe they'll set a watch over me, make me feel anxious, as that time when tools and seeds and a lot of seedlings in pots vanished, and suspicion fell on me. Suspicion. There was always someone behind me, someone keeping an eye on me, day and night; he'd come out from under the trees in Danes' Wood as I was breaking off the bulrushes by the big pond, come out and then at once creep back into the shadow, he followed me through the plantations – there were rustlings and twigs snapping all around me – wait for me in the fog by the river, listen at my door, and always he managed to remain unrecognised.

If they now engage someone to follow me I shan't keep it to

myself: I'll tell the chief, and he'll know what's to be done, he who once called me his only friend. In the last resort I can lock myself in here, the two safety locks and the bolt can be relied on, they won't be so easy to break down, and everything coming my way will have to stay outside and wait. They won't use force, of course not, but if they do I could give them quite a surprise. A single cut with my bill-hook would be enough: just bend the neck backwards, then a hefty crosscut from left to right.

Potato salad and rissoles: how light the rissoles are, how crumbly: Lisbeth has surely used too many breadcrumbs. The rissoles in the waiting-room are harder, older and harder. If the chief's word were really no longer to count, I suppose Lisbeth would be leaving Hollenhusen tomorrow already. She and I would be the first to go, but it's still him who decides who can go on living here in the toolshed, and his wish is enough to make sure Lisbeth keeps her room over in the stronghold. There are a lot of empty rooms there, I don't know just how many now, but at the time they moved in it was clear there were several rooms to spare. But that's none of my concern; for me there was no staying in the stronghold: I shall never go back to that basement.

Oh, Ina, I can still hear you, on that evening before the move, as we were sitting in the Kollerhof surrounded by bundles and crates, making sure you'd be allowed to furnish your room just as you wanted: only the men from outside who were helping us with the move went into the room, and the looks they exchanged out in the corridor already told me they'd seen something they weren't accustomed to seeing.

I was the first person you showed it to. Maybe you wanted to test by my reaction the impression your room would make – should make – on others. Come along, Bruno, just for a moment, and then you led me in. Out of doors: I was not standing in a room, but out of doors, for the walls were covered with big coloured posters you had kept hidden from us all. I found myself surrounded by meadows in which horses stood rubbing their necks together, wild ducks were swimming through a landscape of reeds, and over there beehives stood in a tidy row beneath blossoming fruit-trees; you could even rest your eyes on a forest clearing in which a perspiring company of people had seated themselves down for a meal and a rest. Of the walls themselves there was hardly anything to be seen.

Nicest of all, though, were your drawings, Ina. You had hung them up side by side, they were all the same size and they were pictures of all of us: Dorothea and the chief and Max and Joachim and me and you. The chief's face was almost lost in the crown of a walnut tree, and Dorothea: she was hung all over with brambles; Max and Joachim had their eyes screwed up, as if the sun was dazzling them, and you yourself were looking out of a mirror. I recognised my own face at once – you had painted it on a paper kite – and I was so delighted I straight away asked you to give it to me, but you said no. And you also said: In my room I want you all staying together. That made me very pleased, and I asked you for permission to come and sit in your room now and again, and you agreed and said: You know, Bruno, that my door's always open, and that won't be any different here in the stronghold. And then you wanted to come down with me to the basement flat the chief had provided for me, you wanted to help me furnish it, and were quite surprised when I told you there was nothing to help with, because I'd long ago got it all done.

From my window I couldn't see the chief's bright and airy office on the ground floor, but I could see all the people who came to visit him. They were mostly men wearing jackets or green overcoats, less often couples; they drove up in cars, in delivery vans, and what first drew their attention was not the office itself, but our plantations, stretching right to the horizon. How they stood there, how they shaded their eyes, how they nudged each other and pointed their fingers towards something they recognised! The minister who visited us one Sunday afternoon stood there just like that: he too shielded his eyes and explained to the people with him things he'd recognised in the distance.

Waiting is all the same to me, but the others, they get impatient if they have to wait just half an hour, especially Joachim, who that day kept hopping out to the terrace and searching the main road with his binoculars until at last he made out the two black cars. They drove up the main path, and the minister was the first to get out and to shake everyone by the hand; by mistake he also gave his hand to Ewaldsen, who had just put down a load of pine twigs and was standing watching. Then the man the chief called a great garden-lover cast an eye over our plantations and nodded approvingly and said something to his escort. The garden-loving minister had a youthful face and grey-white hair with yellowish strands running through it; his hands were warm and fleshy, and on one finger he wore a clumsy-looking signet ring with a pale blue seal; his small mouth was always slightly open, just as if he'd been surprised by something. The reason he walked with a stoop must surely have been his tallness: he towered over everyone and had to bend down to the person he was speaking to, and he made a point of speaking to everyone standing close by. He asked me what I liked doing best and I said: Staking Colorado firs, and he gave a surprised nod, as if that was what he too best liked doing.

He must have got to know the chief somewhere before, because he took him by the arm in a familiar way and said with a glance at the stronghold: A nice place you've built yourself here, my dear Zeller, and at one point he also said: One hears a lot of good things about your work here, there's even been some mention of miracles. To that the chief replied with a shrug of his shoulders: Nobody can escape rumours, minister; that's all he said. They decided to sit down to Dorothea's coffee table spread later, after the inspection, after the sightseeing tour: the minister wanted first to see something, and he and the chief walked on ahead. I simply tagged along with the people the minister had brought with him.

They were silent, friendly people, except for one, the thin man dressed in dark blue who was always weaseling around in a high state of nerves – nothing must be allowed to escape his attention, no ministerial word, no ministerial wish, he must always be standing by, just so he could agree with anything the minister said. He didn't like me being part of the procession, that's for sure, often enough he gave me a suspicious glance out of the corner of his eye, but, since the chief bore with me and a few times called on me to help with the growing frames and the polythene tunnel, he didn't dare ask me anything.

He'd have had no difficulty getting a job with us, the minister, for he knew a great deal: that there was hardly any demand for various kinds of poplar, that he knew, that forest shrubs were getting slightly dearer and fruit and decorative bushes went best of all, that he also knew: whatever they talked about or wherever they stopped, the minister knew what he was saying. He even argued with the chief once, that was when they were exchanging views on rootstocks for grafting lilac: the chief thought the best rootstocks should spend two years in the seedbed, for in this time they could be relied on to develop eyes; the minister on the other hand was all for transplanted wild plants, even if their rootstock is quite hard.

The things he found and picked up and examined: flimsy beetles' wings, a dried-up grasshopper, a tuft of hair from a rabbit-skin, pods and panicles and the skeleton of a very small bird – whatever it might be, he would pick it up and hold it close to his eyes. In our currant and gooseberry sectors he asked the chief for an explanation, wanting to know what was responsible for bringing the plant into blossom, and the chief said: The leaf, of course, the blossoming time is decided by the leaf, and, when the minister gave him a questioning look, the chief told him what he'd told me long ago: that the leaf had hidden inside it a clock that measures the length of the days and nights to come and, once it has established that the day's length is right for blossoming, it gives the necessary instruction.

Through some kind of substance. Through a chemical messenger substance. Even if a plant is not ready to blossom, it will immediately follow the instruction as soon as you graft on to it a leaf that had fixed a favourable blossoming time for some other plant. The centre of activity lies in the leaf, the chief said, and after a while the minister said: There are several different views on the matter, my dear Zeller, but yours is without doubt the most persuasive.

And all of us except for the thin man sat down on my stacked wall and gazed across the beds and the young plantations. The chief told the minister how we had opened up the old training ground bit by bit and put it to use; he also said I'd helped him from the very start: Our Bruno was present throughout. That made me happy. While the chief was speaking, the minister was twisting an empty cartridge case between his fingers, one he had found himself. First he rolled it and scratched it, then he blew a bit of earth out of the inside, and during a pause he suddenly asked whether the danger was now finally past; he asked this without looking up, and the chief said quietly: Not yet, they haven't given up yet. The minister said: According to my information several generations of soldiers were trained here, the famous 248th. The chief agreed this was so, then said softly: Several generations, yes, but it was all for nothing, for absolutely nothing. And after a moment's reflection he added: We shall not leave here of our own free will.

The minister nodded. It was an approving nod: he could well understand that the chief would never give up of his own free will after all he'd done, but you could see he knew more than he was permitted to say. Cautiously, and in words that provided no certainty, he mentioned a so-called provisional clause affecting the sale of land controlled by the military, and he also mentioned something else which I'd never heard of before: alliance obligations and defence commitments. Not that he was trying to influence the chief, all he wanted to do was to give him something to think about, but the chief seemingly knew all about it, had long ago thought it all over and decided on a course he wished for the time being to keep to himself. Through narrowed eyes he regarded his rows of trees and pressed his lips together. Whenever he kept silent like that, whenever he sat so unmoving, I'd know at once that there was something at stake for himself and for us, and, though I didn't know what it was, I felt uneasiness rising up inside me, and uneasiness like this always presses on my stomach. I followed his gaze, looked out over our rows of conifers, and felt that something was about to happen. I shouldn't have been surprised to see a few soldiers coming out of the sparse shadows, but nothing moved on the land: all was as on any other Sunday.

That things could happen of which I knew nothing I realised when the minister suddenly asked if the commission had already been here, and the chief replied, as if his mind was far away: Yes, it was here, the commission. And? the minister enquired. The chief shrugged his shoulders and said: Questions, notices, declarations, but nothing has arrived so far, nothing final; we're just waiting. Well, the minister said, nothing has been decided yet, and as he spoke he tapped the stone wall with the cartridge case, there's still hope, Zeller, and then he said something else that I couldn't understand, for my throat had swelled so I could scarcely breathe, there was a throbbing in my temples, and I could feel sweat gathering on my chest. And darkly, as if coming from below the ground, I suddenly heard the minister's other voice, the voice he used when talking to himself, and it said: The situation is bad, my dear Zeller, it looks as if the district military authorities aren't prepared to give up the land, but you do have me on your side.

The minister laid a hand on the chief's shoulder and they both slid off the stacked stone wall and set off without a further word along the path to the stronghold, followed by an escort that probably didn't even notice that I stayed seated, stretching out my neck as I struggled for air. Soldiers came bounding over the horizon, they burst out of Danes' Wood, crossed the Holle, stormed over Lauritzen's meadows, overran one plantation after the other. All at once there were ploughs everywhere, motorised double ploughs which the soldiers eagerly set going, to plough up everything our land had to show, all the broad-leaved trees, the conifers and the fruit-trees, and what they ploughed up at once turned black and began to wither as I watched, while a whole company of soldiers ran behind the ploughs, collecting the branches and piling them up. When an officer was given a lighted torch, when he threw it into the touchwood, I could stand it no longer, I ran after the chief and the others, but tell what I'd seen, report – no, that I couldn't do. At one point I managed to give the chief a secret sign, we drew a little to one side and when he asked me: Is anything the matter, Bruno? I couldn't find any words, all I could do was catch hold of his arm and press it. At that he gave me a smile and whispered: Keep calm, lad, we'll soon be alone again.

Beside the chief's rose-bed – his hobby bed, as he called it – the minister came to a halt. He noticed at once that the chief was particularly fond of old-fashioned sorts, of tea-roses, Noisette, and guessed that all the varieties were grafted on dog-roses – but that magnesium and potash had been added to the soil, that he didn't guess. He examined the flowers at leisure, praised their growth, the strong shoots, asked about frost resistance and rest periods, and then he crouched down and put out a hand: he had discovered the rose without a name, the chief's pride. He fell completely silent, he plucked off a petal, rubbed it, smelled it, carefully cupped the flower in his open hand and drew it towards him, and in all he did he showed his escort how fully you can admire a thing without saying a single word. Seemingly reluctant to put a direct question, he just turned on his heels and looked up at the chief, who said slowly: A back-cross, I thought I'd try it out, a back-cross from the polyanthus back to the wild rose; not much can harm it, it flowers till the frosts come. It must go into the register, the minister said, it's good enough for the register.

It wasn't the minister, but the thin man in his escort who asked for the rose's name, and the chief said: We take our time here over things like that. The thin man wanted to know whether any name had yet been considered, at which the chief looked at him in surprise and asked in his turn: Do you want to make a suggestion? The thin man gave a forced laugh and amid curious contortions of his body made a dismissive gesture, saying it had just been a question, a modest hint that this might be a favourable time for a christening ceremony, if he might be permitted to point this out, a name-giver happening to be present. The chief behaved as if the hint had not penetrated, after a pause he said: Everything here has to earn its name, has to show itself worthy of it, if you understand what I mean. He said nothing more on the subject, but instead invited the minister and his escort to go indoors, where Dorothea was awaiting them at the coffee-table. I walked with him as far as the main entrance and, when most of them were already inside the stronghold, the chief came back. He gave the impression of having forgotten something, but he had forgotten nothing, he drew me quickly to his office door and asked: What is it, Bruno, what's the matter? and this time I could tell him what I'd heard. He looked at me consideringly, his face grew dark, then he ran his hand over my hair and warned me: Don't think so far ahead, lad, and hurried back into the house.

I'd already eaten my Sunday cake after lunch as I walked along. Dorothea had baked it herself, a crumble cake with a layer of vanilla cream. The way she makes it the bits of crumble look like sun-drops, like dried, crisped, gently browned drops of sunlight: I have to close my eyes every time I put them in my mouth. I didn't go down to my basement, Bruno wandered across to the big black cars. The minister's chauffeur beckoned me and offered me a peppermint and, while still holding the packet out, wanted to know where to go for a leak. During his absence I took a good look at the car. Even today I can't understand why the horn suddenly set up a wailing that wouldn't stop. All I'd wanted to do was to hold the steering-wheel and feel what it's like to be a driver, a chauffeur, and suddenly it started belling like a stag, howling and screaming, I suppose it was more than one horn I'd set off, their sound was painful, going down to the roots of my teeth, and I slid out of the driver's seat and ran off; it wasn't until I reached the big pond that the noise abruptly ceased. This heat. This burning in my skin. Stabbed: that's how I felt, and I walked slowly to the big pond, lay down on the ground and first of all drank.

The squiggles of light were already paler, less defined, they weren't rocking and flashing any more beneath the surface, and the little dips made by the wind were being smoothed out. It's always like that as evening approaches: a fine haze begins to spread, things that had been clearcut begin to swim, to flow as if being pushed along by a steady breath, turning back into something that can only be felt, not seen. The haze cast a bluish light over Danes' Wood. My stomach felt heavy, and it rumbled. If I kept completely still I could hear the pond breathing: it sucked the air in, right down to its depths, and then, relieved, breathed it evenly out, causing reeds and water plants to sway gently. Now I could also hear, coming from far away, the voices and groans of the wounded Danish soldiers – but muffled and only when the wind gathered itself up and blew in gusts through the treetops. It was then I saw them.

They came out of Danes' Wood, Ina and Niels Lauritzen, both of them in moss-green clothing, they walked out and at once exchanged a look, just as if both wanted to make sure they were really standing side by side on the edge of Danes' Wood, but soon they began looking in different directions, in a rather strained way, uncertain what to do next. Luckily, something darted out of the brambles, I couldn't see what it was, but it darted away, and Niels Lauritzen spun round and pointed with outstretched arm into the wood, and I suppose he said a few words, silent as he normally is, though always so friendly. It was damp under the alder bushes, it squished and squelched, but I crept into the bushes, supporting myself on the hoops of an ancient fish-trap that lay rotting there.

Molehills: once Ina began kicking down the loose molehills, Niels joined in, and they sometimes ran at the same molehill, making me think they must surely collide, then either catch hold or tumble over each other or something like that, but just in time Niels Lauritzen would brake – it was always Niels who put on the brakes – leaving the destruction of the molehill to Ina. Frogs were croaking on the other side of the pond, they were lying among the creeping plants and croaking and, when Ina and Niels had tired of kicking in molehills, they went across to the frogs, creeping up on them so as not to dislodge anything: one little disturbance of that kind and the whole golden-eyed band would dive under. They watched the frogs, they pointed out to each other what they were seeing in the water. Then Ina looked for and found something she could throw, a batten, a piece of scantling somebody had lost here, she hurled it among the creepers, I suppose at the frogs clinging together there – oh, Ina, I still remember how you once called for stones, for missiles, when we were standing there together, and the sight of all the many frogs clamped together was making you feel sick. A splash, and the whole band dived out of sight, and in the same instant Ina bent over, spread out her hand, examined it, put a finger in her mouth and sucked, while Niels, who didn't know what had happened, stared at her, went right up to her, but didn't dare touch her.

You, Ina, held your hand out to him, showed him where the splinter or the nail had torn the skin open, and Niels took your hand and gazed at it so long and with such interest you'd think he'd never seen a hand before, but in the end he decided the right thing to do was to fetch out his handkerchief and bandage the modest wound – Niels Lauritzen, who was always friendly towards me and never forgot to include me in his greetings. Why you went back into Danes' Wood I don't know either, all I know is that he put an arm round your shoulder and, shortening his steps, led you off protectively. You were willing, through my curtain of leaves I could see you were willing to walk with him along the path he had chosen for you both.

And in the evening you brought him to the stronghold for the first time. We were having our supper – in the early days I still ate with the family at the big table – and Joachim couldn't leave off nagging at me. He only needed to catch sight of me and at once he found something to pick on. A drip mark: he had found a drip mark on the scrubbed floor and a bit of black dirt I'd maybe brought in on my boots, and that started a hail of reproaches and accusations. Must I make a pigsty of everything? he asked me, hadn't it got through to me we were no longer living in the Kollerhof? I had to wait a long time before the chief said to Joachim: Now that's enough, calm down, and all Dorothea said was: Let's have some peace now, Bruno will clear it up after we've eaten. But he kept up his niggling – though it was not continuous and not aimed directly at me – until Ina pushed the door open and said gaily: Look who I've brought. Astonishment was the very least they showed around the table: they stopped eating, stared at the unexpected guest and got to their feet only when Niels Lauritzen, drawn forward by Ina, stood by the table, smiling uncertainly and maybe considering an apology, though that was something no one wished to hear. Niels was greeted in a friendly way and invited to join in the meal. I had long noted the trail of dirt Ina and Niels had left between the door and the table, damp black marks much more noticeable than mine, maybe even enriched with small clods of earth from the molehills. I saw them, but I said nothing, just waited to see what Joachim would say. When at last he saw the pattern on the light-coloured carpet, he cleared his throat and asked Ina: Haven't you seen our footscraper yet? Ina, who was in the act of putting two plates and cutlery on the table, looked down, saw the trail of dirt, gave a laugh and said to Niels: Look, we've left our visiting card, and to Joachim she said: There's no dirt more honest than that – house-warming dirt, and that's all she said.

Niels Lauritzen ate only one slice of bread and drank only

one cup of tea, he said little and on this evening asked only one question. He wanted to know how Doctor Zeller was doing, and the chief said Max would probably be carrying the cares of the world on his shoulders as always, and for that reason would be doing well; in the silence that followed he also said: The more dissatisfied with the world's condition Max is, the better he feels, and then he passed the bread basket around and urged us to eat some more.

Ina couldn't resist showing the little wound on her forefinger. It was no longer bleeding and she didn't want a plaster on it, but she also didn't want to give the handkerchief back at once: first it must be washed and ironed. The reason she gave for her injury was correct. How hard she tried to infect us with her gaiety! She never stopped talking, told us down to the last detail where she had been with Niels and what they had seen and heard – a badger, it must have been a badger we startled in the brambles. She was so wound up that she didn't even notice the way Joachim was sighing and drumming on his knees with impatience. And when he could stand no more of her chatter, he didn't ask her to stop but turned to the chief and asked abruptly if the stocktaking was to proceed as planned, and the chief just gave him a quick look and asked in his turn: What else? And all the other jobs? Joachim wanted to know, and the chief in slight surprise: Why not? Tomorrow is a quite ordinary day. Dorothea, always ready to take Joachim's side, felt it right to remind the chief that the question was a reasonable one. Perhaps we should wait until everything's settled, she said, but the chief quietly decided: We're carrying on, Dotti, everything must go on as usual, that's our safest course.

No doubt Ina felt the seriousness, the tenseness in the air, for she looked with concern from one to the other, put both hands round her tea-glass, hoping, I suppose, that one of them would tell her more, but when nobody offered to put her right, she simply asked whether the visit had brought bad news, asked too: What happened anyway during the visit from on high? They all just looked down at their plates, and it was only when Niels got up and didn't seem to know whether to go or stay that the chief raised his head. He gestured to Niels to sit down again and said: You won't believe it, Ina, but I made the minister an offer as he was saying goodbye. As he was praising everything, I jokingly invited him to start work with us, and he didn't find that funny, he even said: Maybe, my dear Zeller, I'll one day take you at your word. The chief didn't stay with us much longer, he had to go to his office, and, as he gave Niels Lauritzen his hand, he invited him to come again when he had the chance. That he did say.

Birds: always mistrustful and alert, always with an eye on the others, as if everything depends on what the others do. Even when taking a bath in a puddle they watch each other, push themselves forward or take fright: it's always the other one that has the best place and must first be chased off. Our birds always bathe singly: though the puddle is so big that six to eight of them could bathe at the same time, they never do, they huddle round it, eying the one who hops into the middle and with wild nods scoops the muddy water over itself. Not too many drops to start with: probably just enough to wet its feathers, then, when sufficiently sprinkled, it really gets down to it, ducks deep under, spreads its wings and sets them quivering in the water, beats them so fast that they raise a little storm and the air is filled with flashing spray, it whips and thrashes around as if it can never stop. Then all of a sudden another bird flies at it: a shadow, a warning peck and the first bird hops out and stands in an untidy, sticky bundle, water dripping from it, its wings hanging down. No bird could look more forlorn, it's a miracle it can even lift itself off the ground and fly away.

They all fly up and away: the motor has driven them off, the ambulance: yes, it's an ambulance that is slowly driving up to the stronghold. Surely it can't be coming for the chief? He's certainly not ill like Ewaldsen's wife, who has to lie on her back, who now and again sits out in the sun, thin and yellow as a lemon, then has to lie down again. The chief is just disappointed, he's feeling bitter, solitary, maybe discouraged as well, but he'll get things straightened out here, if that's what's needed; they can't just say he's ill and send him off to hospital and then order and arrange things here according to their own ideas: he'll never put up with that. But if they really must take him away, if something has happened to him as it happened to Detlefsen, the old council clerk, who suddenly one day at breakfast couldn't raise his coffee-cup to his lips and couldn't in fact eat or drink at all – if it has got to that stage with the chief, then I can start packing right away, for my time in Hollenhusen will be over.

Two people get out. They surely can't be ambulancemen: maybe they've come here by mistake. I must wait till they drive off again. In earlier times, in the Kollerhof, it was nice being ill: I would lie alone in my room and everyone would be good to me, they'd come to see me and bring me things. In earlier times each spoke as he thought, and when Dorothea said: Now, Bruno, let's sleep this illness off, then I'd go off to sleep at once, and when I woke up the illness would have got smaller.

Ina: she's going up to the men, she's talking to them, and now here's Max, leading Lisbeth. So it's Lisbeth who's being taken away: she probably can't move any longer without being supported. She's got no eyes for the men who take her in charge and steer her into the ambulance, no eyes for Magda, who is carrying a big suitcase. Magda in an overcoat. She gets in too. She'll tell me what has happened, she must tell me, she'll knock at my door sometime tonight, she's promised that.

Maybe after all I shouldn't go off to the coast and shipbuilders, but rather to a small town: there it should be easier to see what's what, so it shouldn't take long to settle down and, if Magda were to come too, we'd find something for ourselves before the day was out.

In a town together we'd soon find our way around. She could take me to the public gardens, where there must be work I can do, and, with all she's capable of, she'd very soon find something for herself, that's for sure – Magda, who grew up in a small town on the coast and knows exactly how to look after herself.

She doesn't like talking about her home town on the west coast; whenever I've asked her about her past life, she has never said more than she had to, but I was always content with the little she said, for I could see the old town clearly enough: the narrow-chested houses with here and there mallows growing in front, the cobbled streets, the lime-trees struggling to survive in the sea winds, the shipyard to which only fishing boats now came for repair. There she grew up in a humble grey house. Her father was a ship's carpenter, his boat went under during a trial run and he was drowned; her mother couldn't bring herself to accept his death and sat for hours at the window, passing many a winter that way, unbelieving, hoping, till one day she developed a fever and, after a short illness, died. Magda was left alone with her younger brother and sister, Jan and Clara, who were still at school.

To keep them from starvation she took a job with a chemist, whose wife had a goitre and also a fad – a fad about dust. All day long she'd be chasing after Magda, instructing her, watching her, scolding her, and each evening before going home Magda had to report to her. Magda was allowed to eat only what this woman gave her, and immediately her plate was empty she'd be told: Work doesn't like waiting. And she was never finished with it.

One day Magda saw the woman take the dustbag from the vacuum cleaner, open it slightly and deliberately shake some of its contents over an armchair and the leaves of a pot plant. Though she'd seen her, Magda said nothing, but then, when the chemist's wife made her usual inspection, when she started telling Magda her work wasn't worth the money she was getting for it, she came in for a very big surprise. Without a word Magda took up the dustbag and scattered all it contained over the pot plants, so they looked as if powdered with dirt, and then she pressed the dustbag into the woman's hands and left the house.

The smokehouse owner: she also worked at one time for a smokehouse owner who was a widower and lived alone in a roomy house covered in ivy. By this time her brother and sister had left school. The room in which she lived was filled with the sound of birds nesting in the ivy, she worked without supervision and was allowed to eat as much as she wanted. There were bottles standing all over the house, on cabinets, on cupboards, on windowsills, fine-looking bottles the smokehouse owner had drunk empty, and, so that he'd remember whom he'd drunk it with, each of the bottles bore a little label with just a name and a date on it. On the nights the smokehouse owner had drinking companions with him Magda felt easy and content; after spending a little time listening to their voices, she could go easily off to sleep, sleep without waking and then next morning write out the labels. But she was always apprehensive when no visitor came, when the smokehouse owner sat by himself, making speeches or moaning or venting his anger on the nearest things in reach. At such times Magda would lie awake, feeling the fear rising inside her as he began to roam around, up the stairs, down the stairs. Every time in the course of his wanderings he would come to her door. At first he'd keep quite still and just listen, but sometimes he'd turn the door handle to see if Magda had locked the door. She always had locked it, and she would pretend to be asleep, not answering when he softly called her name.

The moment he left home the following morning, she ran down to the harbour and out to the end of the mole, where she'd throw a bottle into the sea, a bottle with a message in it; she would just take one of the bottles standing on the cabinets and windowsills, remove the label and stuff a message inside. Magda didn't want to tell me what was written in the message, but I can well imagine she was hoping to get a reply from some far-off place. Though she spat three times after the bottle as it bobbed away, though she was certain her messages were being carried by wind and tide out to the open sea and westwards, never once did she receive an answer.

One night the smokehouse owner rattled Magda's door, having stolen up to it in stockinged feet: he didn't just turn the handle, but rattled the door and shouted and ordered her to open up. It wasn't much use then her pretending to be asleep, she had to answer him, and she begged him to go to bed, she also said she was feeling feverish, but that meant nothing to him, he was determined to get to her and wouldn't be sent packing. When he threw himself against the door, she gave him a warning, and when after a while he took a crowbar to it, she warned him again, but he took no notice, just went on levering and applying his weight.

I can easily picture Magda looking for a way of escape. I clearly see her feeling her way across the dark room and smashing one bottle after another on the floor, scraping the fragments of glass together and arranging them in front of her bed, a wreath of glass splinters; then jumping into bed and sitting there waiting for him.

The moment he came in he trod on a splinter. He yelped and hobbled out, then, after managing to get the splinter of glass out of his foot, slunk off downstairs without a word.

By breakfast time he had got his apology ready. He was already sitting at the table when Magda came down, and he beckoned her over and asked her to sit down beside him. But she just shook her head, put the house and cellar keys down on the table and left.

Magda: when I saw her for the first time I didn't know who she was, nor that she belonged to us, but she certainly took my attention, sitting at a corner table in the railway waiting-room with that girl and that young soldier. As we'd had only a vegetable soup and an egg, I needed to pay a quick visit to the waiting-room during the afternoon. It was very hot and close, and I straight away ordered two bottles of lemonade to drink with my rissoles. The heat was shimmering over the rails, the station was quite deserted, and I was surprised to see the three of them sitting there, the two girls and the soldier, since there was no train due for a long time. They looked to me more or less the same age, the three of them, but it didn't escape my notice that one of the girls was boss: Magda, in a white frock with blue stripes, Magda with a necklace and a bast basket covered with a cloth. The very way she sat there showed clearly enough what she called for in the way of respect, a respect the others willingly granted her. Her pensive air. Her earnest way of asking questions. Her terse words of encouragement and protest, the good-natured smile she sometimes gave the others as she listened.

When the pale woman behind the counter came over wanting them to order something, it was Magda who replied, and she it was too who handed out the plates that were put in front of them, who pulled the tureen closer and filled the plates with soup, the soldier getting the most; she also passed over to him the slice of bacon that had landed on her own plate. From her bast basket she took out two bread rolls: the soldier got a whole one, while she and the girl shared the other.

My rissoles were long eaten and my lemonade drunk, the time was long past when I'd planned to be on my way down to the Holle, but still I sat there: I don't know why, all I know is that something was holding me back and I couldn't make up my mind to go, maybe it was the pleasure I got just watching them.

Later on they ordered apple juice, two bottles and three glasses, and suddenly they drank up very quickly, jumped to their feet and ran out to the platform, where Magda slipped each of them a packet, both the same size. As the train drew in, it started to rain a bit, large lone drops that just splashed in the dust or trickled away. First Magda gave the girl a kiss, then the soldier, and pushed them up into their compartment, slapping each of them on the bottom with the palm of her hand as they mounted the steps. I've never seen anyone wave as those two waved when the train drew out: they hung out of the window, one on top of the other, the wind ruffled their hair, the rain, now falling harder, beat on their faces, but they didn't pull in their heads, they continued waving, fast to start with, then slower and slower, but they kept in time with each other until the train vanished behind the curve leading to Schleswig.

My windcheater: she came in under my windcheater, though her thin frock was already wet through. At first she didn't understand what I was saying, since the cloudburst was making such a noise, but in the end she lowered the basket with which she'd been trying to protect her head from the rain and allowed me to hold the waterproof jacket over the two of us. On the far side of the rails she first made sure that the path really led to our plantations, then kept close to me, just watching her footsteps and leaving it to me to lead the way past the dispatch shed and the new toolshed. Once, when my arm touched her shoulder, she flinched aside and walked a bit faster, and I took care it didn't happen again. She looked at me in amazement when I stopped in front of my door and fished out the key. She clearly had had no idea that I belonged here too, but, as I was unlocking the door, it must have dawned on her, for she said: Are you Bruno, maybe? Yes, I said, and I invited her to come in and wait for the cloudburst to pass. She accepted, hesitantly.

Water was streaming and dripping from her, and I'd dearly have liked to stand her in a washing bowl. I had to talk her into sitting down on the stool and, after she'd reluctantly done so, I offered her some of the things lying on the windowsill for my night hunger, but she didn't want anything. At the sight of my clock she smiled, noticing at once that it had only one hand, and she said: I suppose it runs by the moon. But the marble casing – she did admire that; she turned it over carefully in her hands, wiped over it, did a quick calculation in her head and then said: They'll soon be in Schleswig, and when I asked: Who? she said: My brother and sister, it was their first visit to Hollenhusen.

We sat for a while in silence, the heavy clouds moved off towards the Baltic, the sky cleared as quickly as it always does here, outside it was now just spitting. Then suddenly she wanted to know if I was happy here, and I told her how the chief had brought me here and how I'd been with him from the day he first began cultivating the old training ground. I told her too that I couldn't even imagine living anywhere else.

Whether she enjoyed being with us she couldn't yet say: when I asked her, she shrugged her shoulders and said: I'll see how it all goes.

I didn't talk to the chief about Magda. At that time we were only rarely alone together, since he often had visitors and was always having to go off to Kiel or Schleswig. In the stronghold there was a constant coming and going. There were people from Hollenhusen as well as strangers from little places nearby: the way we attracted them you'd think we were making some special offers, and when they left the chief would send many of them on their way with a handshake or a cheerful shout.

But we did meet when the loading-ramp was officially opened – the railway had built it especially for us, and it must have been the only ramp near and far. We were standing close together, and he pinched the back of my neck gently and said without looking at me: Remember, Bruno? To all points of the compass – and now we're there. What we're growing here is going to all points of the compass. I told you how it would be, and now it's happening. Before I could answer, he was obliged to join the uniformed railway inspector, with whom he inspected the flat crates and boxes in which the balled plants were packed, shrubs and parent stocks and ground coverers. I could only wonder at the eagerness some people were showing to exchange words with him, and how quick they were to agree with all he said, just as if they were dependent on him. Certainly some of that was due to the fact that all over Hollenhusen, on trees, fences and the walls of barns, posters had been stuck, and on these posters was a photo of the chief. Two photos in fact: on one of them he was looking serious, on the other he had thrust a spade deep into the soil in order to plant something, the sapling lying beside him.

They had put him up for election, they wanted him to become mayor of Hollenhusen, not all of them, but at any rate those who thought there might be something in it for themselves. As Max told us, they kept on at him until the chief at last agreed; and from then on he was away a lot, travelling around, and the lights in the stronghold burned later than usual. He could no longer look after the manuring of our pot plants; that job he entrusted to me, and I did it exactly as he did, gave each the kind it needed and as much as it needed. I talked to the plants, and in all I did I listened out for the sound of growing which the chief had heard hundreds of times and which I heard too one morning, a very, very faint rustling. He had often said to me: Funny, Bruno, you hear everything else so well, but the sound of growing, you don't seem to pick that up. Now for the first time I heard it and I was filled with joy.

Magda was not in the 'Deutsches Haus', and probably I shouldn't have been there either if Max hadn't taken me along with him, Max, who visited us only on public holidays and for special occasions. On our way back from the judgement lime, where he'd questioned me almost to death, he suddenly said: This evening, Bruno, you must be there, you'll see the chief in a new role, I shall certainly be going. Max also offered straight away to take me with him, and I waited for him at the railway crossing and then walked at his side into the 'Deutsches Haus', where the whole of Hollenhusen was gathered, together with many others from neighbouring villages, more men than women. The crush, the greetings, the cigar smoke and all that green cloth forcing its way into the large, dimly lit hall! They sat down at long tables, as far to the back as possible. We went at once to the front, where there were still a large number of empty seats, and Max gave his order to the waitress: a beer for him, a lemonade for me; he also ordered a pot of tea for Dorothea, who was coming on later. I couldn't count all the people there, for some of them kept moving about between the tables, whispering behind their hands; some might go outside, returning with others in tow, or they'd lean across to other tables, where they themselves would have something whispered in their ears. No attempt to count them came to anything.

Dorothea had only just sat down with us, hardly had time to catch her breath, when the chief was led into the hall by two men. It grew so quiet that you could hear their footsteps on the wooden floor. No waving, no big scenes of recognition: even when they passed close by our table we exchanged no signals. Nobody clapped. The men led the chief to a podium with a tub plant to either side, he was asked to sit down, and one of the men stepped up on the podium and greeted the audience in a humorous way. This was Tordsen, the grocer, well known to everyone in the hall, and he expressed his pleasure that hardly anyone was missing. He considered it unnecessary to introduce Konrad Zeller, he wanted just to remind them that this man – most times he said: this man – had come here immediately after the war with the huge flood of people from the east, a man who had done his duty and lost everything, but was not by any means prepared on that account to give up and to stand aside, but, as many here could witness, he had, though a stranger and without means, through persistence and experience, built up something that had found recognition everywhere, not just in Hollenhusen. We owe this man our thanks, Tordsen said, and he said too: We believe in this man, in him and in his party.

After him the chief mounted the podium, and now some people clapped, not loudly, not for long, but they clapped. When I went to join in, Dorothea stopped me with a look, and Max pulled my hands under the table. The chief was very earnest, his gaze wandered past us right into the dimly lit corners of the hall. Of all the things he said I did not understand a great deal, but I did gather that it had to do with Europe, with its working together in various fields, he spoke of sacrifices and changes and announced that these would have to be introduced and put into effect in Hollenhusen as well, particularly in the agricultural areas, particularly on the smaller farms down to the very smallest, and certainly a lot of people would be well advised to prepare themselves for sacrifices and changes. Max cradled his head, while Dorothea cast a searching look over the faces around us, all those hard, sceptical faces that could keep to themselves most of what they were thinking. They listened unmoved as the chief spoke first of the good north-south relationships in our country, then of the bad east-west ones; he suggested the building of a bypass, connecting with the road to Schleswig; and when talking of the redistribution of land, he suggested building a new school on the common, a school with the proper number of classrooms and a hall for gymnastics. The chief didn't read from notes: it came straight out of his head. Now and again he would close his eyes in order to collect his thoughts and, when he turned his head to one side, I could see the sweat pouring down his face. It was surely not excitement that made him grip the edges of the desk so firmly: he was quite calm, like someone who always believed what he said. He spoke calmly and confidently about drainage works and the amalgamation of the two old-fashioned dairies, was often prepared to repeat a sentence, and at the end he thanked everybody for their attention.

The discussion: I remember that after scanty applause drinks were brought in for the following general discussion. One man wanted the lights turned up in the hall – he called loudly for this to be done – but the dim lighting remained as it was, and so did the seating arrangements and the size of the audience: it was only the usual silence and placidity of the Hollenhuseners that changed. While the chief was speaking, there had not been a sound from them, no word of disapproval, no exclamation, no query, so that anyone who didn't know the people here might easily have thought the speaker had convinced them all, but the discussion showed that in Hollenhusen silence doesn't mean consent.

First of all they wanted to know how the chief would pay for the suggestions he'd made, and they weren't to be fobbed off with rough estimates and the prospect of financial support from the state, they insisted on exact figures for the school, the gymnasium and everything else. The chief told them what he knew, but he also admitted there were things he didn't know. The chief didn't get ruffled. Even when someone sitting in a dark corner asked about the 248th, he didn't get ruffled, but explained in a calm voice that the return of the soldiers would bring some advantages, no doubt about that, but on the other hand it would mean too many changes in our life here. That's all he said; the man in the corner and some of the others would probably have liked to go on questioning him, but they held back the insinuations and suspicions they had in mind to throw at him, and the chief had no wish to add anything on his own account: he always knew the right answer to give someone.

All the same, he was astonished when from the furthest window a man came forward, a thin old man who without haste walked stiffly past all the tables, stubborn, his head held high; at one point he stopped and seemed confused, as if he'd lost his way, but then he purposefully continued his path up to the podium, where he took his time before saying what he wanted, just fixing relentless eyes on the chief. He demanded additional information about Europe and the sacrifice he himself would have to make: he'd gathered there was no future for small farms, and he came from a small farm of less than twenty-five hectares; yet on this little bit of land his people had existed more than two hundred and fifty years, and what he wanted the chief to tell him: what was now to become of him and others like him? At that several people in the hall sprang to their feet. The old man had spoken for them, and he got his applause. I flinched when I heard their fists drumming on the tables, and Dorothea looked around in concern, seeking Max's eyes. The chief's voice hardly changed. It just sounded a bit sadder as he assured the old man that he could understand his feelings, the bitterness, the anger and despair. He said: I know what it is to lose everything, and he also said: We are always on the move, nowhere is it written that things must always remain as they are. These words did nothing to satisfy either the old man or those for whom he'd spoken unbidden, they demanded certainties, they had to know what they must be prepared to face, and the chief was at once ready to sit down with them to discuss it, later, in a smaller group.

We walked back to the stronghold together, I and Dorothea and Max. We were each of us occupied with our own thoughts. We trotted one after the other along the flint path, without the chief, who had stayed behind to explain remaining matters to the discontented and the curious. Once we had slipped through our thuya hedge we walked side by side, and Dorothea, who now and again shuddered as if hit by the cold, took us both by the arm and shook her head and murmured: Why is he doing this, why does anyone let himself in for such things? Max said quietly: There's nothing so laborious as trying to convince other people, and nothing so unprofitable. Why does he do it then? Dorothea asked, and Max: Someone must do it, if we are to get on. Max was in favour of what the chief was doing, he praised and defended him, he had even admired his speech, at least, he had not thought him capable of such a speech, all the same he believed it wouldn't be enough, despite all the chief's exertions, for he had made a mistake that no one can afford to make: frankness, disarming frankness. With that he's said goodbye to his chances, Max said, you'll see.

We didn't see. Max was wrong: just a little while longer and they elected the chief mayor of Hollenhusen, narrowly maybe, but elect him they did.

That's not Magda's head-scarf: it'll surely be that one-eyed woman who lives behind the abandoned brickworks. This time it's not haws she's pinching, but rhododendron cuttings – snick, in the sack, snick, in the sack, over and over again – all for that pilfered garden of hers that every stranger stops to admire. Once I gave her a real good shock: I crept up on her and startled her so much that she dropped her sack and froze. She stood there like a scarecrow, unable to move, but, while I was still wondering whether to take her to the chief, she turned round slowly and looked at me through her single eye, and I couldn't find much to say. You're stealing here, Bruno said, and that was all. I threw down the club I was holding in my hand and waited to make sure she went away. For lack of knowing what to do I entirely forgot to take her booty off her.

The way she's filling her sack, just as if she were doing piecework for us! She moves from one cutting to another, searching, bent low without keeping watch. What I'd most like to do is challenge her and then take her to the chief to decide on a punishment, but no, I'm not going outside now, I shan't show my face to anybody till evening. Jays fly up. A magpie flies up. Somebody is coming up the transport track, that's for sure: maybe he'll surprise her. The woman has still not noticed anything, she's pulling up the cuttings, shaking the soil from them and popping them into her sack regardless: now it would be too late for her to run off.

Joachim. Joachim by himself and without his dog, and he has still not caught sight of her. Joachim has eyes only for Mirko, who is on his tractor towing a seed-sowing drill. A signal: I must give her a signal. Joachim calls to Mirko and points towards the pine-trees. She doesn't throw herself down, but drags her sack across to the rainbutts, where she hides it, then calmly starts cleaning her shoes, while keeping an eye on Joachim, who is walking beside Mirko's tractor towards the toolshed.

They elected him mayor of Hollenhusen, though Max thought he hadn't a chance; it was the closest result they could remember here, but that didn't worry the chief, he accepted the office and was quite happy to be called Mister Mayor in the council offices. Even Dorothea would sometimes say: Come, Mayor, have another sausage. He always knew what work needed to be done on the plantations and, though he couldn't be with us as much as before, he let us know through Ewaldsen and Joachim what should be given priority. As we worked on the things he considered most urgent, I would try to picture what he'd be doing at that moment, and I'd see him on visits of inspection or hear him speaking to people from a black podium; now and then he'd be listening to requests from the Hollenhuseners.

At one time he opened a grand festival of riding at the ring, to which competitors came from all over the place, old men and young farmers, but schoolgirls as well. They came riding down to the Holle, where Lauritzen's meadow had been turned into a fairground with flags, race tracks, booths and stalls. There they lined up, and the chief climbed on top of a box and opened the contest of riding at the ring. He didn't speak for long, and I couldn't understand what he was saying, for I didn't want to get too close, but it must have been a merry opening speech, for there was laughter and he got a lot of applause. The riding gear, black and white. The lances with their pennons. The decorated horses with roses behind their ears. Whitewashed poles, on which the rings were already hanging. Rope barriers everywhere. The huge faded marquee: the biggest mushroom ever seen. Ina, who ran me to earth in the shelter of my wall, just took me by the hand and tried to drag me along: Come on, Bruno, come on, this happens only once a year. No, I said, from here you get a nice overall view. Down by the rope barriers I was not to be found, I watched from the wall, sat in front of the alder clump and, when the qualifying heats started, I went down as far as the wooden bridge, but I never went closer, never close enough to see the horses' eyes.

Doughnuts and roasted almonds, a few times Turkish delight – these I got Heiner Walendy's small brother to fetch for me: he had no money at all and was willing to run down to the foodstall for me, just for the share he got in return. I couldn't watch the contests all that long – when I'd had enough of the clatter and drumming of hooves and the snorting and neighing I went back to our plantations, to the hollow, in which all the sounds of the fair could be heard, but only faintly, and there I was when Ina cried out to me: Niels – if you keep your fingers crossed for him, he'll win, he'll be king, and I at once helped her in her wish and kept my fingers so firmly crossed for Niels that three days later he did in fact become king.

Of my own accord I'd never have gone into the marquee, but the chief, the mayor, wished it. He commanded: Today the family will stay together, and he himself led us to the table which had been reserved for us in the huge tent: he called it our strong point. And after we had sat down on the folding seats, he laid both hands on the shoulders of each of us in turn, just as if to make sure we remained stuck.

Most of the people were in riding gear, and several had their lances propped up against their table. On a platform a three-man band was unpacking their instruments. The tent flaps swung heavily to and fro, white clouds drifted across the sky, bulging like pigs' bladders, promising a strong wind. Whoever wanted something to eat or drink had to fetch it himself from a sales counter on wheels.

I could see it coming that I should be the one sent to fetch it all, and, while I was still trying to make sense of their orders, Niels came up to our table. He was already wearing the pin and breast regalia that marked him out as king and, when Ina congratulated him with a kiss, he asked quickly what he could bring us. We went together to the sales counter, I gave our orders while Niels looked on from the side and said admiringly: How you manage to remember it all, Bruno! I've already forgotten the half of it. And later at the table, after we'd disposed of the trays, he said once again: I'd have needed to make three trips at least, but Bruno, he remembers it all. He moved as close as he could to Ina and shared a seat with her. Their wobbly perch worried neither of them: now and again they would wave their arms and clutch hold of each other to stop themselves falling over.

How he had come to be king he could explain neither to the chief nor to Dorothea, who kept on asking him. The most credit he gave to Fabian, his old horse, whose gallop was the smoothest you can imagine; sitting on Fabian, he said, is like sitting in a rocking-chair and, if you allow for the movements, all you need do is hold the lance out and it will go through the ring by itself – any of his opponents could have won on Fabian.

The family didn't stay together all the time: people came up to our table from time to time to speak to the mayor; a few times, too, they took him away with them, and I then saw him sitting at other tables, raising his glass in a toast. When the band began to play, Niels and Ina left us too. Since Niels was king, the first dance was his – the king's waltz, as Dorothea said, but he didn't dance like a king, that's for sure. Maybe it was on account of his riding-boots that he couldn't keep time; he made little hops and was a shade behind the beat through the whole dance, and you could see his relief when it ended. How swiftly he took Ina off! Before even the clapping had ended he had vanished with her into the crowd at the marquee entrance. I'd never have thought Joachim could dance so well: he danced two or three times, but only with Dorothea, smiling steadily and keeping his eyes fixed on her throughout. If Dorothea hadn't got so short of breath, he'd surely have taken her on to the floor more often.

The procession: I can still see it advancing on us through the haze, the clouds of smoke – someone was being dragged along by his outstretched arms, he was struggling, bracing himself against the forces pulling him, tearing and jerking and trying to break free, not with all his strength, but trying all the same. I could see at once he was putting it on a bit, his resistance, for old Lauritzen could have freed himself if he'd really tried, so I suppose secretly he didn't object to Niels and Ina dragging him up to our table. I can imagine they'd been working on him for quite a while, and it was only when they saw him sitting there just like a spoiled child, surlily refusing even to glance over at our table, that they made their plan behind his back and on a given signal grabbed him and carted him off for their own amusement. They brought him to our table and held him tight, one on each side as if he were a prisoner, and he, who was rather bent, straightened himself up and sought the chief's eyes. The chief rose slowly to his feet, his eyes fixed too on the man confronting him. So there they stood, weighing each other up with a persistence that strained the patience of us all.

Old Lauritzen was the first to open his lips. His voice raised slightly in question, he said: Zeller? And the chief replied: Lauritzen? And then they stared at each other again, until Lauritzen could stand it no longer and growled: Mayor, eh? But not my mayor, not mine. Never mind, said the chief, a simple majority's enough for me, and, taking a firm grip on an empty chair at a neighbouring table, he placed it between himself and Dorothea and invited Lauritzen to sit down. He, after reflecting a while, made a dismissive gesture and then sat down. Instantly a filled glass was standing in front of him, instantly Dorothea and the chief were inviting him to clink glasses. But he wasn't willing yet, first he had to ask: The timber in Danes' Wood, that can still be used, can't it? To which the chief replied: It can be used, no better and no worse than all the stones we were made a present of during the night. After that they gave each other a nod and swallowed the stuff that smelled of aniseed.

The amount they could put away, and the things they could

say to each other without raising their voices! Both unloaded all they had pent up inside them, words flew to and fro across the table, one charge gave rise to another, neither man spared the other. Earlier, Hollenhusen was a pleasant place to live in. When was that – earlier? Before you came, the hordes from the east, it was quiet here, everyone knew what belonged to him, no one helped himself to property that wasn't his. In place of that, we've shown you how life can be lived and what can be done with this land no one wanted. All the same, we were content here. Yes, those of you who had it all, you were content. Back in your home all you learned was looking after yourselves and dancing mazurkas. Right, and you've made do just with the first. A cuckoo's nest – that's all we were to you. Cuckoos don't have nests, as far as I know. In any case, but for you Hollenhusen would have been a different place. Right, still as it was before Noah's ark.

So it went to and fro between them, but occasionally they would give a hidden smile, and in the pauses between they would raise their short-stemmed glasses to each other. Neither of them raised any objection when Niels put a new bottle in front of them as a greeting from the king of the ring-riders; old Lauritzen opened it himself with his knotty fingers and filled glasses without asking, among them Dorothea's, though she would drink only on condition that nobody asked her to dance. All this hopping around, old Lauritzen said, dancing's silly rubbish, and that was all. He raised his glass to us for the last time, rose to his feet in a series of jerks and got himself balanced, then felt his way along the table and walked off stiffly, but before doing that he leaned over the chief once more and whispered something in his ear. Joachim had at once to know what Lauritzen had whispered, and the chief said: Nothing new – he invited me to his house.

The marquee was emptying and under the table Dorothea had already got her feet back into her too tight shoes and told me to drink up my lemonade, when I saw him and recognised him. He was standing in the tent entrance, leaning casually up

243

against a pole, his narrow face raised as if in search of something: Guntram Glaser. I knew at once he was looking for us – yes, Ina, I knew it, and when he discovered us and came across, I was uneasy rather than surprised. I couldn't have said what caused my uneasiness, it just rose up inside me and made me point to him without a word. When the chief recognised him, he beckoned – here, over here – and Guntram Glaser waved back briefly and hastened his step and greeted us politely. It was for the following day he had been invited to the stronghold: he had arrived too early. Never would I have imagined he would one day be manager here, no, Ina, I'd not have imagined that.

What shall I say to him if he comes over? He's already looking in my direction, I suppose he caught sight of me from the terrace, and maybe he has decided to explain to me personally why he drew up and signed that deed of gift, that contract in my name. Don't be too quick to say yes or no: that was Magda's advice. I'll open the door to him at once and listen to him: he'll surely tell me everything, even if it's secret, even if it's just what he's thinking inside himself. As soon as he says: Now you must stop listening, Bruno, I know something is coming that is meant for my ears alone. He waits a few more moments, takes a few steps, looking past the plantations to the old pines beside the railway cutting. How wearily he's moving, how carefully! I suppose he's frightened of falling, as recently in the sand-pit when he was overcome by giddiness: he just fell down and was gone. I stayed with him till he was able to get up and to speak: Not a word, Bruno, do you hear? Not a word about this to anyone.

His gun, he's got his double-barrelled gun slung over his shoulder: maybe he doesn't intend coming here. He's crossing over to the steps now: he descends them carefully, casts a long look back over the stronghold, no, there's nobody to be seen in the windows. He *is* coming to me, to tell me exactly what's going on: now I can open up. I shan't tell him what I know, what is being said. Unless he asks me, I won't let on, for it could hurt him, and I don't want to say anything that will hurt him or make him feel sad, nothing at all.

No, he's not coming to me, he just walks by without even looking, unapproachable, turned in on himself. I'd better not call out to him. Walk along behind him, that's what I'll do: follow him secretly and, in some spot where no one can see us, just catch up with him and be there. The chief surely knows I've been invited to the stronghold this evening, and maybe he also knows what they want from me. If he's there it'll all be easier, since he'll answer for me whenever necessary. He'll also answer Murwitz, who has threatened me with a lot of trouble coming my way.

Lock up quickly and then to the tall-trunked plantations, where Bruno can't be seen by others, but can see everybody through a cage of tree trunks. The Hookman doesn't hide here. I used to think that the Hookman, who some nights bends our stems according to a plan known only to himself, took cover in the tall-trunked plantations, but the chief proved to me that he must come from further away, for during our patrols together we never found any trace of him.

It's because of you, Bruno, that's what Magda said, it's also because of you they've started these legal proceedings, since the deed of gift provides that after the chief's death the most valuable land will come to you, a third of everything together with an appropriate part of the installations: that they can't consent to, Magda said. If it's all true, the chief had his reasons for it, he has always had his reasons for everything he does.

Why doesn't he drink from the outside watercock in his usual way? Rarely does he pass the cock without turning it on, letting a little water drain off, then drinking from the spring he himself discovered and can't praise highly enough on account of its taste. This time he pays no attention to the watercock, but walks past with dragging steps and heads for the railway cutting. The leather strap on his gun seems to be slipping, and he hoists it once more back over his shoulder. It's a long time since I saw him walking through the plantations with a gun. I only wish I knew what he's after: the rabbits have gone, black-feathered birds he has at last decided to leave alone – maybe he just wants to try out the gun he hasn't used for so long.

Among these young tree-trunks it's impossible to fall over: they stand so close together that you'd simply stay stuck upright if your legs failed you or you were shot, the trunks hold everything up; topple over dead and you won't fall to the ground, you'll just be hung out to dry.

It may be he means the gift just as a way of thanking me. It's only very rarely the chief has had occasion to criticise me, no one has ever carried out his instructions more willingly, often he didn't even need to speak them to the end, I'd already grasped what he wanted and how it was to be done. Once he even told me: You seem to be able to read it all in my eyes, Bruno. Far above the rest as he is, I never needed to ask, I helped him and carried out all he asked of me – whether it was to sink the dead hound in the big pond, to throw the planks of the wooden bridge into the Holle or to drive cattle on to the wrong meadows, he could always depend on me. I didn't even ask questions when he told me to burn his stained jacket, and the baskets full of good things he sent to the Ewaldsens I delivered so stealthily that no one ever found out where they came from.

And he did more than just approve of my work on the young plantations; quite a few times he called our new workers together and told them: Watch how Bruno does it. That's the way you should pot on, stake, graft. It may well be the chief wants to thank me for everything; it's also possible he thinks: Bruno has learnt enough and, if he takes the land over, he'll do it all my way and nothing will change, not in the soil care and not in the planting schedules. Bruno will see to it that every- thing we've done here will remain recognisable for all time. Though he has never said anything to me about it, it's not impossible that's what he thinks.

He's going to the gravel-pit, to the place where we used to fetch sand for pre-sowing. Without once looking round, he sets off down the worn transport track, and it's clear he's paying no attention to the sounds around him. He, who has always become aware of things long before I did, is now not stopping at all, not testing and making sure in his usual way. He'll soon reach the thuya hedge. Though he would never put up with any of us forcing our way through the hedge, he now forces his way through it himself, dives out of sight – ah yes, I know: he'll now be stumbling down towards the pines, maybe there'll be a shot soon – but no, the rooks haven't come home yet.

There he is, sitting in the place we both sat many times back in the early years, when there was more to be done than now, yet still we found time to tell each other things and to await the rooks' homecoming. Often we were still sitting there in the dark, with just the railway lines gleaming down below us. I mustn't startle him. He has laid the gun on the ground. He is staring steadily in one direction, at the Kollerhof, which is still empty. His bent back. His hands in his lap. He didn't call out to me as I was tearing the needles from the spruces and sucking them. I must approach him slowly, as if I just happened to come along, and stop beside him, because he has never liked anyone standing behind him, speaking to him from behind.

Hullo, Bruno, what are you doing here? he asks. No look, hardly a movement: he has recognised me just by my shoes, out of the corner of his eyes. Come, sit down by me, he says, and taps the earth lightly, sit here. There's no tightness in his voice, he is speaking as he once used to. His face looks calm, with just a little hint of surprise. What has to be said he'll surely bring up of his own accord: never before has he forgotten the things that matter most.

Do you know what this is, Bruno, here in my hand? Berries, I say, and he: the mistletoe berry, the one they all chase after, birds, martens and even bats; they all like the mistletoe berry, for its flesh tastes better than anything else. He tips two of the berries into my hand. I feel like trying one of them, but before doing so I scratch it with a fingernail. How sticky it is! But never mind, it'll slide down all right. I've never eaten a mistletoe berry before.

248

Bruno, Bruno, the chief says, shaking his head, I hope it won't stick the walls of your stomach together, the seeds are used to make bird-lime, but we all know you've got a stomach like a thrush. He looks at me in a fond way, fond and curious, as if heaven knows what might happen to me, but the berry is still stuck in my throat. Funny, he says, the birds spread the stuff that's used to catch them: they wipe the remains of the sticky pulp off on twigs or they leave droppings on the branches, and thus sow the seeds for new mistletoe plants – the thrush above all. There's an old saying: The thrush cacks its own doom. The berry has gone down now, with the help of a lot of spit: it's done now. In thrushes, the chief says, it takes the seed only half an hour to pass through the body. It tastes sweetish, I say. Yes, Bruno, sweetish, but mistletoe plants are nasty parasites: if they get to your pear-trees, your walnut and pear-trees, then the host will be in great danger.

Again he gazes across the rails and the land lying between us and the Kollerhof. He said – your pear-trees, meaning my walnut-tree too. So it *is* true! Over there, Bruno, in the Kollerhof, we were quite happy on the whole, weren't we? I've no idea what to say, so I just nod and join him in gazing at the place where we were once quite happy, and he asks nothing more, he seems satisfied. Do you still remember his name, that old man with his snares and spring traps and that stuffed polecat? Yes, he was called Magnussen. That's it, Magnussen, and I believe he was happy there, because no one made demands on him and he made none on others.

Here come the first of the rooks, an advance guard flying in from the big rubbish dump. Now they've caught sight of us and are turning aside, croaking and turning aside; some of them have frayed wings, as if they have already been struck, hit by bullets or slugs; in a moment they'll be warning the main flock and guiding it round to the avenue of poplars. It's ravens, not rooks that are a bad sign, but there's only a few of those around now, and none has yet strayed this way. I clearly feel he wants to say something: maybe he's searching for an opening. But now something has come into his mind: he sits up, taps and fingers the outside pocket of his jacket, feels inside the little waistcoat pocket and finds it. He brings it out inside a clenched fist and reaches for my hand: Give me your hand, Bruno. It is warm and round and heavy. Acorns, two silver acorns hanging on a silver chain, they are solid and make a clicking noise when they touch. How pretty they are! say I. The little plate between them is inscribed 'From Ina on the twelfth of the twelfth', the number on the reverse side is too small for me to read. Keep it, he says, put it in your pocket, so you'll have something to remember me by. But there's something written here, I say, an inscription. I know, Bruno, and so you'll just have a bit more to remind you. Those are indeed the prettiest acorns you'll find anywhere.

Max's voice, right behind us: he must surely have been watching us for a while, lurking behind the thuya hedge and listening. So here you are, he says loudly. Maybe he was even following me while I was following the chief, he comes up close and again says: So here you are. He won't sit down, the way he's standing there he just wants to announce something, his quick appraising look is all-knowing, a look of mistrust that his smile does nothing to soften. The acorns in my hand grow warmer, the silver acorns, they are beginning to burn. I should dearly like to give them back to the chief, but how can I do that, since he hasn't stood up? He has turned away and is gazing over the rails towards Hollenhusen station. As far as he's concerned, Max isn't even there, not once has the chief looked in his direction. The train will soon be leaving. Murwitz is here, Max says.

The chief seems not to have understood him; without stirring he is staring across at the train, where some people are running about and dragging things and the man with the signalling disc has already slammed a few doors shut. Murwitz is waiting for you, says Max. He stoops down, goes to pick up the gun, the chief notices it at once and puts a hand on the barrel. Nothing escapes him: he even knows what goes on behind his back. The train moves off, passes the lowered barrier, behind which a few cyclists and Heiner Walendy's stepfather's delivery van are waiting, people at some of the train windows are waving back towards the station. They've often waved to me here too, though they didn't know me. I shouldn't like to sit in the last carriage, it is rocking as if it's about to jump off the rails. Doctor Murwitz wants another word with you, Max says, talking to the chief's back, not in a pleading or embarrassed way, but coolly and insistently. The chief quietly turns round and lifts his head and gives Max a single look of surprise, his lips twist, his shoulders heave, and now he is pushing himself upright, ignoring the hand stretched out to help. Remember the mistletoe berry, Bruno: the thrush cacks its own doom. He says nothing more, but walks to the thuya hedge, his gun on his shoulder, not bothering about how far Max is behind him – Max, who says to me just: Till later.

The acorns must be got rid of. I can't carry them around with me: with these silver acorns I'd just attract attention. Over there in the sand-pit I've already buried the cartridge cases and the grenade splinters, beneath the trailing pine-roots. But first they must be further off, the chief and Max: I must redouble my guard, for who knows whether someone in the stronghold isn't keeping an eye on everything I do? Maybe they've even appointed someone to trail me; he could be lying behind the hedge, behind the pines.

How many shades of colour there are in sand! Here brown like rust, there bleached by the sun, and where the sun shines the sand is lighter and finer. In earlier times I used to amuse myself now and again burying ants and beetles beneath little sandhills, and every time they came crawling out. No spade: I shall have to dig with my hands as I've often done. I'll put the acorns in one of the cans, among the splinters and the cartridge cases – the cans must be here under the trailing roots, I made an exact note of it. They surely can't be buried any deeper – when will they show up at last, those two cans? With all that weight inside them they couldn't have wandered off by themselves, and in all these years we have never fetched sand from this side of the pit. Somebody has dug them up and carried them off, but who? They can't have dissolved of their own accord: somebody must always be behind me, even after dark, probably he starts trailing me the minute I go outside and accompanies me everywhere, so as to find out all about me and gather proofs.

That's it: they're out to gather proofs against me! Keep calm, Bruno. I must fill the hole up again, not hastily, but as if I'd just been doing a bit of digging here for fun: if I take a twig and brush it over the sand, whip some up, it'll hardly be possible to see where I've been digging. The acorns I shall have to hide at home: the best place will be inside the clock. There's room in the marble casing for the silver acorns: I can't risk burying anything more in the earth.

I must get moving, mustn't stand around. I must walk more slowly. No one can stop me walking in the middle of the track, nor can they stop me drinking a little water, as the chief has done; there's no better water than ours anywhere. Not even Joachim can say anything, for it's now after working hours, and I have a right to wander around here and to do what I consider necessary. But Joachim is anyway the last person I'd expect to meet: they surely can't do without him in the stronghold, where they're now all sitting facing the chief. From now on I'll have my bill-hook on me. I'll carry it wherever I go.

Nobody has been tampering with my lock. Everything is in its proper place, and the pillow is also untouched. The acorns will be safe in the clock, safer than under the mattress, a hiding-place from which quite a few things have already gone missing: the diary Dorothea gave me, the ointment pot I bought off the gypsy woman – when I went one day to get them out, they'd disappeared.

Iron: how long the taste of it remains in your mouth! The water from our outdoor system tastes of iron, and that is good, the chief has always said.

The water from the well dug according to his instructions has always tasted of iron, but the iron content was still greater in the water Guntram Glaser got them to pump up for his irrigation plant during our hottest summer here, when everything was withering and turning yellow as never before. Hardly a soul would ever have thought there were such rich streams of water under the old training ground: it was only Guntram Glaser who suspected it. He hadn't been with us long, but he soon smelled it, unlike Joachim, who simply didn't want to believe it and several times advised the chief to put an end to the test borings and to give up the idea of an irrigation plant altogether. Though Guntram Glaser had not yet been made manager, he was allowed to live in the stronghold, in a couple of rooms not in use, and at weekends he was even admitted to the family table, and we all enjoyed listening to him when he talked about the plantations in Elmshorn where he had worked, and of his eccentric uncle there, of whom all kinds of stories were told. Joachim had often listened to Guntram Glaser's tales, which he scoffed at often enough, but Guntram Glaser had always succeeded in having the last word, at the same time showing he was more than a match for Joachim. Whenever I was invited to the family table I always looked forward to Guntram Glaser and the stories he would tell; the fact that sometimes Joachim would then get up very soon and leave the table worried nobody except Dorothea.

Once the chief had installed him in his new job Guntram Glaser preferred being alone in the plantations. Now and again he would send away the man who had been detailed to assist him, and, when I offered to walk around with him a bit and tell him how it had all been at the start, he just smiled and said: I was here before you even began, Bruno; I've known this land longer than you. His khaki trousers, his dark shirts. He was so thin and his hands so little hardened that you'd hardly have thought him capable of work on the land, but the heaviest wheelbarrow cost him no more trouble than Ewaldsen or me. His short fair hair that stayed smooth even in the wind. His handsome wrist-watch, his narrow eyes that never wavered, and the assured way he could answer any question. And he never sweated: even in that hot summer, when even just to stoop down would leave the rest of us bathed in sweat, his face and his thin body stayed dry, and he never peeled off his clothes as we did, but sat on a box in his khaki trousers and dark sports shirt and smoked and, still smoking, watched us dashing half-naked through the jets of spray from his irrigation plant. Sitting, walking, working, he never stopped smoking, and he frequently spoke with a cigarette dangling from his lips.

During one lunch interval, when we were freshening up in the revolving jet, the chief and Joachim came by. They stopped and watched us pushing each other into the spray, and after a while Joachim asked when the shower cubicles were to be built. Guntram Glaser said: It's our own water, at which Joachim said: Handy anyway for freshening up, and was about to say more, but the chief made a sign with his hand for him to be quiet. He nodded to Guntram Glaser and said: I've been analysing the contents. For the fertilisers we must take into account the amount of potassium and sulphates in the water and adjust as necessary. I've already made out the plans, Guntram Glaser said, and he also said: The chemical weedkillers should also be more effective now. The chief laid a hand briefly on his shoulder and went off satisfied, but Joachim couldn't bring himself to speak a parting word: he just walked off with averted face. It was clear he found the respect the chief had for Guntram Glaser hard to stomach. We too soon noticed there wasn't very much you could tell him: he did a lot of things differently, but what he introduced was good, and we could learn a great deal from him, that we really could.

One day during that hot summer I caught sight of him at the edge of the damp ground. I got up from the shade of the wall and went over to him, and I saw that he was prodding around, examining the glistening, oily puddles. He would push a stick into the bog, turn it a few times and watch as dirty water rose close to the stick and soon filled a hollow, a hollow left by a hoofprint. The sun baked the churned-up mud, which formed a crust, then crumbled. It smelled rotten; horse-flies and other flies with green and gold armoured bodies swarmed above the piece of marshy land the chief had still not dried out, though old Lauritzen was no longer making any claims on it.

When Guntram Glaser recognised my shadow, he raised his head and smiled and said: I don't know, Bruno, whether we should drain it, I just don't know. He quickly drew me away from the damp ground, I realised he didn't want to stand there with me. We walked to the erratic block, where nervily he lit a cigarette and breathed out the smoke with a long hissing sound. He crushed the empty packet in his hand and buried it. I asked him if I should fetch him some more cigarettes from Hollenhusen, at which he said: That'll be difficult, it's Sunday today, but I said: I know where I can always get them, and took the money from him and ran off to the waiting-room at the station, and I was back much sooner than he expected. You're a friend in need, Bruno, he said as I gave him the cigarettes. He then smoked two or three more. We stood leaning against the erratic block, gazing over the rows of drooping plants. The initial feeling of uneasiness that seemed to rise unbidden inside me whenever I met him was no longer gripping me, and so I asked him whether it had been pleasant, the time he spent on this land as a soldier, and he had to think a while before saying: The further back a thing lies, Bruno, the firmer it sticks. He only needed to close his eyes, he went on, and the plantations were swept away and the dummy houses were there again, the practice tank and the dwarf pines, from which almost every attack was launched, and, never mind how still the air, after a little while he would hear the barked commands, the battle cries and the rattle of gunfire, whether he wanted to or not. The training ground – he just couldn't get it out of his mind.

And then Ina called out to us from the wall, and we went over to her and found her in cheerful mood, covered in sweat and with a few insect bites on her face and legs. Ina had a small trowel in her hand, and in her plaited raffia basket were grasses, rushes and weeds, either plucked or dug up complete with roots and a bit of earth. And she got us to identify what she had gathered beside the big pond, in Danes' Wood, in the meadows and on the banks of the Holle, sitting all the while in front of us with just a thin blouse on and very short trousers smeared thick with mud from the many times she'd wiped her hands on them. I could identify almost as much as Guntram Glaser: camomile and crowfoot and frogbit, cotton-grass and sow-thistle and couch-grass and charlock; frenchweed and dandelion were also there. Ina intended to draw them all, and together the drawings would make up a tribute to weeds.

Ina tried to prove to us how beautiful weeds are, and she praised the spiky, the lobed and the feathery leaves and the various panicles and umbels. Guntram Glaser listened with a smile on his face, and then he said: No one enjoys hearing his enemies praised. And Ina predicted we'd soon change our minds when we saw her coloured drawings, for there everything would be turned into faces, and each weed face would speak for itself. And Guntram Glaser said that in plant communities, as elsewhere, there were unfortunately rogues that held back the growth of others and limited the yield and the quality, and so there was no other way but to keep those that threatened others under strict control. They argued a bit about it, but they enjoyed arguing, and I could have listened to them for hours on end.

Then Guntram Glaser said what he least cared for was meadow foxtail, and Ina at once looked to see whether there was any in her basket. There wasn't: meadow foxtail was missing from her collection, and that worried her so much that she thought of going to look for it. Guntram Glaser said it wouldn't be easy to find this otherwise common weed, for fortunately it had proved possible to keep it down. At that Ina gave me a questioning look – Ina, for whom meadow foxtail seemed suddenly to mean more than anything else in all the world. I saw what she was thinking and said of my own accord: Then I'll get going, I know where I can find it. And Ina thanked me and promised to make it up to me. She said: I'll think of something nice for you, Bruno, and winked at me.

Oh, Ina, first of all I went to the damp ground, where swallows were skimming the puddles and drawing patterns in the air. When I turned to look at you, Guntram Glaser was just helping you down from the stacked wall; he had already grabbed hold of the basket, ready to carry it for you.

There were times Ina forgot having promised me something – to this day I am still waiting for the handbook on trees, also for the secondhand ludo set I was to get for my errands to Niels Lauritzen – but she didn't forget having promised me something for the meadow foxtail. I was cleaning shoes, had just finished cleaning all our shoes when Ina brought me her soft leather boots and asked me if I'd ever been to a cinema. I said no, and at that she asked if I'd like to go with her to the 'Deutsches Haus', where for the first time in a long while a film was being shown. I said yes, and that meant I was invited. Good, Bruno, then we'll sit together.

And we did sit together, I on Ina's right side and Guntram Glaser on her left. There were no tables in the big hall now, just rows of seats, and at the front, where the podium had stood, there hung a screen of stretched canvas. Guntram Glaser had a bag of roasted almonds with him, and he held it out to us, saying he'd already seen the film once, but it was well worth seeing a second time; beyond the title he wouldn't give anything away. The film was called 'On the River'. Guntram Glaser could hardly believe I'd never been in a cinema before, he shook his head and said: Then it's high time, Bruno.

The river, the rain over the river that never stopped, the water surging past the posts of the crooked wooden landing stage, the clumsy tarred boat moored to it and swaying this way and that, the faded tarpaulin that suddenly sprang to life: a man crawled out (he must have been sleeping under the tarpaulin), his round unshaven face rose above the gunwale, his eyes searched the riverbank mistrustfully, and he ducked down when between the wooden houses he caught sight of a policeman pushing his bicycle in a leisurely way towards a birch copse.

The water was rising, it tugged at overhanging grasses and branches, it splashed over the wooden landing stage, planks and bottles and uprooted trees came drifting by in the middle of the river on their way to the delta. People in the wooden houses stood at the windows watching the water rise: that's to say, the children and the young people did that, while the old people rummaged around, packed things together and dragged all sorts of stuff up to the loft; they carried up beds and crockery and wall clocks and, when they stopped for a rest, they raised their heads to listen to a distant far-off muttering in the air and a dark rushing sound; they exchanged glances, as if confirming something to each other.

Before the policeman reached the birch copse he met up with another policeman, they pushed their bicycles along together and compared notes, each had his own suspicions, but in the end they decided to search the river bank once again, the sheds into which the water was already licking, the moored boats. They left their bicycles by the houses and walked down the flooded towpath. The flimsier boxes were already afloat and the water was stirring washtubs and worn-out nets from beneath. The policemen waded round them, peering into the gloomy sheds, they inspected everything, closely watched by the man they were looking for, the round-faced man in the tarred boat. Before the policemen reached his level, he crept back under the tarpaulin and lay doggo, but he didn't realise that one shoe and a bit of his convict's jacket were showing under it, and by those they recognised him. Without a word they took their rifles off their shoulders, called out to him and ordered him ashore.

He didn't obey, just stayed where he was, pretending to be dead. The policemen exchanged a few quiet words, then one of them edged carefully along the slippery landing stage, which was already under water, grabbed the rope and tried to pull the boat alongside against the strong current. Whether he slipped, or whether the man in the boat gave him a push was impossible to make out, so quickly did it happen, but at any rate the man in uniform fell into the water, and the convict, who had suddenly thrown off the tarpaulin, severed the rope with a single cut and drifted off and away. The few shots fired after him came too late and just raised harmless splashes.

The water rose and rose, the entire land was submerged, a grey wilderness out of which treetops jutted and a few dismal farmhouses, and the clumsy boat drifted across this wilderness, the man sometimes punting, sometimes rowing, now and then he got entangled in spinning branches, but always he managed to free himself. At one point he pushed himself clear of a drowned cow, at another he got stuck, probably on a wire fence, and he jumped into the water to help the boat over the obstacle. He was happy to have made his escape, but happier still when he could steer alongside deserted farms, half submerged, tie his boat to a window-frame or skylight and swing himself inside the house, where there were all kinds of things to pick out and carry off, cutlery and tools and shoes. In the dark suit he had taken from a cupboard in a loft somewhere he looked exactly as if he was off to a wedding.

When someone waved to him from a skylight he stopped rowing, hesitated, not knowing quite what to do, but after a while he came to a decision and laboriously rowed over to an old wooden house which had a dwarf pine growing on its mossy roof. A boy was standing in the open skylight, up to his ankles in water; skilfully he caught the line the man threw him, wound it round a roughly trimmed beam and pulled the boat in so close that the man could get out. Their steps in the dark. The noises. The stabbing beam of a flash-lamp, which wandered swiftly across a pile of things and came to rest on the boy's face.

With a sudden shock I saw it was no strange boy standing there in the attic: it was I myself. I felt the cold draught, felt the water round my feet, and it was not just *my* hand shielding my eyes from the blinding light, it was also *my* voice that asked the man to shine the light on the stairs. There a body was floating, floating face downwards, rocked gently by the still rising water: my grandfather. I said to the man: That's my grandfather, and he bent down and turned the body over, quickly drew a watch out of the waistcoat pocket, dragged the corpse over to the skylight and pushed it out into the grey wilderness. Then he wanted to know where he'd find the valuables we'd wished to see rescued and, when I shrugged my shoulders, the man said: Come on now, find your tongue or the river will get it all – this time it means business, you can take my word for that.

I led him over to the pile of things, but it wasn't blankets, furniture, crockery or carpets he meant, but coins and cutlery and jewellery, and so I showed him the casket and helped him to break it open, and he tested each piece in the light of the flash-lamp and set aside whatever he thought valuable. He carried it all to the boat himself. He wanted to get it to a safe place, he would fetch me later. That's what he said. And went to the skylight. And grabbed the rope to loosen the knot.

I watched myself as I walked along behind the man. I too seized the rope and then quietly asked to be taken along at once, at which the man nodded and winked at me, then suddenly hit me so hard that I fell down. He got into the boat and was just about to push off with the pole when I got to my feet, shook myself, measured the distance he'd already gained, gathered up my strength and jumped through the skylight, jumped and reached the gunwale, to which I clung with both hands, up to my chest in water. The boat rocked. If the man hadn't used the pole to counter the effects of the violent rocking, he'd surely have capsized. Then he knelt down. Then he hit my fingers. Then he pushed my head under water. I snorted, clung tight and paddled with my legs, I was unwilling to let go, to sink, a voice that was neither mine nor his was calling to me in desperation, someone prised my fingers apart, bit them, a few slaps right and left on my cheeks, then two searing blows, I was pulled upright, dragged away, not knowing where I was.

The tree: I was sitting on the ground with my back against a tree, and beside me Guntram Glaser was crouching, he was passing a hand over my hair in the way the chief often did and rubbing my shoulders. He said, as if from far away: So, Bruno, you've come to at last, and after a while he asked me whether I trusted myself to get home alone, and I said yes.

Next morning Ina waited till we were alone, then she came over to me and silently took my hand and examined my fingers. On one forefinger there were just a few reddish-blue marks to be seen, shallow dents, nothing more. She nodded in satisfaction and said: Pity, Bruno, you didn't see the film to the end, for it all turned out happily – nothing happened to the boy and the man rescued a woman and got the reward he deserved. Oh, Ina, we never again went to the cinema together.

I'd like to know what's going on in the stronghold. Maybe Elef has again been handing in a petition, maybe he's even brought an invitation. Elef, who on certain occasions needs the company of his people – wife and daughter and wife's sister: they pass by in procession.

Once, when Dorothea was at the dentist's, Elef also turned up there, he had a swollen cheek. Six of his people were with him, and they waited patiently outside the surgery until they could take him home.

There's a light in the chief's room, and lights are also burning where the rest of them are sitting: from a distance the stronghold looks like a lighted ship gliding through the plantations. Now I can start slowly to get ready. Don't be too quick to say yes or no. Above all, listen. And don't stand like that with your shoulders bowed, Magda said. Ask questions, if you have to, and take care to remember every word of their replies, for, when Magda comes, she'll want to know it all. If only it was over already and I was now back here!

He's not there. All the others are gathered together, but the chief is not yet there. Ina and Max beside each other on the sofa, Joachim by himself on the upholstered stool, Dorothea leaning back in the winged arm-chair: they're all surely waiting for the chief. He's waiting too: Murwitz, who seems to have just finished reading something from the papers lying in front of him, beside the teacup. They've all got teacups in front of them, though clearly no one has yet taken anything from the biscuit bowl. Maybe I should quickly slip away and not come back till the chief, who has always spoken for me, is there, but Murwitz is already peering in my direction, Max is beckoning me in; I must keep quite calm and wipe my feet once again, carefully, so even Joachim will notice.

Here's Bruno, sit down beside me, Bruno, would you like a cup of tea? Yes, please, I say. The skin on your face, Ina, how stretched it looks! I can see you've been crying, that you didn't get much sleep, you're feeling your temples for the second time already. No fingers could be more delicate, more bony – much too delicate for the two soldered wedding-rings. The biscuits are here, Dorothea says with her old cordiality. She pushes the bowl towards me, then at once leans back again. Why is Max nodding at me like that? Why is he winking? There's been no secret arrangement between us, he has no call to soothe me down. Maybe there's something noticeable about me? I haven't even touched my cup yet: maybe he wants me to take a drink first. That big oil painting behind him – a half-rigged sailing boat, with a lighthouse casting a dim beam on the entrance to a harbour – twice before it has fallen down: boom, and there it lay on the floor, without anyone having touched it, and each time guests had been present.

I must pay attention, must be on my guard. Dorothea, with a single look, has invited Murwitz to begin and he has understood her. He looks at each of us in turn, as if about to count us, he lowers his head, soon he'll begin talking in his husky voice, and he'll point out that there's still one person missing.

Well, then, all of us are aware of the distressing motive for this meeting, he says. He doesn't say the chief is still absent and we ought to wait a while longer – that he doesn't say, which means they've arranged to settle things without him. I suppose they don't need him, since what they have in mind will anyway be done over his head. Herr Messmer has already been apprised by me of the existence of this deed of gift, Murwitz goes on. He has also been informed that the deed will take effect on the death of Herr Konrad Zeller.

Why are they all staring at me? I haven't seen the deed, I wasn't there when the chief signed it in Schleswig, why do they eye me as if it's all my fault, what do they want from me? In so far as it concerns him, Herr Messmer has been initiated into the clauses contained in the deed, Murwitz adds, and he looks down at his papers.

Dorothea: she has always been good to me, always taken my side; I must keep close to her, she knows almost as much about me as the chief himself. With what concern she is looking at me now, how sadly she smiles! All of us, Bruno, she says, we are all of us concerned about the chief, he has changed a great deal recently, he has given us a lot of problems to face. Perhaps you have also noticed it, certainly you must have done, for with no one does he spend more time, enjoys spending his time, than with you. It must surely have become clear to you that he is no longer the person he was. Do you understand, Bruno, what I'm trying to say?

I just nod, and she is satisfied with that. If I only knew what they're getting at! They must have some plan, and, if I disappoint them, they'll send me away, that's for sure. Joachim, no doubt, would like to do that straight away, he can hardly contain his impatience. At times he fidgets with his foot, and now he's looking me straight in the eye. He softens his expression, the fidgetting stops and he says: You must understand, Bruno, there are times one has to do something with a heavy heart, it becomes necessary to do it in order to prevent something worse happening, and we are all of us convinced it has to be done now. The chief needs our help: he is no longer the person we knew of old. We believe some illness has changed him, an illness, you understand, that sometimes prevents him realising what he is doing. And, in order to help the chief, we must know everything, you must tell us what you've noticed when you were alone together, and you're bound to have noticed something or other, isn't that so? Yes, I say – and now I've said yes without thinking, I didn't mean to say it, but now it's done. Then tell us, Bruno, you'll be helping the chief.

What shall I say? That now and again he seemed shy? That he fell down and was out for a while? That a few times he tried to avoid me? His uncertainty. His lengthy brooding. His gifts, with which he properly put the wind up me. That in the middle of his work he would suddenly start talking to some invisible being, each time uttering brief warnings, abrupt commands. No, I say, I've never noticed any signs of illness in him. It's important that you try to remember, says another voice, says Murwitz, for it's a matter of averting a considerable danger.

Listen, says Joachim, we were both there, you and I, when the chief refused for the first time to go into Danes' Wood: he didn't dare enter it, and he sent us in and stayed outside. Why? Because of the trees: he couldn't look up at the crowns of the trees because he believed some of them might fall on him. I say: Trees do sometimes fall. Maybe he thought of that, maybe he was frightened he wouldn't be able to jump out of the way quickly enough. Have you ever seen a tree simply fall down, he asks, tumble over without warning, just like that? Knocked over, yes, sawn down, ploughed up, torn out, yes, but Bruno has never seen a tree fall without some cause, like a bolt from the blue, not in all these many years. It was something the chief was just imagining, Joachim says, or what do you think? I don't know what to say, they're all looking at me, it is pressing on my stomach, but now Dorothea is saying: Your tea, Bruno, it's getting cold. I can't – the cup rattles as soon as I go to pick it up – I can't drink.

And that box, Joachim says, what happened to the box with those ancient tools in it, you must know what I mean – those stone axes, those scrapers, those arrow heads – well, do you remember? We put them all in the box, the chief and I, at the time we were working the land. All those Stone Age tools were washed, labelled; after each find we would take a short rest and he would tell me how the people here lived in the beginning, in thick mist, among placid animals: he knew a story about every scraper, every axe, I could never have enough of it, but one day he said he'd take the box to Schleswig, to a museum. Later, he either forgot or changed his mind, anyway it remained in his possession and moved house with us. You took it out into the grounds, says Joachim, you were carrying the box one evening and the chief was walking behind you. Yes, I say, that's what the chief wanted. You see, Bruno? And now tell us what you did with the tools. Why does he want to know that, when he already knows the rest? When we were alone together in the plantations the chief walked ahead of me, his eyes on the ground, he had a short-handled spade in his hand, and with it he dug a hole and said: Here, and in another place he dug a second hole and said: Here, and I took from the box the first thing I touched and laid it in the opening, which he filled up at once. Buried them, I say, we buried the tools

265

separately, all the things we found in the first few years; that was what he wanted.

How do they come to know all this? It seems their eyes are everywhere, they're trailing me and the chief, nothing escapes them, I must be more cautious, for now once again they've been signalling to each other with their eyes. Maybe I should ask where the chief is, whether he's still coming; but I feel they wouldn't like that, and it's not my place to ask questions here.

If I've done my sums correctly, Bruno, you've been with us something like thirty years, maybe even more; after so long a time one knows where one belongs, one has struck roots, one feels a part of things and assumes a certain responsibility as a matter of course. It is Max speaking; he takes a short breath and goes on: You have no grounds for complaint, I think. We have shared with you what it has been in our power to share. Mother has done so, and the chief of course: you are quite simply one of us. But precisely because of that you too must recognise, as each of us does, that one has certain responsibilities, for instance – and not just to a single person, but to us all.

You mustn't bully Bruno so, Dorothea says. She gives me an encouraging smile and wants me to drink my tea. Very well, Max says, we're not expecting the impossible from him, all we are trying to do is to remind him that we all owe each other something: frankness, for instance. This is no time for secrets. The way he's looking at me, so severely, so expectantly! In earlier times, under the judgement lime, he'd often make me feel quite dizzy with all his questions. There's no reason you shouldn't tell us, Bruno: the presents the chief has given you in recent months, they've come as a very great surprise to you, haven't they? I mean those large, unusual presents: you must surely have been surprised by certain things the chief has slipped into your hand. The watch, that valuable watch, which would at once have drawn attention to me; but I gave it back, he put it in his pocket, confused, as if he'd made a mistake. I say: He once wanted to give me his watch, maybe so I should always be punctual, but I didn't accept it, no, I didn't. But the pendant, Bruno, the silver acorns, the chief's last gift – you did accept that?

They know everything, there's no point in trying to hide things. Ina's silver acorns – 'From Ina on the twelfth of the twelfth' – the perplexed expression on her face as she looks at me – one of her eyes is inflamed – Ina can't believe it. Yes, I say, the chief gave me the silver acorns, but not to keep, he said nothing about that. Shall I go and fetch them? Max shakes his head: Stay here, Bruno, we can settle that later. Regrettably, Max says, regrettably we have to assume that the chief has given you several other things, just slipped them in passing into your hand. No, no, certainly not, just the watch and the acorns, nothing else. Take your time, Bruno, think back, quite a lot depends on it. We must start from the assumption that the chief has given you other things as well, you and probably some of the others here. He gave with the best of intentions, let's put it like that for the moment, with the best of intentions. I was to take them as a reminder: the chief gave me the acorns and he said: So you'll have something to remember me by; that's all he said. Listen, Bruno, listen very carefully: when the chief gave you these valuable things, weren't you surprised? I meant to say nothing, but I say: The inscriptions – I couldn't keep the presents because there were inscriptions on them. You see, Max says, and therefore we must admit to ourselves that the chief has no feeling for the particular significance of his possessions – or would *you* give away something that has been inscribed to you personally? And now, I suppose, you'll understand what is of great concern to us and what we are unfortunately forced to acknowledge: because the chief himself is changed, his attitude towards things has also changed. He is no longer in control of his actions, he is insufficiently aware of his obligations, he hardly feels any responsibility for the things that belong to him.

Dorothea: how laboriously she rises to her feet, turns away, walks with short steps to the window! In the dark there's nothing to be seen. Maybe she's listening and waiting for him to come down, as I'm waiting for him. It's so hard to think with all this tightening and throbbing in my head: what I most feel like doing is knocking my head against the doorpost in the old way, just a few times, until it all quietens down, but I mustn't move. I have to see him.

It is open to you, says Murwitz, it is open to you to interpret the deed of gift in any way you think fit. Joachim: I hope it is now clear to you that the chief could not have appreciated what he set down there and signed, he had simply not realised what the consequences would be. Take your time, Bruno, and don't be too quick to say yes or no. However you have decided or are about to decide, says Murwitz, you will not be able to avoid assessing the deed of gift in relation to the personality change that has occurred in Herr Konrad Zeller. No one is suggesting that you initiated or encouraged this deed, but you must be fully aware that its coming into effect will not be allowed to pass unchallenged, for it bestows on you such far-reaching rights that there is a distinct possibility of the family property being put in peril.

The family property. In peril. Joachim is holding his hands out to me, his friendliness, his concern: You surely understand, Bruno, what this means. If the property is split, everything here will lose its value, the work of many years will have been for nothing; only by staying in one piece can the Hollenhusen plantations continue to exist, and that's what you want too, isn't it?

Why don't they fetch the chief? Why won't they let him say whatever there is to be said? He always has his reasons for what he does, and he would explain to them why he made out this deed.

Now let's be quite frank, Bruno – that's Max's voice – just between ourselves: you have helped the chief from the beginning, you have been in on everything, and what you've been given to do you have always carried out satisfactorily. But can you see yourself doing all that needs to be done here on your own? Deciding how the land is to be cultivated? Calculating, giving instructions, managing, planting, can you see yourself doing that? I don't know what to say, what they want me to say, I haven't yet thought about it, my one feeling is that each of them knows more than I do, I can feel that, and I've already noticed too how they are closing in on me. Well, Bruno? To stay where I am, I say, that's all I want, otherwise I want nothing, as long as we stay together, the chief and all the rest of us.

How swiftly Murwitz straightens up, how surprised his expression as he looks around! Obviously I've said something that pleases him. He is leafing through his papers, but he hasn't yet found what he wants. And now he's looking at me: If I have understood you rightly, Herr Messmer, the continuation of your activities here means more to you than anything else, which means that under certain conditions you would be prepared to give up all claim to the gift this deed bestows on you. If that is the situation, a disclaimer on your part would go a considerable way towards ensuring the continued existence of the Hollenhusen plantations. Is this how we may interpret your statement?

I've no longer any idea of what I said, my throat is swelling, I can feel it closing. I couldn't cry out now, cry out to the chief, but maybe he'll sense how badly I need him: he must speak for me now. We'll draw up a statement for you, says Joachim, a disclaimer, no one need know anything about it, all you have to do is sign it, and that will be that – everything will stay as it's always been. Think it over, says Max, and he also says: We shall of course compensate you for your withdrawal, you'll not be expected to sign it for nothing.

It's my sweat that's tasting so sour. Max seems to have noticed my face is all wet, for he's offering me something white, a paper handkerchief: Here, Bruno, take it. His eyes, the watchfulness at the back of his eyes, I understand, understand and hear ever more clearly what you're thinking, what your other voice is saying: Dimwit – that's what you called me – dimwit, when will you realise what you owe to us? Never in your life will you measure up to the task here, and you can

269

thank your lucky stars we're coming this far to meet you; so make up your mind and agree, otherwise we'll have to pull other strings. I don't want his handkerchief. What a rumpus! Provisional disclaimer, all you need do, it's enough, how long have you been like this, idiot, come on, answer our proposal, what are you dreaming of, do you want to be your own chief, we must stick together, Bruno, it's up to you whether things here stay as they are. Who is saying that? Which of them thinks that? I no longer recognise their voices, they're trying to force me into a corner, that's what they're doing. To him, that's what I must do, go to him – not rush out, just calmly get to my feet and behave as if I'll be returning directly, quite controlled, as if I just need to be excused for a moment, then up the stairs and along the corridor to his door. We're waiting, Bruno, says Max. Yes, yes, but first away from here – out.

It's just my arm that's trembling and jerking so, I must hold my breath, walk steadily. It won't occur to any of them that I'm going to him; you go to him only when you're called – I, at any rate; not once have I gone to him of my own accord. But I must now, must ask him for information and, knowing him, I'm sure he'll understand. Step by step, slowly, so my breathing can calm down, now no one can see me, how long this corridor is, but keep quiet, so my two pests don't open the door, there's light under their doors, mustn't knock too loud.

Is he sitting in the dark? That was his voice: Come in, he said. There he is, sitting beside the little lamp. Hullo, Bruno, is somebody after you? But first calm down. He is not surprised to see me, he isn't angry with me for interrupting his thoughts.

Pull yourself together, Bruno. What do you want? I shan't stay long, I say, they're waiting for me downstairs. Ah, he says, then I suppose you're all holding a council of war – or are you already dividing up the bearskin? Sit down, Bruno. No, no. Are you in trouble? he asks. He gets up and takes me by the sleeve. How shall I begin, the deed, the land, his rights being taken away, where begin? The effort it's costing him to stand, he sways a little, wanting to return to his chair: It's all right,

Bruno, it's all right. What is it then? The deed of gift? Yes, I say.

Why is he smiling? Why does he nod, as if to himself? Maybe he doesn't yet know what they want and what they've already started, maybe he doesn't know that. Look, Bruno, when one is as old as I am, one has to make arrangements, and it's best that matters still undecided should be settled in good time. Everyone has been taken care of, Bruno; the arrangements for you are on deposit in Schleswig, and what the deed contains will be revealed to you at the proper time, at the proper time. I don't want the land, I say, all I want is for things to be arranged so we can stay together. I see from the look he gives me he is not of my mind, he says: Just wait, don't talk so much with other people and don't listen to them, just wait and see.

Know: he must know what they've started in the courts, and he must know that they want to draw up a disclaimer for me, which I only need to sign. Don't listen so much to others, Bruno, the really important things you must do by yourself. Something has been started in the courts, I say. He is in no way surprised, he just raises his face a bit towards me, he has surely known for a long time what's being set up against him, what's to be taken from him, but there's no grieving, no anger, just this twitching of his lips. That's how it is, Bruno – the time comes when you find yourself alone, and there you stand with all your experience that's no longer of any use to you. They are not prepared to fall in with my arrangements, they refuse to acknowledge them: we shall see who wins in the end. I can still stand up for myself. I'm not what I was, Bruno, but I can still defend my corner. After all that's happened things can never again be as they once were, I suppose we're all of us a little to blame, and that's why there can be no return to the beginning. You must take each day as it comes, Bruno, and don't expect it will all be easy and go through without a struggle.

They want me to sign, I say, a disclaimer, they want me to

sign that. Don't, Bruno, for the time being you'll sign nothing; you'll concede or promise nothing to anybody, you'll go on working as usual, and beyond that do nothing at all. Do you understand what I'm saying? Yes, I won't sign, even if they send me packing. No one will send you packing, not as long as I'm in charge here, you needn't have any fear of that. And now come here, come closer, that's right, now give me your hand. I can depend on you, Bruno, can't I? Yes. We must stick together now. Yes. If I knock on your door, you'll open up to me? Always. Good, Bruno, I'll be coming shortly – it's a long time since I visited your place. And now you'd better go.

He will come to me, will stand by me and smooth things over and, if I follow his instructions, nothing can happen to me. Why doesn't he watch me as I go? He has already turned away, no wave of the hand, he is staring down at the empty table top and mumbling softly, his shoulders sagging lower and lower, and now he sweeps his arm across the table and sighs and moans; as far as he's concerned, I've already left the room. Careful, now, I mustn't startle him, the heavy door closes quite easily. So yes, the northern part of the land from the hollow to Lauritzen's meadow, set down in writing and signed, so yes, it's true what they told me.

That was Max: I recognised him clearly, his head, his shoulders. He's been looking for me, that's for sure, maybe he has also been listening. He'll be waiting for me at the bottom of the stairs and will take me back to the others. No, I won't sign, I must stick to what I've promised.

So there you are, Bruno, we thought you weren't feeling well, come, drink your tea. How they eye me, weigh me up, just as if they suspect me of something! Only Dorothea looks concerned, she pushes the biscuits towards me and takes a sugared star herself to encourage me. They're your favourite biscuits, Bruno. The crackling and crunching – surely they must be hearing this noise in my head! I must take a sip of tea: it's all right, the trembling in my hand is almost gone, and the cup doesn't clatter as I set it down. I won't have to go away –

not that; as long as he's in charge here, I can stay. Some time you must take into account, says Joachim, some time you must get it into your head that business hasn't been exactly satisfactory over the past two years. There are various reasons for that, and you may even know what some of them are. Anyway, you must realise that things can't go on in the same old way. We must save on our living expenses. We must save on machinery. On labour costs we must also save. I hope you understand what I'm saying, Bruno. How serious his tone as he says that! His eyes stay fixed steadily on me, he's trying to caution me and get some answer from me, but I've got nothing to say to him.

Do you understand that all of us share the responsibility now? Yes, I say. Is it clear to you that you too must play your part? he asks. Yes, I say, and I don't mean to, but I say: The disclaimer, I can't sign that.

I see I shouldn't have said it. Joachim just shakes his head, as he always shakes his head over me, and clearly what he'd really like to do is get up and go. Max clicks his tongue and turns his eyes up to the ceiling. Only Murwitz gives no sign, just looks at me without stirring: I hope, Herr Messmer, you realise what you are bringing on yourself with this decision, he says, as slowly as if each word had to be taken down in writing, and Max at once adds: All right, Bruno, we know now whose side you're on, but don't be surprised if some things begin to change here, you yourself have not wished it otherwise. Please, says Dorothea, please, you mustn't bully Bruno so.

Stand up – now I suppose I can go. If only I were already outside or at home! Ina's lips are moving, but I don't catch what she's saying. Oh, Ina! I back towards the open sliding door: what a friendly nod Dorothea gives me! Bruno? Yes? Don't forget the presents, Max calls out, the acorns and the other things you'll find in your room, we'll be expecting them. Yes, I say, already beneath the chief's father looking guiltily out of his frame; his picture has never fallen down like the other one, he has to keep a watch on the apple bowl, the entrance.

I could help ensure the continued existence of the Hollenhusen plantations, that's what Murwitz said. Bruno needs only to sign the disclaimer, but the chief doesn't want me to, and he knows better than anybody how the continued existence is to be ensured. Never before has he extracted a promise from me in such a way, with so much solemnity and urgency, I can still feel the pressure of his hand, see his ice-blue eyes: he can depend on me, yes, that he can. Those are my own footsteps I'm hearing: I only need stop and all is still, no, there's no one walking behind me. He's put out the light: I suppose the chief sits in the dark so he can think things over in peace. There's smoke in the air; always, when a gentle breeze is coming off the land, there is a smell of smoke. We must stick together, the chief said, and he said he'd visit me.

Today I'd rather not put the light on. If I push the armchair over to the window I'll be able to keep an eye on the path along which Magda will come. When the slow clouds drift clear of the moon I can see the older plantations – my plantations, for according to his wish this part as far as the railway cutting is to belong to me, everything the moon is now lighting up. Can you see yourself cultivating the land? That's what Max asked, Max, who has surely learnt from me myself that I'm not allowed to use machines and technical instruments, and that I'm not there when planting schedules are drawn up. Why did he ask me that in front of the others? I am always surest of myself when the chief is near; if I work together with him or under his supervision, I succeed in more things than otherwise

Once – I suppose because the chief wanted to find out how much I had learnt from him – we made a tour together through the fruit bushes, a Sunday tour of inspection. I didn't have much to say, but it was simply a pleasure to walk beside him and to listen to him. We examined the shoot tips, the pliancy of the branches and the lateral buds and, without my suspecting anything, he asked me what it meant when branches showed swellings, furrows or twists, and I said it was probably a canker; he just looked at me in surprise. Then he asked me what early autumn colouring and premature growth of lateral buds meant, and I knew at once it was due to leafy gall and told him so. This didn't go so far as to astound him, but when I proved to him that I knew all about illnesses such as rubbery wood and stony pit that causes dents and bumps, especially on pears, then he was truly astounded, and he said: The day will come, Bruno, when you'll have nothing more to learn here. And that evening at supper he said once again: Soon nobody here will be able to pull the wool over Bruno's eyes, he knows his way even around the virus diseases.

Ewaldsen: maybe he would help me cultivate the land; Elef and his people would do it too, and there are surely others in Hollenhusen who would be prepared to work to my instructions. But I don't know who could do all the office work, and it's in the office, after all, that the value of the plantations is reckoned. The chief didn't need a stocktaker even: during the growing season he would just estimate the number of plants that would be good for selling, and his estimates, always correct, were filed in the office. Later, by comparing one with another, he could always see at a glance which plants had been raised on which piece of land, and where there was a danger of soil exhaustion. Often enough he decided inside the office what needed to be done outside.

Ill: why do they just tell me he's ill and sometimes doesn't know what he's doing? Dorothea once complained to Ina that the chief was taking less and less care of himself, Magda clearly heard that, and Magda herself also confirmed that the chief's things had never until recent times been so dirty, his shirts as well as the crockery in his room, and one morning even his bedlinen. But Magda has never said the chief is ill – at most it's just old age, she said. Feebleminded – whoever could have come on that idea? I'll do everything exactly as he wants: listen and wait and sign nothing, nothing at all.

There's this car again. How slowly it moves up the main drive, how the beam from the headlights sweeps over the plantations, brushes across the stronghold and comes to rest on the chief's rose-beds. It may be Magda coming home. Yes, it's Magda, and she's alone, so she must have left Lisbeth in the hospital. She walks quickly through the beam, casting a long shadow across the terrace. She'll surely be wanting to tell the others about it before she comes across to me. If it's in any way possible, she'll bring me something to eat, but I shan't be unhappy if she comes to my door without a parcel, without her basket.

We won't pull the blinds down. We'll sit in the moonlight. First she'll tell me about Lisbeth, then I'll tell her about the chief and everything else. And when all has been told, we'll go to bed. No need to bet who'll be asleep first, for she's always the first to drop off. She has to take off her necklace of wooden beads before sleeping. Knock: today she won't need to knock seven times, I'll wait till she comes out from behind the rhododendrons and, as she raises her hand to make the first knock, I'll open the door very fast and pull her inside.

No, no Ewaldsen, I didn't oversleep, it's just that I had an interview with the chief, and there was also something to be cleared up with the others. Then I had to deliver something to the stronghold, and that all took time, had to be thought about. But it's all done now: I'm coming. The shady house: let's go to the shady house and give the nets another tightening. You want to know how the chief is getting on? How should he be? He's always got his plans, and at his age there's a lot to attend to, but I think he'll be showing up again in the plantations soon. That's all right then. He knows something, that's for sure, and he has his own opinion: someone who looks away like that and smiles to himself has long ago made his mind up about the things he's heard, and everyone here has heard something, no doubt of that. You take the other side, Bruno, I'll stay here, Ewaldsen says, and starts by lighting up his battered pipe.

The chief had said often enough during our Sunday rounds of inspection that we could do with a shady house, but it wasn't until Guntram Glaser joined us that it was built. He saw at once that the young plants needing shade or half-shade must be protected against the harsh light, and he also knew the house would be a good place for wintering. Bruno and I will build the house, he said, and followed that up by handing me an axe and loading the little motor saw on his own shoulder. Not wasting further time on words, we went off to Danes' Wood, where we cut down eight trunks to act as pillars, and stakes as well for the sides. How well he could gauge where a tree would fall! He would walk round the trunk just once, pick out the best spot for it to lie, measure everything by eye, and then down the tree would crash – exactly where he wanted. As we were setting up the pillars Joachim came along, greeted us silently, then just stood watching without giving us a hand. But his advice: that he couldn't resist giving us, and after he'd done enough watching, he suggested the house should be covered over with trellis battens or simply with pine twigs. Guntram Glaser didn't accept his idea; he had long ago got hold of something much better: a disused camouflage net which he had bought from the soldiers in Schleswig. This was already lying in the toolshed, an earth-coloured net under which they'd once hidden cannons and tanks, big enough to cover the whole house and give the sensitive young plants all the shade they needed. Joachim said nothing more then and went away, but, while we were spreading and stretching the net over the pillars we had bound firmly together, he returned with the chief and asked us to consider whether trellis battens or bamboo sticks mightn't after all be better to use as cover: the camouflage net, he thought, would go slack very quickly, would sag and provide no reliable shade. Then we'll just have to tighten it from time to time, the chief said, and he walked round it, praising our work and Guntram Glaser's brainwave. At one point he even took a few steps in the direction of the erratic block, just so as to examine the shaded hall from a distance. Now we'll have no more people come spying on us, he said with a laugh. A certificate: the chief was awarded a certificate for the rhododendrons grown in our shady house, and it hung for a long time in the office beside all the other certificates and rosettes and prizes. Many people stopped to read and admire them, and he would probably have left them hanging there for ever, but after he'd been given the final order to destroy all our oak-trees, he took all the certificates and awards off the wall, and no one has seen them since.

When Ewaldsen stands quite still and the shadow pattern

falls on him, he looks as if he's been caught up in the even mesh. Small birds can easily fly through it, but magpies and crows, they can't manage it. He sees me watching him and asks: Anything the matter, Bruno? And I say: Guntram Glaser built this house — it's lasted well. He makes no reply; he's never had much to say about Guntram Glaser — I don't know why either. All I know is that he was the first to foretell what then actually happened. He was standing beside the sanding machine, and I ran over to him immediately the chief left me. I felt I must pass on what I'd just learnt, and Ewaldsen was the first person I saw. Get it sorted out in your head before you begin, he said. I told him the chief had decided to engage Guntram Glaser as manager: not as second foreman, but as manager. Ewaldsen just looked at me calmly, drew his head back and then said: That would be the first step. Why the first step? I asked, and he replied in the same calm way: I see what I see. They'll be giving out more news soon, Bruno; he'll soon be part of the family. Ewaldsen saw it coming.

They've also said of me: Bruno is part of the family, and of Lisbeth too they said: She's been part of the family for the best part of a century, she worked for the chief's father. That was Lisbeth, who has now sent her regards to me. At first I couldn't believe she would do that, but Magda was with her, Magda went to the hospital with her and was given a present, a black crochet shawl. Lisbeth doesn't want anyone from the family to visit her — well, the chief himself can come, of course, but she doesn't wish to see any of the others at her bedside. That was her final word to Magda, and Magda doesn't know how to tell them in the stronghold. Lisbeth has water all over her body, in her lungs, in her legs, she can hardly move, and her gouty fingers, which look like big spread claws, can keep hold of scarcely anything. She won't be coming back to us, Magda said, and she cuddled up to me and breathed evenly, but just as I was thinking she'd gone off to sleep, she said softly: We'll take everything as it comes, Bruno, that's what we'll do.

To produce an even deeper shade in one corner Guntram

Glaser laid an old disused fish-trap over the camouflage net. This was finely meshed and in good order, and it wasn't long before the first jackdaw got tangled up in it and was pounced on by Ina's cat. Ina's grey and white cat often lay in wait in the shady house. It would pretend to be asleep, but it would be watching everything through the slits of its green eyes, and, the moment a bird came in sight, it would leap up and startle it and drive it into the net, but only rarely did it catch one. Once, while stalking a bird, it fell into the fish-trap itself: it crept along between the narrowing bands until it was wedged at the end of the bag, then it wriggled and yowled, and the more it tried to right itself, the more entangled it became; Guntram Glaser had to untie the knot at the end of the bag to set it free. Ina took the cat in her arms and cuddled it and comforted it; the patterns the fine mesh had made in its fur soon grew fainter, and they vanished entirely when Guntram Glaser began stroking the cat, at first with short upward strokes, which made the hairs crackle and stand up straight, then with a long-drawn-out smoothing motion from the head down to the tail. That's doing her good, Ina said, she's purring again, she'll soon have forgotten it. Next day the cat was back lying in wait in the shady house, but the moment it lifted its head or got ready to leap, a little bell would ring: Ina had fixed it on a collar round the cat's neck.

Oh, Ina, when you were cuddling that cat, when Guntram Glaser was stroking it and you were looking at each other without saying a word, it was then I began to suspect something, and when one evening I discovered you sitting alone together at a window table in the 'Deutsches Haus', I knew Ewaldsen's prediction would be proved right.

After work we took a load of fir branches to the 'Deutsches Haus'. We just laid it down in the big hall, for they wanted themselves to weave the garlands for the ball that would follow the shooting match. As we were leaving – and I was the last to leave – I took a peep into the dining-room from the darkness of the hall and I saw the only remaining guests, I saw you. The big-bellied table lamp. The wine glasses. His hand. The little circle of light. His hand. You raised your head and saw he had moved his hand towards you. Your wavering smile. And then you laid your hand in his, and you looked into each other's eyes. Not a word. Pike: that's what you were eating, smoked pike.

Leaves suffer less damage here in the shady house, simply because the effects of the changes of temperature are slightly reduced. The chief soon noticed this and was pleased, and he said: We should have put it up ourselves long ago, this house, shouldn't we, Bruno? Yes, I said, but we probably wouldn't have thought of covering it with a camouflage net, we'd have used trellis battens or pine twigs, I suppose. That's true, the chief said, and he said too: He's taught us a lot of things, my manager has, he's proved that one never stops learning.

We were sitting on wooden boxes, and there was a dampness in the air, you could almost think it was the light itself that was drizzling down, softer and much finer than rain. The chief pulled a face, as if to show he didn't wish to be spoken to just now, at a moment when there was something so unusual to be heard. But all at once he gave a sigh and turned towards me, he wiped a hand over his forehead, over his eyes, as if he wanted to say something but wasn't yet sure whether he should. But then after all he couldn't keep it to himself any longer, and he told me in confidence that something was about to happen shortly, and I must be the first to know: Ina was to be married. I remember that, as he said that, he shrugged his shoulders. I remember how he opened his mouth, and his lips twisted slightly. He didn't want to know what I thought about it, there was no question in his eyes, but rather a mounting wonder that I wasn't surprised. He rose briskly and said just: It's still between ourselves, then he went off, went to Hollenusen, to the new council offices where during working hours he left his door open, and anyone wanting a word with the mayor could just walk in.

First it was to be in the 'Deutsches Haus', then in the

stronghold, and finally in the 'Deutsches Haus' once again, mainly because it contained the biggest hall in Hollenhusen, and after the decision had been made Ina did nothing all day but sit with the list of guests in front of her and fill out her invitations cards, ticking off names and writing, writing endlessly as new names occurred to her or to Dorothea or the chief. We must ask . . . mustn't forget . . . if those, why not these? On all her invitation cards Ina drew different kinds of fruit, prettily coloured. They hung over the names, glistening in their ripeness: cherries, blackberries and plums, quinces and raspberries too. Two shining walnuts hung above my name – I don't know why either. When I asked her if I could weave the wedding garland, she said nothing, just gave me a quick tight hug, and then I knew it was all right and got the chief's permission to gather all the fir branches I needed and all the roses and zinnias and blue and white ribbons. I started work in the old shed down in the hollow.

That Guntram Glaser would surprise me there was the last thing I'd reckoned with, but he appeared unexpectedly outside the little window, peeped through the smeared pane and then came in. Cigarette in mouth, he hoisted himself on to the rickety working table, dangled his legs and watched me, forever nodding his head in admiration. He knew and could do almost as many things as the chief, but weave a garland, that he could not. Never before, he said, had he seen such a fine garland, ceremonial and yet at the same time gay, and he was already looking forward to walking under it with Ina; when that time came, the photographer must take a picture of the three of us.

And then he suddenly asked why I was always following him with my eyes, staring after him as if unable to take them off him. He said: Maybe you don't even realise it, Bruno, but at times I have the feeling that you're watching me or have got who-knows-what in mind; if there's anything the matter, you must tell me. All I said was: No, and again: No, no, and with that he was content for the moment, he smiled and pointed out all the good things he'd already heard about me, my work on the plantations, my good memory, my green fingers. That he did, and he hoped that some time in the future we might be working even closer together: he had an idea for cultivating half and quarter standard fruit trees, and I could help him with that, but first of all we should shake hands on getting along well together. Before leaving, he held a bit of the garland in his hand. I could see he was happy, and he praised me once more and promised me this garland shouldn't end up on the compost heap.

All I wove into that garland I kept to myself: not even Ina knew. How many wishes lay hidden in those green fir twigs! I made the wish that she would never have occasion to fear and would always find a cause, however slight, for happiness; I surrounded rose petals of a velvety blackness with the fiery glow of zinnias, just to ensure Ina would experience no great disappointments, while blue and white ribbons and tea roses were to shield her from sickness. Many were the wishes I wove into that garland, among them that Ina might recover everything she had mislaid, and also that she might sometimes think of me. The garland was not my only gift. Since I had some idea of what would give Ina pleasure, I bought a little box of coloured crayons. It stood all by itself on the long gift table, but, since I'd forgotten to attach a card with my name on, Ina didn't at once know who had given her the little box. Her delight. Her need to give the crayons a quick try.

It was Dorothea, not Ina, who put me in charge of the gift table. I was wearing the dark jacket the chief had worn only a few times, I stood a few paces behind the bridal pair and looked on as the guests pushed forward, lighthearted and in high spirits, to speak their good wishes and hand over their gifts. What a spectacle of congratulations and embraces and winks! I lost count of the number of smacking kisses Ina received. Each gift was passed over to Bruno, and I would weigh it in my hand, weigh it and try to guess what was hidden in the cardboard boxes beneath the coloured wrapping paper. I guessed a lot of glasses and glug-glug wine decanters, tureens and cutlery without end, a set of flower vases, an assortment of brushes, nutcrackers, a gramophone and time and again something soft and light: woollen garments. The pile grew and grew to quite a height and needed very careful stacking.

If Joachim had brought his gift along – that blue garden hammock – I'd have run out of room, but he had already handed it over in the stronghold, as Max had also handed over his – a shining silk tapestry with hunting scenes. The white stag. The leaping, baying pack. The childlike faces of the huntsmen. Pastor Plumbeck provided the handiest gift – a New Testament in black leather – and the heaviest was brought by old Lauritzen, and he made it clear as he handed it over that it came also from Niels, who was unable to be present: it was the most elegant corner cabinet you can imagine. As I took the cabinet from him and cautiously set it down, he cast his eye over the gift table, smiled and said: You'll soon have a waggon-load together, eh? And it was a waggon-load: the loading floor of our transport truck was only just big enough for us to take it all to the stronghold in a single journey later on.

I'm sure it was Ina's doing that at the wedding-breakfast I was allowed to sit at the head of the table. I sat with my back to the hall, at the corner where two table-legs almost touched, I had Ina and Guntram Glaser well in sight and, if I bent forward, I could see all the others and (except when the noise in the hall got too great) hear almost everything that was said. Guntram Glaser's mother was sitting, silent and sleepy, beside the chief. His uncle, about whom so many stories were told, sat a bit to one side opposite me, a gigantic, fleshy man who could never stop tugging at people's clothing, fumbling with his own and winking. He gave me quite a few winks, making it look as if we'd plotted something together. My idea of an airman was something quite different, but Guntram Glaser told us his uncle had been an airman during the war and, since he found it impossible to give it up, he had enlarged a machine shed to make room for his old double-decker, a rickety two-seater in which he took off, usually on Sundays, and had been reported missing more times than you can count. Dorothea, who was sitting next to him, was alarmed when he invited her to go on a round flight with him the following day, and she refused at once, telling him with a laugh that she'd no wish to see either the mud-flats or our plantations from above, no, thank you. The only person prepared to fly with his uncle was Ina, but Guntram Glaser was against it. He put an arm round his wife, pulled her close and said: That would just about suit you, wouldn't it – making a forced landing on a sandbank with Ina? And he also said: As long as I've any say in the matter, she won't get inside your elastoplast bomber.

To start with there was melon with ham, sweet melons with thin slices of smoked ham, all so tender there was no need to chew. I'd made up my mind not to be the first to finish, but all the same I did finish first, eyed in wonder by Guntram's uncle, who had been watching me for some time. He laughed, shook his head, then asked me if I'd never heard that pips could take root in the stomach. After that there was a soup containing bone marrow and meatballs, a rich soup of many colours that stayed hot right to the end. While we were consuming it, wine was poured out, and those who didn't want wine were given mineral-water; everyone had to have something to clink glasses with or at least to look at while the chief was making a quiet, halting speech.

I didn't understand it all. It had to do with partings, the many little partings that life brings. Each of us, the chief said, takes leave many times of himself as well as of others. And one day, the chief said, the moment comes when we have to leave those who for a long time were very close to us, who belonged to us and shared everything with us; at some time they will drift off in another direction, and that is as it should be, for we all have the right to our own experiences. Turning to Ina and Guntram Glaser, he said: When two people are so united, so determined, they have every reason to look on it as the beginning of something new, they can insist on their right to make their own experiments and to put aside the inconvenient store of experiences made by others. The most important thing is that you should stick together. To end with he said: Whether you believe it or not, whoever sees the need to conspire against the world – and that happens to us all at some time and in some way – will succeed best as a pair, and with that he raised his glass, and we all stood up and drank to Ina and Guntram Glaser. The applause afterwards seemed to go on for ever, and we clapped in time with each other as Ina put both her arms round the chief's neck and leaned so heavily against him that he was in danger of losing his balance and had to hold tight to the back of his chair. Guntram Glaser expressed his thanks with a handshake.

His uncle seemed to be well-disposed towards me, I could feel that without looking. He was watching me, and all of a sudden he asked me whether I didn't intend to get married, and I said: I don't know. He went on to ask whether I hadn't already looked around in Hollenhusen, and I said: Not yet. With what concern he eyed me then, as if I had deliberately left out the best thing in life, but then he grinned and nodded in the direction of Ina and said: If you wait long enough . . . almost every girl has a double . . . if you only wait long enough. Oh, Ina, after he said that I no longer dared look at you.

That bit of bad luck: why did it have to be me it happened to? Through my pain I can still see Joachim's mocking face, the shrug of his shoulders that was meant to suggest that with me people must be prepared for anything, on any occasion, not excepting a wedding.

The main course was pheasant served with white cabbage that had been soaked in wine. The airman saw to it that the dish of mashed potato and the gravy bowl came round to where I was sitting: maybe he knew without telling of my perpetual hunger, for he urged me to take a good helping, just in case. It was the first pheasant I'd ever eaten. I cut deep into the dry breast meat, dipped the strands in the gravy, speared a chunk of pineapple, and found it so delicious that I had to close my eyes. And the cabbage soaked in wine – who had dreamed that up to go with it? I saw the uncle was gnawing the breast-bone, so I also took mine in my fingers, twisted the thigh-bone off as he had done and prised the meat away from the pale sinews. It was only the bits of small shot I couldn't put on the side of my plate as he did, for my teeth discovered none – I suppose I'd swallowed them all.

Nobody had warned me about a pheasant's long bones. I didn't even know pheasants had bones like that, bones that break easily and are as sharp as a needle, so sharp that, when they get stuck in your throat, you feel only a slight prick, a very thin kind of pain that doesn't at once make you fear the worst. I just flinched as the splintered bone drove its point into my throat, all I felt to begin with was some resistance to swallowing, and I thought it would disappear if I took a few more hefty gulps, would be carried down by dollops of cabbage and chunks of pineapple. But, however much I swallowed unchewed, the splinter was not dislodged, it stayed stuck. The pain grew greater, it thudded and passed in waves through my head, and in the place the little bone was stuck I felt a burning, a sizzling heat that brought tears to my eyes. I tried to put it out with a glass of mineral water, but it was no use: my throat swelled shut, the thudding grew more violent, I was choking. Without meaning to I seized hold of the tablecloth, upsetting my glass. I tried to say something, but couldn't, and then the airman realised something was happening to me and knew at once what it might be.

Nothing helped, neither the dry bread he sent for nor the thumping, not even a large glass of mineral water. My throat was blocked, I strained and retched and heard a woman's voice saying: He's changing colour, the poor young man, and through a haze I saw Ina, who had jumped to her feet and was watching me in concern, and I also saw the chief get up and walk the length of the table to the middle of the hall. He and Doctor Ottlinger took me outside. From Max I got a well-meaning cuff, Joachim followed me out with his mocking smile, and then I was lying in the wide armchair, my hands gripping the armrests, my head against the back, and over me hung the face of Doctor Ottlinger. Not a word: he didn't say a word. When he wanted me to open my mouth wide, he simply forced it apart with his fingers. How he got the splinter out of my throat I've still no idea, but I do know I beat back my urge to be sick and didn't fill the basin in the hotel office with vomit.

Oh, Ina, how I should have liked just to slink away, to the boat skeleton or to my hut! I didn't want to show my face again at your wedding. For a long time I sat alone in the office, hoping you'd all forgotten me, but someone suddenly ran a hand over my head, and there stood the chief. He didn't say much, just that three portions of ice cream were waiting for me, guaranteed free of bone splinters, and he pulled me to my feet and led me back to you – not to my former place, but to a chair beside Max, who just sat there drinking red wine and sweating and keeping his eyes fixed on you, Ina, because you seemed quite strange to him, strange and beautiful.

Yes, Ewaldsen, I've finished, I've tightened the net on my side, so our shady house is once more fit to be seen.

That humming, that low, swelling hum advancing over the horizon: it sounds like hundreds of powerful motors all running at the same time. Do you see, Bruno? Over there, towards Schleswig. Yes, I see them now, they're planes. Manoeuvres, Ewaldsen says, there's a big exercise going on here, last night some tanks drove through Hollenhusen, the whole house shook, but you probably didn't even notice it here.

How steadily they fly, these heavy black planes! They're approaching upwind, leaving tattered clouds behind them, the sun glinting in the cockpit windows. They're not flying very high. There are at least fifteen of them, some with a slender double fuselage, and the body in the middle looks like a fat cigar. Where can they be going? Ewaldsen asks, and he also says: Anyway, they won't spot us here under the camouflage net. Over the Holle, over Lauritzen's meadows, no, they're already over the Erlenhof, and the humming suddenly becomes quieter. Something falls out of the last plane and is swept away at an angle, things are falling and tumbling out of all the planes and being swept away, and whatever it is dangling behind each of the black points first turns white, then opens. Parachutes, look, they're all parachutes! The whole sky is speckled with objects swinging and drifting in the wind, circling and sinking down to the ground. A dandelion-clock, a gigantic dandelion-clock has, in a sudden gust of wind, scattered its seeds, and they are floating around on white parachutes. Heavy crates are falling from the planes, bulky containers, above which two or even three multi-coloured parachutes spring open. They too are drifting on the wind towards us, though they're not swinging as much as the bodies, which are now growing arms and legs. How they paddle and kick and twist to guide their fall, how they swing and jerk in the middle of their ropes, just to land quicker, closer to their chosen spot! They've got it wrong, Ewaldsen cries, the wind's blowing them into the plantations.

The sky is still full of them, some drifting so steadily that they'll probably land somewhere on the coast, but the first ones are already coming down, falling on our land, bowling across the nurserybeds, getting tangled up in cordons, shrubs, the wind inside the parachutes blows them up and pushes them along like waves as the men tug at the obstinate material, gather it up and throw themselves across it as if trying to overpower some living beast. Everywhere in the first-year plantations things are snapping and breaking or being ripped from the soil, they land with a thump among the pears, are flung down on the morello cherries and the grafted apples. From all sides come cries, cries of communication, cries of relief, and now one of the heavy crates hits the ground bang wallop in the middle of the soft fruit. There, Bruno, there, someone caught up in the pines! I must fetch the chief – he's just got to come. Get down, mind your head! Ewaldsen shouts.

A rush of wind, a shadow: one of the big containers crashes down hard, tears a hole in the bed of young rhododendrons, is dragged along by its parachutes and ends jammed up against the water tank. We must fetch the chief, I say, and Ewaldsen: He'll have seen what's happening, he'll be here directly.

They gather on the narrow transport tracks between the plantations, in growing numbers soldiers come running up, here and there they are already opening the containers, lifting weapons out, instruments, a gun on rubber-tyred wheels, it seems they no longer need to find out where they are, their officer just points in one direction and off they trot in small groups into the cover of our plantations. There are two men hanging up in the old pine-trees, kicking out in their efforts to get down, others are landing on Lauritzen's meadows, and I'm pretty sure one or two will be ending up in the Holle. They've beaten us, Ewaldsen says with a laugh and puts his pipe in his mouth. He points to a parachute a soldier is laboriously salvaging and says: Best quality silk, you could make something worth having with that. A few are crouching behind the erratic block and in the shelter of my wall, in their camouflaged uniforms they can hardly be seen, and those in the plantations it's impossible to make out at all, you can only guess where they are by the way the young trees bend, then spring upright again. Tim and Tobias, my two pests, are of course the first to arrive: you'll always find them wherever there's something going on, and already they are creeping up behind some soldiers, bent double and full of their own importance, copying everything the soldiers do. But they won't see the planes any more: they're right out of sight by now. Come, Bruno, quick, says Ewaldsen, and he pulls me along with him to the spot where the transport tracks come out on to a main path. There the soldiers have gathered in a ring round their officer, and then – no doubt after getting their instructions – they vanish, one troop after another. Ewaldsen is anxious to get near, to hear what Joachim will say, Joachim, who has run quite a distance, but is now approaching the soldiers rather uneasily. He waits until the officer has sent a few more of them off.

They shake hands and exchange names. Joachim asks: Are you the commanding officer? at which the soldier just nods and points up at the sky, making a helpless gesture as if to say you can't put your trust in the wind. Then he waves a hand across the plantations and expresses his regret for all the damage. He says: The meadows were our landing target, but the wind forced us over here, and then immediately adds: All the damage will be assessed, quickly and without too much red tape: within a week it will all be settled.

A machine-gun: from my wall a machine-gun is being fired, how dry the shots sound! And from afar, towards the Erlenhof, there comes a muffled bang, a cannon maybe, a tank gun. Excuse me, the young officer says, and he turns away, aiming to disappear into the plantations with the rest of his soldiers. But he doesn't get far: a shout holds him back, a terse command from the chief: Wait.

There he stands, the chief, unshaven, wearing muddy boots and a woollen cardigan buttoned in the wrong holes. The spade he's carrying he must have picked up as he came. The officer begs his pardon, stops and makes his excuses, repeating what he told Joachim: a valuer would come and assess all the damage quickly and without too much red tape, that the wind was to blame for all the devastation. I need your name, the chief says, and I need the number and location of your unit. The machine-gun fires, the officer casts one look at the wall and then looks at the chief, who stands calmly awaiting an answer, and without a further word the officer searches in his wallet for a piece of paper and writes down the details required of him. Silently he holds it out to Joachim, but the chief takes it from his hand and asks: How do you intend to make good what your men have done here?

It's plain to see the officer is in a hurry, he must join his soldiers, it's clear he wants to advance with them and to win, but the chief's unyielding manner holds him back. Are you the owner? he asks, and the chief replies: That I am, and that is why I wish to know the basis on which you handle claims for damages, you or your valuer. As far as I know, with a generous outright payment, the officer says, and seems to think this answer must satisfy the chief, for he raises his hand in a farewell greeting and turns once more to go, no doubt encouraged in that belief by Joachim's nod of agreement and his remark: It'll be all right, surely.

No, the chief says firmly, it will not be all right. There can be no question of an outright settlement, not in this case. We shall draw up a list of the damage, each item separately, we shall add up what you and your men have done here and, when your valuer comes along, he will be presented with a detailed invoice, that's what he'll get. In view of all that has been done to us, we have no other choice. The officer nods, turns and vanishes with the last of his waiting soldiers, and, before Joachim can say a word, the chief beckons Ewaldsen across. They go to the pear-tree plot, point out this and that to each other and discuss it, hammer on a metal container, finger trunks and branches and gaze from the path over the damaged nursery-beds. We can't do this, Joachim says softly, it's unreasonable, pointless nit-picking – what do you think, Bruno? I don't know what to think, I still don't know, and I'd sooner not say anything at all to him, for he's shaking his head over the chief in the way he has so often shaken it over me. Anyhow, it's just like him, Joachim says and goes off slowly. The chief has left Ewaldsen and is going off too, but going his own way: not once does he turn to watch Joachim, who, after standing undecided on the main path for a while, finally resolves to follow the soldiers.

All right, Ewaldsen, I'm coming. I've a pretty good idea of the job the two of you have thought out for Bruno: I know before I start that we'll be making a tour of inspection together, to note down all signs of damage, however small, every broken twig, every uprooted plant. We'll do it just as the chief wants, Ewaldsen says, he gave me this pencil and some paper. You,

Bruno, will call out the necessary details – just species and damage – and I'll write it all down, okay? From the way Ewaldsen is telling me what to do I can see he doesn't think much of the chief's instructions either; probably he too feels like shaking his head over the invoice they're leading towards, but he doesn't dare, he just gives me a sign and murmurs: Let's get started.

He's right: where are my eyes? I've missed yet another broken stem, but that comes from having to keep looking at the chief, who is walking across his land with bent shoulders – bending down low as if he's examining the crumbly soil. Maybe after all I should give up my claim to everything he's leaving me, maybe in the stronghold they'd then come closer to an understanding, and things would be as they were before. But he himself doesn't want me to sign the disclaimer, and he has always known what's right. The crowns of the morello cherries here have been shaved clean off. Who knows if that was also the soldiers' doing?

Some people used to think the chief could never take delight in anything, but I know he often enough found reasons for delight, reasons maybe at times small and modest, but they made him happy or good-humoured or at any rate cheerfully content. For him it was enough if a planting scheme turned out well, if a binder did its job properly or if cuttings struck root and formed leaf buds: it didn't have to be more than that. Since he was more open with me than with other people, he often enough showed his delight, even at times his anticipation of it; now and again as we were working he would give me a tap and just say: Come along, Bruno, time now for our reward, and from his step and his way of touching things in passing – a watercock or a fence or a twig, which he'd bend and watch spring back – I could tell he was in good spirits and looking forward to something.

Come along, Bruno, and I left off what I was doing and went with him to the railway station. We didn't get into the open car he usually used to drive to Hollenhusen, but went on foot, along the railtrack, where grasshoppers were chirping, over the level crossing and boldly over the rails – just as he wanted. The stationmaster saw us crossing the rails, but he didn't shout at us or threaten us, he just greeted the chief and praised the sunny weather. Most of the other people we met also greeted the chief, even the woman in the waiting-room, and, without our having said a word, she brought us what we wanted: a lemonade for me, a Weizenkorn for him. He raised his glass to me, then shrugged his shoulders and seemed unsure of himself, yet all the same pleased. At one point he said: We'll recognise him, I think, our guest – nobody remains long unknown in Hollenhusen.

His friend: we had come to pick up a friend the chief knew from many letters, but had never yet seen. He was coming all the way from America and was to stay a few days in the stronghold. Out on the platform, before the train arrived, the chief said: There'll be something doing in the early evening, Bruno, and I want you to be there. That's what he said.

Then the train came in and there was a lot of hissing and shouting and slamming of doors. A lot more people than usual got out, strangers, hesitant, on the look-out for someone, there was already a jam around the ticket barrier, here and there people waving and rushing towards one another. The chief stood quite motionless, running his eyes along the train and inspecting each person as he got out, and at last he decided. There he is – that must be him.

An old man wearing a black hat was standing beside his luggage at the far end of the train, waiting patiently. That's him, Bruno. We ran. We waved. Leslie, the chief said in greeting, and the old man said: Konrad, and then they just took each other by both hands and regarded each other; there wasn't a lot, I suppose, that needed saying between them. As I shook hands with him, Professor Gutowski gave me a friendly nod, just as if he was greeting an old acquaintance, and I felt at once that the chief must have mentioned me in one of his many letters. Bruno pounced on the suitcase, the chief insisted on carrying the holdall, and together we strolled along the platform, waited for the train to draw out, then all three of us crossed the track under the eyes of the stationmaster. The chief asked whether the journey hadn't been too strenuous, and the visitor spoke of a ship as big as a town in which he'd kept losing his way during the first three days; but, wherever his straying footsteps led him, he always ended up in a brightly lit dining-hall with every kind of food you can imagine, shellfish, hams, poultry, everything. There was a band on board and films and lectures. The old man sometimes forgot entirely that he was at sea.

They walked ahead of me, arm in arm. They'd never seen each other before. In order to hear what else they were talking about, I walked close behind them, and in our plantations heard them speaking about trees, the ability of damaged trees to keep going and sprout anew.

They'd never seen each other before, yet on their first walk together they were already talking of all the things trees can put up with. The stumps that came with dormant buds, the frostbitten olive-tree that will sprout from the roots. The old professor had been practically everywhere, had seen all there was to see. Eucalyptus trees, which have a tinder-dry bark, yet can adapt so well to the regular forest fires in their native land that searing heat and flames mean nothing to them. The trees in Africa that surround themselves with coral-tree shrubs as a protection against fire. Plants with underground stems. A tree on some volcanic island that is often buried in glowing ash, yet still retains its power to sprout again. The bare, charred trunks which before the air-raid had been trees and which, though all their branches and twigs had been torn off, bring forth leaves only a few months later. But once they are really dead, they vanish quickly and totally – turned to powder and put to use by all the things that live on them, and the number of things that live on dead trees is almost beyond imagining.

Now and then they would come to a standstill, but the wish to stop came alone from him, from our visitor, who gazed out over our plantations up to the screen of thuyas or down to the Holle pursuing its dark course through the meadows. The moment they came to a halt they'd fall silent, and the old man seemed to be lost in thought under his black hat, while in our light his skin took on a rosy glow. They stopped longest in front of the stronghold, our visitor regarding it searchingly: he must surely have been looking for something, maybe comparing it with the photo of it he'd once received.

And then it was time for him to answer Dorothea's wave. She had already spotted us and was standing on the terrace beside the canopied table, waving and holding out her arms – Dorothea, who had never seen our visitor before either, but who greeted him now with an embrace, saying: Welcome, Leslie, welcome.

The old professor had brought no gift for me, but Dorothea got a wine-red brooch, a serrate leaf in a very thin gold setting, which she at once pinned on, and the chief five small silver goblets that fitted into each other, little drinking-cups for which there was also a leather case. With a meaning glance at his suitcase the visitor said: I think I'll leave my official task till later, and that suited Dorothea, who wanted first to hear about his journey over a cup of coffee.

How I should have enjoyed listening to him! I'd have given anything to be allowed to stay, but the chief reminded me of a school class coming for a conducted tour of our plantations and said: You take it for once, Bruno. On a fine day like this you'll manage all right. And he also said: Don't forget this evening – I want you here.

They were already waiting at our wooden entrance gate, twenty to twenty-five children, chasing each other around, lounging against the gateposts, shoving and skipping, and however much the young schoolmistress strove to call them to order, the mixed class was in a constant state of movement, yelling and squealing. No, I said, I'm not Herr Zeller. Herr Zeller has a visitor from America, and that's why I'm here; my name is Bruno. The children weren't all of the same age, and my eye fell at once on a few very small, smartly dressed girls who were holding each other by the hand; they were well-behaved and earnest – unlike some of the boys. When the teacher had managed to round them all up, she announced: Now then, children, listen and think of what we've been learning, and then our group, stretching and closing like a concertina, pushed and pulled its way to the hot-beds, where I showed how conifers are propagated by cuttings, how cuttings root themselves. Later on I showed the restless bunch some eye-cuttings and some leaf-cuttings. By the erratic block they all sat down, and I demonstrated grafting to them, cleft and rind grafting, which interested some of them so much that they took out their penknives and copied me. What they found least interesting was soil care and planting schedules, and they were not interested either in how we divided up our plantations: say what I would, they were always looking in the opposite direction or messing around with each other. In the machine-house, however, they swarmed out straight away, tried out levers and movable rods, hid, jumped out on each other and clambered aboard the machines.

In the machine-house: suddenly I seized one of the little girls round her hips, lifted her up and put her down on the driving-seat of a tractor, stepped back and left her sitting there. Instead of enjoying it, the girl let out a yell. She yelled as if I'd done goodness-knows-what to her, she slid and wriggled around on the seat and in a moment was awash with tears. It's all right, I said, it's all right, and went to lift her down again, but she backed away and hit out at my arms: she didn't want me to touch her. The teacher had to come, to place the little girl back on the ground and to comfort her. Gradually the girl stopped crying, she moved close to her friend, who was watching me with an expression of mistrust and fear. Both of them, and a few others as well, drew back as soon as I approached them. At some stage I put out my hand and said: Come on, let's make it up, but the girl began yelling again, the teacher had to lead her away. When she quietened down, the teacher came across to me and asked me not to touch the children. What's the matter? I asked, and the teacher said: Fright, can't you see? Some of the children are frightened of you.

She gave me a friendly smile, but it was no help: I could already feel a little storm rising inside my head, and my one thought was: to the entrance gate, all you need do now is get them as far as the gate, for that's what the chief expects. I walked ahead of them, not worrying whether or not they were able to keep up with me. The polythene tunnel I just ignored, though otherwise I'd have enjoyed explaining it to them: I just piloted them to the big wooden gate, nodded to the teacher and then went quickly home, turned the key and fastened the bolt and chain. That's what I did, and then I knelt down – not in front of the washstand, but by the window – and at once banged my head against the windowsill, again and again, until the roaring was answered by another roaring, until I felt the liberating pain that broke it all up and forced it back. Then I lowered myself to the floor. The only taste in my mouth was of sour water. I made no attempt to get to my feet, just lay there trying to get my thoughts straight, but I didn't succeed; sleep took over before I came to any decision. Beneath the windowsill, my back against the wall, I fell asleep.

The chief didn't knock seven times: he hammered against my door, again and again, he hammered with his fists, making the whole place shake, and kept calling my name and threatening in such a way that nobody would have dared lie doggo. The look he gave me from the doorstep! The way he advanced on me! I thought for a moment he was about to strike me, for the first time ever, but he didn't do that – he has never done it. Gently and without a word he pushed me down on to the stool and felt my forehead, examined it and felt it, then fetched my bread-knife from the drawer. He dipped the blade in my water jug. Then he pressed the flat blade against my forehead, moved it up and down a few times and then suddenly threw the knife on the table and went to the door. Remember this evening, he said over his shoulder, and that was all.

Except for Max they were all there, and almost all of them wanted to know what had caused the bumps on my forehead. Dorothea would have liked to fetch her miracle cure right away, and Guntram Glaser quietly recommended what the chief had already tried: Put a knife against them, Bruno, your bill-hook. I was glad I'd put the chief's dark jacket on, for the others had also smartened themselves up, were wearing their Sunday best, ties, necklaces, and there were a lot of candles burning. They all had a word to spare for me, even Joachim greeted me with a click of his tongue. She was the only one who looked right through me, displayed neither surprise nor distaste, but just looked straight through Bruno: Frau Sasse from the Bodden estate. In her green dress, with long wavy hair, she didn't look at all like a famous dressage rider, but that's what she was, and Joachim, who called her Maren, wanted, I suppose, to be like her, all the time he was fussing around her and taking care she lacked for nothing. The old professor clapped the back of my hand and said: Here's our friend, and afterwards offered me the plate containing morsels of fish and sausage that Dorothea had put in front of him – I don't know either why he immediately held it out to me. We stood in a circle round him and listened to what he had to say about flowering. He called flowering a dreadful business that ended badly for the flower itself: it either withers after pollenation or is cast off. He, who had travelled around a lot, had seen a cactus that closed its flowers five seconds after fertilisation, simply in order to show the insects that the shop was closed. A species of speedwell changes its colour from blue to purple as soon as there is no more nectar to be had, and the dwarf box turns red after fertilisation, he told us, red. Many flowers lose their seductive fragrance shortly after pollenation, thus informing visitors: it's done, don't bother any more. Yes, the old man said, flowering is a problem.

All of a sudden he stretched out a hand to pick up some papers from a side table. He called the chief over and asked him to stand very close to him. The chief, who in the usual way can run rings round anybody, looked a bit embarrassed as he did what he was told. He wasn't too happy about it all and had to suffer a prod from Dorothea: Go along, now.

First of all then, the diploma. In the name of the Association of North American Rhododendron Growers – thus the old man began, but then he thought better of it, shook his head and started again: Dear Konrad, ladies and gentlemen. Nature shows us a great deal, he said, it overpowers and corrupts and dazzles us, it amazes us with its accidents and checkmates us with its laws, and on top of all this it soon lets us know that it hasn't yet laid all its cards on the table. The old professor paused to consider what he'd said, and he was not satisfied with that either. He began again from the beginning, just turning to the chief and saying: My dear friend Zeller, and then he spoke of plants having been around long before human beings and having got on well enough without them, for they were always able to change and to adapt, they were always ready to experiment and were in no particular danger. They became gravely endangered only when human beings gained control over them and were concerned only with what they yielded. That was quite understandable, as was the need for increased growth through selection and other such methods. Nevertheless, the most beautiful yield the plant world gives us should not be forgotten: it is delight, the great unexpected delight that comes from amazement, admiration and a feeling of well-being.

Then he spoke of the good fortune of having agents of the plant world who could show that beauty also has its uses, agents moved by love to ensure that the miracle survives. He spoke softly, occasionally closing his eyes. I should dearly have liked learning each of his sentences by heart, especially when he called the chief an agent who recognised the usefulness of beauty and who was working across all frontiers for what we all need in life: pleasure without ulterior motive. At this Dorothea clapped her hands, a bit too early, but she clapped, and I at once came to her aid and clapped too.

And so to the Cecilia: The Association of North American Rhododendron Growers was awarding the chief a diploma in recognition of his work and in particular his Cecilia. The diploma, which Professor Gutowski now presented to him, was an expensive, richly decorated scroll of many colours, depicting the delicate flesh pink and dull mauve blossoms and the leathery elliptical leaves of the Cecilia, which the chief had cultivated and developed to withstand the winter. Now everyone clapped, and the old professor embraced the chief and whispered a few words in his ear that Dorothea must have overheard, for she laughed and said: Not a secret love, Leslie – Cecilia was the name of Konrad's grandmother, he took the name from her. Then a second diploma was presented. This was just in black and white, and it confirmed that the chief had been elected an honorary member of the North American Association. And that, my dear Konrad, the professor said, is one of the rarest honours we bestow.

They all wanted to take the diplomas in their hands straight away, or at least read the inscriptions, but the professor was not yet finished. He took up something else from the side table, looked to see where I was and said: As with all honours we bestow, we should spare some thought for those who contribute modestly and reliably to that success, the silent assistants who have to make do with the half-light. This is a certificate of appreciation, dedicated personally to Herr Bruno Messmer for all his loyal and sensitive work. I felt quite dizzy and my legs began to tremble, but the chief, who had surely known all about it beforehand, dragged me forward and, as I took the certificate, he clapped, and Dorothea and Guntram Glaser clapped too. Clink glasses: they wanted to clink glasses with me and look at the certificate. It was a photograph with a wide margin in which the words of praise for me were inscribed. The photo showed one of the most splendid rhododendron stems imaginable, four, if not five metres high, and the blossoms were dark red, corymb in shape.

They had to wait a while, for the chief had yet to speak. He was much moved, he was happy, and it took him a long time to find words to express his thanks. Then he spoke of Cecilia, his grandmother, who had known all about plants and pressed between the pages of her bible all she found in the fields: herbs that kept fleas away and stopped the devil crossing the threshold, but also flowers guaranteed to make you dream of summer meadows. She had taught him that, to be transformed and to see things others couldn't see, all you needed to do was carry a piece of rhododendron root on your chest, fastened with a thin string. To end with he said: I'm glad Cecilia has been given such recognition.

If only I knew what has become of my certificate! It just vanished like so many other things, like the gifts and the things I found in the earth. Though together we searched for it, Magda and I, we couldn't find it; but it was presented to me on the evening the chief was also honoured, that I know for sure. I had to show the photo around, Ina read the words of praise out loud, they all admired the rhododendron plant and its blossoms. Frau Sasse was the only one who found nothing to admire, she just glanced indifferently at the photo and then asked Joachim for a light for her cigarette. Her weary, dismissive look. Her peevishness. She found something to object to everywhere, and she couldn't listen to anything without raising her eyebrows. I took care to stay out of her way. Magda knew the Bodden estate didn't belong to Frau Sasse, but to her brother, who gave her everything she wanted: he had even set aside a practice ground for her dressage. I soon noticed from his manner that the chief had little time for her. He had a very particular form of politeness for people he didn't care for, and this forced, irreproachable politeness was now directed towards Frau Sasse. However, she, who had already been twice married, wasn't put out by it.

Accustomed to having her say wherever she was, she didn't keep herself in check in our house either; whatever she wished to ask, she asked, and she seemed never to lack listeners.

How she came to clash swords with the old professor is something that simply escaped my notice, but I did hear her ask him where he came from, being of the opinion that his name was in fact a European one, and, when the old man agreed, saying: My grandfather was born in Modlin, she nodded and said: Just as I thought – the good things in America come invariably from Europe. Professor Gutowski smiled and made no attempt to give her an answer, but Frau Sasse was not content with his faint smile, she wished him to tell her what in America was American, and he said quietly: Feeling, perhaps, our feeling for life. She ignored that and wasn't to be shifted from her view that America had Europe to thank for all that was best in it, the many immigrants, their many varieties of knowledge and skill, their culture, their sense of history – that's what she said: sense of history.

The longer the old professor kept silent, the more aggressive she became. She had been to America once, she knew the country and its towns – and the only things that had reconciled her with the continent of gun law were the traces of European origin, the European heritage.

I could see the chief was becoming uneasy. He emptied his glass, then at once filled it again, involuntarily he moved closer to Frau Sasse, preparing to say something, but the old man, who had noticed, waved him lightly aside and gathered himself together and said quite calmly that he was familiar with almost everything that was being said against America in all parts of the world, almost everything. A lot of it had given him food for thought, that he didn't deny, but each time he would then ask himself how it was that for many people throughout the world the name America was a symbol of hope and encouragement: harshly criticised, its reputation blackened, accused again and again, it still represented for many the support and affirmation to which every human being is entitled, and particularly those living in want. He had experienced that not so very long ago inside his grandfather's homeland, he said, and he also said: We are dependable lessees. At that point the chief intervened, handed the professor a glass and bade him drink with him at long last.

Never in my life would I have imagined that on that very night Joachim would move out of the stronghold. For most of the time I was standing by myself eating the sandwiches Ina was plying me with and drinking the fruit juice she poured out for me, and Joachim, wherever and in whoever's company I saw him, didn't strike me as being in any way different; he'd lost none of his high spirits or his superior airs. Probably he wasn't aware yet himself of what was brewing, he spent his whole time fussing around Frau Sasse, was happy when he could do her a favour and pleased when Dorothea spoke to her. Even when I left – and I was the first to go – I would never have dreamt that on the following day Joachim would no longer be living in the stronghold. Who after me was the next to leave I don't know, but I do know from Magda that in the end only the chief and Joachim remained. Magda said that was no accident: she believed the chief had been waiting for Joachim, who had insisted on accompanying Frau Sasse a part of her way home.

It seems their talk was hardly even heated: they neither of them raised their voices. The chief informed Joachim that for the first time in his life he had had to apologise to a guest, and to apologise for the behaviour of another guest who, with her arrogance, had transgressed the simplest rules of hospitality and had even taken pleasure in doing so. Joachim professed surprise, didn't understand or didn't want to understand, and so the chief reminded him of Frau Sasse's behaviour and repeated her remarks, which had been designed to provoke his friend, the guest of honour, quite without cause. Joachim at once leaped to her defence, playing down her remarks and observing it was only that Frau Sasse was used to speaking her mind; she made no secret of her thoughts: even when they were talking between themselves they said everything straight out, literally everything.

The chief had nothing against that, he acknowledged Joachim's right to his freedom and independence, he questioned nothing and demanded nothing, all he requested was just one thing: that Frau Sasse should never again turn up in the stronghold, neither in Joachim's company nor alone. Joachim wanted to know whether that was meant as a kind of ban, and the chief said he hadn't issued a ban, he had just spoken a wish. They went on arguing, then suddenly Joachim got to his feet and said: Very well, if you forbid me to bring to the house a guest for whom I care particularly, then you should find no difficulty in doing without my presence, and, since the chief gave no reply to that, Joachim added: I see it's clear what I must do. Then he packed a few necessaries and moved out. In the middle of the night. Without saying goodbye. Moved out.

Of course he could have lived at Bodden, where there were even more rooms than in the stronghold, but I suppose he didn't want to, it seemed to him more proper to live in Hollenhusen. He rented some rooms in the shopkeeper Tordsen's new house and allowed Ina and Dorothea to visit him there. From the chief he received no visit. I wouldn't care to know how often Dorothea tried to persuade him to return home, she probably wheedled and begged him, but he refused, and every time she had to leave Tordsen's house by herself.

One afternoon I heard Dorothea say to the chief: Won't you come with me? Today is his birthday. I've thought of that, was all the chief would say, there's a parcel lying on my desk; you can take it along with you. He said nothing more, and Dorothea went off without a word. Often, when I saw Joachim's car, Frau Sasse would be with him, and they were either driving towards Bodden or coming from there. While out riding, it was only rarely they strayed in our direction, I didn't see them more than twice.

Sticking it out: when once I wanted to prove to myself that I could stick it out alone in Danes' Wood at dusk in a strong wind, in spite of my fears, it was then they almost flushed me out like a rabbit. Inky clouds with snow-white linings pushing and shoving across the sky. The rushing wind rising to a whistle that each time made me duck my head. After lying down on the edge of the big pond and taking a long drink, I'd dearly have liked to go straight home, but I wanted to prove to myself once and for all that I could stick it out alone shortly before nightfall, and so I went over to the tree stump on which the chief had sat that time before, settled myself comfortably and listened. It wasn't long before I was hearing the murmurs of wounded soldiers who had once sought shelter here, and when I listened more closely I could also hear the wails and groans and a sort of heavy breathing out. Things rubbed against each other, crunched, rattled, suddenly the rasp of a saw, metal jaws snapping shut, and the knocking inside my head – that came for sure from fists drumming on the ground.

They rode out from under the elms, Frau Sasse first with Joachim behind her, they rode quite slowly along the edge of the pond and, at the spot where I'd been lying, they dismounted and let their horses drink.

They stood there side by side, watching their horses, and then Joachim put an arm round the woman's shoulder, hesitantly, as if just trying it on, and, since she didn't move, he gathered up her short thick hair in one hand, holding it loosely as if about to weigh it. He played with her hair, combing it a bit with his fingers, and still she stood motionless. Then he gripped her by both shoulders and turned her towards him. He tried to draw her close, but gave up at once as quickly she raised a hand and, holding her head erect, laid the point of her riding whip on his chest in warning.

It looked as if nothing was said, they just took each other's measure with their eyes, and then she suddenly gave a brief wave, and Joachim put his hands together, stooped down subserviently and helped her on to her horse. How she pulled it round, how she rode towards the wood, heading straight for me! I quickly tumbled off the tree stump and pressed myself down against the ground, making myself small.

Very few of us here missed him at all, that's for sure. Ewaldsen and I, we often didn't mention Joachim for days on end, and Magda too rarely asked after him: he had left and was no longer any concern of ours. Even when one of us found a picture in a Schleswig newspaper – it showed Joachim with Frau Sasse and some other dressage riders – we just looked at it, there was no talk of his coming back, not that. Whether the chief missed him and regretted his absence was something I never found out: what the chief wanted to keep to himself he kept to himself, however hard you tried to worm it out of him.

Most noticeable was the effect on Dorothea: the longer

Joachim's absence lasted, the quieter she became. At times she would just sit sunk into herself, she uttered no words of good cheer, of enquiry, of encouragement as she used to do, her clear face became gaunt. She could get up from the table without having touched her plate, and outside the house she might suddenly come to a halt and then set off hastily in the opposite direction, and a few times this may have been in order to avoid the chief. If we happened to meet, she had nothing for me but a worried smile; no longer did she come up with jobs she wanted done urgently. Every meeting left me feeling sad, and I couldn't help remembering our days in the Kollerhof and wishing for their return. I wasn't surprised when one day she fell ill.

Magda had never before heard of this illness either: it was simply that Dorothea couldn't keep down anything she ate, not even chicken broth or steamed fillet of fish. Hardly had she swallowed it when she would retch, back it would come, and she would have to vomit. Often it happened so quickly that she couldn't reach the toilet or the nearest drain, and, because it was always a race against time, she took care to see that soiled towels were everywhere within reach, as well as small buckets containing a little water. Even then it could happen that she lost the race and had to be sick into her hands or on the floor. She insisted on clearing it up herself, nobody was allowed to help her. Gradually she found it more and more difficult to remain on her feet. Doctor Ottlinger began coming more often, he would sit a long time beside Dorothea's bed without ever saying much, and on one occasion Magda believed he fell asleep in his chair. The chief too sat often at Dorothea's bedside, and he hadn't much to say either.

Oh, Ina, if it hadn't been for you, you with your impatience and your strong will! You always knew how long things could be allowed to go on and how long they couldn't, and now, when you felt the limit had been reached, you drove off with your big tummy, first of all to Joachim's apartment and then, as he wasn't there, straight to Bodden, to the practice ground.

In my mind I can see you as you got out of the chief's jeep, groaning under the weight of your baby, simply fetched Joachim down from his horse and, allowing no questions, ordered him to go along with you, in such a way that he hardly had any time for extended farewells, but crouched there beside you and never even thought of taking over the wheel. You drove him up to the front door of the stronghold – I saw that myself – and, when he held back for a moment, all you said was: Come on, keep moving, or something will happen, in that tone of voice of yours which surprises everybody and nobody dares challenge. His uncertainty couldn't save him: with a look you forced him on through the hall and up the stairs to Dorothea's room, and, although you were already quite a bit out of breath – it was only a month later that Tim came – you then searched out the chief and ordered him too to come with you, in such a way that he didn't even ask where you were dragging him.

So there they were at last, standing opposite each other. Magda told me the silence was complete, not a word, not a sound to be heard, and when at one point she brought in the rosehip tea, they were each standing either side of the bed, reluctant to sit down, but also reluctant to leave. Ina waited downstairs in the hall, stretched out in an armchair with both hands on her tummy, and the longer she waited without hearing anything, the calmer she became. She stayed like that until both of them, the chief and Joachim, came down the stairs, then she went across to them, and before a word was said she could see that her brother would soon be moving back in. However, on the day he returned at last, the chief was not at home: it was certainly very convenient for him that on that day he had to go to Elmshorn.

If only I knew when Ewaldsen would get his job done and come and fetch me! He surely doesn't have to hand in more than a provisional list of damage, and there's not all that much to write down and reckon up. But already I've got the feeling, I can already imagine that once again he's forgotten me, simply left me sitting here like so often before. Once he said: That's how it is with you, Bruno, one doesn't even notice you're not there. He's no longer sitting on the water tank, he hasn't gone down to the main path, maybe he has just slipped off into the conifers and will be back in a moment. Those are the conifers from the bottle, as the chief calls them, because he'd mixed the seeds from which they grew with powdered charcoal and stored them away in bottles and, though some of us found it hard to believe, they kept their power of germination a full three years.

What's that gleaming over there? What are those ripping and rasping sounds? That can only be Ewaldsen. Yes, I know, I can see: he is ripping a parachute apart, dividing it into several pieces. So he has found another one and put it aside for himself; it's the best silk there is, he said. He is cutting into the silk with his knife and then ripping it, jerkily to begin with, then with an even movement of his arms out as far as they'll stretch. The silk makes a hissing sound as it breaks, hisses like a rubber tyre on wet asphalt.

You made me jump, he says, and asks: Why do you always creep up like that? Without paying any further attention to me, he measures out a length of silk and wraps it round his body. It looks as if he has already wrapped quite a few lengths round himself: if he now puts his jacket on over them and buttons it up, no one will spot he's got a torn-up parachute there. Come on, Bruno, take a piece too, it's come down from heaven and so it belongs to us. It's expensive stuff and will make a good present. Stop, stop, I say, but he has already pushed my shirt up and is winding a strip of silk around my hips. He tears off another length and throws it across to me: Get started then, Bruno, and I pull the material tight and stuff the ends of it into the waistband of my trousers. The straps and cords mustn't be left lying here, or they might one day give us away. Hardly has that thought struck me when Ewaldsen says: The remains here – you must bury them, Bruno, but don't just cover them over: put them deeper down where the plough won't reach them. Yes, I say, and now he's walking away, and I can feel the parachute silk pressing into my skin.

But now it's mealtime, and I can bury the remains later: first Bruno is going off to lunch. Magda won't learn straight away what I'm carrying under my shirt for her, white and gleaming, that she won't. This evening, yes. When she comes I'll make her guess what I've got on me and, after she has guessed wrong often enough, I'll invite her to undress me. Magda will see at a glance that this is the best silk to be had. She'll be suspicious, as she is with me from time to time, and I expect she'll first want to know where I got this expensive material. I shall tell her it came down from heaven, and that'll be the truth.

Brussels sprouts: I can already smell the sprouts over which Magda always rubs a little nutmeg, and with it there'll surely be a grilled chop and potatoes with melted butter – I only hope that this time she'll leave the fat on the chop. The kitchen hatch is open: Magda's head appears in it as in a picture frame and her expression isn't friendly. She looks at me as if she's inherited the sighing and the strictness from Lisbeth: So you've come at last, have you? I mustn't give her a sign: here everybody's supposed to think there's nothing between us – even when we're alone I mustn't wink at her, and touching her is quite out of the question. Have I washed my hands: she asks that as automatically as Lisbeth, my plate is already on the hot-plate and she hasn't filled it very lavishly, the sort of helping that could have come from Lisbeth, who often called me Greedyguts. The way she looks right through me as she puts the plate down in front of me, how careful she is not to come too close! I'd dearly like to unbutton my shirt and give her a quick glimpse of the shining white stuff under it, but that would be to betray our agreement.

There seems to have been a lot of excitement outside, she says, and that's all before she turns away. All sorts of things have been falling from heaven, I say, the wind brought soldiers in parachutes down in our plantations, a lot of things have been smashed, but we've made an exact list of the damage. She nods to me through the hatch, turns away, goes back to her work. I'd like to tell her more about the planes and all the things that were hovering above our heads, but I'd have then to call each word out loudly, and I'd rather not do that – she wouldn't want it either. I hope I can have a second helping of gravy and potatoes.

That can't be him, surely? When everything is now carried up to his room? The chief must have lost his bearings. In earlier days he did now and again come breezing in, but not for a long time now. The chief is wearing the same things he had on in the plantations. He greets me with a wave of his hand and says: Enjoy your meal, Bruno, and at the hatch he says: Just the usual apple, and now he turns and comes across to me and sits down without a word. Even if he were to sit down beside me in pitch darkness, I'd always know at once it was him – I can just feel him. He wipes his face wearily, lightly rubs his eyes. His mouth opening and closing. The soft click of his teeth. The faint smile – due, I suppose, to some memory. He stares at my plate, asks suddenly: Is that enough, Bruno? And he calls out towards the hatch: Is there anything more for Bruno? That is his way: he has always shown thought for me. Even when he has a lot of things to think of and to settle, he doesn't forget that it takes a bit longer to fill me up. His pocket flask of Wacholder: Your good health, Bruno, would you like to try a drop? No, no.

Magda puts the glass dish down in front of him carefully, and he starts eating straight away, snatching each time at the spoon: he doesn't bring the spoon up to his mouth, but snatches at it with his eyes closed, a habit he seems to have got into recently. How unthinkingly he gulps it down! You can see it gives him no pleasure to put something between his lips, he leaves himself no time to taste it, just lets the stewed apple with cinnamon and cream slide down his aged throat – he who once said to me how bad it would be if we could no longer enjoy our food. I myself couldn't have got through his stewed apple quicker than he did, and now he is getting to his feet. He has some important matter to settle, that's for sure, now that most of them are against him. I should like to say something to him, to promise him something, but I don't know how to begin.

His friendly push against my shoulder. Seven knocks – that's right, Bruno? Yes, I say. I'll drop in some time. Hiccups – that now of all times my hiccups have to start, jerking my head back: I can't take in everything he's saying. Something about smoothing things down, making an effort to straighten things out, because he has thrown a visitor out, some man from the law courts who professed to have come just for a chat, but in reality wanted to snoop around a bit. This is what we've come to, Bruno: somebody comes along to put me under the microscope, maybe to judge how frail I've become, and that in an official capacity. I told the fellow all there was to tell, briefly, and then showed him the door. I suppose he's sitting with Joachim now, the chief says, and making his report.

Know – he must know he can depend on me: I have kept my promise to him, nothing has been signed, and I've given nobody any information. I say: I've stuck to what I promised, and he gives me an encouraging nod. He does know, he knows everything about me. He puts the glass dish down beside the hatch, calls out a word of thanks to Magda and doesn't forget to remind her that I need a second helping. That's all he says before going out like a man with every reason to feel confident.

I won't open my door to anyone who doesn't knock seven times, never mind who it is and what he wants to question me about, I shall know nothing as far as he's concerned. If people are already coming to pass judgement on the chief, it won't be long now before they send someone to me, someone from the law courts, and all I hope is that he doesn't catch me out in the plantations when I'm alone. What I'd best like to do now is go home and lock the door and act as if I'm not there, and then nobody will be able to write a report on me. Just finish my second helping, and then let them see if they can find me. Once you figure in a report, there you'll stay; once you've been noticed, you'll be the first to be noticed a second time, and so I'll make myself scarce and keep quiet.

There it is again, that field mouse. I suppose you think I'm asleep, but I'm just lying here quite still on my bed, thinking. All I've done is take off my shoes, the raw leather boots you already know from the inside, since you once fell head over heels into one of them in the moonlight, in bright moonlight. Letting yourself be seen during the day shows how hungry you are – or how reckless, for so far you've never come out of your hiding-place behind the skirting-board before dusk. So sharp, so noiseless, and all this darting to and fro, like clockwork. You must have got that from the one before you, the one that never lost heart, but darted about until she found something, a crumb on the window-sill or under the table. That one never lost her timidness: at the slightest sound she'd whisk away behind the skirting-board, wait there a while and then come sniffing back. If I put down a bread crust or half a boiled potato, she'd bring her whole family with her, and then what a scrambling and squeaking and dancing there'd be! As soon as all the food was polished off, the whole family would dance for me.

I've got nothing for you, except maybe a few grains of maize. I'll pick them off the cob for you. Now don't go running away whenever I move, when the grains are pattering and bouncing on the floor: you're bound to like them. But just as I thought: timid like all the others, but now I'll keep still again and you can come out without fear.

Tomorrow or the day after, anyway very soon, I shall lay in

a stock, I'll keep it on the rack behind the curtain, and then I'll be able to hold out here for a long time. I'll go to Tordsen's shop and – let him think what he will – I'll buy as much as I can carry, that's what I'll do. That smoked sausage whose skin is wrinkled with so much sweating. A jar of pickled meat and a jar of jellied eels. A big bag of raisins and crispbread and a flan shell of short pastry. I'll buy apples, a whole pile of them, and also honey and a tin of mackerel in tomato sauce, that's for sure, and cheese and liquorice I certainly won't forget either. I'd best go to Tordsen's shop very early, wait till he opens up, and then buy it all at once before the other customers arrive.

So there, you see, you're back again. Now look for the grains and try them: the Hollenhusen maize is floury and it tastes so sweet. Closer to the bed, come closer, and don't dart around so much. Why are you listening now? Are you afraid? You know you don't have to hide from me.

Somebody's coming to visit me, maybe he's creeping up on tiptoe, but the mouse has heard the footsteps, has flitted off behind the skirting-board and is keeping still, waiting. Max? What does Max want with me now? He's coming straight towards my door, he'll soon be knocking, calling out my name. He won't look through the window, Max has never yet done that, but I won't let him in, for he'll surely be bringing a new suggestion to please everybody, or, if not that, he'll just be wanting to put more questions to me, dozens of questions I can never answer as he wants. He knocks and stands waiting with lowered head, but I won't open up. How softly he calls, almost as if he's afraid of disturbing me! Joachim would hammer on the door with his fist and order me to open at once, Max never. He's already shrugging his shoulders, turning away. Go and look in the plantations if you like: this time Bruno is not at home, you won't talk him into anything, as you've already talked so many others!

He once even managed to talk over Heiner Walendy, here in my home, one evening as lightning flashed over the plantations and a cloudburst was finding all the cracks and holes in the roofing felt. Suddenly drips were coming through everywhere, and we had to put bowls under the leaky places to catch the water. Heiner Walendy had already been hiding in my home for a few days. He had lain in wait for me in the dark, not far from my door. Maybe if he had knocked I wouldn't have let him in, but he just stepped out of the thuya hedge, took hold of my hand and begged: Put me up, Bruno, just for one night, out of old friendship and for the sake of that scar on my back.

I saw at once he was in trouble and I took him inside, where he didn't want me to put on the light. He sat down on the floor in one corner, his legs stretched out, his head against the wall. The first thing he said was: I shall never forget this, Bruno, and he also said: I could always depend on you, and then he ate some of the bread I still had left over, grateful, not asking for more. They'd arrested him by mistake and sentenced him by mistake: that's what he told me. The whole blame belonged to Frau Holgermissen, of whom we all know, though hardly any of us have seen her, for she only rarely leaves the fine big house in which she lives alone with her melancholy daughter.

Frau Holgermissen has everything done for her, the shopping, the cooking, the laundry, everything, and many people in Hollenhusen have worked for her, one of the last having been Heiner Walendy. He offered to cut down the ancient beech-tree whose crown made the rooms dark and whose roots were pressing against the walls. Together with another man he chopped off tips and branches, felled the trunk, dug out the stump and sawed and chopped up the wood for the fire. When he had finished his work, Heiner Walendy was invited into the house for the first time, and all the things he saw there made him quite speechless; among them he even discovered a little elephant made of silver. Anyway, he stood there looking around until Frau Holgermissen came in and gave him an envelope containing his payment.

It was not the sum they'd agreed on – anyway, Heiner

Walendy himself could remember that more had been promised him, and so one evening he went back to fetch the rest, not knowing that Frau Holgermissen and her daughter would already have gone to bed. So nothing: he was to get nothing more for all his work. Since he had a right to more, he simply searched for the money-box, rummaging through everything and, in order to do that undisturbed, he tied Frau Holgermissen and her daughter securely to their beds and took what was owed him.

That he'd be arrested on Hollenhusen railway station was something he'd never reckoned on; they took away his ticket and the money and a few other things he had on him, though he had no idea at all how they came to be in his pockets. That he had taken a brooch and the little silver elephant Heiner Walendy put down solely to his excitement and haste, and he would gladly have returned them of his own free will, but they refused his offer and took him to Schleswig. There, by mistake, he was sentenced. Luckily for him, he was sent several times each week to work on the land; his warder was an old man, and it didn't cost Heiner Walendy much effort to slip off behind his back one day and to make for the railtrack, where slow goods trains came jolting by at frequent intervals. That's the kind of thing that can happen to a person, Heiner Walendy said, and he advised me never to do anything for Frau Holgermissen.

He was unhappy, he was exhausted, and I felt so sorry for him that I offered to let him sleep in my bed, but he refused and couldn't thank me enough for being willing to put him up at all for one night. He slept on the floor, in the damp clothes that were too small for him and pinched all over, and it didn't surprise me that next morning he felt unwell and asked me to hide him during the day as well; he would leave in the evening, he promised. So I locked him in, saved a bit of my lunch for him, wasn't cross when he owned up to having taken some of my dried apple rings, and, when evening came, I brought him bread and rissoles for his journey. However, he didn't yet feel well enough to venture outdoors, and so I kept Heiner Walendy in my home and allowed him to sleep in my bed. He was content with everything, though he'd have liked a bit more to eat.

One Sunday Max came over; he had already arranged to take me with him on a walk to the judgement lime, and, since he knew I was at home, I went to the door. Heiner Walendy couldn't hold me back – he begged and threatened, but hold me back, that he couldn't do. In the moment it took me to slip out Max caught sight of my guest, looked at him without recognising him and then stood in silence as I locked my door. We walked down to the Holle and along the muddy path leading to the judgement lime. He kept on offering me his wine-gums and, if he opened his mouth at all, it was just to talk about age, about growing older. There was nothing on that subject I could say to him, I could offer him no consolation for the disappointments he was suffering as he grew older. Everything gets on in years, he said, not just we ourselves, but other people too and everything we have ever thought and stood up for. Ideas get on in years also, he said, and hopes and expectations – they become encrusted. Getting on in years means changing, whether you will or not. We must guard against that, Bruno – that was something else he said. As we passed the clump of willows he wished to have a little stick cut for him, I sought out a straight, flexible branch, topped it with my bill-hook, carefully removed the inner bark, and made a handle. He didn't ask a single question about the guest he had seen in my home. I suppose he didn't really want to know anything about it, but as time went on I could no longer keep it to myself, I just had to tell him I had taken in Heiner Walendy, the boy from the neighbouring barracks in earlier times. And I told him what Heiner Walendy had gone through with Frau Holgermissen and how he'd been arrested and sentenced by mistake. Max wasn't surprised, he simply nodded a few times, as if it were a familiar story.

The rickety bench beneath the judgement lime was already

occupied, we could see that from afar, but all the same we kept going and came on an old woman and a fat, friendly girl, who at once moved aside to make room for us. It was only on my second look that I recognised my old teacher, Fräulein Ratzum. She had a very small face covered in liver-spots, her hands were also spotted and her eyes looked milky, as if boiled out. I told her I was Bruno, the Bruno of former times, she searched her memory for a short while, then spread her hands in apology; she couldn't recollect exactly, had a few vague memories, but not enough to build questions on. On the other hand, she had heard of Professor Zeller and was pleased to meet him, if only here out of doors. Her sight was gone, she said, but fortunately Marlies came on occasional Sundays; she took her around a little and told her how everything was getting on and what had changed, so she managed still to keep up to date. They went off hand in hand, and the further they went the harder it was to make out who was the leader and who the led.

All of a sudden Max felt the urge again to ask questions in his usual way. His first question was so odd that I felt I must have heard it wrong, for what in fact he wanted to know from me was: who owned the land behind Lauritzen's meadows, the entire land between the railway cutting and Danes' Wood. I said: It belongs to the chief, of course, who else? And before that, Max calmly continued to ask, whom did it belong to before that? The soldiers, I said, when we began here it was a training ground, which the chief at first just rented, then bought. I was surprised he was asking questions he could easily have answered for himself, but he often did that – I don't know why either, all I do know is he always began with odd but easy questions that then became harder and harder.

Good, Bruno. And before the soldiers? Whom did the land belong to before the soldiers? No idea, I said, and he: Just try to imagine it. Maybe it all belonged to a general, I said. At that Max smiled and looked at me out of the corner of his eye and said: Not at all bad, Bruno. Let's assume the general had acquitted himself so well that his king gave him this land as a reward. He used it for hunting and leased it out, and, when he was very old, he sold it to the army as a training ground. But before that? Who owned it before him and before the king?

That's a long time ago, I said, and then I said: Maybe it belonged to a farmer, who grew oats and barley in his own particular way, which made Max shake his head and remind me there'd been no free farmers at that time, only tenants, all of them heavily in debt to a powerful owner. At that I asked quickly: And he? From whom did he get the land? From smaller people, Max said, from whom he'd swindled it, confiscated it or perhaps even bought it.

Step by step with his questions he led me down to earliest times, now and again I had the feeling that there'd soon be no solid ground left, for we were descending ever further down into the past, things were growing ever darker because of that, and my head was in a proper muddle. And before that? And before him? And before that person come on the scene? His questions carried us right down to some far-off, misty period in which the land was its own master, with no footprints crossing it, no fences dividing it up; everything was self-sufficient, it flourished and it withered and was content with its lot. Then, when the first man turned up, when he stood maybe on the command hill and looked out over the land, where there were no houses, no roads crossing and no railtrack cutting through, he may have thought of this and that, but surely not of making the land his own. Originally, said Max, everything belonged to all. Even when a second man arrived, then a third, to none of them did it occur to lay claim to something just for himself, to separate it off and defend it against rival claims: what was there was regarded naturally as common property.

And then he wanted me to tell him whether it wouldn't be a good thing if each of us took for himself only what he needed, and I said: Some always need more than others. Then he sighed and asked whether it wouldn't be a good thing if what we needed for living were to become common property once again, and I knew no answer to that.

Max shook his head and struck the bench with his little stick. I could see he was not satisfied with me, but that didn't last long, and, when I suggested we should wash our muddy boots in the Holle, he was at once in favour. He sat down on the riverbank and I washed his boots, dipped a clump of grass in the Holle and rubbed and scrubbed. Now and again I pulled a bit too hard or raised a leg too briskly or turned a foot too far sideways, and then Max would tighten his lips and let out a little groan as if in pain. Not so rough, Bruno, he said, not so rough.

It was his joints that hurt him. I got that out of him as we were walking towards Danes' Wood and he kept sighing and stopping, always looking for an excuse to stop. I couldn't show him my root people: they were gone. The hole in which they'd been hidden was still covered over and looked untouched, but the man on stilts and the kraken-man and the witch with three legs had vanished, and I've never seen them since. The two-headed snake I once gave Max was still in his possession; it was lying on a shelf keeping watch over his books. That's what he said, and standing beside the empty hiding-place he also said: Maybe they've declared their independence, your root people, have just moved out and are wandering around somewhere.

He, Max, had once himself had a collection, that was back in the eastern plantations, but what he collected as a boy was neither cartridge cases nor odd root formations, but something living that he kept in three wooden boxes his grandfather had given him.

You won't believe what my short-lived collection consisted of, Bruno: they were caterpillars. In one box he had the green pine-moth and also the yellow and grey drinker moth, he had the black-veined white butterfly and the tiger moth, and with their bright colours, their spines and their horns they gave him a lot of pleasure. Hardly was he out of school when he would slip out to the shed in which he'd hidden his living collection, and the ever hungry, ever nibbling and sawing caterpillars would be given the leaves and pine-needles and other things they liked. The boxes were hidden behind rolls of wire netting the chief had bought to protect the young plants from the gnawings of wild rabbits, and one day when he went to unroll the wire, he found the collection and first of all carried it outside: then he called Max over and asked him to explain why he was fattening and pampering such dangerous foes. Max couldn't understand his attitude, he pleaded for his caterpillars, swore he'd keep so close a watch on them that they couldn't do any damage, but the chief was not to be moved, he answered each word with a shake of his head and, though Max seized his arm, tugging and begging, he carried the boxes over to an open fire and tipped them out. Just tipped them out. Some curled, some reared up. The bright hairs vanished in a twist of flame. The bodies blistered and melted and charred and in a flash were gone. And that was the end of my collection, Max said, and that was all he said.

I was already thinking he'd be walking the rest of the way in silence, for now he was sunk into himself, his eyes fixed to the ground, his hands holding the little stick behind him. But when we came to the plantations, he asked me all of a sudden what I understood by happiness, at which I looked at him in such a puzzled way that he had to smile. But after a while he asked me again: Tell me what you would consider happiness. I didn't have to think long before saying: Staking Colorado firs. Then he asked: Nothing more? And I said: Yes – when the chief's satisfied with my work, when he comes and examines it all and says: Nobody does that as well as you do, Bruno. At that Max gave me a friendly cuff on the shoulders, he was suddenly as cheerful as I could wish, but at the same time he seemed surprised, as if something had just dawned on him. And when we reached my home, he didn't say goodbye at once, he made a silent request to come inside, and I unlocked the door and called out a word of reassurance to Heiner Walendy.

Heiner Walendy had long seen us coming. He was standing beside the entrance, pressed flat against the wooden wall and ready to take to his heels. If I hadn't been expecting that and blocked his way as I entered, he'd have been out and away for good. Grudgingly he sat down on the bed. I could feel his reproach, and I didn't fail to notice the wary look he was directing towards Max. Nothing I could say had any effect on him, he didn't even relax when I told him who it was I'd brought in. He ignored the wine-gum Max offered him, but he did take the cigarette, accepted a light and drew the smoke in greedily. He didn't want to talk. When Max asked him how long he'd been here with me, he just pointed towards me and said: He knows, he knows everything, and when Max told him he'd heard the whole story of his misfortune from me, Heiner Walendy said: Then you can arrange for somebody to collect me. A phone call will do.

Speaking more to himself than to Heiner Walendy, Max said it was a risky business trying to win for yourself by force the justice you feel has been denied you. You could try – good, there were even times when you had to try – but it's better not to forget what the consequences might be. When force stems from desperation or great suffering, it must be acknowledged and understood, but here that was not the case. Heiner Walendy started to grin, he grinned and looked at me in a harassed way and asked: What's going on, Bruno? Are we being given extra lessons? If so, I'm off.

A different person: suddenly there was a person quite different from the Max I knew standing there. Even the manner in which he turned from the window towards Heiner Walendy showed his superiority: a threatening, ominous calm I'd never seen in him before. He narrowed his eyes and said sharply: Don't put on airs with me, my friend. You've got no reason for it. You seem to forget what you owe to Bruno. That found its mark all right: Heiner Walendy looked not just surprised, but dazed as well, and he forgot to draw on his cigarette as

Max tested the flexibility of his stick, bending it down and then letting it spring back as he started to speak.

He'd already heard enough, he said, and he believed very little of it. It might be that a price for the felling of the beech-tree had never been fixed at all, and that he, Heiner Walendy, had felt underpaid only because he wanted to provide himself with an excuse for helping himself to a few things in Frau Holgermissen's house; if it had been otherwise, he'd have made do with the missing payment and refrained from taking some valuable articles along with it. Such things are done, Max said, and we both know the sort of people who do them. I noticed that Heiner Walendy was looking queasy and would dearly have liked to leave – something he hinted at when he said: Pity it's not yet dark. That just made Max laugh: he laughed and asked whether a clear conscience depended on the time of day. Listen, my friend, said Max, I know you better than you'd like to think, and, if I can give you a word of advice, vanish, go back of your own free will to the place you came from. There's nothing else you can do, for the reasons you give for doing what you did are not convincing; you thought them up after the event, and that's hypocrisy – you won't get away with it.

What support could I give Heiner Walendy? He was hoping for something from me, expecting it even. Rarely had he looked at me with such urgency, but I could think of nothing that would help him now, as he sat there so abjectly, his shoulders drooping.

Max gave me a sign and I followed him outside. I was not allowed to lock the door as we went off to our evening meal in the stronghold, I to Magda, he to the others. That Heiner Walendy might make off during our absence he considered out of the question. He'll stay, Bruno, he'll open the door just once, take a look outside, and stay – and not only on account of the thunderstorm. All sorts of things were gathering and jostling for position in the skies above us, black clouds full to bursting were coming in from the northwest, but the mobilisation was not yet complete, the corvettes and the sloops were still lying in wait behind Hollenhusen, as happens now and then.

My supper was already laid out on the table and the hatch was closed – a sign that Magda was engaged elsewhere – and so I could eat as fast as I pleased. While eating I could think of nothing but Heiner Walendy and the manner in which he had been crushed. Though I reckoned he would have made off during our absence, I wrapped some bread and sausage up just in case. In spite of everything, I felt even sorrier for him than at the time he'd had that accident with his stepfather's delivery van and all the fish were scattered over the field of rape.

Heiner Walendy had not gone: he was sitting motionless on my bed, and he didn't even turn his head as I came in, but he did take the bread I held out to him, and ate it without a word. Then he demanded the key, and I saw at once what he was planning and said no. He then asked me to lock the door, but I didn't. Since I could feel how afraid of Max he was, I tried to rid him of his fear by telling him some of my own experiences with Max over the years, but it wasn't much help. When at one point he got up quickly and tore the door open, I thought he would rush out, but he just stared out into the rain and shut the door when there was a huge crash of thunder and a flash of lightning.

Max arrived in a raincoat, carrying a cellophane bag he threw over to Heiner Walendy so unexpectedly that he instinctively caught it. I saw apples in it, and two or three small packets that surely contained something fried. That's for the road, Max said curtly, and he also said: It makes a good impression when you return of your own free will. Why he stood looking down on Heiner Walendy so intently and for so long I don't know, but I do know he suddenly straightened up, as if he'd received some comforting assurance, then waited for a few further flashes of lightning before leaving with a brief goodbye. Plop, plop, went the drips from the ceiling. I placed bowls under the leaks, as many bowls as I could find. We said nothing more to each other. After I had locked up Heiner

Walendy crouched down in one corner, the cellophane bag beside him. He refused my bed, which the last few nights I'd allowed him to take over, and, when I woke up the following morning, he was gone.

I wouldn't care to know how many people Max has already talked over – no one can match him at that. First he asks and listens and makes you believe that all he himself wants is to understand: you can see him thinking it over – and he never lets you see that he knows beforehand what you'll say and a lot more besides. And just when you're thinking he's become unsure himself and would like to let it all rest, he takes the subject up again and moves in closer with his questions until there's nothing much left to consider: you have to acknowledge and agree with what he says. Then, as he continues probing deeper and deeper, always as if just seeking a firm foothold for himself, the cords begin to tighten. Max properly ties you up, and in the end you feel like a pepper and salt moth spun fast inside its cocoon. So you're stuck, and all you can do is say yes, or do the only thing that's left for you to do.

How flabby his face has become, how flabby and puffy! Once when I fetched him from the station he said to me: I've got fat, Bruno, haven't I? But it's easier to face the world with a bit of fat on one's bones. We all need a buffer of some kind, and this is the one I've made for myself.

Though Max can talk people over, he couldn't become chief here. Joachim, yes – or at least he could make a pretence of it, but not Max. Yet who knows? Maybe they've both been dreaming of taking over one day and, if they're prepared to go to the length of depriving the chief of his rights, they must surely also have considered who will take it all over and run it: it must be one of them. Max, no, never in a thousand years, he doesn't even know how the cotyledons develop in marrows, and the fact that in some plants the water is forced up by root pressure, that's something he couldn't even grasp – at the time I won my bet against him. I got my jar of honey, which had been my wish, for the chief himself confirmed that some plants force their water up with a pressure of eight atmospheres. Of course Max might have just let me win, he might have lost on purpose, I wouldn't put that past him, and I'm certain *he* won't send me away. Two bets I've already won against him, and the stake for the second was also a jar of honey. It happened beside the big anthill in Danes' Wood, the teeming castle of ants he was seeing for the first time.

Max didn't believe anyone would dare sit down on this hill, he thought the nipping of thousands of tiny pincers would be enough to put anyone off, so I asked him what he'd give to see someone do it, and he said: A jar of honey at least. I got it. Like a shot I sat down on the loosely-built hill and kept quite still. The ants at once gave the alarm, dropped their white eggs, crawled out of their work passages and swarmed over my hands and shoes and legs. Some of them strayed on to my back, crept up to my neck and examined my ears – the ones trying to get into my mouth I blew off. Not one of them bit me – at least, I felt no pain, no burning – and Max, who was watching thunderstruck, had to hold tight to a tree to bear the sight of me. Later, after I'd taken off my clothes and was picking the confused ants out of them, Max said: There's something quite special about you, Bruno, I don't know what, but it's certainly special. I got my honey.

If Max comes back and knocks again, I'll open up after all. It's possible he wants to tell me something important, maybe he has to leave already and just wants to say goodbye: Max has never once gone off without saying goodbye to me. All the same, there are times when I can't make him out. It's much harder to see inside him than any of the others: he must have several layers, like our land here. If he were really to become the new chief, he'd be dependent on me to a large extent, at the start he couldn't get anywhere at all without me. But what is putting such ideas into my head? I'd be better taking a little rest than thinking such thoughts, for it's more likely our plantations will take off into the sky than that Max will be put in charge here.

Stay awake for ever, that's something I'll never be able to do. I've often wondered what it would be like if I could always stay awake, day and night, indoors and out, and a few times I've even tried to ward off sleep by imagining all kinds of things, fires and shipwrecks and runaway horses, but not even the things that strike fear into me could hold back my tiredness, in the end sleep would overtake me wherever I was. Not in my stomach or chest, but first of all in my eyes, which I have to close, whether I want to or not. I still hear almost everything, but there's less and less to be seen – no, it's not like that, rather that what there is to see moves backwards and becomes blurred, it loses its sharp edges, its solidity, sometimes I even seem to be looking down on things from above, on the Holle, on Danes' Wood. Alertness: maybe a person could stay awake for ever if sleep didn't take away his alertness. That's what the chief once said: The miller stays awake only as long as his mill-wheel is not turning regularly.

It can even be painful to try to force yourself to stay awake, that's a thing I've sometimes noticed. Very slowly a kind of pressure builds up behind your eyes, your skin begins to smart and there's a hot feeling inside your head – as now. Pinching yourself helps for a while, but not always. That night when Bruno was keeping watch with the chief, when we were sitting in the pear plantation, I pinched myself goodness knows how many times in an effort to stay awake, but sleep overcame me shortly before dawn, and when the man with the shivers climbed over my wall and moved in an odd, tottering way across to the erratic block, the chief had to nudge and shake me sharply.

It may be I'd fallen asleep because in all the previous nights nothing at all had shown up; we patrolled, we lay in wait, we stood stiff as storks among the shadows and lay on our stomachs between the nursery beds – but all for nothing: we never came face to face with the people who were clearing out our plantations, making off with whole cartloads.

Once my eyes are open, nothing lingers behind: no dreams, no heaviness, my head is clear. I don't need time to adapt, like Magda, who always wakes up grumbling and can't bear being spoken to, but a nudge from the chief, a little shake, and I'm awake and ready for anything.

Over the chief's outstretched arm I saw the man as he climbed over the wall and, without looking round, made off towards the erratic block, struggling along in his peculiar manner of walking, and I thought he must surely have been sent on ahead to test our alertness. And when the chief gave me a sign to cut off the stranger's path, I felt certain we had at last caught one of the elusive band that had been taking things that didn't belong to them, always on nights when none of us was outdoors. Things of all sorts they took – hardwoods, softwoods, fruit – they knew exactly what could be easily sold, and they helped themselves so generously that the chief had a fresh stocktaking made after each of their nightly visits – not just a rough estimate, but done with a calculator. The Hollen-husen police could find no traces either, Duus contented himself with walking a few times in full view through the plantations and making a note of our losses, that's all he managed to do; we had to keep the nightly watches ourselves, I always with the chief, Joachim and Guntram Glaser each by himself.

The escape route: there'd been no need for me to cut it off, for when he saw me he waved, beckoned me over from the top of the erratic block, glad to see another human being at this hour of the day. I waited until the chief had made a detour and come up behind him, and only then did I go towards him, go up to the thickset man who greeted me in a very friendly way and politely invited me to sit down beside him. I said nothing, leaving it all to the chief, who had come up quietly and who called out so suddenly that the startled stranger slipped off the block. There he was now, looking at both of us in turn and not knowing how to explain his presence there. If only we'd had some idea of who it was standing there so awkwardly before us, if only we'd known! When the chief pointed out that he was on private property, he nodded and said: I know, gentlemen, I know; and then he made a vague gesture over the land and shook his head, as if he couldn't believe how greatly everything had changed in the past few years. The chief asked him if he had come from Hollenhusen, and he replied: No, no, from farther away, and with a smile he added: I enjoy walking early in the day. He had words of admiration for what he saw on our land, he was impressed by the neat cordons that ran along the level ground and down into the hollow, the imposing house on the hill – he didn't say command hill – and he liked the wall I had stacked up in the early days, and I realised then that it was all familiar to him from the past. He begged pardon several times for his presence here, regretted having taken us away from whatever we'd been doing and repeatedly drew our attention to the tracks he'd left behind him, which showed with what care he'd walked over the land. It was probably the chief's silence that made him keep on talking; he'd sooner have made off, that's for sure, but since he wasn't certain what we meant to do with him, he stayed there voicing his admiration and his regrets.

And suddenly, in the middle of a sentence, he gave a violent start. As if struck by a bullet, he bent double, felt his way with outstretched hands across to the block and there sank down in a crouching position. His panting breath. The fidgetty grasping movements with which he tried to clasp his hands together.

The swaying, shivering jerks of his upper body. He looked helplessly up at the chief, helpless and at the same time as if ashamed, and I was surprised how calm the chief remained, he said nothing, just at one stage brought the stranger's hands together, so he could clutch his knees, and that was all. The sucking movements he made with his lips were in vain: I guessed at once he was asking for a cigarette, but we had none on us, and it wasn't long before the shivering stopped and he could get to his feet without our help. His parting words were brief, and spoken in a thick voice, and the chief's reply was even briefer. We watched him as he stumbled off towards the stone wall and over the damp ground down to the Holle. I suppose the chief could see I wasn't happy just to let the stranger go, for he said: Not him, Bruno, he's not one of them, but I'd like to know what he wants here. Maybe they just sent him on ahead, I said, to which the chief replied: Not with those hands, Bruno, and anyway he's got palsy. But what if he was just pretending? I asked. He wasn't pretending, the chief said, he picked it up somewhere, maybe during the war, maybe he was buried like my dispatch rider, who also became palsied.

I crept along behind him. The chief didn't think much would come of it, but he didn't object to my following him, for this was the first person we'd challenged since starting our nightly watch. Since he never once looked back, I didn't need to stay under cover the whole time among the trees or in the long grass. I followed him, stooping low, and watched him make his way to the makeshift wooden bridge, those muddy boards and planks across which Lauritzen's cattle would trot. There he sat down and followed the course of the Holle with his eyes. On the horizon narrow strips of reddish yellow light were filtering through, bringing a faint glaze to the meadows and a sparkle to the black waters of the Holle. The stranger sat there as if waiting for sunrise; now and again he threw something into the river, stalks and leaves probably, and watched them drift away. I was hardly in any doubt that he knew our river well, and I knew it for certain when he stood up and moved along the bank to the cattle's watering place, behind which the river is at its deepest – a grown-up person can just about stand there. The water doesn't flow swiftly at that point; from the depths it sends up whirlpools which run in towards the bank, and whatever happens to be floating on it is spun around a few times before being caught again by the current and moved on. The stranger stayed there longer than by the bridge, just staring down at the water until the sun came up, and then he went off in the direction of Hollenhusen railway station.

The chief shrugged his shoulders, he couldn't explain either what the stranger wanted on our land by the river, this man with the shivers whom we encountered for the first time during that watch. The chief's thoughts were occupied much less with him than with the others on whose account we'd spent yet another fruitless night, and his disappointment and bitterness showed in his face. He thrust his spade into the earth with a grating sound, and I knew that was the signal to break up. We walked along in silence, each with his own thoughts, but before I left him he said: We'll catch them yet, Bruno, one day they'll fall into our trap, for we shall hold out longest.

We didn't catch them. In spite of all the time spent outside, we never caught sight of any of them, either because they'd gone by the time we arrived, or because they waited to cart the plants off until we had abandoned our watch. We were forced to the conclusion that they had an eye on us at all times and even overheard what we arranged between ourselves. The chief kept a register of all the losses in his office, he was beside himself, couldn't think what to do, and at times he lost his self-control. I wasn't surprised when one night he decided to sling his gun and to hold it on his knee during our watch. I believed him capable of anything then, anything.

Once at dawn he shot a magpie and didn't bother to retrieve it – something he'd never done before; I had only to tread on a twig or to sigh and he'd be shushing me or giving me a warning look. Some night I didn't even dare speak a word, so gloomy and so silent was he as he crouched there beside me, and, if he then suddenly said something, it would often make me jump. I sensed how his mind was for ever working, and I felt quite certain that – since up till now he had always managed to get to the bottom of everything and set it to rights – he would one day manage to close the trap. Whether at that time he had his suspicions I don't know, but I do know he got into the habit of asking everyone he met about his work or casting long brooding looks at people's backs; he even looked that way at Joachim and Guntram Glaser. Bruno wasn't the only one to notice quite a lot of people taking care to keep out of the chief's way.

The nightly visits ceased in winter, a winter of much snow. It went to work like a pastrycook in our plantations, setting hoods and caps on all our plants. What glittering white clouds then flew up as the wind rushed through or a swarm of rooks dropped from the skies! The unseen invaders took nothing more, the few tracks on the ground were always our own, and we began at last to think of other things instead of just our stricken plantations. But there was one who couldn't forget, wherever he was, standing or sitting, and that was the chief. He couldn't take his mind off it. What worried him most was probably that he hadn't been able to catch anybody; he gave no indication that the losses meant a great deal to him. This brooding, this absent-mindedness, this probing and questioning – even on New Year's Eve, during the fortune-telling, you could see what was occupying his mind more than anything else. Cupping his glass of grog in both hands, he sat by himself in a corner staring at the damp ring his glass had left, and hardly listening as we looked for meanings in the odd shapes the molten lead made when poured from a spoon into cold water. When Ina called him a spoilsport, he gave a troubled nod.

She it was, Ina, who took charge of the spirit-stove and the washing-bowl filled with water; she also dealt out the lead piping that had been cut into little strips, placing a bit of it in the old-fashioned soup spoon for each person in turn. All each of us had to do was to pour the molten lead into the bowl and then fish it out. How she could laugh and hop up and down with joy, particularly when Guntram Glaser thought up meanings for the gleaming shapes. Though everybody said something about the molten objects, no one could read into them such funny and such strange interpretations as Guntram Glaser, and his predictions for the future were beyond compare.

Now let's look at what Joachim has come up with: a horse doing a handstand – I mean a hoofstand of course, and these bullet-shaped heads, those are seals clapping: Joachim will win a prize! He told Dorothea she'd cast a waterfall, which meant strength and trustworthiness without end, and the scattering of grey was the wreckage of a boat belonging to someone who hadn't allowed for the current. The things the lead, after falling with a hiss into the bowl, was capable of showing! A pump with a hat, a wreck on the sea-bed, exploding pine-trees and one-legged herons: all of these could be seen in the lead, provided you looked long enough.

I don't know why I trembled as I held the spoon in the flames. I felt I had to get it over as quickly as possible, and that's why I didn't wait for the grey slab of lead to turn into a single silver tongue, but tipped it into the bowl too soon. Now let's take a look at what Bruno has produced. A wave, said Max, breaking against a harbour wall and making a grand splash. Looks to me more like a dog squashed flat by a car, said Joachim. No, said Dorothea reprovingly, Bruno has succeeded in making a very splendid juniper bush, a copybook Noah's ark juniper. I was pleased with that, but Guntram Glaser, who had been sizing my shape up from all sides, could see no juniper in it. He said: Bruno has produced a rarity, a cloud in fact and, better still, a cloud on wheels; that, if I'm not mistaken, is the sign of a journey: Bruno will be making a combined journey over land and sea.

Ina – she managed in the end to fetch the chief out of his corner, to coax him into holding the soup spoon and get him to hold the lead in the flame – something none of us others could have done, that's for sure – and, before anybody else could comment on the shape the chief made, she had the answer: A volcano, a good-natured crater, but one practising how to erupt again. Off target, little sister, said Max, right off target: it's a fountain, but it seems to me to be coming from a burst pipe – that's it: we must look out for a burst pipe. The chief regarded the shape he had made with only lukewarm interest, rubbed it a few times and held it closer to the flame, then he screwed up his eyes and murmured: I think it's a landmine exploding, and that's all he said. He twisted and bent his lead figure out of shape as he drifted back to his corner, where he sat tight-lipped, pearls of sweat gathering beneath the grey stubble of his hair. I was fully expecting him to leap to his feet and leave us, but he stayed, breathing heavily, forcing himself to stay.

Then suddenly I myself was finding it harder to breathe, my throat was swelling shut from the inside, and my temples felt as if gripped in a clamp. I had to turn to him, and though he was not moving his lips, I heard his voice, and his voice said: One of you must be part of it, one of you is involved, I can feel it, and I shall get to the bottom of it. Since at that moment they were all grouped around Ina, I slipped quickly out on to the terrace, made a snowball and rubbed my neck and face with snow. The heat died down, but I felt no calmer – not even after eating the extra portion of doughnuts and apple turnovers Dorothea pushed towards me.

Ina and Guntram Glaser also left me the remains of their New Year's Eve goodies, and it was quite a job emptying all the plates, but I did it and won some applause – though not from Joachim. His impatience, his restlessness: for him the old year couldn't be seen off quickly enough, he even went to the length of filling up our glasses well before midnight, and when we turned to face the grandfather clock, you could see how dearly he'd have liked to give the minute hand a bit of a push. He clinked glasses as fleetingly with me as with the others, saying just: To the new, Bruno, and that was all he wished me; then, since I was the last person he drank with, he pressed his glass into my hand and left me standing. He went out to the terrace, while we stayed drinking each other's health and exchanging all sorts of wishes for the New Year. Max had the most wishes for all of us, the chief the least: he just nodded in reply to all that was said to him. He gave Dorothea just a quick kiss on the cheek, to me he held out his hand with the remark: Take good care of yourself, Bruno.

All at once the fireworks began. Joachim had prepared them, and it was surely the biggest firework display Hollenhusen had ever seen. Three thunder-flashes set it going, three explosions whose waves rolled across the snow-covered plantations and must have roused all the creatures hiding on our land, the hares, the birds and all the rest, from their sleep. In the snow below the terrace bottles had been stuck, in them the wooden sticks of the rockets. Joachim was leaping from one to the other, holding his burning lighter to the fuses, and one after another they flew upwards with a hiss to burst and release revolving moons and silver rain and stars of all colours that drifted slowly across the white land, producing moving shadows from the plants under their burden of snow. The cries of admiration and merry squeals of alarm and the reflections of the spraying suns, all colouring our faces and casting shadows over them – just from watching our faces you could have made out all the things that were bursting and flashing and raining down over the plantations.

If only I knew what's coming, whether I shall have to leave Hollenhusen, if only I knew more altogether about what they're planning and preparing and whose will is behind it all! Sometimes I feel I am getting quite close. Among the wheels of fire and the bursting stars of Joachim's fireworks I tried to discover signs of what the New Year would bring us: I sought the chief in the light of a trailing comet, I hoped to find Ina in the silver rain, quickly I let it be March and then August and thought of Dorothea and Joachim, but I could make nothing out. Smoky darkness held everything hidden; and then, while I was still looking out for signs, squibs started hissing past our ears and jumping crackers exploded with a rattle among the snow-covered roses and sprang up at us: you had to watch out you weren't hit. The chief was the only one who was not hopping about. He stood by himself in the terrace doorway, watching it all. Not a sound came from him, no excited word, but no disapproving one either when one or two of the rockets shot off along the ground and burned out in the pear plantation. Nor had he anything to say when we were all praising Joachim's fireworks. All he wanted was to get back to his corner, to his glass of grog, but before he could sink down there, Dorothea restrained him by taking his hand.

She led him back the way he'd come, led him once again to the terrace and then, unnoticed by him, she gave me the signal we'd agreed on. I sped up to Dorothea's room, lifted up the new rocking-chair, the handsomest chair you can imagine, and carried it carefully down into the hall. Max helped me place it on the floor. Ina had already decided on the position for it, we removed the last of the cardboard wrappings and gazed in wonder at the chair with its black, dully gleaming leather, its polished rockers – the things Dorothea would bring back from her shopping trips could always make you gaze in wonder.

We gave Dorothea a sign that all was ready and she steered the chief back into the room. As she led him closer and closer to the rocking-chair, his face showed neither eagerness nor expectancy, just a sort of gruff good humour. Before the rocking-chair she let go of him and stepped to one side: There, a surprise for the New Year – for you alone.

I was expecting him to sit down at once and try it out, to make himself comfortable and then let us see what pleasure you can find in a chair by rocking it gently, but he didn't do that. He just stood there sizing the chair up, then he glanced across to the light-brown sofa, in the corner of which he usually sat, raised his shoulders and said: It almost seems a pity to sit in it. Aren't you pleased? Dorothea asked. It's the best to be had in Schleswig. You can see that, said the chief, and he also said: A chair for feast-days. For relaxing in, Dorothea said, and she went to push him down into the chair: It's meant just for you alone, to relax in. Now come along, sit down.

And then he sat down, hesitantly, stiffly, cautiously, as if he was afraid of damaging the chair or at any rate soiling it. He didn't venture to lean back, let alone rock backwards and forwards, just sat there awkwardly for a moment, then, getting up, voiced the opinion: It's certainly good value for money, this chair.

Dorothea: all of a sudden Dorothea had tears in her eyes. She said nothing and she didn't really weep properly, just stood there with tears in her eyes. Maybe she was waiting in the hope that in the end the chief would say something, some word to show his pleasure, his thanks, but nothing came, and then suddenly she went out, went without a glance at any of us.

No one moved, all of us conscious, I suppose, of the gloom in the air. It was so quiet that I could hear the ice clinking in Max's glass. And it was Max who first broke the silence, saying: The New Year – now it has truly begun, and then he drank from his glass and put it down so loudly that it sounded like a starting pistol. I should dearly have liked to run after Dorothea and bring her back, but it wasn't my place to do that, there were others with a better right, even Guntram Glaser, who was just staring in front of him, embarrassed. Then Ina went across to the chief and took him by the arm. Come, she said, please come, we'll fetch her back together. Still holding him, she put out a hand for his glass and gave it to him, saying: We can't start the New Year like this, can we? The chief took a sip and said: You go then, you can manage it alone, Dotti listens to you. She's waiting for you to come, said Ina, a word of apology from you and it'll all be forgotten. The chief shook off Ina's hand, he smiled bitterly and quietly asked: What for? What should I apologise for? Maybe for not being able to take pleasure in anything? And in a louder voice he said: A surprise – and this time for New Year. Not a week has passed recently without a surprise of some sort. I think it's time we gradually began to get used to what we already have.

You're overlooking something, Ina said, and she also said: You're unfair, for Mammi's not doing it for herself, she wants to give you pleasure – you. How can you take pleasure in something you don't need? the chief asked softly, and it was almost as if he was talking to himself. He took another short sip and then he said: Let's understand one another, Ina – I've got nothing against surprises, but a thing must have a use, there must be at least some need for it, we can't just indiscriminately buy and pile up things that happen for a moment to catch our fancy. To that Ina showed no wish to reply: she pressed her hands together, she closed her eyes, and all at once turned and walked out. She didn't come back, not during the time I was there.

Rarely have I been sadder than on that night. I didn't go straight home, but walked through the snow-covered plantations, collecting up the tattered cardboard remains of squibs and rockets. I trudged up to the erratic block and stood on the hump from which I could look down on it all. There was the stronghold, massive, lit up, but the lights didn't burn evenly, they flickered and blinked and, together with the light of the stars, tinted the snow a soft blue. I hadn't been standing there long when a light flared up in the chief's room. I couldn't make out his silhouette, but I knew he had left the others, knew too that he hadn't gone to Dorothea. What I should then most have liked to do would have been to return secretly to the stronghold, just so as to be close to them and, since I couldn't bring them together again myself, to wait there until Ina or even Guntram Glaser succeeded in doing it. I would have done anything, anything, just to see them back together again. The lights didn't go out, I trudged through the snow to the old pine-trees, which were creaking softly, I picked up a heavy branch and dragged it along behind me, so that my tracks were

340

almost wiped out and, leaving hardly a trace behind, I wandered over to the wall and down into the hollow and then in a wide circle around the stronghold, and as I walked I thought of Ina, trying with my wishes to help her.

When for an instant the front door opened and a shadow slipped out into the night, I thought it was Ina. I at once dropped the branch and followed the figure, which kept in the shadow of the frozen rhododendrons, crossed the open bit of path as quickly as it could and didn't stop till it reached the shelter of the thuya hedge. Since I had already recognised Magda, I didn't call out, I kept her in sight and let her scurry on, right up to my door, where she stopped to listen for a moment before knocking. It gave her a proper start to find me suddenly standing behind her, it wouldn't have taken much to make her go away again, so annoyed was she. We'd hardly got inside before she made me promise never to scare her like that again. As a punishment she put the paperbag she'd been hiding under her coat down on the table carelessly and without a word, then waited sulkily until I'd pulled the blind down and poked the stove and put on fresh fuel. After that all she said was: Since it seems you're not going to say it: Happy New Year.

After we'd made it up, we sat down together to eat up the dripping-cakes she'd brought. Magda read my palm a little, but – as usual – couldn't tell me what the future holds, since one of the planetary mounts is missing on my hand and there's a misleading cross-line. She found my future so obscure that she let go of my hand with a shake of her head and looked at me in a worried way.

The warm, sweetish air was making me sleepy, but Magda wasn't at all tired. She stared straight ahead in a brooding sort of way, she sighed, her forehead wrinkled in reflection, she couldn't stop thinking of Dorothea, of the one and only Frau Zeller, as she called her, she had heard her weeping at the start of the New Year and was convinced we must be prepared for all kinds of things in the near future.

How tenderly she stroked the brooch, the silver seagull in flight Dorothea had given her for Christmas! How obstinately she persisted in calling the chief unjust and peevish and bitter! I didn't even try to contradict her. Then suddenly she wanted to know what I thought was the most important thing in life, and I suppose I must have looked at her in such a puzzled way that she had to smile and run her hand quickly over my hair. Independence, she said, believe me, Bruno, there's nothing so important as independence. Once you've achieved that, you've got the best in life. And she also said: I have thought about it a lot, and maybe you should think about it too.

All of a sudden she put an arm round my shoulders, and that was so nice I scarcely dared move. After a while she began to stroke my back, gently, as only she can, at the same time keeping her eyes fixed on the window of my stove, through which a steady glow was coming. The chief himself had sought out this stove for me, because it kept its glow for a particularly long time – sometimes ten hours. Very cautiously I leaned towards her and laid my face against her, but her necklace of wooden beads so dug into my cheek that I moved to lean just against her arm. Magda has a bunion, just like me; I saw that when she kicked off her shoes and hoisted herself further up on my bed. A faint noise came from the stove, the embers fell inwards and settled, we turned off the light, for enough was coming from the little yellow eye in the stove. We didn't say much, just at one point she asked me where my perpetual hunger came from, I didn't know, and when she asked if I'd ever been so full that I could get nothing more down – truly nothing more – I had to admit I couldn't remember. She thought she could manage it, and I could feel her already planning something, turning it over in her mind, thinking something up that would completely satisfy my hunger, but she didn't say what, she just left me with the promise that one day she'd stop up the hole in my tummy, so help me God, Bruno. Confident and content, she stretched out, wriggled her way out of the hollow in my bed and breathed evenly as if just waiting for sleep. I too stretched out and cautiously, tentatively put an arm round Magda. I was amazed how soft she was. Our hands touched and clasped each other. That was the first time she stayed with me. It was only for a few hours, for she had to return to the stronghold early, and after she'd gone I thought of summer and the solitude of some of our plantations, but above all I thought of her and of me. To begin with Bruno couldn't think of any name at all for this particular feeling, but I did find it in the end: it was simply lightness, a soothing lightness all over. That was it.

The beginnings were the nicest, and because the beginnings are the hardest, they lead to the greatest pleasure, and, because nothing is yet fixed and planned, you can try out all sorts of things of your own: that gives the greatest satisfaction.

Somebody is knocking: that's Max's way of knocking. So he's trying again, and this time I'll let him in, this time I must. Just a moment. Elef? What does Elef want with me, how does he know I'm here? The cardboard is already showing through the peak of his cap. How small he looks in his crumpled drainpipe trousers, and how easy to see in his face that he's come to offload some worry on to me! Come in, Elef. He doesn't want to disturb me at home, he hasn't come about knives or saws or because yet another pair of shears must be reported lost: he has something else on his mind. Sit down, Elef. Never before has he been so agitated. How he shifts from one foot to the other, searching me with his dark eyes! He can't make up his mind whether he should come out with whatever it is that's brought him here. Come on now, tell me what's the matter. Herr Bruno knows much. Yes, yes, go on. The chief, he says, it is told the chief very ill . . . No one knows exactly, maybe Herr Bruno can give him some information. So it's come this far: someone has picked it up and passed it on, they're whispering it to each other in the plantations, the wooden houses. From whom, Elef, from whom did you hear that? He points this way and that, meaning he's heard it from several different directions, it doesn't matter where, all he wants to know is whether it's true. If the chief very ill, then no party on Sunday, he says. What shall I say to him in reply? And how much can he be permitted to know, when it's certain he'll pass it all on?

I was with him, I say, I was speaking to him yesterday, he doesn't feel altogether well, but he'll soon be out and about again. And I say: The party can be put off if necessary. How closely he considers my answer! He can't hide his doubts, hardly anything escapes his keen sense of hearing. Honest, Herr Bruno, a new chief is coming? Who has suggested that, I ask, and he: When new chief comes, we maybe all go home, get sent home. You needn't worry, Elef, the chief's still here, he's still in charge and nobody's thinking of sending you home. I've heard a number of things too, there's always a lot of talk, but as far as I know you have nothing to be afraid of: I wonder who started that rumour? Once more he ponders my words – they twist and turn everything they hear, these people – must do, I suppose, in their position. The pleading deep down in his eyes, the appeal to be told what he needs to know, so he can see where he stands. Yes, Elef, as soon as anything has been decided, you'll hear of it from me, you can rely on that. Good, good, and thank you.

He hurries across to the toolshed. So it's got as far as Elef already! I suppose all over the place it's being said that there's something wrong or something brewing up there, and I wouldn't be surprised if they already know what the chief is planning to do with me, has set aside for me; maybe some of them believe I already have some influence here, that's quite possible. No one passes on exactly what he's heard, he always adds a bit of his own to it, and so it puffs and swells till instead of a hazelnut you've got a whole hedge.

Elef is testing the rubber belts on the grubber. Even these machines have been improved by the chief: he thought and thought until he came up with the vibrator that shakes the soil off the young plants that have been trimmed and grubbed up. I promised him I wouldn't confide in anybody. But I must get

344

dressed, must go outside, now I shall pay even more attention to orderliness: there's still time before Joachim makes his tour of inspection, but from now on he'll no longer be shaking his head over me, not from this day on.

Little pests, you're in for a surprise: from now on I won't let you vex me any more, cook up what you like in your hiding-place there behind the old tractor. Maybe you think I don't know where those dry clods of earth are coming from, bursting against the plough I've just cleaned. I saw it long ago, also that one of you is shooting with a catapult – not at me, but at the disc-harrow and the ploughshares. As long as you don't hit me I shan't even look up. I'll wear you down and see you off just by taking no notice of what you get up to: I'll just go on working with my steel brushes and my rags, scratching off the mess you've made, polishing what you've soiled.

What I'd most like to do would be to seize them by their scrawny necks and bang their heads together so hard that they'd give me a very wide berth in future, but I'm not allowed to touch them, it's forbidden. Once, when they'd stolen into my home – I knew at once someone was there, and I found them crouching behind the rack curtain – I grabbed them by their necks and dragged them out to the path, and then I was accused of having tried to throttle them, and Bruno promised Ina never again to lay a hand on her children.

The chief – he gave it them in a way they've never forgotten. Since that day down in the hollow they've never dared play him up in their favourite way: as soon as he comes on the scene, they do their best to keep out of sight, and when he calls them they put on innocent expressions and wipe their hands.

346

The way they crept up on him as he was sleeping on the worn old bench and plotted in whispers what to do: I saw that through the grimy window of the shed. I stood quite still and watched them go up to the chief, who was sound asleep, and then, just for fun, take all sorts of things from his pockets, a knife and a magnifying glass and his shabby old wallet. With their slender fingers they also drew out a folded sheet of paper, they danced around him on tiptoe, and what they'd filched they hid in a redcurrant bush.

Even that wasn't enough for them; they each had with them a length of thin waxed string, which they knotted together and silently from behind laid over the chief's chest and arms, then looped loosely over the ends of the bench. The idea was good, but in their impatience they pulled it all together too soon and too hard, and the chief woke up. He woke and tried to sit up, but the bond held him tight, and the two kids skipped around and doubled up with laughter – though not for long, for it took the chief only a few jerks to free himself. He massaged his wrists and felt himself all over, and it was then he must have found out his pockets were empty. Since the two kids were skipping and hooting in even greater enjoyment, he knew at once who had relieved him of his things as he slept. He considered a while, his eyes fixed on them, then suddenly he rushed at them and took them by the scruff of their necks, lifted them up high and shook them till their eyes started out of their heads and they began to whimper. Then, without letting go of them, he asked where his things were, and they pointed as well as they could to the redcurrant bush. They kicked and struggled in his grip and I kept still, glad to see them getting what they deserved. After making them fetch his things out of the bush and hand them back to him, he took hold of them once more, in order to make sure they understood once and for all what he was about to say. Woe betide you, he said, if ever again you interfere with a sleeping person or a man lying on the ground; and to emphasise the seriousness of his words he bumped their heads together – maybe a bit harder than he meant, for they both began to snivel as they ran off.

All right, keep going – you won't bother me.

The chief didn't watch them go, he sat down again on the bench and drew the paper out of his pocket and read it and reflected, and, when he called me over, I was expecting to be reproached or sent on an errand, but he just held the paper out without looking at me and said: Read that, Bruno. His resignation: he was submitting his resignation as mayor of Hollenhusen. He needed only a few lines to do it, for he gave no reasons. I read the letter several times, not knowing what he expected me to say, and when he turned and looked at me questioningly, I couldn't speak a single word.

He wasn't disappointed, he just smiled bitterly and nodded to himself, just as if realising that even he had to bow to the inevitable or at least to acknowledge that not everything could go according to his will. He took the letter from my hand and folded it and put it in his wallet and, maybe because he felt the agitation that was rising up inside me, he patted me on the shoulder and said: We'll have more time for ourselves now, Bruno.

And after a while he let out that he stood alone in the Hollenhusen council, quite alone, because he couldn't bring himself to vote along with the others for a return of the soldiers to Hollenhusen. Unlike the others, who saw some advantage to themselves in the return of the sappers and so wanted things to be as they'd been before, the chief couldn't approve this plan. He was against it – against, even though the council assured him the sappers would be offered another piece of land as a training ground: a part of Lauritzen's meadowland and a marshy field and the stunted wood behind the dolmen. It was just that he didn't want soldiers back in Hollenhusen. He was determined to resign – even though he was probably the only one who already knew the Hollenhusen council's wish would never be granted. How he came to know that I could never make out. There's no danger of that happening, he said, and that was all he said about it.

As he got up, his joints cracked – maybe it was time, as he himself once put it, for another drop of oil. He looked at me in mock alarm and waved his hand in a dismissive gesture before walking off stiffly towards the plantations.

No, no, I'm not throwing anything back, neither this lump of clay nor this chip of brick: you can wait till the cows come home, you'll no longer be taking the mickey out of me. I notice you're already not quite as cocky as you were. That's because I'm not doing you any favours: not behaving as you want me to behave, and not just patiently putting up with it all like your father.

The things Guntram Glaser would accept without a murmur! How still he'd remain, even when you were hurting him! That little rattle-gun that shot arrows with rubber plugs – plugs that clung by suction: you had to try that out on him straight away, the moment after he'd given it you as a birthday present. You didn't even wait to finish your chocolate cake, but on a given signal slipped off your chairs and made for the birthday table to goggle at, to fiddle with and to try out all the gifts laid out on it. Since the boys' birthdays were less than a week apart, they were always celebrated together, both getting their presents on the same day. They'd accepted the picture-books and the meccano sets from the chief with a bow and a polite handshake, but they took hardly any interest in them, nor did they care much for Dorothea's xylophone. Ina's little puppet theatre aroused their curiosity, but the biggest impression of all was made by the two rattle-guns Guntram Glaser had given them.

I saw and heard each of them push an arrow into the barrel and wind up the spring, and then each let off a trial shot, one against the floor vase, the other against the glass door to the terrace. Woof, the rubber plugs sucked themselves tight, the red arrows quivered. Their second shot was directed at Guntram Glaser: he was just lighting a cigarette when Tim and

Tobias took aim at his back and shot. He jumped as if he'd been stung and got quite a shock, but he gave them no more than a friendly warning. It didn't do much good. Unlike the chief, who warned them in advance, just in case, and was then spared any attempt to make a target of him, Guntram Glaser had to suffer a number of bullseyes. He bore it good-humouredly, a bit sourly, but good-humouredly all the same. It wasn't until Ina told them there'd be no puppet theatre performance if they kept on shooting that they were persuaded to abandon their game. With the guns slung across their shoulders they sat down to finish off the cake, showing clearly by the looks they gave me that I was marked down as their next victim.

When Guntram Glaser put on an act in the puppet theatre, when he spoke in five different voices, when he imitated wind or a running fire, when he brought on treasure-seekers and robbers and circus equestriennes, then all else could be forgotten. Probably no one was looking forward to the first performance in the new theatre more than I, for Guntram Glaser had announced a very special play: a birthday play. It was to be about a cunning old bear that comes by accident on a merry party of bear-hunters – he wouldn't reveal much more than that. When he announced it, I wasn't the only one to clap my hands, Ina clapped too, and she said at once: I'm sure Bruno wants to see it, you'll be very welcome, Bruno. It was decided that the performance should take place following our birthday coffee, and the chief, after a few words from Dorothea, decided to stay for it too. Joachim was the only one to make his excuses: he claimed to have urgent matters in the office to attend to. We rejoiced too soon.

I still remember his astonishment, still remember his annoyance when Magda came in and said there was a telephone call for Guntram Glaser, and not just that: in reply to his question who was on the phone and whether he couldn't be put off to the following day, she had to tell him it was a close friend who was just passing through – he didn't want to give his name.

How worried Ina looked as Guntram Glaser reluctantly rose, promising to keep it short. The chief and Dorothea exchanged glances too, and one of the children called out: Come back quickly, or we'll shoot.

Ina poured out more coffee – rather shakily, I thought – and had no answer to the chief's question who this close friend might be. Time passed and still more, or maybe it was just that we felt it to be an age before Guntram Glaser returned, and, when he did at last appear, he was looking very sombre. He didn't come back to the table but, halting some paces away, said he had to go out for a while to settle something that unfortunately couldn't be put off, but with the jeep he'd soon be back. The children at once wanted to know when the theatre would begin and whether they'd be seeing anything at all, and he promised them a lengthy performance in the evening. He showed no wish for Ina to accompany him out to the car, but all the same she got up and ran after him, and those of us still at the table remained silent until the engine started and the wheels crunched hard against the pebbles. All right, said Dorothea, now let's go and have a good look at all the presents.

But not even Dorothea could lift the damper that had fallen over the birthday party: the edge had gone off it, and it was no great surprise to me when the chief suddenly remembered things that still had to be done before evening. He went off with a kiss for Ina, who kept going across to the terrace door in the hope of seeing Guntram Glaser returning. He took leave of the birthday boys with a cuff apiece and a warning finger, and he was just about to give me a shove when he discovered a job for me: Come along, Bruno, we must get an express packet down to the station.

So take note: this is how I'll be dealing with you in future: I'll just carry on as if you weren't there, I won't chase you, won't throw things back and won't get angry, then in time you'll grow tired of it. You're always quick to tire when what you're doing doesn't have the desired effect. I can see your spindly legs there behind the tractor: I could easily catch you and bang your heads together – something you richly deserve, for even on that birthday of yours you saw to it that people behind me nudged each other and laughed, first of all on the plantations and then at the railway station in Hollenhusen. The way people would often nudge each other as I passed and stare after me, that was something I'd long got used to, but why they should burst out laughing, that I couldn't understand. Even Michaelsen, to whom I handed over the express packet at the station counter, even that fishface grinned, without letting on why. When children started to follow and gaily poke fun at me, I at last realised something on my back must be the cause of all the laughter, and in the station's advertisement mirror I saw what it was: a scrap of paper was stuck to my back and on it they'd written in red: Fresh Paint. With that I'd been running around for all to mock at. Though Tim and Tobias denied having stuck the paper on my back, there's no doubt in my mind that it was them, my two little pests, these two angel-faces here.

To escape from the jeering I could think of no better place than the waiting-room, where you're allowed to go only if you've got a ticket or order refreshments. There I could shake off the children and the laughter, and so I fled inside and ordered my usual: a lemonade and two rissoles.

They were sitting in the darkest corner: Guntram Glaser and the shiverer. They were taking no notice of the few travellers around them, but were talking without pause to each other – Guntram Glaser, who had his back to me, demandingly, vehemently and at times harshly; the other man, who had almost emptied his beer glass, in a worried way, as if pleading for understanding. At one point Guntram Glaser sprang to his feet, determined, it seemed, to go off, but when the shiverer held an open hand out to him, a wheedling hand, he sat down again, drew something from his breast pocket and read from it to the other man.

So as not to be seen and recognised, I turned to one side and bent low over my plate. I quickly gulped the rissoles down and just sipped my lemonade: fears were rising up inside me, warning me to get a move on. Guntram Glaser mustn't be given a second chance to say there were occasions when I was watching him.

When the family in their Sunday best at the table next to mine rose to leave, I pretended to be one of them and crept out under their cover. Outside I had to stop and take a few deep breaths in relief. Get away as quick as you can, I thought to myself, but I couldn't resist peeping once more through a window on the shady platform, and I saw Guntram Glaser push something across the table towards the man opposite, an envelope that surely must have had money in it, for the shiverer prised the envelope open and looked searchingly inside, as if counting money. He didn't seem particularly satisfied, just put it indifferently in his pocket. Guntram seemed to have nothing more to say: he got to his feet and looked down at the shiverer, his expression one single warning, and then he went off, leaving his untouched beer glass on the table, left without a parting word.

The train: if the train hadn't come in at that moment I'd simply have crossed the rails and got into our plantations near the loading ramp: at any rate I'd have kept out of his sight. But, since the barrier came down and we all had to wait at the level-crossing, he had time as he sat at the wheel of the jeep to look around. He saw me straight away, waved and called, and I had to get in beside him.

I told him at once that the chief had sent me to the station with an express packet. He just nodded, showing no interest in what the packet contained and to whom it was addressed; he put on an air of good humour, of relief and, without looking at me, told me he'd been meeting an old friend who had suddenly turned up from nowhere, a poor chap to whom he'd been obliged to give a little help. He said: To a certain degree one is, after all, responsible for one's friends, and he also said: Strange though it may be, a shared past does impose certain obligations. He wanted to know whether I didn't feel the same, and I thought at once of Heiner Walendy and his secret stay in my home, and said yes. He seemed satisfied with what he'd achieved, he took the matchbox out of my hand and showed me that you can light a cigarette in an open car, even when travelling at speed. You're coming to the performance, Bruno?

On the narrow transport road, where we had to stop behind a tractor, he looked down at my raw leather boots and a trouser leg that had ridden up and asked if it was true I wasn't wearing any socks. When I admitted I wasn't and told him my socks wore out too quickly, so I saved them for cooler days, he shook his head and said: Bruno, Bruno, and couldn't bring himself to believe me. Suddenly he brought out his wallet, took a twenty-mark note from it and held it out to me: Here, take this and welcome, it'll buy you at least three pairs of socks. I thanked him, but didn't take his money. He grabbed my hand and tried to force the money on me, but, since Bruno made a tight fist, he didn't succeed. That left him puzzled, and he didn't know what to make of me. In the end he accepted my refusal and put his money away, but he couldn't let the matter of my going around without socks rest: he informed me he'd take it up with the chief at the first opportunity. The chief has known about it for a long time, I said, he knows and has no objection. At that Guntram Glaser became rather thoughtful and murmured something I didn't understand.

What I'd really have liked to do was get out of the car and walk on by myself, but I didn't dare, and we'd hardly got moving again when Ewaldsen stopped us and asked us to go with him at once to the broad-leaved lime-trees, to the lime seedlings that had all drooped, that overnight had been attacked by the drooping sickness and were now lying flat on the ground as if asleep – that's how it looked. Ewaldsen was unhappy, he crouched down and felt a seedling. He knew what had caused the illness, had even seen it coming: if it had been left to him, he'd have waited with the *tilia* seed. Too early, he said, they've just been planted too early, and then he informed

354

us that he'd voiced his doubts in good time, but nobody had taken them very seriously, they'd just stuck to the planting schedule. He didn't need to mention Joachim's name, we knew at once whom he meant and that he was accusing him of not listening to the voice of experience. The only thing that surprised me was that Ewaldsen, who normally just listened patiently to instructions and then did what he himself held to be right, had worked at all as Joachim wished.

Guntram Glaser didn't agree with Ewaldsen, as I'd been expecting. He scratched the ground, picked up a handful of earth and rubbed it between his fingers as the chief sometimes did, then examined some of the seedlings and came to the conclusion they certainly hadn't been planted out too soon. No, he wasn't ready to put the blame on Joachim: he soon found out that the soil had been disinfected two years earlier, and then he knew exactly where he was. That's always the way, he said, in the year following the treatment the soil fungi can't do much damage, but by the second year they've either recovered or developed from resting spores. As Ewaldsen had in addition to admit that the seeds had not been treated, Guntram Glaser had all the facts he needed to explain why the drooping sickness had struck us, and, when he saw what trouble the whole thing was causing Ewaldsen, he tried to console him a little, advising him to give the seedlings plenty of nitrogen to help them over their critical period. By the time your seedling becomes woody above the root, it'll be out of danger.

If only I knew what a person must do to make himself impenetrable, to make sure nobody will see at first glance what is occupying or disturbing his mind and making his heart heavy – if only I knew that! How often have I longed to be able to conceal things like Max, who can look at you without letting on what he's thinking! The chief doesn't always let you see either what's on his mind, and no more does Ina, who now and again has so surprised me with her ideas that she might almost have been a stranger.

With me everyone sees everything at once: I just cannot keep dark the things I wish to keep to myself. I don't know why either, I must simply accept that all I carry around inside my head can be read in my face, whether it's a plan or a mood of sadness or a bit of secret knowledge. How often, when there's something I want to keep to myself, have I been surprised to hear it said straight to my face, and the one who has most surprised me in that way is the chief. In the morning he'd only need to look at me out of the corner of his eye to know I'd had a bad dream that I couldn't shake off, and, to help me get over it, he'd at once give me a job of a more strenuous kind to do. Once, when I was full of confidence in myself – it was on one of our Sunday walks through the plantations – I wanted to ask to be allowed to work with machines and mechanical tools like the others. I suppose I spent some time beating about the bush, but I was just about to come out with my request when he said: Later, Bruno, one day you too will be driving the machines, but for the present I need you for another important job. Nothing can be kept secret from him: just a single glance, and he knows what's in my mind.

I hadn't yet decided whether I ought to tell him what I'd seen in the waiting-room. I didn't want it said of me that I was a second pair of eyes for the chief, I didn't want that, and so, instead of returning to the stronghold, where the performance was soon to begin, I came here to the toolshed, where I thought I'd be alone, but found I wasn't. I was just about to climb into the driving-seat of the old tractor when I heard from one corner the sound of a hammer, the sharp blows of a big nail being driven into wood.

It was the chief doing the hammering. In three places he drove in nails, and on each nail he hung a bunch of yarrow, smiling as he did so with a strange sort of satisfaction and winking at me. After hanging up the last bunch he said from the stepladder: There, Bruno, now let's see whether the old wives were right. I knew yarrow was a remedy against bleeding, what I didn't know was that it was hung over working

356

tools to prevent accidents. The chief had done it because once again one of his men had been injured by the harrow, badly injured. He said: The important thing now is that our people should be told why the yarrow is hanging there.

Then we walked to the exit door. Then he looked into my face. Then he stopped and narrowed his ice-blue eyes and asked: What's the matter, Bruno, what's crossed your path? I still wanted to keep what I'd seen to myself, but he said: The one person you don't want to meet you meet in the waiting-room, that's it, isn't it? After that there was no point keeping it secret any longer, since he'd surely have come in a moment on what I'd seen.

How still he could keep when he was listening! His eyes were fixed on the ground, now and again he drew a sharp breath, but otherwise he showed nothing, no agitation, no surprise, gave no sign either of suspicion or of growing bitterness, asked not a single question as I told him what he maybe already knew. And at the end, after he had listened to it all, he had no word of thanks for me, he just gave me a tired look, laid a hand briefly on my shoulder, then turned away and walked off. Something was slowing his footsteps, and I could feel that his gift of knowing in advance, which usually gave him an advantage over others, was this time weighing him down. This searing feeling, this giddiness, this state of helplessness in which he had left me – I didn't know what to do, a sudden fear held me tight in its grip, fear of some far-reaching decision that was about to be made. I sought refuge among my Japanese cedars.

There was no performance: the play about the cunning old bear that comes by accident on a merry party of bear-hunters was not staged, either on that evening or any other. For a while I was expecting them to send someone to fetch me, but no one came, not before darkness fell. When you came, Ina, it was already very dark, no moon, low clouds, I wouldn't have been able to recognise you through the window in any case: nothing was recognisable. Even before you knocked I heard the whimpering, and I knew at once that the person out there whimpering was you, I was at the door at once, and I called out to you and pulled you into my room. The state you were in would have alarmed anybody and led him to expect the worst, you were so scratched, so covered in mud, your clothes so torn, and everywhere you were bleeding from little wounds, on your face, your arms, but you probably hardly even noticed, at any rate you paid no attention to them. Hardly had you sat down in my armchair when you were seized by a weeping fit. All my questions were in vain: you couldn't speak. I thought: Let her cry herself out, and very cautiously I stroked you and dabbed with a cloth at the places that were bleeding. When I discovered the thorns in your arm, I at once knew you'd run through the chief's rose-bed and fallen over there. I pulled out the thorns, and you didn't once flinch. I don't know how long it was before you managed to speak and how much longer before I could understand bits of what you were trying to say, a lot of it I had to piece together for myself, since you kept stumbling, speaking only half a sentence and hiding your tear-stained face in your hands.

This much I did understand at once: that you were in fear of some disaster. Oh, Ina, you wiped your tear-stained face with my towel, then looked at me as if from afar and said in a small voice: A disaster, Bruno, I believe there's some disaster on the way. And after a while you said: Look for him, Bruno, you must find him, he went to see that man. What man? I asked, and you: Guntram wants to bring him here, I don't know who he is, he wants to see him and force him to do something. At that time you surely knew just as little as I did, you asked a few times: What's going on, Bruno? For God's sake, if you know anything, tell me, and as you spoke you looked at me searchingly and held tight to my arm.

For you, Ina, I went to Hollenhusen, just for you. I could easily have lost my way in the dark plantations. I slid down the slope of the railway cutting and walked between the rails, first to the waiting-room: nothing there. Then along the platform: nothing. I searched through the lighted streets and put my head in at the 'Kiek in': nothing, neither there nor anywhere. I hoped I might find him in the 'Deutsches Haus', he and the shiverer, about whom I told you nothing because I didn't myself know what the connection was between him and Guntram Glaser. Neither of them was there, only a few of the familiar Hollenhusen faces sitting drinking, and they grabbed me and wanted to make me drink – a beer into which one of them had swiftly tapped his cigar ash, the stupid ox.

All of a sudden Hollenhusen seemed so huge, offered so many possibilities that I almost lost heart. I searched and searched, speeding past the school, not omitting the market-place, even along beside the cemetery and in a circle round the council offices: Guntram Glaser was nowhere to be found. I don't know how late it was when I finally reached home; my door was on the latch, the little lamp was alight, but you were no longer there: I suppose you couldn't bear it any longer. After a while I went out again. A lot of lights were burning in the stronghold, many more than was usual at this late hour, but your room was in darkness.

Those are his footsteps, the hissing sound of his leather-trimmed breeches gives him away at once: Joachim is making his round of inspection as usual, as if nothing had changed here – they must be feeling very confident of things going the way they want. He mustn't be allowed to push the door shut, I must let him know someone is still at work here: this wire brush makes a fine rasping noise when I draw it sharply across a ploughshare, enough to send shivers down your spine. Yes, it's me, I'm still here. It's long past knocking-off time, Bruno, he calls out, but I say nothing, let him come up to me, let him watch me working, working to methods of my own. It's all sparkling, Bruno, no one looks after the tools as you do. Wire brush, I say, scraper and wire brush and oil-soaked rags. A method of your own, I take it. Yes. But you should knock off now and help me push the door shut. He's not carrying his little stick, just the tubular flash-lamp. How careful he is to avoid shining it directly at me in his usual way! He just directs the beam of light into the corners and doesn't dazzle me. Come along now, Bruno, that's enough. That's the other, the old tone of voice, that's the Joachim I know: take away his irritability and his discontent and he's no longer himself, but there's one thing he can't do now – make me feel helpless and uncertain of myself. Shall we try it together? The door moves so easily, I say, you can do it with one hand.

Off home already, Bruno? Come with me, he says, we can look together to see everything's in order. Why this invitation? Never before have I been on a round of inspection with him. No doubt he wants to sound me out, and if not that, to talk me round. But I can't just refuse his offer, that I can't do. We're going in your direction anyway, Bruno. Yes, all right.

How fleetingly he casts his light around! The beam of his flash-lamp just flies along, circles over the beds, sways across the green wall. The ray of light hasn't yet got its stiff, pillar-like outline: it doesn't get that till it's really dark. Those gleaming eyes in the thuya hedge: that's the wild cat – goodness knows how it found its way here, but lucky Joachim didn't spot it. Whether I've heard anything of Lisbeth, he wants to know, of our Lisbeth, he says, and I say: No, nothing. I've been to see her, Bruno. I had something to do in town, so I looked in on her. A sad sight, I can tell you. Just imagine, she showed no pleasure, just lay there staring at the ceiling and didn't speak a single word. I almost got the impression she didn't recognise me. And now he wants to know if I can explain that.

No, but maybe she was too tired, or she was in too much pain, I say. It's not till a heavy body like that comes to a standstill that the weaknesses and the sufferings begin to show. Maybe you're right, Bruno. He says that in an absent-minded sort of way, and I can feel his mind is busy with something else, some plan, maybe, from which he hopes to gain: now he's even forgetting to point his lamp at anything in particular. Listen, Bruno, how would it be if we were to visit Lisbeth

360

together some time, would you like that? You never seem to go anywhere, as far as I can remember you've never even been into town, and this would be a good opportunity, wouldn't it? I'll take you there in my car. Well, what do you say? Why not? I say. So that's agreed? I don't know yet, I say, and he: Think it over, Lisbeth deserves it.

He'll be puzzled when on his second visit Lisbeth still says nothing to him. She doesn't want people coming to see her, she told Magda to pass the word round, it's only us two who would be welcome, the chief and me. Maybe we should take the chief with us, I say, if he was with us Lisbeth would be pleased, that's for sure. He's already been to see her, Joachim says curtly, as if he disapproved, yes, he was with her all by himself, no one knows how he got there. Joachim had seen the moment he went in that the chief had been there already: The proof, Bruno, was lying on her bedside table, a present from the chief, a medal.

Joachim switches the lamp off, stops and, standing now very close to me and whispering as if we might be overheard, he says: That medal, Bruno, was one that had been presented to the chief himself. I'm sure he'd just forgotten it, I say, he showed it to Lisbeth, laid it down on the bedside table and later forgot it. But he knows better: He didn't forget, he gave it her, gave it away without thinking, as he's given so much else. You won't believe it, Bruno, but there are matters in which the chief no longer possesses the power to judge, it's as if he's lost the proper attitude towards certain things, and since there are aspects he can't recognise and assess, he can't answer for them either. That's how it is with him.

If only I knew how to answer him! It would have been better if I'd gone straight home, where there's fresh milk waiting, a pickled herring and a currant loaf. Now he's passing the beam of light over the nursery beds; he turns away and walks on and says over his shoulder: Everyone knows, Bruno, how you stand by him, what my father means to you, and for that very reason you must be prepared for changes. Perhaps you too have long been aware that the chief is no longer the man he was – you must have noticed it. We at any rate have had to realise he's doing things for which there is no justification, we have all realised it, independently of each other. What he has done and is doing could put us all in danger here, including you, Bruno, and, since that is so, we must with heavy hearts do something, in sheer self-defence.

He falls silent, he's waiting, hoping for a confirmation, but I won't say anything, I'll stick to my word. It could be, Bruno, that you'll soon come round to our way of thinking. You're with my father often enough: just keep your eyes open, compare and consider, and, if you think we do have some reason to be concerned, then come to me, I'm always ready to see you. Do you understand me? Yes, I say and add at once: Here we are, I'd better be off home now. How easy it was to say that! He doesn't even shake his head over me, just comes to a stop and watches me go and shines his lamp on my door to help me find the lock more easily.

Still no whistle from the railway, still none. And I planted an almond tree for him, at Ina's request. Maybe the night train is running late. And she stood there in a black dress and just silently watched as I placed the little sapling in the soil. But maybe it has already gone through, the night train, and I failed to hear the whistle – it does happen now and again that I fail to hear or see something. And she thanked me and went off by herself even before I watered the little almond and trod the soil down. Once the night train is through I can go off to sleep more easily, I don't know why either, all I know is it's been like that for a long while. And after that I met her only once more by his grave, when I was pruning the little tree.

It doesn't worry me if now and again I have to wait some time for the engine's whistle. I lie quite still and listen: in my mind I can already see the engine as it labours along beneath the old pines. And at first Ina too thought it had been an accident, as did Max and Dorothea and I myself. Pastor Plumbeck, who gave the funeral address, knew no different either, and he spoke of a tragic misfortune.

A finer day for a funeral there can never have been – not at any rate in Hollenhusen: there was not a breath of wind, the sky was as blue as a freshwater carp, a smell of drying grass hung in the air and the gravel on the main path gave off so much heat that some of the men surreptitiously unbuttoned their jackets. But the birds: I'd dearly have liked to pick up a few pebbles to throw at the chaffinches so loudly proclaiming the bounds of their territories, and I'd have liked to chase off the two blackbirds as well. Four men lifted the coffin in which Guntram Glaser lay on to a small rubber-tyred cart, and after that they hardly needed to exert themselves, for the touch of a hand was enough to set the cart rolling down the main path to the road and to the grave lined with greenery. Ina walked immediately behind the cart hand in hand with her children, behind them came the chief and Dorothea and Guntram Glaser's mother, and after them Max and I and Joachim, with the other mourners some distance behind. Ina without a veil, Ina slight and bony, her face grey. The two boys proper little gentlemen in long trousers. Dorothea with a white handkerchief in her hand. The chief thin-lipped, head erect, stiff: he already knew the truth. And Max sighing in the heat and Joachim with drooping shoulders.

Heaped up beside the grave were greyish-black humous, greasy clay, a layer of mixed clay and sand. We grouped ourselves around the grave, the procession of mourners broke up and spread out, some mounting benches, others even showing half a mind to climb on gravestones in order to get a better view, though in the end they didn't risk it. The sun was dazzling, on our side we had now and again to close our eyes, the chief too: he had stamped down the greasy clay to give himself a firm foothold, and he took me a few times by the arm as if feeling the need for support. The coffin was lifted over the grave and set down on planks laid across it, the ropes lay ready, Pastor Plumbeck mounted a small hillock of earth and began to pray – and in that moment I recognised him, recognised the shiverer.

He came out from behind the brick chapel, close to the ancient gravestones, and was watching over the heads of the mourners. Now and again he turned away, as if afraid of being discovered; it looked as if he was just content to take part at a certain distance. During the prayer the shiverer came closer, warily, step by step, it was as if he was being drawn in, but it wasn't enough for him just to join the mourners, he pushed his way past some of them, past Ewaldsen, who was wearing a black jacket, and past Magda too. At one time he went out of sight behind a bush, at another he was obscured by a group of people standing close together, but he didn't escape me, I kept my eyes on him – I just had to, though it meant I took in only a little of what Pastor Plumbeck was saying over the coffin. He spoke of the prime of life, that I remember, and I also remember that he said: All flesh is as grass, and all the glory of man as the flower of grass. Ina did not shed tears, but Dorothea was sobbing, shaking from head to foot, and Max had to hold her up.

Suddenly he was right up front, standing behind Ina and the two boys, and it looked as if he meant to stay there, for he bowed his head and folded his hands. He was truly mourning, as anybody could see, and maybe that – his grief – was the reason why nobody close by took any interest in him, though he was wearing a suit with a herringbone pattern and looked pretty shabby. Then all at once the chief became aware of him. The chief felt for my hand and held me round the wrist. I looked at him and he caught my eyes and guided them towards the shiverer, then whispered softly, so that no one else would hear: Over there, Bruno, there he is, get hold of him.

That was easily said. I considered and calculated. Pastor Plumbeck was talking about inscrutable counsels, Dorothea was sobbing even harder, the mourners were standing motionless, listening, their eyes fixed on something or other, and he himself, the man I was supposed to grab, seemed completely absorbed in himself and deaf to the world. I couldn't just leap across at him, no, I couldn't do that. The trowel, the little trowel with which the mourners would throw a bit of earth down on the coffin, lay near me, I picked it up and took a step backwards, as if I was taking it to Ina and the boys, who had the right to use the trowel first, and I slipped across without attracting too much attention, pushed the trowel into the clay, stepped back and positioned myself beside the shiverer. He, sunk in his grief, probably didn't even notice me at his side; a faint shiver passed through him from time to time, and again and again he hunched his shoulders and gently shook his head. What he was murmuring had no connection with what Pastor Plumbeck was saying, and I thought he must be making a funeral address of his own – that's how it seemed to me.

In the middle of the final prayer he looked up and drew himself upright, he looked at me, a timid smile crossed his face, then suddenly he gave me a nod and went off, walked slowly and in a dignified way past the mourners and on towards the brick chapel. There he vanished. The door of the chapel was open, drawing me inside, and I found myself standing before a mountain of wreaths and a floor covered with bouquets: the scent of the lilies almost overpowered me. I couldn't see him, but since I could feel his presence, I went up to the wall and waited, and after a while I called out softly, but he didn't reveal himself, gave no answer at all. I thought he might have hidden in one of the two side-chambers, so I tiptoed through the rows of chairs and opened the first door. I found myself peeping into the deep shadow of a storeroom. I didn't go down the steps leading to it, but opened the second door, already reckoning on drawing a blank. The second side-chamber also served as a storeroom, and a cold draught was blowing towards me. I decided to go down the steep stone steps and groped around for a handrail, but found none. A shuffling noise made me turn round, too suddenly maybe, I don't know; I turned round and hit against something, or rather I thought I'd hit my head against something, in reality it was the push he gave me. As I fell, I just had time to think: Now I'm falling over, and I could also still think: I must put out an arm to lessen the impact, but the crash with which I landed, that I no longer felt.

I scattered no handful of earth over Guntram Glaser's coffin. Later, at Ina's request, I did plant an almond tree, but I wasn't there when they lowered the coffin and threw earth down on it, neither was I at the funeral reception in the 'Deutsches

Haus', where there was apple pie and crumble cake. Though things were sloshing and splashing around in my head as if they'd been torn loose, I managed to creep out of the side-chamber without help. Outside in the fresh air I felt a terrific throbbing, and I don't know how often I had to stop, had to go down on all fours as I made my way home, but, since that was my one thought, I made it in the end. The only thing I didn't do was lock the door behind me: I simply forgot.

The chief was the first to visit me. He shaved off some of my hair and cleaned the wound and stuck on a plaster that he himself fetched from the stronghold. He didn't want me to tell the others what had happened, and I fell in with that and just said I'd had an accident. His silence as he sat there beside me. His downcast manner. The restlessness that overcame him at times and forced him to get up and walk a few paces. Dorothea came to see me too, and Max and Ina – she just brought me a bunch of grapes, gave me her hand and went away – but nobody came as often as the chief, or stayed as long. Sometimes he'd say no more than: That's how it is, Bruno, and that would be all. At one time, after work was over, he said the moment he came in: What do you think, Bruno? The shiverer has given himself up to the police in Schleswig. Then he sat down and awaited my comment and, I suppose because what I had to say wasn't enough, he added: He's admitted everything. And then he took a sip from his pocket flask and made me drink too, and I obeyed because the offer came from him, who knew all before we did.

He knew that the shiverer had spent a part of his time in the army here, when the land was still a training ground, and he also knew they were in the same barrack-room, the shiverer and Guntram Glaser, and that they shared a bunk and were inseparable mates. With what care the chief spelled all this out to me! It was just as if he was trying to put what he had learnt into my keeping or commit it to my memory, for reasons only he himself knew. They had once been inseparable, they stood in for each other, what happened to one also happened to the other: if someone had to do extra drill, the chief told me, or attracted attention at rollcall, it was never just one of them, but always both together – their company had already become used to it.

Once they had to go out on a night exercise. It was autumn, it was raining, they had their groundsheets slung round their shoulders and more or less slithered over the soft earth – I know those autumn nights, the overcast sky, the wind getting in everywhere. Nothing much could be seen, they took their bearings from the creaking and clattering of the baggage they were dragging – dragging over the whole training ground as far as the hollow. There they assembled and stood and waited, and in due course it was explained to them that an attack would soon be coming from the Holle, from the meadows, and their job was to fight it off. And they were further told they should fall in for a counter-attack as soon as they saw three flares above their heads. They then split up and took up their positions.

The shiverer and Guntram Glaser were together as always. They crept into the dwarf pines – where our deciduous conifers now stand – and dozed and slept a little, and when the attack began and the air was full of the crackle of guns and rifles, they too joined in the shooting, but without taking aim or leaving their hiding-place. On the counter-attack they were missing, for the simple reason that they didn't see the flares, which the wind carried off low: they stayed in their hiding-place till the night exercise was over.

Their sergeant flushed them out. He didn't say much – he never said much; he ordered them to fall down and crawl on their elbows in front of him, and they crawled with their packs to our damp ground. There he made them go through the counter-attack on their own by chasing them a few times through the boggy patch, through the water-holes, through bubbling mud, at the same time making them utter battle-cries so he could hear them. When one of the shiverer's boots was sucked off, he made them search for it in the mud, and they prodded and bored without finding the boot, and, since a soldier can't be allowed to get away with a loss like that, they had to continue the search next day, a Sunday.

The sergeant had a very low opinion of them, for they attracted too much attention and were a constant disgrace to him, he said. He only needed to set eyes on them and he'd find something to object to, and he had a wide choice of punishments to inflict on them. Guntram Glaser and the shiverer made no complaints: they did what he ordered them to do, for after all they were very young. Now and again they let him see he'd never get the better of them, and that had the effect of making the sergeant lose no opportunity of teaching them the extent of his power.

The Holle: he made them cross the Holle while it was in flood, they and the other soldiers in their squad. Since an enemy was occupying the wooden bridge, there was only one way of getting to the other side, and so they had to wade through the water with their weapons, one after the other, among them the little weakling they called the baker on account of his paleness and his dough-like skin. His pleas that he was suffering from stitches and couldn't swim were no help at all: at a sign from the sergeant he too had to wade into the Holle, holding his rifle above his head. Fog swallowed up the noises, the sucking, the gurgling and splashing: an enemy on the other side would hardly have noticed them as, twisting and turning, seeking with groping steps for a foothold, they moved against the current towards a flat part of the riverbank. But the cry: the fog couldn't swallow that – the cry for help, the despairing cry. Someone let it out as the baker – probably because he suddenly found no ground under his feet – disappeared beneath the surface with the rifle he couldn't bring himself to let go. The baker simply sank, weapon, steel helmet and all.

Those who were near him tried at once to find him, feeling and groping around, always with one eye on keeping their weapons above water. In their search they lost their balance, and more than one dipped his rifle under, but they didn't find the baker, for the current had at once carried him a few metres further downstream. Hearing the cry, the sergeant came to the water's edge, he saw at once what had happened and he didn't wade, he sprang into the Holle at the spot where the water reached up to his chest. Then he dived under, in full uniform he dived and swam down river and only a few moments later came up again, holding the baker in a firm grip. He dragged him to the bank and then on to dry land, where he knelt down beside him and applied those movements through which water is forced out of the lungs, lightly pressing and pumping. Some of the men standing around him he sent back into the river with orders to look for the baker's rifle. They couldn't find it, and so it was now up to him to seek it. He did so the moment the baker was back on his feet, and it wasn't long before he brought the weapon up.

That noiseless crossing of the river: the chief told me they didn't have to go on practising it after that. They marched, or rather staggered, back to the barracks, with the shiverer and Guntram Glaser taking care of the baker, who walked between them, hardly able to hold himself upright. They were allowed to go to their rooms and change their clothes, and afterwards they sat round a table cleaning and polishing their weapons, among them the baker, who had not yet quite recovered his wits and so didn't know what he was supposed to be doing. The shiverer helped him clean his rifle, and it was the shiverer who couldn't let what had happened in the Holle go unchallenged. He kept on asking himself and the others whether something oughtn't to be done against a superior who treated his soldiers in such a way, and now for the first time the shiverer asked himself whether the sergeant hadn't earned a beating-up after all he'd done, but no one else was keen on the idea, not even Guntram Glaser.

When they felt done in, drained and embittered, the sergeant would sometimes say to them: Preparing you, that's all I'm trying to do: harden you and prepare you for times when you'll be spared nothing, and he also said: Maybe one day a few of you will feel grateful to me. On his free Sundays he would now and again go to the 'Kiek in', where he'd sit by himself and smoke and drink a few glasses of beer.

And he was sitting there on the afternoon Guntram Glaser and the shiverer came in with the girl they'd just gone to the station to meet. She was the shiverer's fiancée, she was paying her first visit and they were all in high spirits. They saluted their sergeant, saluted him and then made for the table farthest from him, but before they settled down they heard a sharp order: not Guntram Glaser, but the shiverer was to go back to the sergeant's table and repeat his salute, doing it the way he'd been taught. With a shrug of his shoulders, just to get it over and done with, the shiverer gave another salute, but the sergeant wasn't satisfied with that one either, nor with the next and the one after that – probably bitterness was making the shiverer stiff and awkward and preventing him doing what was required of him. But he succeeded at last and was allowed to return to his table. His face was pale, he was shaking, and for a while he wouldn't drink, and later, there at that corner table, he said to Guntram Glaser: That I'll never forgive him, never.

For weeks the shiverer carried his plan around inside him and, when he felt enough had happened to bring the matter to a head, he confided his plan to the baker and to Guntram Glaser. He'd have liked all three to be involved, but the baker spoke against it, he didn't want to take part, though he'd also got a score to settle. So it was just the two of them, and they set off as usual and under the sergeant's eye practised an attack on the dummy houses, and under his eye crept up to the buried practice tank and dealt with it as he instructed, and disguised themselves as bushes and dug narrow holes from which to defend themselves without presenting a target. They'd discussed it and come to an agreement and were patiently awaiting their opportunity. Just a beating: that's what they had decided. At last, after a long wait, it was dark enough and quiet enough, they waylaid him at the foot of the command hill, rushed at him, knocked him over and set to work on him without a word, for he mustn't be allowed to recognise them. But he managed to free himself from their grip and get to his feet, and not only that: he started to fight back, hit first Guntram Glaser and then the shiverer too. They had had their warning, but it was too late for flight, since he had already recognised them.

And then suddenly he fell, uttered a groan and fell to the ground. The shiverer bent over him, his arm raised as if to strike, but he lay there and didn't move, didn't even lift his hands to defend himself. Stop, that's enough, we must get away. Guntram Glaser knelt down and ran his hands over him, felt something damp on his fingers and then heard the sound of a bayonet being pushed back into its scabbard. Do you know what you've done? he asked. And they crouched and stood in the dark beside the motionless body. Do you know what you've done? They listened out, they explored their surroundings, then together they lifted him up and carried him a few metres further on, cut away the turf and dug a deep hole. They took away everything he had on him, including his identity disc, and together they laid him in the earth. At the end they put back the turf and trod it firm.

The chief told me all this, and he also knew that a wide search and investigation had very soon begun, not only at the training ground but in Hollenhusen and neighbouring villages as well. Enquiries were made and search parties sent out, the station staff was questioned, even the big pond was dragged and Danes' Wood combed, but it all led to nothing, nothing was found. And when they got their marching orders and left, the search was finally given up, other soldiers took over the barracks and trained on the scarred land that gave nothing away.

Guntram Glaser and the shiverer didn't remain together for long, they lost touch during the big retreat, each gave the other up for lost, and their secret: that they carried off in different directions and lived with it, each in his own way.

How worried was the chief's expression as he looked at me! He got up and walked about, raised his arms and then let them fall. Don't you see, Bruno? he said. A man can have courage enough, but what's the use of it if he doesn't have the courage to speak out when he should? And then he shuffled across to the window and looked out over the land and related – so softly that I had difficulty in understanding him – how one day the shiverer had turned up here, with a group of primary schoolchildren Guntram Glaser was conducting round the plantations, to which he had simply attached himself. Many years had passed by then and at least one of the two had no thoughts of a reunion. The shiverer walked along with the group, keeping out of sight, and listened to Guntram's talk. They did the big tour, as we call it among ourselves, and to end with went into the cold store, where they were told about jacket cooling, in which there is no moving air and the plants don't need any additional damping.

To demonstrate that plants in the jacket cooling store don't dry out, Guntram took a rose bush from the wooden rack, and through the gap it left he suddenly saw the face of the shiverer, recognised it and forgot what he was about to say.

They met in the waiting-room, beside the Holle, in Danes' Wood, and it was always the shiverer who fixed the meeting-place. Each time they met he came up with the story that he couldn't go on any longer and would give himself up, once and for all. His main reason for wishing to give himself up was the nature of his fits.

In the years immediately following his misfortune – during their retreat they had blown up a railway embankment and he had been buried – the fits came only rarely, but as time went on they became more frequent, and in the end they were arriving promptly as if on cue: he had only to think of a certain happening and the shivering would start, forcing him to his knees, and, since he didn't want to think of what it was causing his fits, he couldn't escape doing it all the more.

And Guntram Glaser helped him, helped him get back on his feet and gave him all the money he could spare, for he didn't want the shiverer in his distress to go and give himself up. At each meeting he would talk to him and try to convince him that it wouldn't be of any help to anybody to reveal it all now, so long after, and for the moment the shiverer would agree – for the moment. Now and then he would go off on the train, he never said where, he just vanished for a few days without a word, but Guntram Glaser had given up hoping he'd stay away for ever; suddenly he'd be there again, making his presence known. He stayed in the 'Kiek in', in one of the low-ceilinged rooms he paid for with Guntram Glaser's money, but only rarely could he be found there, because he was always wandering around at unusual hours, along the Holle or through our plantations. The people in the 'Kiek in' were already wondering about him and asking questions behind his back. That they certainly did, and what they wanted above all to know was the connection between this stranger and Guntram Glaser, and why they met each other in out-of-the-way places where they couldn't be overheard. And since they found nothing definite, they came to certain conclusions of their own and spread them abroad.

The last time they were seen together on the platform in Hollenhusen they were walking up and down, talking together; neither of them had bought a ticket. The shiverer seemed determined to give himself up, and Guntram Glaser, feeling that this time neither appeals nor reassuring words would stop him, offered him all the money he had, on just one condition: that from then on they would stop seeing each other. He was thinking it over still, the shiverer, when a train came through, a goods train that would always slow down, though it didn't stop. He stood there, staring at the waggons as they rattled past, and all of a sudden he seized the thin iron rail that leads up to the brakesman's box, jumped on to the running-board

374

and clung tight. Not a word as he was borne away, no waving. Clinging tight, he stood looking back at Guntram Glaser till the train reached the old pines.

Some of our people saw Guntram Glaser coming up from the rail track and walking over the land in an unseeing way very unusual for him. He ignored all greetings, did not linger as he normally did in the young plantations, but made straight for the stronghold. Then, before he reached it, he changed his mind and disappeared along a transport path that led down to the hollow. The people with whom he came face to face saw him there for the last time. He was not looking for the chief. He went down towards the old shed, but had already passed it when the chief caught sight of him and called out, bidding him come into the shed, where at that time he often went to investigate the causes of dormancy in seeds – what it is that sits in the fruit pulp or in the seed kernel or in the skin and arrests sprouting.

A single glance, and he who misses nothing, who scents and sees through everything and knows most things before anyone else – he saw at once that here was someone at the end of his tether, and he drew him into the shed and pushed him down on the stool. For a while they sat opposite each other in silence. I suppose Guntram Glaser couldn't yet make up his mind whether to tell everything and get it off his chest; but once you find the chief looking at you like that, with such persistence and with such a willingness to understand, you do suddenly start speaking of your own accord, often to your own surprise. As if setting up in judgement against himself, he described his part in the happenings, excusing nothing, underplaying nothing and leaving nothing out.

Never before had the chief listened to anyone so intent on heaping blame on himself. They didn't notice the failing light. They sat opposite each other in the dark, and they remained seated after Guntram Glaser had come to the end. Maybe he was waiting for something: the chief was not sure about that. He asked the first and only question that came into his mind on the spur of the moment, and Guntram Glaser, instead of answering, stood up and walked outside the door in silence, as if to think it over. And, since his silence continued, the chief also went outside, to get his answer. No one was there: Guntram Glaser had gone.

The chief sat down beside me and said he had waited in the shed for a while before returning alone to the stronghold. He asked at once for Guntram Glaser, but nobody there had seen him, and none of them suspected that he was already sitting on the railtrack waiting for the night train. He saw no other way out, the chief said, looking down at the ground, because I now knew almost everything about him, I wanted to know the rest as well, and that is why I asked him whether the shiverer had had anything to do with the thefts on our land.

I shouldn't have asked him that, Bruno, not that; for he really had no part in them, that I know today. I feel sorry for him, I said, I feel sorry for Guntram Glaser, but the shiverer – I'm sorry for him too. I suppose my words didn't reach him, for he just stared straight ahead without moving, and then all of a sudden he pulled that unopened letter out of his pocket, a letter the shiverer had written to Ina shortly before he gave himself up. I suppose the chief had doubts whether Ina should read it and had been keeping it back, I don't know – all I know is that he suddenly got up, gave me a nod and went out with the letter in his hand, as if he felt the time had come to hand it over.

You and your eternal pity, Magda said at the time, whatever a person is like and whatever he does, you'll always find something to make you sorry for him. Even the shiverer, even Heiner Walendy, even Joachim on the occasion when that falling tree tore off a bit of his skin: a person's only got to be in some sort of trouble and you're bound to feel sorry for him. I shook my head and she demanded to know somebody I didn't pity. Come on, she said, give me the name of someone for whom you've never felt sorry, and I thought for quite a while without coming on a single name. You see, she said.

It must have already gone through, the night train, I suppose I missed the whistle, the mournful whistle the wind carries across the plantations. Haws: I'll swear I put out some haws on the windowsill, a whole handful for my hunger in the night. I suppose I must have eaten them without noticing. When I'm deep in thought I may eat without noticing I'm eating, and afterwards I've forgotten all about it. Why do I always have to eat before I can get to sleep?

The chief isn't asleep yet, there's still a light in his room, and there he is at the window: that's his figure. Maybe he's looking across to me here and deciding when to pay me a visit. There's someone else as well. Ina. Ina and he.

He simply will not go away. There he stands with his briefcase and watches me so persistently and intently you'd think he was wanting to learn to pot by hand himself. At the same time he asks so many questions that I feel like pretending to be deaf and dumb. He's called Grieser or Kiesler – I didn't catch his name properly, because he always turns his head aside when he talks, wearing a permanent smile that isn't really a smile at all. If only I knew what he wants to discuss with the chief so early in the day! His briefcase isn't all that full, he's got plenty of time, and to place orders you don't have to wear a dark suit and comb your hair in the peculiar way his is combed: not forwards or backwards, but from side to side. Maybe – who knows? – he's the man the court has sent along to examine the chief, the one he threw out of the room, or maybe someone officially instructed to spy out the land: it wouldn't surprise me if they're now starting to gather proofs in their own particular way – that wouldn't surprise me at all.

Why do we no longer use clay pots, he asks, surely in earlier times young plants were put into clay pots? For reasons of watering, I say, clay pots are porous, the water evaporates quickly, it stays longer in our plastic pots. And now he also wants to know why we use square pots instead of round ones, when all the time he can see from my work-table that square pots make better use of the available space. The questions he asks! A planting machine. Yes? I had a look at your planting machine, three men sitting side by side, planting. The time's gone when we worked with hoe and spade. Whether there isn't also a machine for potting, he asks: that could surely do more than I can by hand. No, the machine doesn't do much more, we've tried it; the chief put a few of us on piece-work, potting by hand, and set the machine going beside us to compare: we only just lost. Who'd have thought that, he says.

The way he eyes the compost, fingers a pot, surveys my working-top! No doubt he wants to show me what an impression everything is making on him. He's the man – he must be – they've sent to write a report on the chief, and it looks as if he's trying to question us to begin with. One can only stand and admire all the things Herr Zeller has brought to fruition on his land – he did actually say 'fruition'. Nobody can show him what to do, I say, one look is enough and he knows what's what – and on top of that he's familiar with the secret language. What secret language? the smiler asks, asks in the tone of amazement I'd fully expected: he can't hide from me what he's really after – anyone wanting to pump me about the chief will have to get out of bed early. So what secret language? What shall I tell him? How can I best oblige him? At any rate I mustn't look at him, must carry on potting, saying it all as if by the by.

It's like this, I say, Herr Zeller is the only person our plants and trees converse with. I've seen it myself – many times. He hears in passing what they have to say, and he takes note of it and does what they ask. Does he perhaps hear voices? the smiler asks. Once, I say, as we were walking through the plantations, when there was no wind at all, the pear-trees began to rustle, they rustled their leaves, which were hardly yet unfolded but were already curled and deformed, and Herr Zeller listened carefully and took a few leaves in his hand and said to me: It's a fact, Bruno, they're complaining that red spider mites have settled on them and are sucking them dry, the only help is acaricides. Or at another time, I say, he suddenly stopped and listened, as you do when you hear

379

someone calling. I couldn't hear anything, but he nodded and went over to the tall-stemmed trees, and when I came near him I thought I could hear it too, though I didn't understand: that very soft scraping and clicking, I didn't understand it. Those tree trunks, whether you believe it or not, were drawing Herr Zeller's attention to tiny traces of wax wool: that's the stuff mealy bugs give off. We saw the danger looming, and the chief at once got in some propoxur.

It's only because he understands this secret language, I say, that he's able to achieve so much. I can well believe it, the smiler says, looking as if he's considering something, and he licks his lips. Could it also be, he asks, that your plants and trees recognise him as he goes by? Certainly, no doubt of it, there's proof of that. I believe you, he says, I don't doubt it at all, otherwise it would be impossible to explain certain results.

He looks at his watch, and I hope he'll soon leave me in peace. If there's anything else he wants to know, he should turn for a change to Ewaldsen, who never has more than three words to spare for strangers. I have one more question, he says: this secret language, is it by any chance in print somewhere? What is he getting at? If only I knew what he now has in mind! But he doesn't want an answer, he just grins and says goodbye and strolls off – it looks as if he doesn't take the things I've just told him seriously.

Max, that's Max waving to him, I wouldn't be surprised if they want to talk things over before the smiler enters the stronghold. Maybe the story of the secret language will now be passed on. It's all the same to me what they make of it, whether they believe it or not: for the chief I could make up all sorts of different stories, for him I'd do anything. He'll win in the end, that I know, for there's nobody can hold a candle to him, he has brought us through worse things often enough already. The losses in the big frost. The death of a hundred thousand oak-trees. That was probably the worst of all in his eyes: the wiping out of our oak-trees; it was a long time before he got over it, and the memory can still cause him pain.

Sometimes, when we are lining out, his face will suddenly darken, the old anger returns and he'll say, loudly enough for everyone nearby to hear: I hope all the trees here have got their Aryan passports, or God help you all.

At first I had no idea what he was doing, that time he came out of Danes' Wood holding in one hand a three- or four-year-old oak he'd broken off in there. When he saw me, all he said was: Let's go, Bruno, come with me, and I left what I was doing and joined him. There were certainly more than a hundred thousand oaks in the plot where we'd lined them out between the erratic block and the wall. The chief wanted them there in the deep soil, on the ground which in the soldiers' time was covered with dwarf mountain pines, and, as he'd foreseen, they were growing well. Oh, the way he threw down that little tree he had brought out! He pointed to one of our young oaks and gave me the order: Pull that up, come along! And when I hesitated and just looked at him, he repeated his order with a grimness that frightened me. I took hold of the smooth, thin trunk, tugged, tore and pulled, and the snapping of the roots hurt me inside. Put it down, Bruno, lay them side by side, and then tell me the difference. That's what he said, and, since I still wasn't clear what he wanted me to do, he repeated: Compare one with the other, do as I say. Since there was no difference, neither in the root system nor in the stems, and not in the leaves either, which were long-stemmed and jagged as a sessile oak should be, I didn't need to look long, for the one tree was exactly like the other. Nothing, I said, I can't notice any difference, at which the chief: You see, Bruno? I can't either, but the backroom arseholes in the ministry, they can supposedly show you the difference and, since that's what they claim they can do, let's have them over, those desk-bound stallions, those dry-land swimmers. He shook his head, he sighed and pulled a face, he pressed his fingers together till they cracked, and then he stepped among the little trees and examined a few of those nearest him, and it didn't escape my notice that he now and then gazed meditatively across the whole plantation and shrugged his shoulders, as if unsure what was to become of the oaks. He then called me over, made a scything motion with his hand over the young crowns and said: Think what it will mean, Bruno, if they have to go, all of them. Go? I say. A directive has come from the ministry.

They'd worked out some new regulations, back there in the ministry, and, in order to make them stick, had also dug out some older regulations. The chief said they were the rottenest regulations imaginable: they laid down that all trees must come from German seed, otherwise they were not to be sold. A pedigree, Bruno, just think of that: these experts are demanding a pedigree for each single plant, that's what they've worked out back there in their chambers; they want only German seed sown in German soil. All we need now is for them to stipulate German cowshit as manure. And then he said: Thank God it won't affect us, we've got proofs for everything.

That was all I heard for the moment from him, for Max had come down for a few hours and was waiting in the stronghold. Since it was the chief's wish, I went along with him, and we greeted Max, who that evening had to be in Kiel, where he was to speak in front of a lot of people. We had pancakes with chocolate sauce and also Max's favourite cake, poppyseed slices, heavy and warm. Dorothea saw to it that I was the only one to have both kinds on my plate at the same time. Max just smiled, but there was no race, no sign from him to see who could finish first as in earlier times.

While we were still eating he pushed a present across the table for the chief: his latest book. The chief stared at it for quite a while before drawing it closer and opening it, and, after Joachim had given him his reading glasses, he even began to read it, a bit here and there. He gave an approving nod and spoke the title slowly out loud: A Farewell to Standards. After that he tilted his head as if weighing things up, took off his glasses and passed a hand over his eyes. Well, Max, he said, and held out a hand in gratitude, I'll tackle this at sunrise, it's only early in the day I can keep up with you. Smiling, he spoke the title of the book once more and said: As for us, we're just discovering them for the second time, the standards; they're being pushed through the door in directives from the ministry: here, read this.

And Max read the letter the chief fished from his breast pocket, read it with growing amusement and let out an explosive gasp of disbelief, then, before he could say anything, Dorothea took the letter from his hand and held it up to the light to read it herself. They must be mad, Max said, German seed, German trees: it's all so wonderfully reminiscent of the Nazi race laws – they'll soon be talking of incest between trees. It's purity they're after, the chief said, only the pure can be allowed to breathe German air, the inferior crops must be wiped out – that's actually the word they use: wiped out. Purity! To have to hear that word again!

But it's only to preserve the line, Dorothea said. Anyone wishing to plant trees will surely want to know where they come from. Yes, Dotti, said the chief, that's certainly right, but the authors of these regulations have overlooked something: that it can lead in the end to dangerous inbreeding. They continued for a while to argue, Dorothea recalling the man who bought a large number of French pines without knowing that they came from deformed parent plants, the chief recalling the huge enrichment brought about by the Japanese larch and the Douglas fir from America; Dorothea spoke of the risks with trees of uncertain origin, the chief of crop improvements through foreign seed and plant stock, but they couldn't see eye to eye, not in anything.

But then the chief told Joachim to produce the required pedigree for our seed-corn – the piffling pedigree, he called it – and Joachim, who had always had the job of looking after the seed-corn, ordering it on the chief's instructions from a drying kiln in Klein-Sarup, suddenly began to hum and haw, his throat dried up and he couldn't look anyone in the eye. Speaking down to the table, he came out with the confession that he had bought part of our seed-corn from the new seed extraction plant in Hollenhusen and not from Klein-Sarup.

The sudden silence, the silent dismay. It was Dorothea who tried to defend Joachim, saying: Why shouldn't we get our seed for once from Hollenhusen? Peter Landeck supplies a lot of people, and he's also Joachim's friend. Old Smissen in Klein-Sarup is my friend, the chief said, with him you always know where you are. Joachin wanted to get up at once and go to Hollenhusen to fetch a guarantee form for approved seed-corn, but Dorothea said that could wait till tomorrow, and she filled up our coffee-cups and invited Max, who so rarely came to see us, to tell us more about himself, about his work, his friends. Before he left, he had more or less promised to bring along on one of his next visits the woman music teacher with whom he shared an old house with always something in need of repair. Joachim took him to the station, refusing all attempts to put him off, simply insisting, and that gave me some idea of what he was planning to do in Hollenhusen. The chief of course knew it all beforehand.

I've never found out what it is that helps him see so many things before they happen. I'm not sure in my own mind whether he works out what's coming, whether he sniffs it in the air or just knows. There are times I envy his ability never to be taken by surprise, but at other times I feel sorry for him. I shouldn't wonder if inside himself he already knows whether his deed of gift will remain valid, and also what will become of us, of me, of himself and of the others, that wouldn't surprise me at all.

We were both washing after work under the cold jet when Joachim came along, embarrassed and unsure of himself. I saw at once that he wanted to speak to the chief alone, but the chief didn't send me away and he didn't hurry himself, he washed his neck and dipped his arms in the basin, and then we both drank a bit from the jet. Joachim waited, looking at me, then at the chief, then at me again, but he didn't get what he wanted, for the chief suddenly said: Bruno is one of us, so say

384

what you've got to say. And then he began to speak, hesitantly but with carefully chosen words, admitting to us at once that he hadn't been given the guarantee of approved stock, since only recently there'd been an inspection of his friend's premises in the Hollenhusen seed extraction plant, and during this inspection several things had been discovered.

The chief said nothing. An official inspection had revealed that Peter Landeck had been in quite serious difficulties, and in order to overcome these difficulties he had gone to Rumania and bought seed-corn there at a favourable rate. The chief said nothing. What Peter Landeck bought there had later been mixed with approved seed-corn and nobody had discovered any difference, neither the people in Elmshorn, nor those in Pinneberg, who had all received supplies. Then the chief said: That's it, a lot of us were supplied by your friend. He took no notice of Joachim's apology, didn't even nod and didn't look at him either as he quietly declared that the people in Elmshorn and Pinneberg and in other places had already received a letter from the authorities, an instruction to plough in and destroy all seed-corn of unknown origin, and in particular that supplied by the extraction plant in Hollenhusen. Millions, he said, that means several million trees. A second apology wasn't even allowed to finish, the chief interrupted Joachim, looked him firmly in the eye and said: From now on you'll have nothing more to do with the seed-corn, and he added quietly: We haven't yet received it, this instruction, but maybe you should sit down and work out the extent of the damage, just in case. With that, he walked off, left Joachim standing and walked away, and I didn't at first know what to do, but in the end I ran after the chief and, as I came up with him, heard him muttering. He was talking to himself, but he didn't sound at all helpless or disheartened – rather determined and self-assured and with the hint of a threat in his tone. At one point I think I heard him say: You can't do things like that to us.

The letter from the authorities, though delayed, came at last, a lengthy letter the chief took with him wherever he went. A few times he read it out to men on the telephone – or at any rate he would have it lying in front of him while he was telephoning – and once he even gave it unexpectedly to me: Read that, Bruno. And I read it and couldn't believe what they demanded of us: that we should destroy the whole crop. They instructed us to plough up and burn all our young oak-trees (more than a hundred thousand of them), and, when I said: They can't do that, the chief just replied: They're sitting tight on their regulations, and those give them the right. His indignation, his incredulity, his defiance and that gleam at the back of his eyes: I could see he wasn't prepared to knuckle under entirely, and when he winked at me and went into his office, I'd dearly have liked to follow him, simply to witness how he was fighting back against the regulations.

My plan: at that time, alone in the threatened plantation, Bruno worked out a plan of his own. For the very first time I made up my mind to acquire a piece of land for myself: the damp ground. I would buy it from the chief, and was ready to give him all the money I had: the amount that fell short of the purchase price he could deduct from my wages over as many years as necessary. Then I would drain it in my own way and manure it and prepare it for my little problem wood, in which only things that were sub-standard and unsalable would grow, the deformed, the stunted, the rejected, the things of unknown origin: all the waste from the plantations I would gather together and plant and then leave to their own devices. Why the chief was against it I don't know, all I know is that he smiled in a strange way and advised me to wait a few more years. A problem wood, he said, is something you plant in your old age, and that was all he said.

The letter from the authorities was signed with an unreadable name, but the chief knew it was a departmental head, and to him he wrote a letter inviting him to come here, to examine and to compare; he left it to him to name the day. But the departmental head didn't come. He didn't come because he considered an inspection unnecessary, he was satisfied with the results of the official inspection, he relied on that and demanded once again, so he did, the immediate destruction of our oak crop.

The morning arrived, that morning when the sky was grey and peaceful, no wind in the air, not a breath. Work hadn't yet begun, but suddenly the throbbing, stuttering sound of a tractor sent the rooks flying into the air. The tractor coughed hoarsely, went quiet, then throbbed and coughed again, as if angrily gathering strength to overcome some obstacle. I didn't lose much time in thought, but ran to where the tractor was at work. The smell of oak as I drew near! Rarely before have I breathed so pure an oak smell, and it was coming from all the little trees the tractor had torn down, uprooted and crushed. The smell was the first thing I was conscious of, then I saw him. He was crouching on the seat of the tractor, tense, his face gleaming with sweat, he was cursing, spitting, changing gears with a crash, and the tractor was shaking and at times bucking, but he managed to keep it moving, and not just that: quite deliberately he was breaking through the cordons of little trees, carving out lanes. The slim trunks bent over and snapped, built up, were pushed aside and dragged along – he, the chief, who had not driven a tractor since the early Hollenhusen years, still knew how to handle it.

I gave him a sign, which he didn't see. I called out to show him I was there, but he didn't hear. It wasn't until I sprang in front of his tractor that he stopped and glared at me. Everything about him was vibrating. He pointed to the trees he had run over and to the trailer. He wanted me to begin clearing and loading, and I did begin, collecting up the slim trunks whose bark had been mangled by the hard rubber tyres, gathering branches together and throwing them all on to the trailer. But too many of the little trees still had their roots in the soil, and they were none too easy to pull out, none too easy. I was panting quite a bit and maybe he noticed it, for he suddenly drove backwards out of the plantation and then down to the machine shed, where he fixed the digger plough to the tractor, then came back at once. And now he ploughed the little trees out, row after row, they came out of the earth and toppled over, complete with roots. All I had to do was pick them up.

The trailer was soon full, but as the chief didn't stop ploughing, row by row, I went on collecting the young oaks and piling them up. I arranged them in two heaps, which I trod down from time to time, and when Ewaldsen arrived I asked him to give me a hand.

Ewaldsen: he couldn't believe his eyes, and he asked why we were doing it. If it had been left to him, he said, he'd have sold the little trees as foundation material and floor covering, or in smaller amounts to landscape conservationists: Why have you just given in to them? I could find no answer to that, in fact I couldn't speak at all, since I felt such pressure on my chest and was having to breathe hard just in order to get enough air into my lungs. When the others arrived – they came pouring incredulously from all sides and whispered and nudged each other whenever the chief drove by on the tractor without giving them so much as a glance – Ewaldsen took it on himself to talk to them. All he did was to confirm what they'd already seen for themselves and send them away. He didn't speak to the chief, not even when the tractor stopped beside us and the chief, leaving the motor running, climbed down and poured some coffee out of Ewaldsen's thermos flask into the battered aluminium mug, which, screwing up his face, he then drained. It was almost painful to meet his gaze: he had an uncanny calm that made you fear heaven knows what. Abruptly and without a word of thanks he set the aluminium mug down on Ewaldsen's briefcase, climbed back on to his tractor and drove off with that awesome energy, that obsession he brought to so many things.

Children's voices: there they are again, my little pests, marching towards me in step along the working path, one behind the other, shouting out that nursery rhyme about the cat in the snow so as to make sure they'll be heard. Carry on shouting, carry on marching, but watch out for your white socks and your nice jersey suits. It's too late now for you to creep up on me: I saw you long ago, and if you throw anything, I'll throw it back, this time I'll throw it back – but not so as to hit anybody.

Good morning, Bruno. Well, so there you are again, I say. What are you doing? Potting, as you very well know. Why? So the plant will grow, say I, and add: In fact, you could both do with being potted yourselves; if I had a bigger tub I'd give you a whole heap of compost and then water you up to the brim. They put their heads together, exchange a few words – it's clear they're once more hatching something out for me: Come on then, out with it, and stop giggling.

They want to ask me a riddle, that's what, and if I guess it right the caramel bonbons will be mine. Okay, off you go, but speak it slowly. They exchange a sign and speak together: Who, it is said, has a hat but no head, just one foot, not two, but never a shoe? They'll count up to ten and by then I must have the answer. All right, start counting. (I know it's a mushroom, but I won't say it till you reach eight.) Has a hat and no head – that can only be a mushroom, right? How amazed they are – and annoyed! Particularly Tim. Put your heads together, I don't mind, and ask me another if you want.

And they once again, as with a single voice: What, we beg, has only one leg, no mouth to be fed, but a heart in its head? That's a hard one, I say, it's not everything has its heart in its head, but wait, hold on, maybe I'll get it. You won't, says Tim, and he looks at me, biting his lower lip; he doesn't suspect that I already have the answer, for a cabbage is the only thing with a heart in its head, and it stands on one leg too, a cabbage-head.

He's got Ina's eyes; in that same timid way she looked at me once, that evening when she threw a little parcel tied with string into the big pond just as I came out from under the elms. She too bit her lower lip and trembled as if caught in the act, and softly she said: Guntram kept an account – everything he

389

gave that man he wrote down in a book. Then she turned suddenly and went off.

Eight, nine, ten. The cabbage-head, the cabbage-head, they both cry, hopping up and down in the belief that they've won. Now you'd better be off, I say, the chief will be here soon. They obey, scamper off, as I knew they would: threaten them with the chief and they do as they're told.

There's probably no one here to whom the chief likes giving instructions and orders more than he does to me; others first take a look, they consider and hesitate and ask one question after another, but with me he doesn't have to waste words, to demonstrate, to explain, he just says: Cover the seed tomorrow, or: Get everything ready for the winter hand grafting, and Bruno knows what to do and loses no time setting to work. I don't need to ask questions. Just you alone, Bruno, load up.

Single-handed I loaded up the big trailer with the little uprooted trees. It was long past knocking-off time, there was no one there to see, I trod the young wood down and bound it tight as instructed, not counting the separate trunks. Then I sat down at the edge of the churned-up, ruined oak plantation, and with a knife removed a strip of bark from one of the little trees and chewed it, extracting its sweetness. The chief's dog came up, licked my hands and looked at me. I threw him a bit I'd already chewed and he swallowed it, ran across the churned soil sniffing and dug a bit in the fresh furrows.

Those clamps that suddenly gripped me round the temples and squeezed tears from my eyes! As the pain began to throb, I threw myself on the ground and banged my head against it until he called me, until I saw his muddy boots right in front of me and heard his command: Come on, Bruno, up you get. At his command I stood up, staggered a bit maybe, but was able to do what he asked: he backed the tractor up to the trailer, I inserted the bolt, fastened the safety chain and climbed on top of the lashed-down trees. I was hardly there when off we went, driving in the dark towards Hollenhusen.

We drove without headlights, the trees jolting and rocking on the trailer as if alive. On the uneven road they clamped my hands tight, bounced around under me, and on a bumpy stretch the last scraps of soil rained down from the roots. It was not for me to ask where he was taking the condemned wood: I thought he might be making for the big Hollenhusen waste tip, above which from time to time seething black and white clouds could be seen, a cloud of seagulls and a cloud of rooks, but we didn't drive that far. Just past the level crossing we turned into Lindenallee and right along it to the grand house in which all the council departments have their offices.

Hardly any lights. The bicycle racks empty. Not a soul to be seen on the open square. Here he stopped and jumped down and came running towards me, I saw the flashing in his eyes, smelt his sour breath as I bent down to him: he looked like a man possessed. And then he said: Off with the stuff, and I set to at once, grabbing several trees at a time and hurling them from the trailer down on the paved square, where he worked hard throwing them all together, heaping them up into a funeral pyre. Never have I unloaded anything so fast, and never had he urged me more grimly to make haste. And then I passed the can down to him and heard him sloshing it about, sloshing the petrol over the trees and with the remains tracing a wet stream away from the heap and then hurling the empty can at my feet. The fourth match was the first to ignite: he dipped it in the stream and ran to the tractor, while the fire sped along the paving to the heap and with a sudden whoosh enveloped it, the whole pile, flames closed in over the trees and stretched upwards, lighting up the square.

The trailer skipped and rumbled, the empty can rolled across the floor as we drove off, I turned to look back as the flames gained height, crackling, spitting, throwing up sparks. The flames were reflected in the windows of the council offices, a few figures were running out on to the square. As we crossed the railway lines I was pitched quite a way up in the air and almost flung out and the petrol can flew off and vanished without trace. The machine shed: we drove straight to the machine shed, and there I had to help him drag out the big ladder, which we put against the wall and climbed in the dark up to the roof, but there wasn't much to see in Hollenhusen, just the far-off glow of the fire, nothing more. He was muttering to himself all the time, sketching movements in the air, as if he was cutting something and throwing it away, and at one point he said: Never trust anyone who preaches genuineness and purity, Bruno, the apostles of purity bring us nothing but disaster; and before we climbed down he also said: By rights we ought to send him a cardboard box full of ashes, that fellow in the ministry, the ashes of our un-German trees. He left me to take the ladder down and store it away, and he had no more instructions for me either, he leaned against a post, slapped it a few times, then muttered a farewell and went off to the stronghold.

I'd dearly have liked to return to Hollenhusen, to the fire we'd made. I would have mixed in with the people and watched them put the funeral pyre out, but something urged me to go home and lock myself in. I can still recall my feelings of joy and of satisfaction. And I recall too the thrill that came with the thought that down there on the paved square the big job of solving the riddle was beginning, the questioning and the probing, while already we were miles away.

My joy didn't last long. In the morning I summoned the birds. A sharp hissing sound mixed with mournful whistles brought them along, as it always does – I had found out, quite by chance, that a particular hissing sound makes them fearful and at the same time curious, while a deliberate, mournful whistle makes them fly straight up to me – and I stretched out my hand with bread crumbs and sunflower seeds on it and enjoyed their flutterings. Twelve kinds of birds, including bullfinches and long-tailed tits, fluttered in from the planta-tions, some of them catching bits in flight, others clutching hold of my finger for a split second; they tried to scare each other off, pecking and chasing, leaving tiny feathers to float down around my feet. All at once they scattered; on a tomtit's warning cry they all scattered and, raising my eyes, I could see it was Duus approaching me. Come here a moment, Bruno, he said, dangling our petrol can.

Because I admitted everything straight away, I had to go with him to the police station. On the way there we stopped only once, at the place on the square where the fire had been. He pointed to the paving, blackened by water and ashes, and to the charred tree trunks and shook his head, but he said nothing. Inside the station there was another policeman beside Duus. He sat down in front of a typewriter and kept looking at me in a pitying sort of way, now and again he even risked giving me a smile, I don't know why. I took it all on myself. When I was asked whether it was I who had dumped a cartload of young trees and set them alight, I said yes. When I was asked if I knew what I'd done was against the law, I said yes. And when I was asked why I'd done it, I said: On account of the regulations. According to the regulations our whole crop of oak-trees had to be destroyed.

I said all this, but I soon saw Duus didn't believe me; several times he wanted to know if I'd really been alone and not under instructions, whether Herr Zeller really knew nothing about it, and how had I made off with the tractor without being noticed, and where did the petrol come from – from his questions I could see he wasn't satisfied with my confession. When I suggested doing the whole thing over again to show them how it was done, the young policeman laughed, but Duus looked at me with a serious expression and asked if I had any idea what the consequences of my fire might have been, on account of flying sparks and so on. I replied that live wood and damp leaves don't give off flying sparks, or at any rate only a few once the pile has burnt low. An answer like that didn't please him, he got pretty severe and threatened me with punishment. That scared me, and I promised him it was the first and last time I'd do such a thing. Then the two men whispered together, keeping their eyes fixed on me, and my fright grew.

I recognised the chief by his footsteps. He knocked just once and immediately tore the door open. He stood for a moment on the threshold, panting after his fast walk, then he gave the policemen a nod of greeting, came in and said: So here you are, Bruno. He wasn't surprised. How hastily Duus drew the chief to one side and quietly, his back to me, explained things! He also gave him my statement to read and replied to his questions as he read with just: Certainly, Herr Zeller, we know that, Herr Zeller – that much anyway I heard. And how promptly Duus agreed when the chief asked him to come up to the stronghold: Let's say two o'clock, Herr Duus, I shall then be at your disposal. He gave me a wink that nobody else could see, and then, loud enough for all to hear, ordered me harshly to go with him. There's a lot to be done, he said, and that was all, and we walked out together and got into the jeep. Only by a hair's breadth did the chief avoid running down one of the labourers who were cleaning the paved square with rakes and brooms. They gave us an indignant look as we drove off over the burnt patch.

On a working track in the middle of the fruit plantations he suddenly came to a halt, and I thought he was going to give me some instruction, but he just gazed straight ahead, and after a while – I would never forget it – he unexpectedly said: Thanks, Bruno. And drove on again. Humming to himself. And seeming self-assured and pleased with himself as he spoke into thin air: You know, Bruno, after that I just feel better. We won't get off cheaply, but I feel very much better. I only hope you feel the same. And then he winked at me, and I had just one wish: to stay by his side for ever.

Weeping: Dorothea has surely been doing a spot of weeping. Well, Bruno? Nobody here can pot as fast as you do, she says, and nods to me in the old friendly way and comes up very close to watch. She is carrying something, pressing it to her body as if to warm it, but I mustn't look and certainly don't mean to ask, because it's none of my business. Have you done all those? Yes. You'll soon have them finished. Yes. What a gentle voice she has! I could listen to it for ever. I was with Elef, Bruno, she says, with him and his family. Elef has invited me along, I say, they want to give a little party, and I'm to go to it. I know, Bruno, we're invited too, and we're looking forward to it, but it's not possible at the moment. It's just being put off for a while, I say. Yes, Elef put it off at once of his own accord, for he wants us all there, says Dorothea, and she places down on the side table the thing she's been holding in the crook of her arm.

The partridge family – that's the mother partridge with her five chicks. How black and discoloured the silver is! The chicks all look up to their mother, learning how to peck in the safety of a thicket. Dorothea strokes the little silver partridges, her hand is trembling, she's pressing her lips together, it's clear she's on the verge of weeping, and now she's wiping her cheeks, though no tears have yet come. The chief, I say, those are the chief's – on the windowsill in front of his writing-desk, that's where they always stood. That's right, Bruno, and there we shall put them back. That is Elef's wish too. She says nothing more, but for me it's enough: the chief must have taken the partridge family to Elef, must have given it him as a gift, just as he gave me the watch and the silver acorns, or at any rate tried to give them. There's much that becomes harder as time goes on, Dorothea says, taking the partridge family up again. I used to believe things would become easier with time, but they don't, Bruno, they get harder. Shall I carry it? I ask. No, they're not very heavy; but when you've finished here, the potatoes probably need sorting, both piles. I'll see to it, I'll just finish potting these and then I'll go down in the cellar. There's no hurry, she says in farewell and smiles as she walks away, stepping carefully as if carrying something alive that might fly away.

Not a word about the chief, about what's about to happen to him and to us all here. When silence reigns, things are getting serious, as Max once said. She won't leave us – that she won't do. Dorothea has gone off only a few times, and then she has always come back sooner than intended, simply because she couldn't bear not having us close at hand; but she could turn her back on us, indeed she once locked herself in for weeks on end, refusing to show her face to anyone but Joachim.

When I think of that time I at once see Mistral, the black horse, see the paddock by the big pond in front of Danes' Wood, and Bravo, the chestnut with the white blaze, and each time I feel this stabbing pain between my ribs. The chief had no objection to Niels Lauritzen putting a fence round the meadow by the big pond and turning it into a paddock, all he said was: Go ahead, and he also said: Maybe your manure can come down a bit in price, and with that everything was settled between them. Niels Lauritzen, who has always been good to me, took me with him to the uncultivated land, where I helped him drive in stakes and fix the wire, double and triple strands. When that was done, he led his black horse into the paddock, he himself fixing the pole that closed the fence, then he beckoned me over, and together we watched his Mistral, who stood for a long time with ears pricked and tail lashing, but he then trotted off towards the copse, as if exploring the limits of his new domain. He must in the end have decided things were moving too slowly, for he suddenly switched over to a gallop, his strides became long, clods of earth flew up behind him, he snorted and tossed his mane.

Niels Lauritzen saw me trying to move away, so he grabbed me by the sleeve and held me tight, directing my eyes to the horse who, now close beside the fence, swung his hindquarters round and galloped towards us in a wide curve, still with long strides full of power: the whole land seemed to shiver and shake beneath his bounding hooves. The eyes: at the sight of those wide open eyes I tore myself free. Bruno ran to the elm-trees and from there watched the horse halt and rear up, he moved towards Niels Lauritzen on his hindlegs, snorting and beating the air with his forelegs. Niels stood his ground, raising a hand towards Mistral as if pleading with him, and the horse first shook his head, then, nodding, went so close that Niels could touch his nostrils and stroke them.

Come, Bruno, he called, called several times, but I stayed where I was, nothing could tempt me away from the shelter of the elms, and even later on I was unwilling to be shown how to approach Mistral and gain his friendship. I didn't want it. For several weeks the black horse was alone in the paddock, I observed him only from a safe distance, watched him grazing or rubbing his neck against a post, and now and then – maybe because he'd been stung by a horsefly – galloping with raised tail, always along beside the fence. Then on Sunday Bravo, the chestnut, was there too.

Dorothea talked us into going together to the big pond. Her hints made it clear to us all that she had a surprise in store, and that this was meant for Joachim was made just as clear by the way she kept giving him a wink and looking at him in a questioning way. Though Joachim had only come second in the dressage championships, she never stopped calling him champion, and no doubt she'd have liked the chief to say a bit more about Joachim's success, but apart from congratulations he offered nothing. Does our champion want some more coffee? she would ask, or she might say: As a champion you could look a bit happier. She it was, Dorothea, who pressed us to get going, and outside she linked her arm in Joachim's and never once scolded my two pests, who ran on ahead with their sticks, knocking the heads off everything that had one, burrs and buttercups.

The horses were standing in the paddock as if each had offended the other: they may have been standing very close together, but each was looking over the other's croup, and now and again one of them would shake his head or paw the ground a bit. The coat of the chestnut gleamed in the sunlight. He was the first to spot us, probably guessed we'd come here on his account, for he at once left the black horse and came trotting towards us, whinnying a greeting – not for me, but for the others, who had gone up to the fence. Joachim's praise, his admiration for Bravo. The fetlocks, the withers, the hocks: the things he found to point out and wonder over! The chestnut went straight up to him and, lowering his head, tried with stained yellow teeth to open the pocket of Joachim's jacket. He must have been hoping to find something to nibble in there, a lump of sugar or a crust, but Joachim had nothing on him, he put his arms round the horse's head and for an instant pressed his cheek against the white blaze.

And then Dorothea asked him if he'd like to have the horse for his own, and Joachim stiffened and looked at her in disbelief. And then she gave him to understand that from now on it belonged entirely to him, and he still couldn't move and didn't know what to say. And then she invited him to take possession of Bravo, to introduce himself to the horse, and then he took her in his arms as if he was about to wrestle with her. But on a snort from the horse he let her go and climbed over the fence and patted the animal, ran the palm of his hand over his coat, spoke to him. The black, Mistral, was curious and came trotting up, but he didn't want to be patted; keeping his distance, he just watched what Joachim was doing with the chestnut.

No one had been paying attention to the chief, and by the time we turned he was already quite a long way off. There was something defiant, something pounding in his tread, and we all knew no one would succeed in calling him back. Those short steps – even from a distance you could see he was boiling with rage, or at any rate was in a temper. Without stopping to choose, just more or less as he passed by, he broke a twig from the hedge and gripped it tight. Something seems to have upset him, said Dorothea, at which Ina: He'll get over it.

Because I thought he might possibly need me, I ran after him and soon caught him up, but, though he could feel I was behind him, he didn't look round. Even at the water-main, where he stopped to drink, he hardly took any notice of me, just gave me a fleeting grin, then went on his way to the stronghold. Inside, he sat down at the coffee table, which hadn't yet been cleared, tossed down the remains in his cup in a single gulp, stared for a while straight in front of him and then, when the bullfinch pair made some enquiring chirps, got up and went to the cage. He pushed the point of his twig between the bars, at which the birds began fluttering their wings, raising their fine sand into a dust storm. They hopped and fluttered around and all at once were outside, slipping swiftly one after the other out through the cage door he'd opened. Flying just below the ceiling, Dorothea's birds circled the room until they discovered the open flap of the veranda door – I suppose the draught told them where they could escape – and fft-fft, they were outside and flying to the top of a lime-tree. It was only then the chief seemed to realise I was there and had seen it all. He smiled uneasily, moved the cage door to and fro and laid the blame on the person who had apparently failed to secure it properly. And then he wanted to know whether I would bear him witness, and I said yes.

Rarely have I sat so long opposite him in silence: he had no job for me to do, just wanted me to sit down, and this I did.

His blood-shot eyes. The movements of his lips. As he ran a hand over his stubbly grey hair he looked utterly tortured; when he took his hands from his face, it could suddenly reveal a quite unexpected expression, confident where before it had been clouded. It's a wonder he could stand my gaze for so long, but he did at last get up and, before going up to his room, he said: Here among us too, Bruno – that saying is proving true here among us too: behind the founders and the collectors come the destroyers. And that's all he said.

I can recall my uneasiness as I left him. I felt in my bones that something else would be happening that day, and nothing much came of my efforts at home to carve the old cherry wood; even as I shaped it I knew I'd have to carve the long-handled stirring spoon all over again. The spit I'd managed all right, and the vegetable forks and the wooden tweezers were quite presentable, but the stirring spoon was a failure, and since I didn't want to give Ina something for her birthday that I didn't myself like, I put off the carving till the following evening and just did a bit of sandpapering on the whisk and other kitchen utensils. My foreboding was right: the person who knocked on my door, who didn't impatiently order me to come out, but waited for my: Come in, was the very last person I'd have expected to see. Joachim didn't presume to sit down of his own accord; he who as a rule had nothing but a shake of his head for me stood looking round the room approvingly. The carved kitchen utensils, standing with their handles in a beer glass, so took his fancy that he wanted to order a similar set when time allowed. Oh, Bruno, he said after I'd offered him my armchair, and I could tell from his sigh that he was depressed and needed someone to confide in.

He was depressed and he was worried. He'd left the strong-hold because he could no longer stand the quarrelling. They never stop, Bruno, they're always finding something to throw at each other's head, it has become simply unbearable, he said, and hunched his shoulders as if struck by a cold shower. Never in his life before had he seen his parents like this, he would never have believed they could so lose control of themselves. He said: They literally try to find out who can hurt the other most. The horse: it had all begun with the horse he'd been given. The fact that Dorothea had bought it out of her own savings didn't satisfy the chief: he couldn't understand how in difficult times savings could be used to buy a horse. And now they're taking stock, Bruno, and you've no idea of all they've got stored up inside them and are now bringing against each other. Joachim asked me for a cigarette, but I had none, and he didn't want the bowl of stewed pears I offered him, but he did try a few of the plum stones I cracked for him.

The promise: I distinctly remember he made me promise one day to go alone with him to the paddock. He wanted to prove something to me, wanted to show me how easy it is to make friends with a horse, if only one approaches and confronts it properly. He felt sorry for me and wanted to get my trouble sorted out. His Bravo was friendliness itself: Believe me, Bruno, when you and he have had a good sniff at each other, it won't be long before you'll be sitting on his back. That's what he said, and I was so amazed I couldn't answer. And there was something else he said: You've got something to get out of your system, Bruno, and your surest way of doing that is to face up to it. He of all people was the one offering to help me with it all, and before he went away I had to promise to go with him one weekend to the paddock.

Ever since the horses had been in the new paddock I had stopped going either to Danes' Wood or to the big pond. Usually I went down to the Holle, where I would sit on the planks that served as a bridge, watch the herons and the lapwings, and sometimes dangle my home-made fishing line in the water. I would catch small bream and finger-sized eels, but never a pike. Carefully I would free the little fishes from the hook, allow them to flap about for a while, then throw them back into the Holle.

But once I did go to the paddock, and I did it for your sake, Ina. Since you asked me, I walked around up there looking for

401

the children, who hadn't been seen for most of the day, your Tim and Tobias, my two pests. When one of them needed to be found, it was always to me you came first, and almost every time I could put you out of your misery: you were often quite amazed how quickly I could find the one who had disappeared. I have a method of my own, unknown to anyone else: once I've established the mood in which someone has gone off – whether he was content or excited, in despair or in search of something special – I first of all consider the weather, for the simple reason that when it's raining people decide differently from when the sky is clear, and after that I think what I myself would do, and then off I go and usually trace the person who has to be found. Since you told me the children had taken their catapults, I felt at once they'd have headed for Danes' Wood on account of the wood pigeons, so numerous that not even the chief, who now and again comes home with whole bundles of them on a wire, could keep them in bounds with his gun.

I decided to catch the children red-handed, to startle them, so I didn't call out their names, but crept in the shelter of the elms past the big pond, undetected by the little hunters, but noticed by the two horses, who had stopped biting each other's manes and chasing each other and were now standing with pricked ears watching me. How edgy they were, how ill-tempered! Though I could see something had excited them, I didn't give up my plan of slipping swiftly between the taut wires and running across the narrow strip of paddock to Danes' Wood. When with a clatter of wings a flock of wood pigeons rose up from the oldest oak-tree and flew in a circle round it, I knew in which direction I must go, and in a twinkling I squeezed between the wires and ran, twirling in my hands a piece of squared timber I'd picked up beside the pond.

The black gave the signal: with a whinny Mistral took off and galloped towards me, drawing the chestnut after him. Bravo quickly caught up, and they ran along side by side. Those bounds, that thundering, the swelling and straining of those muscles! I saw I wouldn't make it to Danes' Wood, I'd have to go back, so, hurling the piece of squared timber at them, I ran to the fence. They were egging each other on, that's for sure: their heavy bodies, now at full stretch, seemed to fly along, borne by rage and the urge to win, but I reached the wire first, by a whisker. Then something threw me against a fence-post and everything went black. The wire squeaked and snapped with a loud bang and I heard an awful neighing behind me. Something massive rammed me and forced me to the ground, then an overwhelming weight fell on my legs and jammed me tight. A stabbing pain in my ribs. Right in front of me the coat of the chestnut, who was neither standing nor lying, but resting on the ground with hind and forelegs half stretched. I could feel the burden breathing, share in each movement as with all his might Bravo strove to rise, pawed, jerked, worked himself upright, but each time collapsed and sank back, because his leg, the right foreleg, wouldn't support him. The black was standing beside the broken-down fence, but still obediently within the paddock; he made no attempt to cross the borderline, just stood stretching out his neck and sniffing and time and again tossing his head.

The children found me. I heard their voices in the paddock, also distinctly heard them slap Mistral, and then they came over to me and couldn't make out what had happened. Bravo didn't get up, though they patted and coaxed him, and they didn't manage either to pull me free. They then ran off without telling me what they meant to do, all they said was: We'll be back soon. I didn't move, and the horse didn't seem to know I was even there, not once did he turn his head. He shivered as once again he collapsed and sank back and just lay there submissively, waiting.

Niels Lauritzen pulled me free. All of a sudden he was there, and he grasped at once what had happened. At his word of command Bravo moved – but in such a way that he toppled and remained lying on his side – and I was free and was dragged clear and given an old fish-trap as a headrest. After feeling me over and reassuring me, Niels examined the injured

403

horse's foreleg; he sighed and said to himself: Oh, my God, then again: Oh, my God, then he went to the edge of the paddock, where he searched for clues and prodded the ground. Suddenly his arm sank deep into the ground, almost as far as the elbow: Niels Lauritzen had found the hole, the mole tunnel, in which Bravo had caught his hoof as he attempted to stem his wild gallop. That was it, Bruno, that must have been it – he wanted to stop in front of you and caught his hoof in the hole, and after the double fracture he was unable to check his impetus and so crashed into the fence, taking you with him, said Niels Lauritzen. Leaning on him, I took a few trial steps, but every time I put my foot down I felt a sharp pain in my stomach, and I soon had to take to the ground again. There was nothing Niels Lauritzen could do but leave me by myself and go to the stronghold for help.

So there we both lay, Bravo and I. He lay quietly on his side, breathing heavily, rubbing his neck against the grass, and now and again he moved his broken leg, from which a blood-covered bone was sticking out. He seemed to have given up trying to raise himself. I crawled towards him, moving so cautiously that he didn't once prick his ears to listen – the black stood watching me – and then I was close to him, so close that I could see the short stubbly white hairs in his coat and, without meaning to, I put out my hand and touched him. He twitched, I laid my hand on him and he twitched again. His violent snorts alarmed me and I crawled further away, keeping my eyes fixed on him.

And I should probably have touched him once again if Niels Lauritzen and the chief hadn't come. They came marching at the double over the damp ground, followed by the children, who weren't allowed beyond the meadow; one warning word from the chief was enough to make them turn and trot reluctantly back. He was carrying his gun. The chief was carrying his gun, barrel downwards. The things you get up to, Bruno, he said as he knelt down beside me, loosened my belt, pulled my shirt out of my trousers and pushed it up to my neck. Feeling around, he at once found the place that hurt the most. When he decides something urgently needs to be done, there's no time wasted in considering and searching: he had only to walk through the elms to the pond and immediately he had the board he wanted, and he simply cut the cords he needed from the leaders of the old fish-traps; a few notches, a few knots, and the carrier chair for me was complete.

He laid it down in front of me and went over to Niels Lauritzen, who all this time had stayed with the horse, talking to him and holding the broken leg in his hands. As he and the chief spoke together they walked several times around the prostrate animal, pointing things out, coming to conclusions, and then they decided to bring him to his feet with words of command and physical support. Bravo obeyed, he rolled over, pressed and strained and drew himself up to his full height, but suddenly he collapsed again and fell on his side, the broken leg dangling in the air. The two men conferred once again. And the the chief took up his gun, loaded it and walked right up to the horse. He lowered the barrel, and his hand was steady as he took aim behind the ear and pulled the trigger. The chestnut tossed his head slightly, a shudder ran through his body, his legs reached out as if seeking once more to tread the ground, his tail lashed the grass and little bubbles burst from his muzzle. Niels Lauritzen was stroking his neck. The shuddering stopped and Bravo lay still.

I was told to sit on the board, and they both put the cords round their shoulders and lifted me at the same time, and in this manner they dragged me away from the paddock, sitting between them as if on a swing. I felt sick, and at one stage, when they set me down to get their breath back, the feeling was so strong that I vomited before their eyes. Hardly was I lying on the ground when the stream gushed out, and the chief knelt down and held my head. Out with the fear, he said, spew it all up, and that's all he said. When they lifted me off the ground again, I felt lighter, and I resolved to tell it all as it must be told.

They didn't wish to hear me. In the stronghold deep silence reigned, and at evening light showed through only a few windows. Joachim could be seen only at most from afar, Dorothea not at all. You, Ina, you laid the broad strip of plaster over my chest and from time to time looked in to see how I was getting on, and from you I learned that something had been destroyed and fractured for ever, a pact, a bond, and it was from you I heard that things between us all could never again be what they had once been. No one asked me how it had all come about; what had happened was enough, nothing more was needed to make them turn away from each other. Dorothea locked herself in her room and seemed prepared to stay there for ever. The chief soon gave up calling through the closed door and went his own way. His loneliness. He who is streets ahead of everybody else and forgets nothing seemed at times no longer to know what instructions he had given me, and more than once behind his back Ewaldsen asked: What's the matter with the chief? I felt so sorry for him that I resolved to speak to Dorothea myself; I crept up the stairs and knocked at her door: no reply. But someone else had heard my knock: Joachim, who looked at me mistrustfully and sent me away. One of the two, either Joachim or Ina, then had a word with Max, and he came at once and stayed all day, his manner hasty and irritable, as if he'd been asked to do something for which he had no time. I don't know what he reproached them with, how he worked on them, but I do know that when he left he shrugged his shoulders and pulled a face. However, shortly after his departure Dorothea came out of her room and appeared downstairs at the dinner-table.

That was surely the iron bar? Some of them here were annoyed with the chief for signalling breaks and closing time by striking that singing bar, the vibrations from which can be painful for anyone standing close by. Some of them say it reminds them of former bad times, and they'd rather decide for themselves when to start their lunch break, but the chief is unwilling to do away with the iron bar, for it had once sounded the hours in the plantations of the rising sun, and to him it's just the normal thing.

Another five pots and I'll be finished: Magda will have to wait that long. She'll surely have put together some kind of hot-pot, beans with ribs and belly of pork, or maybe peas with pork crackling, which all the others find tough and leathery, but not me: I can never have enough of it. How often during the winter have I begged her to bring me unwanted crackling, but she prefers to hang it out for the tits rather than give it to me, since she believes eating crackling hardens your stomach. She doesn't like it either when I sit beside her chewing the gristle off the ribs: it seems she can't bear the crunching noise, as of grit or corn being ground. Altogether Magda finds a lot to object to in me, and she even said once: I really don't know, Bruno, why I put up with you. But I must make haste now, and after lunch go straight down to the potato piles in the cellar.

It's sauerkraut with sausages and mashed potatoes. My plate is already standing in the hatch – that's something Magda sometimes does to make me feel her reproach – and now her face appears in the opening: So the lord and master deigns to come at last? That is spoken a bit too loudly, as if meant to be heard. Her wave, her signal: she wants me to come to the hatch to fetch my plate. It's been fixed, Bruno. What has? The date: I didn't catch it all, but a date has been fixed for the court hearing. No, Magda! Yes, a man has been here, he brought some things along and took some more notes; I saw him myself, and he and the others think it'll go through, the loss of his rights. I don't know what to say – surely they can't really mean to take his rights away? Maybe that's his temporary guardian, Magda says, and she says: You must just wait and see, Bruno. You've got nothing to fear, just because the deed of gift is made out in your name. Do you understand what I'm saying? Yes, yes. Then pick up your plate. He won't let them get away with it: one day, when his patience is at an end, he'll fight back, he can still run rings round everybody, he with his knowledge, with his scars. There's nothing I wouldn't do for him. Why aren't you eating, Bruno? Magda calls. Aren't you hungry?

They've burst open, the sausages, but they taste very good, and the little bits of apple and the grapes add flavour to the cabbage, there's not many could do it better, Magda. If only we can stay together, he and I! He looked on, smiling, when I once went down on all fours and held still so the little pests could put that make-believe collar round my neck, on the lawn, in front of everybody. Because you looked at me so encouragingly, Ina, I played along with them, stretched out my neck for the two lads, who at that time were still very small. They could only place the cord round me, the knot had to be tied by the chief, who had just received yet another award. And I barked and sniffed for them and raised a leg against the roses, to their great joy, I sat up and begged, fetched the stick and rushed growling at the legs of one or the other. I didn't wish to be a spoilsport. But then the two of them tugged so violently on the leash I couldn't draw breath, I choked and threw myself backwards, while they laughed. The chief cut through the leash, severing it with his pocket-knife.

You can have some more sauerkraut, Bruno, and potato too, but not sausages – they're finished. No, no, I've had enough. You've been filling your stomach with something else, I'll bet, Magda says, people like you don't even notice they're eating. I hope I'm not running a temperature, the plate already seems to be growing bigger; that's how it's always been when I get feverish: everything changes size or shape or grows bigger, a shoe, an apple, a butterfly.

Here's my plate, Magda. Just put it down. Was it a little man with a briefcase, I ask, with his hair combed a funny way? Who? Who do you mean? You know, the one who is maybe to be his guardian. She looks at me in astonishment. How do you know, Bruno? Come on, tell me – have you met him? He was with me, I say, he watched me while I was potting, his name's Grieser or Kiesler, and all he can do is ask questions, nothing else. The chief could twist him round his little finger. Not so loud, Bruno, don't speak so loud. Will you be coming this evening? I can't, not tonight. But decide, I say, we must decide what to do, and she, turning away: For the time being all we can do is wait. To my word of thanks she makes no reply. So I'll be off now.

The toad must be put out, otherwise I can't start. It must have fallen into the cellar while the window was open, or it took a leap in the dark of its own free will, finding things too dangerous out there in the bright light. I'd like to know what it's been living on. That warty skin with its steady pulse, those gold-rimmed eyes! It can't hop as frogs hop, it pulls itself up, climbs and drags its belly over the potatoes, it can't get up on the shelf, the glass jars and jugs are safe from it, and the smoked ham in its bag. I like holding frogs in my hand, I enjoy the way they brace themselves and stretch and try to find a way out of my closed fist, but I don't touch toads. On the shovel now, come along, get a move on, that's right, now stay where you are, keep still, still, and don't jump, you'll soon be outside and can hide away under the rhododendrons, under the dead leaves.

The wire basket: that's where the shoots must go, they really have begun to sprout, our potatoes, the shoots feel like stiff, whitish worms, glass-like worms that take on a violet shimmer in the light. Cellar paleness, cellar damp: though they try to keep the cellar dry, they can't stop saltpetre coming through. Flowers of nitre, swollen and burst. Here, under the soil, under the training ground, deep inside the former command hill – and maybe not far from the place where they once buried him – here there are surely more kinds of jam than in the whole of Tordsen's shop, and every jar labelled by Dorothea: quince, strawberry, apple jelly and plum, but also blackcurrant and cranberry – we've got the lot. The jar of fruit preserved in rum was put down by the chief himself: he's really the only one with a taste for the stuff: one winter he swallowed three whole bowls of it and afterwards could still get up and walk. The shoots can easily be rubbed off with a thumb, I don't have to snip them off.

That's Joachim's car, he sounds the horn twice, as he always does, and the voice is Ina's voice. She's talking to a stranger, I hear that at once, politely she's saying goodbye, thanking him for his visit. The stranger himself speaks so softly that I understand hardly a word. Joachim will surely be taking him to the station. Maybe it's the man with the briefcase, that could well be so: maybe he has asked all the questions he needed to ask and now knows enough. If only I knew what's going to happen here – to me and to him!

This draught all of a sudden: where is it coming from? I closed the cellar door. Light off, light on, and now footsteps that are not Dorothea's. Someone is coming, creeping down quietly. I must see who it is and what he wants: if I duck down behind the potato pile, duck down low, he won't see me. The chief. He's the only one who murmurs like that when he's alone. He's carrying a little box, a casket: that blue and white ribbon is surely the bow that was attached to the scroll of honour he took off the wall along with all his other awards and decorations after we'd destroyed the oak plantation. He's also got a little packet wrapped in greaseproof paper. He sits down at the foot of the stairs, motionless, staring straight ahead: maybe he's forgotten why he came down. He'll have to know I'm here, I can't just stay watching him, I must straighten up and tell him what Bruno has been sent here to do. But I suppose it's too late now. I hope to heaven he won't run me to earth: I should have made my presence known at once: please God I don't start to cough or get an attack of hiccups.

He bends down over the heavy earthenware jars, drags them cautiously away from the wall, the jars full of pickled plums, cucumber and beetroot. He's got a hiding-place there, that's for sure, he's already scratching, loosening, he reaches down deep as far as his shoulder and lifts something out, all the time muttering to himself. He takes up all the things that are lying on the stairs in one single handful, all of a sudden he's in a hurry, one after the other he drops the things into his hiding-place, taps it, closes it, probably with a stone or piece of broken brick. The scraping noise of the jars. His relief. The jars give nothing away. His face is quite wet from his efforts, but he is satisfied with himself and wipes his hands on his trousers. This time he doesn't creep, he stamps up the stairs. Click, and I'm sitting in the dark and must wait till the door is closed and then a little while longer – just in case. Who knows what he has hidden or placed safely out of reach of the others? Maybe they're documents or old coins, maybe even letters that are one day to be used as proof; he no longer trusts the others, he's frightened they might take from him things he considers important, the chief is afraid of them.

Something is dripping, something gnawing: the minute it's dark something or other will venture out, I only need throw a potato and at once all is still, a tense, humming silence. There's no cellar secure enough to prevent some things creeping in, locks are no use and nor is keeping watch. I've never managed to see in the dark, though I've tried several times. Now and again I thought I was getting close to it, the darkness began to flow and take on a grey colour, but I couldn't recognise anything. It should be safe now to switch on the light.

The ribbon behind the jars can still be seen, that blue and white ribbon: he didn't hide it carefully enough, didn't push it down and cover it up. Anyone coming down to fetch some pickled plums or cucumber will see it straight away, give it a tug and find what the chief has stored away. No, I mustn't go near it, mustn't touch anything, though there's clearly all kinds of things to find and examine, maybe even things affecting me. But no, that's none of my business, it belongs to him alone: no one but he has the right to handle his things. Yet the others: they certainly won't hold back from examining anything they find down here. They'll assess its value and discuss it, and maybe he'll be left standing helpless, not knowing how to continue without the things he hid away, that's possible. I must tell him. He, the person to whom I owe everything, who once called me his only friend, he must be told the blue and white ribbon is showing and giving the hiding-place away to all and sundry. Quick, before Dorothea comes along, for she's bound to come some time, make haste and reach him, so he'll have time to stuff it all away and cover it up.

If the light is out, Dorothea won't come down, she'll just call down into the dark cellar and then find something else to do. I just hope I don't run straight into her arms. Why must she insist on keeping the vacuum cleaner and brooms and heaven knows what else behind the cellar door? How many times have I stumbled over the broomsticks and the buckets! There's nobody at the table, the armchairs are empty, the door to the terrace closed, it all looks deserted, just a puff of wind plumping out the curtains because the door is warped, the wood still working and causing tiny cracks. Wood is never content with things as they are, the chief once said, it never stops working. Only the chief's father is watching me from his glittering frame. The stair carpet muffles my footsteps. Once I'm upstairs no one will catch me. The drawings of broom plants are still there on the wall – Ina once wanted to change the prints, but the chief wouldn't let her, he'd grown so used to them. Quiet, quiet, if I knock too loud, another door may open: better just knock and go straight in, he'll surely forgive me. This dryness in my mouth! He doesn't answer, doesn't call out, but I must see him, must go in.

On the couch, his bed both day and night, he's lying as if asleep, about him a smell that isn't the smell of rum, it's too sour, too stale. He hasn't even taken off his boots, nor has he hung up his jacket – just thrown it over a chair. There is a smell of stale food. The silver stubble on his chin, on his neck, his breathing is laborious, a faint shiver runs over his face.

There he lies with his mouth open and his eyes closed, and he hasn't yet noticed me standing in front of him.

Well, Bruno, what's the matter? What do you want? He recognised me long ago: nothing remains hidden from him, even when he's half-asleep, people like him seem to see with their skin. The ribbon, I say, down in the cellar, in the hiding-place behind the jars, the ribbon's still showing.

In the way he opens his eyes, shakes himself, sits up and looks at me, I can feel what he's thinking, I can see the suspicion in his eyes: I suppose he believes I've been spying on him. No, I just happened to be behind the pile, I say, I was sent to rub the potatoes. He just gives a weary nod, wondering whether to believe me, though he must surely know I've never purposely eavesdropped on him. Oh, Bruno, he says and shakes his head, never before has he looked at me in so sad a way. If only I could prove to him I'd no intention of watching him! I didn't touch anything, I say. I know that, Bruno, but I'm disappointed you didn't say a word while I was down there, just lay doggo and watched what I was doing.

He wipes the saliva from his chin and gives a little smile: he surely isn't taking it all that seriously. Now he puts a hand under his pillow, gropes around and pulls out his flat pocket flask, from which I've already once been allowed to drink the Wacholder he always holds for a long time in his mouth before swallowing. Empty: just a few drops come out and splash his lips, but I suppose he found it enough, for he puts the flask back with an air of satisfaction and beckons me, bidding me come very close. Listen, Bruno, down there lies my secret reserve; I had to start it, for up here everything is bound to be checked in my absence, checked and counted. Our stronghold was once like a glasshouse, with everything lying around open, anybody could find out anything he wished to know. But that's all changed now, as you know; now there are whisperings in corners and secret chambers and hiding-places of all kinds. Everyone tries to camouflage things, for camouflage brings certain advantages to those who use it. I'll put the ribbon out of sight, I say, push it deep down into the hiding-place so it can give nothing away. He approves, is already saying yes with his eyes: Good, Bruno, do that when you can, I know I can depend on you.

Why is he still holding me tight? I ought to be getting a move on, so why does he pull me even closer and raise himself up as if wanting to study me from the shortest possible distance? He pulls me down by my jacket, wanting me to sit. You haven't signed anything, Bruno, no disclaimer, nothing? No, no, nothing signed. And that's just what I expect, he says. The deed of gift has been drawn up, he says, and no one will make me withdraw it. One day you'll get what I have provided for you, and then you'll have to show you can protect it.

His voice is getting fainter and fainter: I can hardly understand what he's saying, and I can no longer see him very clearly, for this sudden veil over my eyes and this feeling of dizziness make him seem far away, it's only his hand that is growing bigger and bigger. I can't help it, I must ask: Why, why can't it be like it once was, like it was when we began? Because we've changed, Bruno, each one of us, and because we've gone through experiences that can't be ignored. Now he must be told: If it's because of me, I need nothing and I want nothing; the best thing would be for the land to belong to the person it always belonged to.

This constriction: there's no chance of forcing any more words through my swollen throat, and my temples are beginning to throb. But his voice, I can hear that more clearly now, this calm other voice: You don't understand, Bruno, you'll never understand, you sleepwalker, but maybe one day you'll wake up. One day you'll have to stretch your limbs, come out from under your cover, shake your head and fight for yourself – I've done all I can. Yes, I say, yes, and he, again from far off: You've no need to look back, for nothing will ever return. Just keep on going, Bruno, till you have reached your hill.

The Kollerhof, I say, that's empty again. I clearly heard myself say that, but he doesn't seem to have understood, he just sighs and sinks back and settles down on his bed. Nothing ever repeats itself, Bruno, you'll come to realise that. His weariness. The weight that is holding him down. He closes his eyes, there is nothing more he can say, though his lips are still twitching, and he moves his fingers as if counting something. A parting word would only disturb him.

The ribbon in the cellar must be got rid of, my first job is to get down there. If only this aching would stop! I could get quit of it on the banisters – bang my head a few times against them till I get an answering roar, then I'll feel easier again. No one was eavesdropping on us, I can walk slower now, go cautiously down the stairs. You're quite alone, Bruno. How cool the banisters are, smooth and cool! The chief called me a sleep-walker, for the very first time.

Get up, make haste, get to the cellar door before she does. But those aren't Dorothea's footsteps. A few moments earlier, Magda, and you'd have caught me with him, we'd maybe have bumped into each other, me and you with your tray. That's just like Magda: she doesn't stop at my signal, just looks at me in a hostile sort of way, warning me not to try to speak to her, no one in the house must be allowed to know. All right, all right, I won't say a word, just watch out with that tea and the stewed apples. How well she plays at looking severe! No one can carry a tray more carefully, nothing rattling or clinking or sliding around. If you only knew what I'm about to do! I've had my instructions from him too – and you can't imagine how secret they are. There's nobody else he'd trust them to, that's for sure, because there's nobody else he can rely on as he can on me.

Away with the jars, push the ribbon down deeper, never mind if it's creased and flattened by the bit of masonry that's big enough to cover it: nobody shall discover his secret reserve, only he and I know it exists, wrapped up in greaseproof paper to protect it from the damp. Maybe one day he'll instruct me to fetch something from his hiding-place without being seen, money or documents or whatever he might need at that moment, he won't have to give me detailed descriptions, a sign will do and I'll know where to find it. Against the two of us, Bruno, no one can win. He said that to me once, but he also said it to Dorothea, back in the Kollerhof at the time we were just beginning and all of us were sitting at the old table, the only one we had. I can hardly think of it without feeling sad.

Cheer him up: I'll do something to cheer him up, not tomorrow, but today. I'll bring him a gift, and maybe that will remind him of times when every day something happened to make us cheerful. Why couldn't it stay as it once was, why did our ways have to part and carry us further and further away from each other? I think and think about that, but I can't quite explain it. I'd do anything, anything, if only I could bring them together again, him and Dorothea.

One pile is almost done, the other must wait till tomorrow: if I'm to buy him a present, I must stop now and go to Hollenhusen, best to Tordsen, who has everything in his shop anyone could want. I know what he needs, what will give him pleasure. He'll look at it unbelievingly, that's for sure, and laugh and poke me in the ribs, that's what he'll do, but so he doesn't see at once what it is, I'll have it packed in a little box which he can first weigh in his hand, turn about and try to guess what's in it. Work will surely be over in the plantations by now and no one will see me, so be off before Dorothea comes and I shall have to give her an answer.

How clean the air is! Washed clean, no longer that earthy smell, and a peaceful stillness among the cordons that are growing according to our plans. And it is his wish that I take over all this land, all this he has set aside for me: from here down to the hollow, then across to the erratic block and the shelter belt and, beside that, the whole stretch from the railway cutting to Lauritzen's meadows – everything lying to the north is to be mine, more than the eye can see at a single glance. That is his wish. That is what he has decided. It's not for me to ask his reasons, I've always just done whatever he's demanded of me. But here, in the middle of the plantations, I daren't let myself think that one day I'm to take sole charge of them, for then everything starts to spin, my hands grow moist, words refuse to enter my mind, and I see them coming from all sides with grins on their faces, standing there in a superior sort of way and waiting for me to give my instructions – from the top of a wooden crate maybe, so they'll see me better. I don't want to be seen, I don't want to attract notice, to be seen. Why am I trembling all of a sudden? Magda said one evening: There's nobody I know can get himself into such a state as you, Bruno.

I'll buy him a bottle of Wacholder: that will surely please him. I can't imagine anyone else will be giving him presents these days. Our old path to the Kollerhof, the private path we trod ourselves, can hardly be seen now. If others after us hadn't used it, probably it would have got grown over altogether, leaving nothing to remind us of the countless times we walked along the edge of the meadow. Now only the wind stirs there, plundering the thatched roof and combing the hedge. The clouds of smoke the peat stove puffed out at us. Crisp potatoes in the world's largest frying-pan, and Dorothea in good spirits and half-smoked herself. And you, Ina, next to me at table, your room next to mine. And the chief said: The period of drought, we'll survive that too. And we did go through quite a few shake-ups in the Kollerhof, but we stuck together and were always of one mind when it really mattered.

How dark the Holle is! There's not a great deal of water in it just now, the arrowheads swing in the current, and only leaves and thin twigs come floating down. There's someone on the makeshift bridge: Niels Lauritzen, and he's watching something. It's probably not drifting paper, drifting pages from a book, like on that day we were both standing there and couldn't make out where those floating pages were coming from. He fished a few of them out, and we could see at once they'd been torn from a book. He read a bit and then with a shake of his head squeezed them together and threw the sodden mass back into the Holle. Why did it have to happen as it did,

Bruno? he said. The sunflower seeds: one morning there were five sunflower seeds lying under my pillow. I didn't know how they'd got there and was no wiser about what they were supposed to mean, but when I examined my seedlings and found they really had developed good roots after I'd made a wound in the outer casing, then I knew: whoever finds five sunflower seeds will be proved right in whatever he may be trying out.

Tordsen's shop is closed. I can already see that from here, but I want to read the cardboard notice on the door, for people like him keep their shops open till the last possible moment to make sure of missing nothing. Closed on account of bereavement. So: on account of bereavement. Well then, the railway station: I've always got what I wanted there in the waiting-room, both from the old manageress and the new one, whom everyone calls just Marion. Quite a few wink or invite her to a glass, but she won't let anyone touch her: whoever does gets his fingers slapped. If she has no Wacholder she'll sell me something else, something the chief drinks now and again in passing – she'll know what it is. Over there, by our loading bay, there are no waggons as in previous years. The scarred wood is sagging a little, no one has found the time or the will to remove the two broken containers: even the chief, who likes order in everything, has forgotten them. Soon there'll be some new state contracts coming along, and then they'll fix the bay up, soon. How anxiously now we count the years! Once we hardly noticed how the years were mounting up.

Nowhere do people more often throw things away or simply drop them than on a railway station. Cigarette ends or used tickets or wrapping paper, it all gets flung on the ground, they even throw down empty icecream cartons and apple cores: here, they think, between arrival and departure, they can let themselves go. How chipped the swing-door is from all the kicks it has suffered, and how it sways to and fro in the constant draught: no wonder Marion's been coughing ever since I've known her. The small panes of the slot machine for bonbons have been smashed in, probably by someone in a rage, because the machine would just swallow all the coins and give nothing in return. Whenever the chief wished to drink here, he would do it standing, just drain his glass, pay and go. Even when the waiting-room was empty he wouldn't sit down: Here there's too much in the air for me, he said, and that was all.

Well, Bruno, the usual? The rissoles are quite fresh. No, not today, Wacholder today, a whole bottle, and wrapped up nicely. I can already see in her sad eyes, round as marbles, that she has no Wacholder: so something else then, I've no idea what, but as long as the chief likes it – Marion nods, she smiles, she knows what's wanted: Weizenkorn, that'll do, he likes that. Is it meant as a present? Yes, I say. With what surprise she regards me, what curiosity – just as if I'd disappointed her in some way, and now she's asking me once again whether she shouldn't bring me my usual, and I say no. Why is she shaking her head over me and looking at me in that pitying way? She knows my order and that should be enough for her. In any case I won't stand by her counter, waiting. I'll be right back. Yes, all right.

The weighing-machine – I'd like to know why they put a weighing-machine here of all places, on the platform where people come only to greet or say goodbye to someone and are always in a hurry. I'll bet no one has ever yet checked his weight on this machine, and I don't intend to be the first. They've really gutted the slot machine for bonbons: the wires are all hanging loose. I'd sooner cart sand from a gravel pit than work on this station, I'd sooner cut turf or dig drains or gather stones on the land as I once did, together with him. Nothing ever repeats itself, Bruno, the chief said, lying there as if under a weight. If only I could help him!

I've been spotted. I can clearly feel someone staring at me from somewhere. Not from the dreary platform, not from the station entrance; he's sitting close behind me in his glassed-in ticket office, over which the curtains are half-drawn. Maybe my closeness is disturbing him: Bohnsack, old Bohnsack, who no one has ever known other than surly and irritable, and of whom Max once said: a born sergeant-major. What are you hanging around here for? he asks, looking at me scornfully through watery eyes, and under his breath he mutters: Halfwit. I can stand here if I want, can't I? Sure, he says and grins, sure you can, but not right in front of the ticket office: that's for people who want to buy a ticket, you can understand that, can't you? His grin, the hardbitten expression on his face: he looks like someone who has suddenly grown old overnight. Or maybe you want to buy a ticket? he asks, tickled by the idea, and he points out: You need money for that, you know. I have no wish to speak to him, but all the same I ask: How much? Tcha, he says, that all depends on where the gentleman wants to go. To Schleswig, I say, give me a ticket to Schleswig. He looks at me quite flabbergasted: he doesn't know now what to do, this born sergeant-major. A twenty-mark note will surely be enough. Here's the money, I say, and I place the note on the turntable and smooth it down. Never have I seen him look so unsure of himself, but he pulls himself together, shrugs his shoulders and says with a grin: Why not? He seizes a ticket as if taking part in a joke, places it on the turntable and flicks it round. Why not? Don't forget your change. Have a good journey.

I mustn't crease the ticket, my first ticket, now growing warm in my hand.

Hi, Bruno, what's got into you? Marion asks, pointing to the swing-door, which I suppose I pushed open too violently. The packet is already lying on the counter. That looks nice, I say, the chief mustn't guess at once what's inside it, he must first unwrap it, and unwrapping is part of the pleasure. I'll pay now. Why does she look at me in that curious way, why once again ask: Is anything the matter, Bruno? There's nothing at all the matter, I just want to be back home before dark. No rissoles, no lemonade? Nothing, I say, not today, for once, at which she: I hope you're not ill, Bruno?

Slip quickly over the railtrack, past the new signs forbidding it. The grass is already looking darker. At dusk everything becomes stiller, turns in on itself and settles down for the night. Now and again as I walk along a gurgling noise comes from the packet, which would look better with a coloured ribbon round it. The first bats are already flitting over the toolshed. You've no need to look back, he said, just keep on going, Bruno, till you have reached your hill. That's what he said. The very thought of him makes me sad, I see him lying there on his bed, silent and as if crushed by it all and not prepared to try again. Maybe he believes his time is past, that's possible; and maybe he also believes that for him there can be no new beginning, because the happiness and the confidence of those early years can't be brought back again. Those mornings then, mornings full of impatience and eagerness, the scarred, pathless land that lay waiting for us and sent us home each evening in a state of contented exhaustion – a beginning like that, he must be feeling, is granted us only once in a lifetime. The packet: I must make it look nicer still for him, there must be a piece of coloured ribbon in my box, among the collection of laces in my old cardboard shoe-box.

I don't need to lock the door, not for this short moment, it'll be enough just to shoot the bolt, that'll do for today. How things grow quieter when I'm at home! Once the blind is drawn and the lamp is burning, it all calms down. The clock that quite a few people have admired: I'll have that repaired. I'll read the book Max dedicated to me once again. The railway ticket, the little brown ticket to Schleswig: they've all been there, the chief, Dorothea and Ina, even Magda was there with Lisbeth's things. Magda: she would never believe it of me; knowing her as I do, she'd just give me an amused look, and that's all. And Joachim, he would certainly be pleased to see me gone, as would quite a few others. The chief: he would be the only one who would miss me and ask after me, maybe he'd even send someone out to find me, for it's his wish that I take over what he has set aside for me. I want to go away. It's because of you, Magda said, if I understood it rightly, Bruno, they've started these legal proceedings because of you, for the deed of gift lays down that you're to get a third of the land with the installations belonging to it. And that they can't and won't accept.

I must go away. Once I'm gone, there'll be nothing more to come between them, they can forgive him and cancel all the things they've started, there'll be nothing in the way once I've gone. Without me they'll surely come together again, they'll take him back into the fold, and he'll be what he always was, he to whom I owe everything. I'll take my tools, all the things the chief picked out and made over to me. My knives, the English tree-saw and the lopping pruners with the long handles: they've all been sharpened and oiled and packed away in the watertight bag. There's still time before the last train leaves for Schleswig. A wonder that my suitcase is still here, when so many things have been lost, were simply not there when I needed them. But the suitcase has stayed with me. Shirts are important, underclothes and the carefully preserved socks – I've no idea how much a person needs when he goes away.

Who, I wonder, will be the first to discover I've gone, simply vanished, never to be seen again? Magda, maybe, and she'll rush around telling everybody, and for a while she'll think me ungrateful, for she'll never come by herself on my reason for doing it. When Ewaldsen realises I'm no longer here, all he'll probably think is: Right then, he's gone, and he'll do all there is to be done by himself. Dorothea: she'll be sad, but she'll soon work out my reason for leaving Hollenhusen, and maybe she'll then go upstairs and knock at his door. You, Ina: you will miss me longest and will best understand that I had to leave. What he'll think, I don't know. It's possible he'll be upset and will send people out to look for me, but it's also possible he'll secretly approve. Nothing remains hidden from him, not even the thoughts you think.

The rack stays here, and the armchair the chief gave me. Who knows who'll ever sit in it again, and who knows who will one day get my table and use my mirror? I shan't need more than one towel, and whoever needs my plate and my cup can help himself. I can also do without the old thunderer whistles, indeed without all the buried treasures from the time when our land was still soldiers' land and we hammered that iron pipe, our earth-borer, into the ground and saw it would be worth our while to stay here and start work. Who takes my pillow and who wraps himself in my blanket is all the same to me: they can share the lot between them, the gumboots, the working trousers, the cap with ear-flaps that always made the chief smile, because I reminded him of a hare when I wore it. Whoever has taken something over from me will probably be asked at first: Where did you get that? And he'll reply: From Bruno, who has gone away. But that's about all the asking there's ever likely to be, for no one feels much like wasting thought on someone who has gone off of his own free will.

I can hear, clearly hear there's someone at my door, and I know it's Dorothea, for no one knocks quite as she does: three short taps with her knuckles. But I shan't open it. If she comes in and sees the preparations I'm making, she'll want to know everything. Maybe even she's come to give me some instruction for tomorrow, but tomorrow I'll be gone. I can accept no further instructions. How things begin to tense and tighten! And this taste in my mouth: it's as if I'd licked the watercock with my tongue. I must see that I get away the moment she's gone. They'll find my present for the chief all right, and, if I write his name on the packet, they'll know it's for him.

No wonder one of the locks won't snap shut: it's grown rusty after all this time. I'll put a strap round the suitcase, twice, so it will hold. The handle is strong and I can tie the bag of tools to it. I shall then be able to carry what there is to carry in one hand: it's always good to have a hand free. Dorothea must have gone off, disappointed at not finding me. I'll get ready. Not much longer and it'll be dark. The door can stay open now.

I'll take the side path, as I've often done, and walk for the last time in the shelter of the thuya hedge, breathing in its bitter smell. And then I'll sit in the train for which I've waited so often before going off to sleep. Its row of lights will glide across the even land, its whistle will scare the rooks from their loveless treetops. I shall see the Holle once more, but our plantations: I shall hardly recognise them, for in the dark they don't look the same. But I shall know they're there, the cypresses and the larches, in their proper places, and the yews and the limes and my Colorado firs, all standing where they belong.